A HODDER CHRISTIAN PAPERBACK OMNIBUS

CORRIE TEN BOOM

In My Father's House
The Hiding Place
Tramp for the Lord

IN MY FATHER'S HOUSE

In My Father's House

The years before 'The Hiding Place'

Corrie ten Boom with C C Carlson

Hodder & Stoughton

LONDON SYDNEY AUCKLAND

*This Corrie ten Boom Omnibus edition first published 1994 by
Hodder and Stoughton, a division of Hodder Headline Ltd*
0 340 630469

In My Father's House

10 9

British Library Cataloguing in Publication Data
A record for this book is available from the British Library

Typeset by Hewer Text Composition Services, Edinburgh
Printed and bound in Great Britain by
Clays Ltd, St Ives plc

The paper and board used in this paperback are natural recyclable
products made from wood grown in sustainable forests.
The manufacturing processes conform to the environmental
regulations of the country of origin.

Hodder and Stoughton
A Division of Hodder Headline Ltd
338 Euston Road
London NW1 3BH

When my parents were married, many years ago, they claimed Psalm 32:8 as their 'life verse,' the promise which they felt was God's assurance for them.

> I will instruct thee and teach thee in the way which thou shalt go: I will guide thee with mine eye.

. . . this promise became the special directive for my life as well.

CORRIE TEN BOOM
From *Tramp for the Lord*

Contents

Foreword

Today I know that memories are the key not to the past,
but to the future. I know that the experiences of our lives,
when we let God use them, become the mysterious and
perfect preparation for the work He will give us to do.

Corrie wrote that in *The Hiding Place*, without realizing that
it had provided the introduction to this book.

As I worked with Corrie, following her around America,
and living with her in Holland, I saw her in many different
circumstances. It is a constant amazement to me how the
Lord uses her. One time my husband, Ward, and I prayed
with her in a small room off a large auditorium. She was ashen
with pain and weariness. When she walked on the stage before
four thousand people, her voice was firm and her message
animated. She was – and continues to be – a living example
of the way in which the Spirit of the Lord works through His
available servant.

However, as *In My Father's House* began to grow, I
became excited to see how this was more than a collection
of memories – more than nostalgia from a rich life. Here we
had the unique lessons of a family preparing for a future,
a future which would demand the power of God's love and
strength.

If we are living in the time in which we believe God's
plan for planet earth is reaching its completion – when the
new beginning Jesus promised would take place – then each
individual and family needs the pattern for living in this present

age. Never before in human history have guidelines been more important.

The applications of various parts of Corrie's life to modern living were impressed upon me, as I savoured those wonderful 'years before'. I've learned so much for my own life and family, as I've lived with Corrie *In My Father's House*. Let's visit together . . .

CAROLE C CARLSON

1

Inheritance

'Remarkable, extraordinary . . . Peter, where did Cook find strawberries in the midst of winter?'

The Dutch merchant summoned his butler and pointed to the luscious fruit in the silver compote. Even in the home of great wealth this was an amazing luxury in the early 1800s.

'It's the gardener, sir . . . ten Boom. He does some miraculous things in that hothouse of his.'

'Ten Boom, you say. Hmm, must remember him. Astounding! Bring me some more, Peter, with lots of thick cream.'

My great-grandfather ten Boom grew those plump strawberries during the chilling months when ruddy-cheeked children skated over the canals. He was no ordinary gardener, but a master craftsman who caressed the soil into performing miracles. He experimented with plants, manipulating them between an ice cellar and a hothouse, until he produced the fruit which was served at the dinner table of his employer, one of the richest men in Hofstede, Bronstede, Heemstede.

Those simple strawberries saved my great-grandfather from jail!

It was during the time of Napoleon; Europe was trembling from the onslaught of the evil little man from Corsica. Swaggering across the continent, victorious in war, the French emperor conquered country after country, and forced men into submission. The government of Holland was ruled by Napoleon's followers and their oppressive regime.

My great-grandfather was an independent man; he had spunk, but not much tact, I'm afraid. He refused to submit to men who denied freedom to other men. However, Hollanders at that time had two alternatives: they were either obedient to those who served the strutting dictator; or they faced what could be very severe punishment.

Tyranny at any time in man's history demands loyalty.

One Sunday Great-grandfather went to his church and heard the minister announce the opening hymn; the theme was from Psalm 21, but as the congregation began to understand the words, one voice after another stopped. They realized it was a pointed description of their political situation. Nobody dared to continue.

But Great-grandfather and the minister sang louder, a defiant duet (translated from the Dutch):

> The evil one considers himself to be free from all bondage, and runs around, while he stirs the people. At the same time, the bad people assume they hold the reins of government, and they are being raised to the summits of honour.

Sad hearts and silent voices were encouraged by the bravery of the minister and the spunky gardener.

When news of ten Boom's traitorous act of defiance reached the authorities, he received a summons to appear at the town hall. He must have been prepared for the consequences, as he addressed the officer in charge.

'What does this Mr Snotneus [snot-nose] want with me?'

First he challenged the regime; then he hurled that contemptuous name at his accuser!

But where do strawberries fit into all this? Before Great-grandfather had a chance to be sentenced or taken to prison, his boss, who was a very influential citizen, interceded and had him pardoned. (A gardener couldn't grow fruit in jail, could he?)

My father told us this story of Great-grandfather and his personal challenge to the Napoleonic regime with a sense of joy.

'I'm glad he was a real man,' Father said.

Over a hundred years later when people said to Father,

'Stop having Jews in your house – you will be sent to prison,' my father answered, 'I am too old for prison life, but if that should happen, then it would be, for me, an honour to give my life for God's ancient people, the Jews.'

From Generation to Generation

Willem ten Boom, my grandfather, was not strong like his father, so he chose a work which was not physically difficult. In the year 1837, Grandfather purchased a little house in Haarlem for four hundred guilders, and set up shop as a watchmaker.

It was in 1844 that Grandfather had a visit from his minister, Dominee Witteveen, who had a special request. 'Willem, you know the Scriptures tell us to pray for the peace of Jerusalem and the blessing of the Jews.'

'Ah, yes, Dominee, I have always loved God's ancient people – they gave us our Bible and our Saviour.'

Beginning with this conversation, a prayer fellowship was started, with Grandfather and his friends praying for the Jewish people. This was an unusual idea among Christians at that time. The Jews were scattered throughout the world, without a country or a national identity: Jerusalem was a city torn by centuries of conflict. The attention of the world was not upon the Middle East, and yet a small group of Dutch believers met in a little Haarlem house, a watchmaker's shop (later called the Beje), to read the Scriptures and pray for the Jews.

In a divine way which is beyond our human understanding, God answered those prayers. It was in the same house, exactly one hundred years later, that Grandfather's son, my father, and four of his grandchildren, and one great-grandson were arrested for helping save the lives of Jews during the German occupation of Holland.

Another strutting dictator, more arrogant and insane than Napoleon, had planned to exterminate every Jew in the world. When Holland was controlled by Hitler's troops, many Jews were killed.

For helping and hiding the Jews, my father, my brother's

son, and my sister all died in prison. My brother survived his imprisonment, but died soon afterward. Only Nollie, my older sister, and I came out alive.

So many times we wonder why God has certain things happen to us. We try to understand the circumstances of our lives, and we are left wondering. But God's foolishness is so much wiser than our wisdom.

From generation to generation, from small beginnings and little lessons, He has a purpose for those who know and trust Him.

God has no problems – just plans!

Beginning With Mama

My mother was a woman with a loving sense of humour and a striking appearance. She had thick, dark, curly hair, and brilliant blue eyes – an unusual combination for a Hollander. She came from a large family, and was left fatherless just after her mother gave birth to an eighth baby. While she was still very young, her mother and her brothers and sisters were forced to earn their own living.

One of her sisters, Jans, started a kindergarten where Cor (my mother) and another sister, Anna, became her assistants. I'm sure this experience helped my mother later in training her own children.

When Jans added a Sunday school to her kindergarten, she began to work with a young theology student, Hendrik Wildeboer, who became her special boyfriend. Cor caught the eye of a handsome teacher in the Sunday school by the name of Casper ten Boom, and they immediately found something in common: their birthdays were on the same day, May 18.

Romance grew between Cor and Casper; when Cor journeyed to Harderwijk to visit her grandmother, Casper was so lonely that he followed her the next day.

About fifty years later, I visited the quaint village of Harderwijk on the Zuider Zee with Father. As we walked along the Bruggestraat, Father said, 'This is where I proposed to your mother. There were cobblestones instead of pavement at that time, but many of the old houses and the sea gate are still the same.'

He paused to remember the youth which had vanished, and his love for the gentle woman with the laughing eyes.

'Did Mother say *yes* immediately?' I asked.

'No, not until the next day, and I spent a very restless night waiting for that decision!'

When I asked him if he had ever regretted his decision to marry Mama, his voice was firm. 'Never! Until the last day of her life, I was just as much in love with your mother as I was on that day in Harderwijk. We didn't have an easy life – we had many sorrows – but God led us by His extraordinary providence.'

A Little Jewelry Store

Grandmother died shortly before Casper and Cor were married. By then, Father had started a jewelry store in a small house in the heart of the Jewish section of Amsterdam.

Once a customer arrived who was a pastor from Ladysmith, South Africa. He came into the shop and asked Father to provide a clock and a bell for his church tower. This was a tremendous encouragement to a young merchant. The order was simple to fill; all Father had to do was to go to the factory in Brabant to make the selection; the manufacturer did all the installation. However, the commission from that sale provided enough money for the young couple to be married.

Uncle Hendrik, Jans's husband, was a minister in a little village near Amsterdam. Mother and Father had to go to the town hall first, to be registered and married in a civil ceremony. The man at the town hall who married them thought they were 'high people' because they came from Amsterdam. He tried to be very dignified, in a manner suitable for this distinguished couple, and began the marriage speech with great airs.

'Honoured bride and bridegroom . . . you are now . . . you are now gathered . . . you are now gathered here . . .' He stopped, looked around, and burst into tears.

Father said, 'I'm so touched by your speech and tears, but we would like to be married.'

The poor fellow finished the ceremony somehow, but Uncle Hendrik conducted the final marriage rites in his church – without tears.

The newlyweds moved into a shabby little house in Amsterdam after their wedding. It's probably just as well that the emotional clerk from the town hall didn't know of their humble means!

Mother had dreamed of a home with a small garden, for she loved flowers and the beauty of colour.

'I love to see much of the sky,' she often said.

The sky was there, if she stretched far enough to see it in the narrow street outside the old house. Their cramped home had a single room on each storey, with worn-out furniture left by my grandmother.

Money was scarce, but happiness was abundant.

The neighbourhood of Jewish people made it possible for Father to participate in their Sabbaths and other holy days. He studied the Old Testament, their Talmud, with them, and was given opportunities to understand and explain the fulfilment of the prophecies of the Old Testament in the New Testament.

My father's love for the Jewish people was nurtured in the Jewish quarter of Amsterdam during those first years of married life. Father and Mother lived on poverty's edge, and yet their contentment was not dependent upon their surroundings. Their relationship with each other and with the Lord gave them strength.

Plan for Parenthood

When the first baby was expected Mother was glad she had learned to sew. She had inherited an old sewing machine from her mother, and every moment she could find she stitched little garments for the baby. A Jewess who lived upstairs couldn't contain her curiosity, and asked Mother if she was a seamstress.

'No,' Mother answered proudly, 'but I'm expecting my first

baby. See the little dress I've made?' She held up a dainty garment tenderly.

The Jewess was astonished. 'You're not sewing the clothes before the baby arrives! That is tempting God!'

Mother was puzzled, but this didn't stop her from preparing for her baby. However, she began to understand why Mary had only swaddling clothes for the Baby Jesus. It wasn't lack of money, but the Jewish custom not to sew the layette before the birth of the child. I've heard that Portuguese Jews maintain this tradition today.

When Betsie, the first child, was born, Mother became quite ill. She asked her youngest sister, Anna, to come for a few weeks to help with the new baby. Those few weeks stretched into forty years.

Mother and Anna had always been close, but when Mother married, Anna went to live with Jans and Uncle Hendrik. Anna, however, became very lonely for Cor, and was delighted when Mother and Father invited her to stay with them in Amsterdam.

Within seven years, four more babies were born, but one didn't live. Father had to look for a cheaper house to accommodate his growing responsibilities.

By the time I was born, they were living on the Korte Prinsegracht, in a house at the very end of the canal, where few people passed the shop. Business was at its lowest ebb.

I was a premature baby, with blue skin and pinched features. When Uncle Hendrik saw me he shook his head sadly. 'I hope the Lord will quickly take this poor little creature to His home in heaven,' he said.

Fortunately, my parents didn't feel the same as Uncle Hendrik. They surrounded me with love and good care. There were no incubators in those days, and one of the greatest problems was keeping me warm. I cried so pitifully from the cold that Tante Anna rolled me in her apron, and tied me against her body; then I became warm and quiet.

Many years later while I was in Africa I met a missionary family whose baby could not be comforted, until a native girl bound the child to her back with a piece of cloth. The baby became calm, secure in the closeness to the body of a person who loved him.

I must have felt that same way bound snugly in Tante Anna's apron.

Throughout the first year of my life I was a poor, sickly-looking creature. Mother told me that once she was travelling by train with a friend who held a beautiful, plump baby on her lap. The baby's name was Rika, and the people in the coach were giving her many admiring glances and comments. They would look at me in my mother's arms, and then turn away, unable to find anything positive to say.

Mother told me this bothered her at first, but then she would hug me and whisper, 'I wouldn't exchange you for anyone in the whole world, you darling ugly baby with the beautiful eyes.'

When Rika was two years old, she began having epileptic seizures. I played with her all through my childhood, but I remember how aware I was that her little face would change so drastically as the sickness would overpower her. Mother was always ready to care for Rika; throughout her life Mother taught us to be helpful and loving toward those who were weak or abnormal.

Haarlem Inheritance

Grandfather Willem died when I was six months old, leaving Father his shop in Haarlem. We moved into the house, which wasn't very large, and poor Mother still didn't have her garden. She put some flower pots on the flat roof and called this her garden. She had geraniums in clay pots, hanging fuchsia, and some ivy climbing the brick wall. She developed a roof garden long before the modern penthouse dwellers thought of such a thing.

Even in the 'new' house in Haarlem, she could see only a small piece of the sky she loved. The roof became her 'out-doors' when she became too weak to take her daily walks in the street.

During those first years of their marriage, the financial situation must have been very serious. Anna worked night and day to nurse Mother when she was ill, and to care for four children. She earned the grand sum of one guilder (about thirty cents) a week. Father gave her this magnificent salary each Saturday, but often by the following Wednesday the finances would become so desperate that Father would have to go to the kitchen and ask, 'Anna, do you still have your guilder?'

Anna always had the guilder available, and it often bought the food for the family on that day. This was certainly 'blessed money'.

This was the beginning of my rich inheritance. When I remember my family life, I realize that my parents and my aunts had truly mastered the art of living. They enjoyed life and they loved children.

'We never laughed so much as when you children were small,' Tante Anna often said.

In our hearts we must have stored some of the memory of laughter to be brought out in later years, when the sounds of happy voices were scarce in our beloved land.

2

Five Is Not Too Young

In 1892, the year I was born, Holland was entering an exciting and important era. In a few years, Wilhelmina would be crowned Queen at the tender age of eighteen. There were signs which indicated that the stability of that latter part of the nineteenth century would soon be rocked by the rattling of German swords. Foreign policy was being shaped around lines of power, as young Kaiser Wilhelm II ruled the country which later played such an important part in my life.

History in the making means nothing to a child, but it was a world event for me when Mother or Tante Anna pinched a guilder hard enough to squeeze out some sugar and butter for those fat little sugar cookies I loved. The fragrance of baking would float from the iron stove into the shop, and tantalize the customers just as it put us in a happy mood.

When I was five years old, I learned to read; I loved stories, particularly those about Jesus. He was a member of the ten Boom family – it was just as easy to talk to Him as it was to carry on a conversation with my mother and father, my aunts, or my brother and sisters. He was there.

One day my mother was watching me play house. In my little girl world of fantasy, she saw that I was pretending to call on a neighbour. I knocked on the make-believe door and waited . . . no one answered.

'Corrie, I know Someone who is standing at your door and knocking right now.'

Was she playing a game with me? I know now that there was a preparation within my childish heart for that moment;

the Holy Spirit makes us ready for acceptance of Jesus Christ, of turning our life over to Him.

'Jesus said that He is standing at the door, and if you invite Him in He will come into your heart,' my mother continued. 'Would you like to invite Jesus in?'

At that moment my mother was the most beautiful person in the whole world to me.

'Yes, Mama, I want Jesus in my heart.'

So she took my little hand in hers and we prayed together. It was so simple, and yet Jesus Christ says that we all must come as children, no matter what our age, social standing, or intellectual background.

When Mother told me later about this experience, I recalled it clearly.

But, You're So Little

Does a child of five really know what he's doing? Some people say that children don't have spiritual understanding – that we should wait until a child can 'make up his mind for himself'. I believe a child should be led, not left to wander.

Jesus became more real to me from that time on. Mother told me later that I began to pray for others, as young as I was.

The street behind our house was the Smedestraat. It was filled with saloons, and many of the happenings there were frightening to me. As I played outside jumping rope, or joined with Nollie, my sister, in a game of *bikkelen* (ball and stones), I saw the police pick up these lurching, incoherent men as they slumped to the ground or slouched in a doorway, and take them into the police station.

I would stand before the *politie bureau* (police station) behind the Beje, and watch the drunks being pushed in. It made me shiver. The building was made of dark red brick, and 'way at the top were turrets with small windows. Were those the cells, I wondered?

It was in that same police station years later that my father, and all his children, and a grandson were taken after being arrested for helping Jews escape from the German Gestapo.

As a child I would be so concerned for those arrested that I would run into the house sobbing, 'Mother . . . I'm afraid those poor men are going to be hurt . . . they're so sick!'

Bless Mother's understanding. She would say, 'Pray for them, Corrie.'

And I would pray for the drunks. 'Dear Jesus, please help those men . . . and Jesus, help all the people on the Smedestraat.'

Many years later I spoke on a television station in Holland. I received a letter after the programme which said: 'My husband was especially interested because you told us that you had lived in Haarlem. He lived in a house on the Smedestraat. Three years ago he accepted the Lord Jesus as his Saviour.'

I read that letter and recalled the prayers of little Corrie. That man whose wife wrote me was one person I had prayed for seventy-six years before.

Does He Listen?

At another time in my later years I was camping with a number of Haarlem girls. Around the campfire one evening, we were talking about the Lord and chatting about the pleasant events of the day.

'Do you know that I am a neighbour of yours?' one of the girls asked me. 'I live in the Smedestraat.'

'I lived there until five years ago,' said another girl.

'My mother lived there,' said a third.

We all began to laugh to discover that all eighteen of those girls, who were sleeping in the big camp tent, had lived on that street or their parents had lived there. They found it an amusing coincidence.

'Listen,' I said, 'I just remembered something that I had almost forgotten. When I was five or six years old, I used to pray every day for the people in the Smedestraat. The fact that we have been talking about Jesus, and that God has even used me to reach some of your parents, is an answer to the prayer of a little child. Never doubt whether God hears our prayers, even the unusual ones.'

How often we think when a prayer is not answered that God has said *no*. Many times He has simply said, '*Wait*.'

The Future Comes Quickly

When we are very young the future is so hard to grasp. My father had one coming event which he mentioned in every prayer. It baffled me. I didn't want to ask in front of the entire family; I thought they might think I was foolish to ask about something I heard several times a day.

I waited until Father came upstairs to tuck me in; this was a time I could ask him anything.

'Papa, you always pray in every prayer, "Let soon come that great day when Jesus Christ, Your beloved Son, comes on the clouds of heaven." Why are you longing for that day?'

'Correman, remember when you saw the men drunk and fighting in the Smedestraat, and they were taken to the police station? The whole world is filled with fighting. You may see worse fighting in your lifetime than what you have seen on the street.'

I hoped not. Fighting upset me.

'In the Bible,' Papa continued, 'we read that Jesus has promised to come to this world to make everything new. The world is now covered with hatred, but when Jesus returns the world will be covered with the knowledge of God, like the water covers the bottom of the sea.'

Thinking of that wonderful day, I knew why Papa prayed for it so often. 'Oh, Papa, then everyone will know about Jesus! I'll be very happy when He comes.'

Let the Children Come

Decades later I was speaking to a group when I challenged parents to 'Bring your little ones to the Lord Jesus. He has said, "Let the children come to me; the kingdom of God is theirs".' (*See* Matthew 19:14.)

Then I told how I had made a decision for Jesus when I was five years old.

After that talk I left the platform, and went into a small

room in the building where I found a father with two little
boys, all on their knees. The father had an arm around both
of those boys, and I moved back quietly while the man told
the boys tenderly that they were not too young to ask Jesus
to come into their hearts.

What a wonderful heritage those boys have, to know that
their father cared enough about them to lead them to a
knowledge of their heavenly Father!

Later I received a letter from a lady who told me the results
in her life of that evening.

I went home after that meeting and went directly to my
little girl, Mary, who was in bed. She knew about the Lord
because she had been to a Sunday school, but that night,
in her bed, she gave her heart to Jesus.

The next morning she said, 'Oh, Mummy, I'm so happy
that Jesus is now in my heart. He made me a child
of God.'

Mary was singing the whole time before she went to
school, and I was amazed that she sang many songs about
heaven.

My husband went to school to pick her up that day,
and as he approached the schoolhouse, he noticed that
a great many people were standing around, and there
obviously must have been an accident. Then he saw what
had happened.

Mary was on the street, her little body crumpled like a
rag doll. She was dead.

As I read that letter my eyes were so filled with tears that
the words blurred.

Mary had passed behind a big transport truck and had not
seen another car, which was coming toward her from the
other direction. She was killed immediately.

My husband brought her little body home. He was in
deep despair, but then he remembered the songs Mary
had sung that morning. I told him what had happened the
evening before, and right then, my husband, who had never

made a decision for the Lord Jesus, accepted Him as his Saviour.

On Mary's burial day many children of her class came to the Lord.

I sat for a long time with that letter on my lap, realizing that I must have a new sense of urgency to talk to parents about the joy of leading their children to the Lord. What a wonderful assurance Mary's parents had to know that some day they would be with her again.

During some of my talks I have often repeated this little poem:

SAFE?
Said a precious little laddie,
To his father one bright day,
'May I give myself to Jesus,
Let Him wash my sins away?'

O, my son, but you're so little,
Wait until you older grow,
Bigger folks 'tis true, do need Him,
But little folk are safe, you know.

Said the father to his laddie,
As a storm was coming on,
'Are the sheep all safely sheltered,
Safe within the fold, my son?'

'All the big ones are, my father,
But the lambs, I let them go,
For I didn't think it mattered,
Little ones are safe, you know.'

AUTHOR UNKNOWN

Praying for Crazy Thys

As a child in Haarlem I prayed for a man most people avoided. His nickname was *Gekke Thys* (Crazy Thys) and he was the town tramp, and idiot. I pitied him and when I was five or six years old started to talk about this to the Lord.

How curious the little minds of children are. Was it my mother or one of my aunts who gave me the advice to cast my burden on the Lord in prayer? Or did the Lord Himself give me this motivation?

Every prayer in the evening and in the morning ended with this request: 'And Lord, be with all the people in the Smedestraat and also *Gekke Thys*.'

My sister Nollie was only a year and a half older than I, but she seemed so much wiser. I remember walking with her through the Smedestraat one day and stopping to watch a crowd of children surrounding someone they were taunting and teasing. As we inched closer to the others, wanting to know what was happening, but a bit afraid of getting involved in something which looked so mean, we realized that poor old Crazy Thys was standing in the middle of the circle, confusion and hurt showing in his face.

I was so full of pity for poor Thys and angry at the cruel children that I shouted, 'You leave him alone, do you hear!'

The children stopped at my bold challenge. Thys looked for his defender and saw a little girl, less than half his size. Suddenly he walked toward me and stooped down. I could smell the unpleasant odour of his unwashed clothes and matted beard. He put his hand under my chin and kissed me on both cheeks.

Nollie was shocked! She grabbed my hand and pulled me home as fast as we could run. Down the Smedestraat, into the alley which ran beside our house, and through the side door we raced.

'Aunty, someone . . . hurry! That dirty old *Gekke Thys* kissed Corrie. Let's wash her cheeks!'

My face was so thoroughly washed I was afraid my skin would fall off. I heard someone say, 'Such dangerous tramps shouldn't be allowed to go so freely in the streets.'

Stinging from the rebuke as well as the face scrubbing, I went to my mother. 'Mama, why was it so bad that *Gekke Thys* kissed me? He's such a poor unhappy man. Everybody makes fun of him.'

Mother took me into her bed and talked quietly with me as I nestled against her soft shoulder. She said, 'Correman, it's good that you have pity for this man. The Lord Jesus gives you love for *Gekke Thys* and for the drunken men in the Smedestraat. Jesus loves sinners, but before they are going to love Him, these men can be very bad. It's wise to keep a little distance. But there's one great thing you and I can do – and you are doing that already – pray faithfully for them.'

Shortly after that incident *Gekke Thys* disappeared from the streets. I don't know how the Lord worked in his life, but a deep concern for the feebleminded was fostered in me.

Fear No Evil . . . Except

A child is not fearless, contrary to what his parents may think at times. A child is often a bundle of unexpressed fears, unknown terrors, and shadowy worries. I was afraid of the doctor's surgery, my family's leaving me, and the mystery of death.

Nollie's nightgown was my contact with security. We slept in the same bed, and I can remember clinging to Nollie's nightgown as long as she would allow me. Poor Nollie, when she would try to turn, she would be anchored by my little fist clasping her tightly.

One time Mother took Nollie and me to visit a woman whose baby had died. I wished Nollie had been allowed to wear her nightgown on that journey, because I needed desperately to hang onto it.

We climbed a narrow staircase and entered the poorly furnished room of one of Mama's 'lame ducks' (the name we children had given to her protégées). Although we often did not have sufficient money for ourselves, Mother always found someone who was in greater need.

In that shabby little room was a crib with a baby inside. It didn't move at all and its skin was very white. Nollie stood next to the crib and touched the baby's cheek.

'Feel that,' she said to me, 'it's so cold.'

I touched the little hand, and then ran to my mother and buried my face in her lap. I had touched death for the first time, and it seemed that the impression of cold remained with me for hours and hours.

When we returned home, I ran up the narrow stairs to my bedroom and leaned against the antique chest of drawers. There was an enormous fear in my heart – almost terror. In my imagination, I pictured the future in which I saw myself all alone, my family gone, and myself left desolate. My family was my security, but that day I saw death, and knew that they could die, too. I had never thought about it before.

The dinner bell rang downstairs, and I was so grateful to go to the big oval table, and get warm again, and feel the security of being with my family. I thought how stupid the grown-ups would think I was if I told them about the fear which was still in my heart.

I ate dinner quietly that night, which was not easy when you are in the midst of such a lively family. Our dinner table spilled over with conversation.

After dinner Father took the Bible, as he always did, and began to read the lines from Psalm 46:2. 'Therefore will not we fear, though the earth be removed, and though the mountains be carried into the midst of the sea' (AV).

I sat up straight in my chair and stared at my father. I didn't know much about mountains, living in flat, flat Holland, but I certainly knew a lot about fear. I thought Papa must have known exactly what my problem was that night.

My faith in Papa, and in the words he read from the Bible, was absolute. If they said not to fear, then God would take care of it. I felt secure again.

3

From Small Beginnings

My doll, Casperina, and I were going to have a party! Mama and Tante Anna were cooking, and I watched their long skirts bustle past me from my perch on the footstool beneath the table. This was a wonderful place to play, safe and secure beneath the red and black tablecloth.

My friend was named after my father, but the resemblance ended there. I loved her very much, but dragging her up and down the stairs of the Beje had left her with a few fingers missing, and a slightly cracked head. Oh, my, why couldn't she look like Nollie's doll, who was immaculately dressed, and didn't have a scratch on her china face? Poor Casperina, she would never be in the same society with Emma, Betsie's doll, who was named after the mother of the Queen.

'Never mind, Casperina,' I whispered to her in the shelter of our little house beneath the table, 'Jesus loves you, and so do I.'

When I was especially happy, I would sing a little song which Tante Jans had composed:

> *'k Zou zoo graag eens komen, Heiland,*
> *In dat heerlijk Vaderhuis.*
> (I should just like to come, Saviour,
> In the beautiful Father-house.)

However, instead of singing *to come* I substituted *to peek*, combining my words with a mischievous look around the fat table leg.

Tante Anna laughed at me. 'Corrie, you'd better not let Tante Jans hear you change the words in her songs. When she writes "I should like to come to heaven," that's what she means.'

Some things grown-ups don't understand, I thought. I meant that it would be great fun just to look around for a moment in heaven, where I knew I would spend my future. I just wanted a little peek; after all, my father-house right here on the Barteljorisstraat was all the heaven I wanted just then.

I clutched Casperina's three-fingered hand in mine and whispered, 'We'll just stay in our own secret place, where no one will ever – ever – scold us for anything.'

A Time to Uproot

A time comes when all children, even a little Dutch girl with her jaw set and her black-stockinged legs rigid upon the staircase, must leave her father's house for a time. I was born with my feet slightly turned in, a defect which the doctor said would cure itself with time and growth.

'Don't worry,' he told Mama and Papa, 'when she is about sixteen, she will become vain enough to turn her toes the right way.'

However, when I turned my toes in even more, and tightened my fingers in a knuckle-whitening grip on the railing, I meant business.

'I'm not going to school. I know how to read; I can learn arithmetic from Papa, and Casperina needs me at home.'

There. *That* was settled.

'Of course you're not going to school alone, Corrie. I am going to walk with you.'

Papa bent over me, his beard tickling the top of my head, and one by one loosened my fingers on the railing. With the release of each finger, I howled a bit louder. By the time Papa had my hand in his, he was almost dragging me down the street toward school. I thought my hand would break – just like Casperina's – and then it would be impossible for me to go to school.

It must have taken great dignity for Papa, with his immaculate suit and erect carriage, to struggle past the homes and shops of his friends with a red-faced child announcing her objections to the entire world.

I knew Father was not angry, but his will was law. I had to obey.

When we arrived at the school I saw a little boy being carried into Master Robyns's classroom in his father's arms. (At least I was walking!) He was crying lustily, even louder than I was. He looked so ugly that I felt sorry for him. But what about me? I realized how I must look to others, and stopped abruptly.

Papa released my hand; my fingers weren't broken at all – only my heart was slightly injured. However, when Papa kissed me gently on the cheek, bringing the familiar fragrance of cigars and cologne, he assured me that when school was over, he would be waiting at home, and I knew I would find that blessed security I needed in the shelter of his arms.

God was teaching a little lesson in a small life, because sixty-seven years later, He reminded me of my fingers on the railing.

I was in a room of *Zonneduin*, a house in Holland, which some friends and I had established first for ex-prisoners who had been in concentration camps, and later for any person who needed nursing and rest. I had been travelling so much and was tired – tired of strange beds and different food – tired of dressing for breakfast – tired of new people, and new experiences. I liked this very luxurious house with its large rooms, and decided to stay, and enjoy the comfortable life in Holland, although I knew that God didn't agree with my decision.

Most of the furniture in the entire house was mine, but there was one room in particular which reminded me of the happy family life of my past. It was a room which held my treasures: photographs of those I loved, mementoes of my family during the years before. Every picture was like the railing on the stairs. My hands grasped the past, and tried to hold on, but my heavenly Father's hands were stronger.

I left the house for a while for some speaking engagements, intending to return to my old room and settle in for good. However, when I came back to *Zonneduin* some weeks later, my pictures were down, and the strange belongings of someone else were on the bed.

My friends had not known of my personal decision to return to this room; my irregular life, my coming and going unexpectedly, was difficult for those who had to manage the big family of patients and staff in an orderly way.

But I decided to stay, and that was settled!

My heavenly Father spoke to me, 'Only obey Me, Corrie. I'll hold your hand. It is My will that you leave your room. Later you will thank Me for this experience. You do not see it, but this is one of My great blessings for you.'

Father's hand was firm, but I knew His love.

I packed up my suitcase again and left for the United States. How the Lord blessed my time there. Meetings began to grow in size, and when I saw people come from darkness into light, from bondage into liberation, I began to see the pattern. I could praise my Father that His hands were stronger than mine.

Blue Stones Can Hurt!

School life did not prove to be as horrible as I thought. I can still remember the sensation of victory when I worked an arithmetic problem, and discovered that the final figure was what it was supposed to be. However, my mind was not always so attentive to details. I was a daydreamer, carrying my fantasies into a world where everyone needed an expensive new watch, and every day was a walk on the dunes with the sunshine warming my cheeks.

The headmaster of our school was a strict taskmaster, insisting upon obedience and discipline without question. He had warned all the children not to step on the 'blue stone', which was a small square stone slightly higher than the rest in the outer yard. I was not paying attention to his instructions and stepped on the stone. Instantly my face was smarting from a sharp slap on my cheek. I can still feel the shame of it, after all these years, for I don't believe the people at home had ever slapped my face. A colour photoplate was impressed upon my mind, which has never faded. The tears covered my face, but I could see the girl who stood in front of me who wore a red dress and a white apron; there was a green door on the garden gate, and the colours all blended with the blazing eyes of Mr Loran, the headmaster.

I couldn't wait to get home that day. Before I opened the door my cries had overpowered the sound of the bell, which announced any visitors to the shop.

Mama took me on her lap and comforted me; and when I had quieted, Papa held me in his arms as he did when I was a baby. I can still feel the sensation of safety as I put my head upon his shoulder. What a security to have a refuge when life is really hard!

Forty-five years passed after the blue-stone incident. The Gestapo had arrested me, and I was being asked the location of the secret room in which I had hidden four Jews and two underground workers. I realized that if I told, it would mean prison and possibly death for the six people who were there, so I didn't tell. The interrogator slapped me on the face, and at the same moment I recalled the backyard of the school, the angry headmaster, and Mother and Father's comforting help.

'Lord Jesus, cover me!' I cried.

'If you mention that name, I'll murder you!' shouted the man. But his hand stopped in mid-air and he couldn't beat me any longer.

What a security to have a refuge when life is really hard!

In dat Vaderhuis (In That Father-house)

Our house was not very big, but it had wide open doors. I don't think that many guests who came to the Beje ever realized what a struggle it was to make both ends meet. As Mother said, 'We must turn every penny twice before we spend it.'

We didn't feel that we were poor, however, and indeed we weren't. The words 'we can't afford it' were not a part of our thinking, because as children we knew something about the status of family finances, and didn't ask for what we knew was impossible.

Many lonesome people found a place with us, where there was music, humour, interesting conversations, and always room for one more at the oval dinner table. Oh, it's true, the soup may have been a bit watery when too many unexpected guests came, but it didn't really matter.

Mother loved guests. Her lovely blue eyes would brighten, and she would pat her dark hair into place when she knew we would be squeezing another visitor around our table – already bursting with four children, three aunts, herself, and Papa. With a flourish she would place a little box on the table, and spreading her arms wide, she would say to our visitor, 'You are welcome in our house, and because we are grateful for your coming, we will add a penny to the blessing box for our missionaries.'

Years afterwards on my trips around the world, when I have been dependent upon the hospitality of others, I believe that I have enjoyed the reward for the open doors and hearts of our home. Here on earth I have enjoyed a 'house with many mansions'.

I often think of that verse which says, 'Cast thy bread upon the waters: for thou shalt find it after many days' (Ecclesiastes II:I AV).

Corrie, Stand Still!

Although money was scarce, the outside world thought we were wealthy. Every member of the family dressed neatly and well. At least – almost everyone. Mother made most of our clothes, until the burden became too much, and Miss Anna van der Weyden, the seamstress, came in to help.

Clothes to me were just something to keep me covered and warm. The endless fittings for a new dress and the inevitable pricks from countless pins were torture to my restless body.

'Corrie, come here, dear,' Mother would call in the tone I knew was meant to be another torturous session trying on clothes.

'If I don't finish this homework, Mama, Master Robyns will make me stand in the corner.'

'Corrie!'

There was no escape. I knew if I didn't subject myself to trying on a new dress which Mama was making, that I would probably be assigned next time to Miss van der Weyden, and her clothes didn't fit as well as Mama's. The whole process was such a bore, and there was no way I could look like Nollie or Betsie anyhow. I just preferred to be me. However, I was a ten Boom and must not bring shame to the family name!

Mother had such a marvellous sense of humour, and having been a kindergarten teacher before her marriage, we profited by her practical knowledge of child psychology. She knew that praising my appearance would not provide me with motivation for my self-esteem. However, when she said, 'Correman, you are such a bright girl . . . I'm sure Master Robyns calls on you often in class. You do want to look nice when you stand up to recite, don't you?' Then she would strike a responsive chord, for I was eager to learn and have recognition in school.

I stood still for Mama, but only briefly. There was so much to do, so many things to learn, so much to live. I had a built-in sense of urgency to cram all that life and love could offer into each precious day.

4

The Many Ages of Love

Children need the wisdom of their elders; the aging need the encouragement of a child's exuberance.

Wisdom and exuberance lived side by side in the Beje, a house filled with the varied personalities of the old and the young.

Tante Bep (Alone in the Crowd)

Children's nurses in the rich houses of Holland were very lonely. They were not at home in the kitchen with the servant girls (who thought the nurses had privileges which they didn't enjoy), and they were not at home in the drawing room with the master and mistress of the house. Consequently, they frequently became bitter with their circumstances of not belonging in any niche of society. Tante Bep was a children's nurse, going from job to job, and becoming more unhappy each year.

She was the oldest of Mother's sisters, and one of the reasons (I realize now) that my mother was very skilled in the art of tact. Mother usually had to steer a smooth course in our family with all of the aunts and their individual views on education and discipline; she knew how to bring the ship between the rocks.

When Tante Bep became too weak to work as a nurse, Father and Mother took her in. She had the same big, beautiful eyes like Mother, but the expression was very unhappy. She was quarrelsome about everything. There was the issue of the coffee, for instance. She told Tante Anna, 'I'm the only one in this house who can make coffee.' Now if there's one thing that was important in our house it was a good cup of coffee. Tante Anna would shift her apron around her ample waist, clear her throat with gusto and say, 'Bep, if you think your coffee is so good, you may just take over all the cooking from now on.'

'Anna,' Mother would say with her soft smile and gentle persuasion, 'we couldn't exist without your fine cooking – and Bep, I know your coffee is excellent, too; so perhaps you would like to make it your way on Tuesdays and Thursdays.'

It was such a small house, it was impossible to avoid Tante Bep, but I tried because I didn't like to be compared to the Waller children. The last place she worked before coming to live with us was the Wallers', and I thought they must have been angels who had their halos polished every day.

The Waller children were always neat. The Waller children never ran in the house. I didn't like to tell Tante Bep anything, because she might say, 'The Waller children would never say such a thing.'

Mother always soothed my insulted feelings by telling me, 'Tante Bep complained about the Waller children when she was caring for them. Love her for what she is, Correman, and remember that she has had a very lonely sort of a life.'

Tante Jans (That's That!)

'Corrie, close the door . . . my feet are cold and I'll be sick with all the draughts in this house.'

Tante Jans was always concerned about her health, and made us very conscious of her needs. She had a diet which was different from the usual fare of the rest of the family; as a child, I sometimes thought it would be interesting to be sick and have my own trays of food and special attention.

Her rooms were special, too. Mother and Father had given her more floor space than the rest of the family, because Tante Jans had a great deal of furniture to fill the rooms which she occupied upstairs.

Her husband had been a well-known minister in Rotterdam, and she had worked faithfully beside him in the church. They had no children, and it was a great loss in her life when he died before she was forty years old. After his death, it was clear that her place was to be in our house.

Tante Jans was not a woman to curl up with grief, and as soon as she had become established in her new quarters, she began all of her many activities which contributed to our buzzing household.

She was a poetess, an authoress, and an unusually good speaker. She started a monthly paper for girls, wrote books with a Gospel message, organized clubs for young women, and even began a club for soldiers.

One time Tante Jans swept into the house, pulling the scarf off her mouth, and proclaimed, 'There are soldiers wandering around the streets of Haarlem with idle minds and mischievous thoughts. I am going to start a club for soldiers.'

That's that! It was settled. When Tante Jans made one of her announcements, the wheels were set in motion. Before we knew what had happened our house began to look like a military installation. They would come alone or in pairs, young men who disliked the street life and were looking for the simple warmth of a home. One sergeant she met on a tram-car was a great musician. When he saw the harmonium which Tante Jans had against the wall of her room, he sat down and began to play, making the thin walls of the house quiver with each crescendo of volume.

Tante Jans folded her hands and listened intently to the talented soldier. She decided that Nollie and I should have him give us music lessons.

Even if we had not enjoyed music, we would have learned because Tante Jans decreed it. Soon I could play hymns well enough to join in the meetings and accompany the singing. It taught me at a very young age not to be self-conscious in the presence of men – although I don't think that was the intent of Tante Jans.

Some people have the gift of raising money by convincing others of the worth of a project, and this was one of Tante

Jans's special talents. One afternoon she had a tea and invited some wealthy women she knew to come to her rooms. We scurried around rubbing her silver tea set until it glistened, and making sure everything was immaculate for the occasion.

I peeked out of the window and watched the ladies arrive, swishing into the house with their long dresses underlined with full petticoats. How could they possibly walk and manoeuvre the narrow stairway with all those skirts? I had a hard time just keeping my feet in front of me! It must be a burden to be rich and have to dress in such fancy clothes, I thought.

Evidently Tante Jans was convincing, for in a short time she had enough money to build a military home. When it was finished and filled with soldiers, she went twice a week to give Bible studies.

Tante Jans didn't move with the times; she marched to her own beat. Her outspoken ideas on behaviour, clothes, and theology were constant abrasives on the surface of our family relationships.

When I was a child, I thought Tante Jans was very rich, because she was a minister's widow and received a small, regular pension. Sometimes she would have an unexpected donation, and we would all share her joy. However, when she bought clothing for us it could be embarrassing – especially for Nollie and Betsie who had their own very distinctive tastes.

'Oh, dear,' Betsie would say as she turned to give us the effect of a drab gray dress Tante Jans had given her. 'Do you think she would mind if I put some lace around the neck – or maybe a pink sash at the waist?'

'Betsie, if you think that's bad, just look at this hat,' Nollie would groan as she pulled a bonnet on backwards, sending us all into suppressed giggles. Tante Jans's taste in hats was somewhere between the style of a servant girl and that of a great-grandmother. Nollie was very fashion-conscious, and the gifts of stodgy clothes were a challenge to her ingenuity.

I didn't care about my appearance; I accepted all she gave me and consequently received the most hats and dresses.

During the First World War most of Tante Jans's income
stopped; it was dependent upon gifts of people who were
having a financial struggle themselves. I remember she was
surprised by an unexpected gift of fifty guilders (about eighteen dollars), and quickly gathered her muffler and umbrella
to go shopping. When she returned, we thought something
amazing must have happened, because she had forgotten to
button her coat to the top. The sight of Tante Jans with face
flushed and scarf loose was as uncommon as seeing the Queen
riding in a tram-car!

'Come in everyone . . . I have something to show you.' We
all followed her into her room, and she spread her packages
on the sofa, and began to distribute them with suppressed
excitement. There was a warm blanket for Mother, a coat
for me (black and shapeless, but practical), a blouse for Tante
Anna, and cakes for the whole family. Any sweets were rare
for us, reserved for birthdays and very special occasions.

I found out later that she had spent more than seventy
guilders on us. I believe she was one of the richest persons
I have known, for she knew how to give to others.

Tante Anna (Sheltering Apron)

Tante Anna, stocky, practical, unsentimental, was our substitute mother whenever Mother was too ill to care for
us. She ruled over her little basement kitchen like one
of Tante Jans's sergeants over his platoon. She was firm
and hard working, but overflowing with love for Mother,
Father, and all the children. When I was very young, I
would stand beside her in our basement kitchen and lick
the bowl of something she had been making. I watched
the legs of the people passing by the kitchen window, for
that was all we could see from beneath the street level. I
began to wonder about all the people in the gigantic world
outside.

'Tante Anna, where do babies come from?' I asked.

She stirred the *alle haphetzelfde* a bit and answered carefully, 'Well, Corrie, when a baby is too small and weak to
live in the cold world, there is a place underneath a mother's

heart where it is kept warm and can grow, until it is strong enough to stand the cold in the big world.'

I could understand that. It seemed like a very good plan of the Lord's.

My question answered in a simple manner, I went on to the more important matters of life, such as investigating with my finger the inside of another bowl. This one contained a special treat – *allusion*, which was a dessert made with stiffened egg whites and flavoured with lemon and sugar. There was more air than substance, but it was good for a big family.

Tante Anna was a good cook, stretching a little far. She would cook a stew on the big, black coal stove until most of the vegetables all blended into each other. The *alle haphetzelfde* meant 'every bite the same', and I know it was a real surprise and a treat when we encountered a bit of meat.

She had her club work, too, and her concern for others reached into the homes of the wealthy who employed servant girls. Every Wednesday and Sunday evening a group of them would come to a clubroom, and bring their sewing and embroidery work. Tante Anna taught them gospel songs and gave them a Bible study. When one of 'her girls' went the wrong way Tante Anna became ill. Her face would become puffy and swell, and we didn't have to ask; we knew that she had received a piece of bad news.

'Tante Anna, who was it this time?' we would ask.

She would take her apron and try to hide her blotchy face. 'It was Betty,' she would say, dabbing at her eyes, 'she wasn't strong enough in the Lord . . . she ran off with Hans . . . he's had two wives before this!' She would become as distressed as any mother would over a wayward child.

'Anna,' Father would say, 'you must not bear this yourself. Cast your worries upon the Lord.'

Nollie (*Mijn Moedertje*)

Nollie was physically the strongest of the three girls in the family. I considered her my elder, although she was only a year and a half older than I. Even when she was a little child, she felt responsible for me; she was my *moedertje* (little mother). As a toddler, whenever she drank water she brought a cup for me, too. I had to drink even if I wasn't thirsty. After all, Nollie knew best. I was shy and she was not; she voiced her needs and views. I waited.

One time, when we were very young, Nollie and I were out for a walk, when a man on a bicycle knocked us down right in front of our house. Covered with mud and shocked, we ran into the sitting room, loudly declaring our presence.

Nollie screamed and everyone came running, brushing her hair out of her eyes, wiping off the dirt, and kissing away the tears. I stood in the corner, watching all the commotion and wondering when I should take my turn screaming – after Nollie was through, of course. I knew my time to be comforted would come.

Suddenly Mother said, '*Hemeltje*! (Little Heaven!) Come look at Corrie.'

Everyone stopped, and for the first time realized that I was standing in the corner of the room, big tears making muddy rivers down my cheeks. Finally I was given the attention of the grown-ups.

The little alley beside our house was the scene of many events in our lives. There wasn't much room for playing in our overcrowded house, so the alley was our yard, our recreation room, and our schoolhouse of life. Once Nollie met a little boy named Sammy Staal. I think there must have been something wrong with his heart, for his skin had a bluish colour and his nose was always red. He was unable to walk, and propelled himself in a wheelchair. Nollie made friends with him, and encouraged by Mother, she would push him for hours and hours while the rest of the children were playing active games. When he died, Nollie was heartbroken.

Nollie's grief was probably a shared feeling. Even when we were very young, we knew that our problems were never too small for the grown-ups; there were many ways and many ages of love under one Dutch roof.

5

Winking Angels

Secrets are for children, and promises are like soap bubbles – easy to make, easy to break. The one time I tried to keep a secret from Mama, my little deception was uncovered. I talked in my sleep.

I was very young, perhaps eight or nine, and very flattered that Richard would ask me to go for a walk through the dunes. He was the nephew of our minister, and quite grown-up – a teenager.

However, I was not prepared for an act of boyish curiosity which surprised and shamed me at the same time. We had reached a valley where we could not be seen, and suddenly he pulled me close to him and started to do very strange things. Even without previous warnings from protective parents, I knew this was wrong.

I pulled away from him, flushing with childish indignation, and stamped my foot, 'Richard, you stop that. Mama would think that's dirty!'

Richard looked frightened, but defiant. 'She isn't here . . . and you mustn't tell.'

'Mama isn't here, but Jesus is and I'm sure He doesn't think it's right.'

Richard was defeated. He stopped immediately and said, 'Promise me never to tell anyone what I tried to do, especially your mother?'

I thought this over for a while. After all, he was Richard, and a very important person in my eyes.

'Well, I guess so . . . I promise.'

As we walked back home, he told me some very nice stories and I forgot about the incident.

At least I thought I forgot about it!

The next day I was ill and had a fever. I talked about the walk on the dunes, but wasn't conscious of what I had said. After the fever was gone, Mama asked me what had happened with Richard.

'A promise is a promise, Mama, and I said I wouldn't tell anybody in the world.'

'Correman, never forget that Jesus is always with you. Every morning I ask Him to keep you and all of my children within His constant care. In the evening, I thank Him that He sent His angels to guard you. Now you and I will pray together.'

I remember Mother folded her soft hands around mine when she prayed. I thought how wonderful it was that she asked Jesus to guard me. She prayed, 'Thank You, Jesus, that You never leave my Correman alone . . . thank You that You protected her during her walk on the dunes. Please lay Your hand on Richard . . . show him how wrong he was and that You are willing to make him a good clean boy.'

How did she know about Richard? I wondered if mothers know everything. Oh, well, never mind . . . Jesus knows, Mama knows, and everything is all right.

Dutch Mischief-Makers

I was no little angel. *Mischief* was my middle name, and Dot, my cousin and best friend, was my willing partner. Her father, Uncle Arnold, was the usher, or verger, of St Bavo's, the magnificent Gothic cathedral which dominates the centre of Haarlem. Its cavernous interior provided endless hours of imaginary play. In the banks (or pews) with their enclosed rows of seats, shut off from the aisles by half-doors, a child could have a private house. We could be pirates, hiding in our caves, or storekeepers in our offices; we could run a school or own a sweet shop.

The pulpit was out of bounds. We were not allowed to go there; that wasn't proper, or respectful. It seemed quite awesome to a small child, because the chair in the pulpit doesn't stand on the ground. It is held up by the bronze wings of an eagle. The font in front of the pulpit is supported by three brass snakes, and that was enough to keep us away without being told.

Our voices would echo in the stone interior, adding intrigue to our games. Sometimes Uncle Arnold would have to hush our exuberance.

'Children, children, there are graves beneath our feet. Step softly.'

The position of usher carried the privilege of living within the cathedral grounds. Uncle Arnold's family had a cozy little house just off the side entrance to the church. I always loved going in through the narrow passageway surrounded by beautiful blue Dutch tiles.

Living within the cathedral didn't make Dot any holier. If I didn't dream up a prank, she would.

We were in the same grade in school and usually walked together to our classes. I was comfortable with Dot, because we were on the same level of academic achievement, which was toward the bottom of the class. Whenever we had difficulty with our homework we asked Josien van Paassen to help us. She was not only bright but also owned a bicycle. A winning combination. Her father was a minister with a regular monthly income, but the earnings of a watchmaker went up and down like the weights on the grandfather clock.

One morning Dot called for me on the way to school, and she was unusually excited. 'Corrie, come here, look what I found.'

She handed me a dime which was broken in half; the coin had probably been run over by a carriage, and the two pieces were wedged on the cobblestones just waiting for a little girl to pick them up. A dime was a great deal of money to us; it could buy ten pieces of candy at the sweet shop on the Begynestraat. Such a rare and wonderful treat!

We skipped off to school, neither one of us admitting that we thought we were going to do anything wrong, and ordered our candies from the jolly lady who owned the shop. Dot slipped the two parts of the dime to me and I placed them on the counter, then made a very fast retreat out of the door. We were running toward school, when we heard the bell of the shop door ring and the owner call, 'Girls . . . girls . . . come back . . .!'

I grabbed Dot's hand and we ran a little faster, my feet having their usual problem of keeping up with my own momentum. We felt so guilty and for weeks avoided going by the candy store. The candy didn't taste very good, either, and in later years when I read this Proverb I thought about that childish caper. 'Bread obtained by falsehood is sweet to a man, but afterward his mouth will be filled with gravel' (Proverbs 20:17). Can candy really taste like gravel?

Another time Dot and I made some solid snowballs and put them in our pockets. It was so cold, they didn't melt but formed hard balls just the right size for mittened hands to grasp and throw. We were walking through the Kruisstraat behind three dignified men, who were loudly discussing their problems. I winked at Dot and we reached into our pockets, drew out our ammunition, took aim, and fired. The top hats flew into the snowy streets, and two sweet little girls raced to pick them up.

'Here you are, sir,' I said with a serious face and very polite demeanour, as I brushed the snow carefully off the hat. Dot picked up the second hat and handed it to one gentleman who had a very bald, cold head. He fitted the hat on his head and said, 'Thank you, young ladies,' as he looked around to see who the rascals were who committed such a crime.

Hats Off

Not all my episodes with hats went unpunished, however.

The director of our school was a very strict man, not the type of person who would tolerate misbehaviour from his students. Father had helped Mr van Lyden start the Christian educational institution, and because of this assistance we didn't pay to attend it, a fact which was a great help to the ten Boom family. When the school was new, many of the disciplinary problem children from other areas were sent there, and several times Mr van Lyden had to send them back to the schools they had attended previously.

I was shocked when a student was expelled. Just imagine how humiliating it was for the parents to have their child sent away from school for bad behaviour!

I must have been about ten years old when this occurred. I sat at my desk, gazing out of the window, watching the wind swirl the dust on the playground. I was thinking about the new hat Tante Jans had given me, a large blue and white sailor, which I hated just because it was a hat. The teacher stepped out of the room and an idea flashed into my mind.

'Listen, everyone,' I said to the class, 'I have a brilliant idea. Exactly at two o'clock we'll all put on our hats or caps. We can smuggle them under the desks so Mr van Ree won't see them. I've got a watch and I'll give the sign.'

The room of sixty ten-year-olds crackled with excitement, and I was the leader. The fact that I had a watch made me very important, because I was the only one in the class who had one.

Two o'clock arrived and the classroom was very quiet. We were working our arithmetic problems in silence, and the teacher looked from one to another, distrusting our unusually good behaviour.

I was sitting toward the front of the class and, after giving the signal, I took my hat from under the desk and put it on. I didn't hear a thing behind me. I looked around, and to my horror saw that no one else had the nerve to follow my example, except Jan Vixeboxe who sat at the back of the room. When my eyes returned to the teacher, he was staring right at me, furiously glaring from humourless eyes. There was terror in the atmosphere.

'Go to the headmaster at once, Corrie ten Boom!' he commanded.

Oh, no, not the headmaster! That was Mr van Lyden, and he expelled students for infraction of the rules.

I slipped from behind my desk, pulling off my hat as I left the room. In the hallway I opened the coat closet and ducked in, hiding myself in a dark corner behind the coats. I don't know how many miserable hours I spent there, but it seemed like an eternity before the bell rang, and I ran out ahead of the rest of the students.

I expected to be dismissed, just as the problem pupils from other schools had been. I thought of all the shame I would bring to Mama and Papa, of all they would have to go through because of my misdeed. How I loved them! I thought of all the care they had given me, of the difficulties we had as a result of sickness and lack of money. We were such a close-knit family that we always shared joys and sorrows, and now this! Dismissed from the school my father had helped organize!

At the supper table that night I was so quiet Mama thought I was sick. I went upstairs early and crept into bed, pulling the eiderdown under my chin. I told Nollie everything that had happened.

'Why don't you ask forgiveness of God?' she suggested.

'I've already done that . . . but do you think He will arrange it so that I won't be sent away from school?'

I asked Nollie the deep questions which were puzzling me, because she was almost twelve! Certainly she would know all the answers.

'I don't know,' Nollie replied, 'but do you remember that boring Psalm that Papa read at the table, where every sixth or seventh verse were the same words? ". . . Then they cried unto the Lord in their trouble, and he saved them out of their distresses"' (Psalms 107 AV).

For the first time since the hats-off incident I began to cheer up. 'Why couldn't we do the same?'

We 'cried unto the Lord' and then fell asleep. The next morning Nollie shook me awake and told me her wonderful idea. We had a little monthly missionary magazine that I delivered to several people as my special work in evangelizing the world. Mr van Lyden was one of the subscribers. Nollie suggested, 'You must manage in some way to go to the headmaster, and personally bring him the mission magazine for this month. It can't do any harm, and perhaps it will do some good.'

That morning, with my heart pounding right through my best school dress and a very pious expression on my face, I went to the headmaster's room and handed him the paper.

He looked at it and then at me. The pause took a hundred years and the silence hurt my ears. He didn't have much of a sense of humour, but I believe the corners of his mouth turned up just a little bit.

He cleared his throat, tapped the desk with his pencil, and said, 'Corrie ten Boom, I don't think you behaved as a very good Christian girl yesterday.'

That was all I ever heard about my crime. The Lord saved me from my distress.

Mice in the Manuscript

When I was about twelve, I decided that I wanted to be a writer. I curled up on my bed, pad of paper on my lap, and wove a wonderful fantasy about the adventures of Nollie, Josien, Dot, and all of Dot's brothers and sisters on a holiday without our parents. It was a beautiful story, filled with more adventure than Dickens, and more vivid character sketches than Louisa May Alcott. How famous I would be!

Betsie shattered my dreams. She came into the room and asked, 'What's that?'

It seemed quite obvious to me. 'It's a book I'm writing,' I answered as smugly as a sister seven years younger could reply to the ridiculous question of a grown-up.

Betsie seldom voiced any words of discouragement, but this time she said, 'How foolish . . . you can't write a book.'

I just won't show anyone my book any more, I thought. So I hid it in the attic and forgot the priceless manuscript for several months.

When I remembered later to take the papers out of their secret niche, there was only one-tenth of this potential best seller left. The rest was eaten by the mice. I was so disappointed that I decided never to write a book again.

The Shadow of His Wings

My security was assured in many ways as a child. Every night I would go to the door of my room in my nightie and

call out, 'Papa, I'm ready for bed.' He would come to my room
and pray with me before I went to sleep. I can remember
that he always took time with us, and he would tuck the
blankets around my shoulders very carefully, with his own
characteristic precision. Then he would put his hand gently
on my face and say, 'Sleep well, Corrie . . . I love you.'

I would be very, very still, because I thought that if I moved
I might lose the touch of his hand; I wanted to feel it until I
fell asleep.

Many years later in a concentration camp in Germany, I
sometimes remembered the feeling of my father's hand on
my face. When I was lying beside Betsie on a wretched, dirty
mattress in that dehumanizing prison, I would say, 'Oh, Lord,
let me feel Your hand upon me . . . may I creep under the
shadow·of Your wings.'

In the midst of that suffering was my heavenly Father's
security.

Reach As High As You Can

My desire to please my papa was one of the basic motivations
of my life. I remember when I was walking home from school,
there was a very dirty wall I passed every day. It was full of
flies, and during the warm weather one of my games was to
run my hand along the wall and try to catch a fly. When the
challenge had been met, I would release it and try for the
next catch.

One day when I was busy with this messy game I heard
a familiar voice behind me, 'Now isn't this a joy to meet my
youngest daughter here on the street.'

I was suddenly very embarrassed about how dirty I was,
for Papa was so immaculate and well dressed that I didn't dare
put my hand in his. He never mentioned my appearance, just
walked along chatting about the visit to Mrs de Vries and his
talk with the servant girl about the Lord, until we arrived
inside the Beje.

'I'm home, Cor,' he'd call to Mama. Then he turned to me
and said, 'And I know, Corrie, that you're going to wash your
hands before you see your mother.'

Such a small thing, but I remember the shame of being so dirty in Papa's presence.

We were always challenged to do our best. When Papa took a watch apart and put it back together again, it was a task he performed without regard to the owner's social status or wealth. He taught us that it wasn't important what you think, or even what other people think, but what God thinks about the job you have done.

When Nollie and I were teenagers, we decided to take sewing lessons. I made a blouse; it was a very careless job, with crooked seams and poorly fitted sleeves. I pulled it on, knowing that I looked very sloppy but not really caring much until I saw Papa's face. 'Corrie, the servant girl may be able to teach you how to scrub a floor, but your mother should teach you how to sew. When you spend your time and money on making something, it should be your best effort.'

Achievement and honesty were such basic ingredients in Papa's personality that there were times when we had to hide the giggles he disliked so much. One of the stories Mama told about him was, 'My husband is so honest that when the children were babies, he wouldn't allow me to give them a pacifier, no matter how loud or how long they cried. He would say, "They think they are getting a drink. That is fooling a child to put something in her mouth which is a lie." '

Mama would sigh with amused resignation and say, 'So my babies never had a pacifier, because my husband is so honest.'

Papa was honest about pain, too. Whenever we had to go to a dentist or a doctor, Papa would come along to comfort us. However, he would never say that we would not have pain. He said that if we had to have a tooth filled or pulled, that we must be brave and strong. Whenever it was possible, he went with us. Holding his hand gave us courage. If the doctor did need his assistance, his strong hands kept our hands or head from moving.

Perhaps it is wrong to tell this today – in view of the permissive way in which many children are being raised – but we were disciplined without spanking. I cannot remember being spanked as a child, but there was no doubt in our family that we were to obey Father. His will was law and we all knew it.

We never spoke about the 'line of authority' in our home – it was simply understood. Father didn't have to stand up and say, 'I'm the head of this family!' He just was. We never felt any desire to have it any other way, because the love and security of all our relationships were built upon the established fact that God was always with us, and He had appointed Casper ten Boom in charge of the mansion in Haarlem called the Beje.

6

Around the Oval Table

Can a piece of furniture be important? The oval table in our dining room was the gathering place for hopes and dreams, the listening place for prayers and petitions, and the loving place for joy and laughter.

But Sunday it was something more – it was the special place for family and friends.

Sunday was an important day for us; it was a day when everything – from the clothes we wore to the spoons we used – was distinctive. My Sunday dress was the new one I received for Christmas, so I seldom had a choice about what I would wear to church. Tante Anna could work magic with that dress, adding a coloured sash or a ribbon in a way that improved my rather careless appearance. It was another of her small gifts of service which said, 'I care'.

When we were ready for church, Father would lead the way to St Bavo's while we trailed along, trying not to scuff our shoes or soil our Sunday outfits.

After church it was good to go home, especially when the weather was chilly, for St Bavo's was unheated, and there were days when my teeth would chatter through the entire service.

At home I would help with the Sunday dinner, first by smoothing a beautiful white cloth over the oval table. I tried to do this carefully, because I knew that Betsie wanted it to hang evenly, and it was a great desire of mine to meet her standards. Everything about Betsie was neat and I was . . . oh, well – just Corrie.

'Good work, Corrie,' she would say, and that was all I needed to encourage me for the rest of the day.

The delicate china, which had been brought from Indonesia by father's older sister, Tante Toos, and Tante Jans's ornate silver service – a gift from wealthy members of her husband's church – were placed on the table. Then Tante Anna would emerge from the kitchen, wiping her hands on the generous apron she used to cover her black silk dress, and ring a little bell.

'Come to dinner, everyone.'

When we were seated, Father would remove his fresh Sunday napkin from its holder, place it carefully on his lap, and bow his head.

'Lord, we thank You for this beautiful Lord's Day and for this family. Bless this food, bless our Queen, and let soon come the day that Jesus, Your beloved Son, comes on the clouds of heaven. *Amen.*'

Our table talk on Sunday sometimes centred around the sermon we had heard, but usually Father was cautious not to say too much. He attended the cathedral near our home because he felt that God had called him to that place, but he didn't hold any position in the church. His views were not accepted by the liberal thinkers who were in positions of leadership.

Conversations around the dinner table were lively because we all had stories or experiences we wanted to share. I believe that the great enjoyment of a family eating together is having this time when each person can be heard.

Father had a special talent in directing our talks so that no one would feel left out. We loved to tell personal stories, but were taught to laugh at ourselves, not to make fun of others.

I remember one time when Nollie was telling about a painting she had done in school.

'I thought the drawing was rather good,' Nollie said, 'but when Mr van Arkel walked over to my desk, he held up my picture and looked at it one way and then another, scowling all the time.'

'Maybe he just wanted to get a better view,' Betsie offered.

'I'm afraid that wasn't his reason,' Nollie answered.

(Studies were important in our family, so each one of us received special attention when we talked about school.)

'What did Mr van Arkel say, Nollie?' Mother asked.

'He said, "Do you know of which Proverb your drawing reminds me, Nollie ten Boom?"'

'I told him *"Honi soit qui mal y pense."* (Disgraced is he who thinks wrong of it.) It's from a motto on a badge of knighthood. Boy, did Mr van Arkel laugh!'

Nollie's eyes twinkled when she told the story. Father really enjoyed a good joke, as long as the girls didn't giggle. Laughter he loved, but giggling was *verboden*.

On Sunday afternoons we frequently had visitors who would stop for a cup of tea and conversation. Sometimes we would go for a walk, but we didn't study, sew, or work on the Lord's Day. The only work allowed was winding the watches which were in the shop for repair.

Father said, 'Even on Sunday, I must milk my cows.'

Father's Friends

Fellowship around the oval table was more than just a family affair. Throughout the years there were many people, young and old, rich and poor, who contributed so much to the richness of my childhood. I loved to have some of Father's friends visit our home, because they laughed a lot and always told wonderful stories.

When Father was a young man in Amsterdam he worked in a mission called *Heil des Volks*, which was in a very poor part of the city. There were three other men who gave their time and energy to this particular outreach and they all became fast friends.

The four men would meet often, sharing their burdens and triumphs, studying the Bible together, and discussing many topics of interest. As a child, I was always happy when they came to our house; it was a time when I loved to listen to the conversations of these great friends and learn from their experiences. The children were welcome to stay during their discussions, and encouraged to participate if we had something we wanted to ask. I can still recall the fragrant mixture of cologne and good Dutch cigars which lingered in the room.

Frits Vermeer was a rather round Dutchman who loved to joke. He was 'Uncle Frits' to us, just as the other good friends were called Uncle Dirk and Uncle Hendrik.

One of the first things Father would do when his friends arrived was to bring out the box of cigars from its place in the desk where the bulky ledger of the shop was kept. From his pocket, he would take the special cigar clipper which had keys for winding the clocks on the other side. It was a very important tool, and many children over a span of half a century sat on his lap and played with it.

Uncle Hendrik was considered the theologian of the group, and was constantly being challenged for a Bible verse to meet some situation or problem. He was seldom at a loss when asked to quote something appropriate for the occasion.

Uncle Dirk, the fourth member of the group, was the only one who wasn't married. However, he loved children very much and was able to express that love in a special way.

On one occasion, when Father's friends were discussing their concerns, Uncle Dirk was anxious to tell about an orphanage where he was on the board of directors. I sat up and listened carefully, because children without parents bothered me so much. I thought how terrible it would be not to have the love of a mother and father.

'I decided to become the father of the orphanage,' Uncle Dirk announced. 'I have been on the board of directors, arguing for better conditions for those poor children, but I have not seen any positive results. I must get in there and work myself.'

Father was delighted. 'Dirk, this is certainly the leading of the Lord for you. He has not given you a wife, but He is going to bless you with many, many children. We will pray about it.'

Father would begin to pray with his friends in an attitude which was so easy and natural that the conversation never seemed to stop; it would flow easily from friend to friend to the Lord.

Many times through the years I remember the wonderful moments I had listened to the stories and experiences of Father's friends. There is a Proverb which says, 'Do not forsake your own friend or your father's friend . . . ' (Proverbs 27:10). I have often thought how wise that is.

Bible Study Was a Game

With the dishes cleared off and kitchen duties accomplished, the oval table could be turned into a place for games. We didn't play cards (for that was considered a form of gambling), but we had a lasting enjoyment in the type of games which taught us something.

Different languages were introduced as a game, not as a forced study. When I was in the fourth grade, we began to learn French. As I remember, I loved the melodious sounds of this beautiful language, but it was and remained a difficult language for me. The next year I started English, which was easier, but I wondered as I struggled with all the different English meanings for words if I would ever go to England or America and have an opportunity to use the language.

Father wanted me to learn English well, and he gave me a little Sunday-school booklet in English which was called 'There's No Place Like Home.' I read it over and over again.

The greatest fun in language-learning came during our Bible study. The entire family would take part, each one of us having a Bible in a different language. Willem usually had the original in Hebrew and Greek; I would have the English; Mother the Dutch; Nollie the French; and Betsie or Father, German. It was a special and joyous time for us.

Father would begin by asking what John 3:16 was in English. I would answer from my English Bible, Mother from her Dutch Bible, and Betsie would reply in German.

When I was so young, it didn't seem possible that Betsie would ever have a chance to use a Bible verse in German. We didn't know any Germans then! However, God uses such seemingly insignificant ways to prepare us for the plan He has for our lives. Over forty years later, in a concentration camp in Germany, Betsie was able to use that verse – and many more – to speak to the prisoners and the guards about God's love.

When Father Prayed . . .

Every room in our house heard our prayers, but the oval table probably experienced more conversations with the Lord than other places. Praying was never an embarrassment for us, whether it was with the family together or when a stranger came in. Father prayed because he had a good Friend to talk over the problems of the day; he prayed because he had a direct connection with his Maker when he had a concern; he prayed because there was so much for which he wanted to thank God.

When Father talked with the Lord it was serious, but unpretentious. He talked to Someone he knew. Once we had a minister in our house, and when his visit was over, Father prayed, 'Thank You Lord, for a good day. We hope everyone goes together in the same way.'

The minister left with a puzzled expression on his face. Could this be the Casper ten Boom so many of his parishioners told him had such a deep understanding of God's Word?

Father always prayed before and after each meal. He included two things in his prayer: the Queen and the Second Coming of Jesus Christ.

The knowledge and anticipation of the return of Jesus Christ was given to me by Father during one of the quiet, thoughtful times before I went to sleep as a small child. As for the Queen – patriotism and loyalty were an accepted way of thinking in our house, as it was in most Dutch homes. However, I never thought that the prayers of the little ten Boom girl would be answered in such unusual ways.

Me? A Guest of the Queen? Not Me!

It was the year 1956, more than half a century after I first heard Father pray for the Queen. I was in Formosa with Dr Bob Pierce, a man whose outreach of love and concern has spread throughout the world. He said to me one day, 'Corrie, I believe it would be a good idea for you to talk with the Queen of your country.'

Bob is an American, and I forgave him for not understanding about proper protocol with members of royalty. How ridiculous, I thought.

'Bob, you don't know what you're saying . . . I can't go see the Queen.'

He looked at me gently and said, 'Just pray about it.' And so I did.

Wilhelmina had been Queen through two world wars; her reign had spanned two generations, and now she had abdicated and given the position of monarchy to her only daughter, who is our Queen Juliana. Wilhelmina chose to have the title of *Princess* from that moment on.

When I was back in my homeland, I wrote to Princess Wilhelmina, and said that I would like to meet her and bring greetings from Bob Pierce and World Vision International. The day after my letter was delivered the Princess sent her car to pick me up.

I sat in the back seat of the limousine, enjoying every kilometre from Haarlem to *Het Loo Apeldoorn*, where her palace was.

Wouldn't Father have loved this, I thought. *All those years he prayed for the Queen and here is his daughter, Corrie, visiting Princess Wilhelmina herself!*

One amazing thing after another happened. I was given the opportunity of speaking with the Queen and meeting all the people in the palace. After a few hours I had to tell Princess Wilhelmina that I had to leave for some meetings that were planned in Germany.

She looked at me and said, 'I expected you to stay several weeks here, and you're just staying a few hours. Why are you going to Germany?'

The war had been over for more than ten years, but its memories were still vivid to many Hollanders.

'I must go to Germany, Your Highness, because God has called me to tell them of His love and forgiveness.'

She dismissed what I was saying with a wave of her hand,

but later when I returned once more to Holland she sent word for me to come and stay in the palace for a longer time. I was allowed on that visit one hour each evening with Princess Wilhelmina. She said, 'I'm too old for too much, so we may either eat together or talk for an hour.' I chose the last part, and had my meals with her lady-in-waiting afterwards. Princess Wilhelmina knew her Bible very well, and we enjoyed those hours in her lovely private chamber. She gave me the opportunity to tell her of the miracle God had worked in my life to forgive my enemies.

I believe that in some way something of Father's prayers many, many years before were answered when God allowed the daughter of the watchmaker to carry His message of love to the Queen.

I had a happy time of fellowship with many people in the palace. I had personal contact with most of them when we talked about the most important Person, our Lord Jesus Christ. But the happiest moments of each day were the hours with that great lady who had reigned over our little country in a time when two world wars had wounded Europe.

7

Seventeen, and So Much to Learn

When Betsie told a story, she wove threads of brilliant colour through the word pictures she created. When she moved into a room, or dressed for a meeting, it was with a special flair. She knew *levenskunst* (the art of living)!

I wasn't what people would call a 'mature' teenager. I was a tomboy during my adolescence – not a 'young lady'. However, I loved imitating and wanted to learn, but it didn't seem possible to me that I would ever have those soft qualities of womanhood which were so natural to my older sister.

Betsie taught me many things, and one of them was how to tell a story. She had a Sunday-school class for many years, starting to teach when she was seventeen. She loved her pupils, and the little gifts and adoring glances she had from those boys and girls proved that her love was returned many times. One day she said to me, 'Corrie, you must take a class, too.'

'What can I teach?' I asked, thinking how embarrassed I would be if someone asked me a question I couldn't answer. There was so much I didn't understand, especially all those Kings and Judges and battles in the Old Testament.

Betsie's answer was, 'Try it! Tell the story of the feeding of the five thousand.'

Now there was a story I knew! So I went with her to her class, believing this was a very simple assignment. What an embarrassment! How inadequate I felt when I finished the story in five minutes. The class was thirty minutes long and I didn't know how to fill the remaining time. Betsie took over and I listened with amazement as she told the same story over to a spellbound class of children.

I was rather discouraged; I didn't know how to tell a story, but after that experience I was determined to learn. As I listened to Betsie I realized that you must weave a tale, leading your listeners on a word journey.

A girl friend of mine, Mina, was a teacher in a Christian school and she promised to help me. We asked permission of the director of the school to allow me to give the Bible story in her class every Monday morning. They were pretty drab at first, but gradually I began to learn how to add those imaginative touches which made them more interesting.

I used the technique of describing one picture after another, leading my little class through the art gallery of the Bible. When I told the story of the feeding of the five thousand again, we visualized Jesus with all the people sitting on the grass around Him. We would look at these people individually, imagining where they lived, what sort of problems they had, and what they might be thinking about this Man with the divine love in His eyes. The next picture is of Jesus and His followers, the disciples, talking about how the tired, hungry people were going to be fed. There was no bakery or fish market within sight, but there was an obvious need for food. The blue waters of Galilee reflected the surrounding green and brown hills, and the luxuriant grass where the people sat to listen to Jesus was flattened by the crowd.

Then I would carry my listeners with me to the climax, as Jesus took the five loaves and two fish offered Him by a boy who had gone shopping for his mother, and '. . . looking up toward heaven, He blessed the food and broke the loaves and He kept giving them to the disciples to set before them; He divided up the two fish among them all. And they all ate and were satisfied' (Mark 6:41, 42).

'What a feast we have when we believe Jesus Christ!' I would end.

I had no idea how valuable this lesson was going to be in later life. If Betsie had told me that some day I would be speaking before thousands of people, I'm sure that the

fear of such a thing would have silenced my clumsy efforts
at story-telling immediately.

From Bach With Love

Music was as much a part of my young life as television is
to the children of today. Mother and Tante Anna had taught
kindergarten, and I can remember their singing to me the
little songs they taught to their schoolchildren. When I was
old enough to sit at the organ called the harmonium and pump
the pedals with my feet, Tante Jans had arranged for one of
her military visitors to give Nollie and me music instruction.

We loved to sing in our house. Nollie had a rich soprano
voice, Willem sang tenor, and I was the alto when we learned
to sing the Bach chorale *'Seid froh die Weil'*. I grew up
loving Bach.

One time Father called us together and said, 'We're going
to St Bavo's tomorrow evening for a great treat!'

I couldn't imagine anything that could be better than some of
the concerts we had already enjoyed at Uncle Arnold's church.
Because of Uncle Arnold's position as caretaker, we were
given special permission to listen to the concerts, sitting on
the bench beside the door which separated his home from the
main sanctuary. Only the people who had money could afford
to attend these fine concerts, and without Uncle Arnold, all
the members of the ten Boom family would seldom have been
able to enjoy such riches.

'Wear your warm clothes,' Mama warned, as we were
getting ready for the mysterious treat.

St Bavo's was a vast, unheated building with footwarmers
for those who could afford to pay, and a hard wooden bench
with cold stone at our backs for Uncle Arnold's relatives.

We all lined up, excited over the anticipation of Father's
'great treat', and went to the cathedral, by-passing the front
entrance and going in the side door to our own special
reserved seats. The smell of moisture and dust, smoul-
dering gas lamps, and the burning coals in the footwarmers
was so familiar, and the excitement began to build. We
sat down, with Father wrapping a wool blanket around

Mother and placing a pillow at her back to make her more comfortable.

A wiry man with unruly grey hair and a drooping moustache passed us before going upstairs to the world-famous pipe organ. I had explored the area where this impressive organ stood and wondered how anyone could learn to play on so many manuals with sixty-eight stops. We had been told that Mozart played that organ when he was only ten years old.

We soon knew why the evening was going to be such a treat. I held my breath as Albert Schweitzer began playing a Bach prelude. He was an authority on organ building, and an organist who could fill the cathedral with exquisite beauty. During the day St Bavo's was a composition in grey, inside and out, but in the evening – with the gas lamps giving a Rembrandtesque light, the pillars pointing upwards in a mysterious glow – the atmosphere of harmony was heaven. I thought eternity must contain this kind of beauty.

Albert Schweitzer was a German philosopher, physician, writer, and theologian. He had gone to Africa as a medical missionary and established a hospital and a leper colony. As his fame grew throughout the world, I often thought of the first time I heard him interpret Bach, and how much Father's treat contributed to my lifetime love of music.

Impatient to Learn Patience

We are not born with patience, and I believe God began to teach me something of what this means when I was in my seventeenth year. Because I was the youngest of the family, I remained childlike for a long time. I loved life intensely, charged with the desire to cram every available experience into each day. Then came a terrible blow which depressed me so severely, I thought I wouldn't survive.

For some weeks I had a slight fever. For a time I managed to disguise how I felt, but soon Mama began to see my listless attitude and called the doctor. He probed and tapped, listened and questioned, and then told me I had tuberculosis.

Death sentence! *So young*, I thought . . . *why would God*

want me with Him when there was so much for me to do on earth?

'You must go to bed, Corrie, until the fever is gone,' the doctor pronounced.

In those days tuberculosis was as fearful as cancer is now. I cried and went upstairs slowly, not looking back. It was the middle of the day and it seemed strange to undress and go to bed!

I cried to the Lord, 'Why must I be ill, Lord? I will live! I will be healthy!' It took many days before I could surrender and accept the situation. I surely had to learn what it says in Colossians:

> We pray that you will be strengthened from God's boundless resources, so that you will find yourselves able to pass through any experience and endure it with courage. You will even be able to thank God in the midst of pain and distress . . .
>
> I:II, 12 PHILLIPS

Through my tears and anger, I would thank Him, but I couldn't understand why He wanted me to lie in bed, imprisoned by the walls of my little room.

At first many visitors came upstairs, but after several months had passed, some people forgot me. I began to feel more self-pity and rebellion, but I prayed every day for peace in my heart and finally the moment came when I could say, 'Yes, Lord, You know best.'

At that time Willem was a theological student at the University of Leiden. He was going to have an examination in church history, and often came home on weekends.

'I get things in my head if I teach them. How about it, Corrie, if I give you some books will you study them?'

It was not the first time I had to assist him in that way. To earn some money in his college time, he gave lessons in Latin to a boy who was a very unwilling pupil. Every morning from seven until eight o'clock he taught him, and I joined the two of them. If the boy didn't listen and was absolutely uncooperative, then Willem taught me Latin. I enjoyed those lessons, and knew that my brother was a good teacher.

I gained a great love for church history during those months of confinement, and it took my thoughts away from my illness.

The doctor did not visit me much; rest was the only cure he knew, and he told the family not to allow me to get out of bed until there was no sign of a fever. One day he passed my room after visiting Tante Bep, who was very old and feeble, and I called him.

'Doctor, I have a pain in my abdomen. It's right here,' I said, pressing my fist on my right side.

He examined me and found an appendix infection, which was probably the cause of my fever all that time. I don't think anyone has ever been so happy with appendicitis! After five months of confinement I left my bed, had a minor operation, and returned to the wonderful outside world.

In the World, But Not of It

Until that time in my life the outside world was very small. It consisted of the streets and alleys of Haarlem, with only brief excursions with Father to Amsterdam, or an occasional visit to a neighbouring village to visit friends.

I began to want to be somebody outside the protection of the Beje – to learn about the world that existed away from the Barteljoristraat. I didn't dream that I could see some of the countries and people that I read about in my geography book, but at least I wanted to experience life outside the shop.

Was I wrong? I struggled with this ambition and decided to ask my Bible teacher, Mrs van Lennep, who was a very understanding woman who counselled well. She said, 'Corrie, it's very natural for you to feel the way you do. You can do something in the world through the power of the Lord.'

The first thing I did was launch into an intensive study of many subjects. I received diplomas in home economics, child care, needlepoint, and others. It proved to be a good background for my first job.

My opportunity came to be 'out in the world'. I heard about

a job from one of the girls at school. The Bruins, who had a magnificent home, needed an *au pair* for their little girl. This position was a combination governess and companion. I knew this was what Tante Bep had done in her youth – and she had become a lonely and rather dour old woman – but this didn't quench my original enthusiasm for what I thought would be a new adventure in living.

Father and Mother gave their permission, and I packed my few clothes in a little suitcase and left with great anticipation for Zandvoort, a village by the sea, about ten miles from Haarlem.

The contrast between my home-life and my new job began with my first glimpse of the home. It was so big! How could just one family live in a house that size?

As I began my job, I tried very hard to please the entire family. At home I had always known fun and laughter, with a large dose of love and affection. Out in the world it wasn't the same. For the first time I was faced with a new way of thinking, a different kind of family life than I had ever experienced.

If this was the way to 'be somebody', I wasn't sure it was what I wanted.

Thursday was my day off, and it was such a relief to go back to Haarlem for my catechism lessons. Going home each week only made me realize the contrast between the security of our family and life in the outside world. In some ways, it was disillusioning to me.

I had determined to do my very best as an *au pair*. I wanted to leave often, but I was not a quitter, so I stayed.

One day, however, Willem came to Zandvoort with the news that our oldest aunt, Tante Bep, had died. She had been an invalid in our house for many years and Tante Anna had the full responsibility of nursing her after I left. Now Willem told me that Tante Anna was very tired and should have a long rest.

I told my employer that I must leave at once because I was needed at home. Freedom at last! In my heart I wanted to rejoice that I was going home, but under the circumstances it really didn't seem the proper thing to do.

As Willem took my little bag and we walked away from that house of luxury, I felt no regret. Willem said, 'Let's go down to the beach – it's such a glorious day!' And then he began to sing Bach music very loudly.

Somehow I felt it was all right to rejoice inside, but I didn't think it was right to let it show. 'Willem, how can you do such a thing? Tante Bep has died and you shouldn't be acting so happy.'

'Of course we should be happy, Corrie. A child of God is a citizen of heaven and the attitude of a Christian must be one of praise when someone has died. Our grief for Tante Bep would just be one of selfishness on our part, of grieving for the sake of ourselves.'

I knew he was right, and when we arrived at the Beje, it was with our hearts at peace with the knowledge of the glory of Tante Bep's new home in heaven. How good it was to be home! There was a harmony there which was such a contrast to the rich home of my former employer. I realized then why Tante Bep had the type of personality she had. Just a small taste of the life she had led gave me more understanding. We never know until we walk in someone else's shoes.

The Everlasting Arms

There were so many times when the problems of the moment, whether they were small or large, would overwhelm me. I remember a time, not long after Tante Bep's death, when Mother became very ill. I was so worried about her, and in addition I knew there was a large bill which had to be paid within the next few days. People were not interested in buying watches at that time, and Father and I were sitting in the dining room talking things over.

I stared at the familiar red and black tablecloth which had seen happy and sad times. I felt so depressed. Everything was wrong, and there didn't seem to be any good thing which could come out of such a discouraging situation.

'Father, what must we do? Everything is so terrible!'

'Don't forget, Corrie – underneath us are the everlasting arms. We won't fall.'

I didn't know that expression and I asked, 'Is that in the Bible?'

'It certainly is. Moses spoke those words to the sons of Israel.'

'How does that help us right now?' I asked rebelliously.

'Girl, it makes all the difference. Moses tells us in the Book of Deuteronomy that God is a dwelling place. We have the promise of security when His arms are beneath us . . . holding us . . . supporting us . . . strengthening us.'

Thirty years later I was lying on a dirty mattress in a concentration camp. It was pitch-dark, and in that restless room Betsie lay so close to me that I could feel her heartbeat. It was irregular and feeble.

I tried to think of something comforting to say to her before we fell asleep, and suddenly I remembered the dining room, the red and black tablecloth, and Father saying in his calm voice, '. . . underneath are the everlasting arms'.

'Betsie . . . are you asleep?'

'No, not yet,' she said weakly.

'Remember what Father told us: "God is our dwelling place. Underneath are the everlasting arms."'

I can't be sure, but I believe she must have smiled in that black barracks.

'Oh, yes, Corrie . . . and they will never leave us.'

8

The Best Is Yet to Be

Our concerns reached beyond the borders of Holland. We all wanted to know more about other lands, different languages, and people from contrasting cultures. This interest was stimulated by visitors from many countries, and by reading good books.

During my late teen years a man came to Holland who focused our attention upon foreign missions. His name was Jan Willem Gunning, and he started a movement for 'mission study advice'. Betsie, Nollie, Willem, and I became involved in groups which he formed. During the summer we went to a conference in Lunteren, a centre in the midst of the woods and heather fields. It was so exciting to meet real missionaries from all over the world.

On the first day of meetings, an elderly missionary led the hundreds of people at the conference in group singing, and our own Nollie was chosen to be a soloist.

'Nollie, isn't it thrilling? Imagine – you're going to sing for all those people,' I said.

'Oh, Corrie, don't remind me or I won't be able to utter a sound.'

It was a new experience for all of us. We listened to the lectures, and then divided into smaller discussion groups. We chose what we wanted to study, and later used the material in weekly meetings at home. Mission students from a large school led these discussions, and we became great friends with some of them.

Many girls we knew were interested in more than the study

groups; the mission students were as new and different as the subjects we were being taught. Unfortunately, there was very little time for dates. In fact, the only time available was two hours before breakfast. I've never been very alert at an early hour, but I learned to accept the challenge of this discipline for the advantages of the friendships.

I slept with a little rope around my toe. When a boy came to meet me when I was still asleep, he pulled the end of the rope which hung outside my window, and I would jerk to attention. Soon we would be walking together over the heather fields of Lunteren, talking about mission activities, and what we wanted to do with our lives. It was innocent enough – but not the part of the conference I would relate to Tante Jans!

One boy, Albert de Neef, had a girl friend who was not very strong. She had gone to her doctor for a physical to find out if she was healthy enough to go to Indonesia, but during the conference she heard that she had been rejected. Those two were very sad, so we invited her to come to the Beje for a visit. She had so much fun with us that she almost forgot her disappointment. However, a year later, during another mission study conference, she was re-examined, and was given approval to go to the mission field.

Because of that little act of hospitality, we became quite popular among the mission students. A new world opened for all four of us when we started a mission study group at home.

We had such good training at those camps. I never dreamed how much this would mean years later, when I became a tramp for the Lord and visited mission fields on five continents.

Beyond the Dikes

My horizons began to stretch. From the camps for missions, we met people from all over the world. Then through the YMCA in Haarlem, we had further opportunities to know people from other countries and other denominations. The Y was only a building where young men could have meetings, but tourists came from other countries, expecting it to be a hotel. The manager didn't speak English, and many times he brought guests to the Beje, where he knew they would be welcomed. We could exercise our English, broadening our interest in the whole world situation at the same time.

I learned more about Christians who did not have the exact beliefs in some doctrines which we did. As a little girl, I had always thought that the Dutch Reformed Church was the only one which had the right theology. Others could love the Lord, I granted, but they really had a lot to learn!

As my interest in a true ecumenical faith grew, I began to learn about Christians who endured so much for their beliefs. Father once told me of Christians in Russia who were called Stundists. They loved the Lord and were willing to suffer for Jesus. They knew the Bible from cover to cover, and were very strict in their behaviour.

Father said, 'God has given Russia a great blessing by sending these Christians to that country. They live in the vast area of Siberia in a kind of community life where young and old are trained to glorify the Lord.'

It seemed so remote to hear about suffering of Christians. We were free in Holland, and it was difficult for me to imagine Christians in another land undergoing persecution.

More than half a century passed after Father told me about the Stundists. Ellen de Kroon, my secretary and companion, and I went to Russia. We travelled all the way to Tadzhik, far inside Russia near to Siberia, and there we found a lively church, so dedicated to the Lord that it was a light in that dreary land. These people were Stundists, and I remembered Father's story.

A very old woman, stooped with age, a lifetime of extreme hardships written on her face, came to me and said, 'Corrie ten Boom, I have prayed daily for you for years.'

I was astonished. 'How did you know about me?'

'Once I got a Care package from Germany. One of the boxes was packed with a page from a Christian magazine, and I read about your experiences and the work you do now. God told me to pray faithfully for you.'

It never ceases to amaze me the way the Lord creates

a bond among believers which reaches across continents, beyond race and colour. This spiritual bond is something man has tried to establish with big national or world councils and organized ecumenical movements, but always misses when the Spirit of the Lord is not present.

Sadhu Sundar Singh

A person who influenced my life in my late teens was a man from India. As a boy he was taught to hate Jesus. He knew about God, but the Bible of the Christians was a book which he believed was a gigantic lie. Once he took a Bible and burned it, feeling that with this act, he could publicly declare his scorn of what he believed were the untruths it contained. When missionaries passed him he threw mud on them.

But there was a terrible unrest inside of him; he longed to know God. He told this story about himself:

'Although I had believed that I had done a very good deed by burning the Bible, I felt unhappy. After three days, I couldn't bear it any longer. I rose early in the morning and prayed that if God really existed, He would reveal Himself to me. I wanted to know if there was an existence after death, if there was a heaven. The only way I could know it for sure was to die. So I decided to die.

'I planned to throw myself in front of the train which passed by our house. Then suddenly something unusual happened. The room was filled with a beautiful glow and I saw a man. I thought it might be Buddha, or some other holy man. Then I heard a voice.

'"How long will you deny Me? I died for you; I have given My life for you."

'Then I saw His hands – the pierced hands of Jesus Christ. This was the Christ I had imagined as a great man who once lived in Palestine, but who died and disappeared. And yet He now stood before me . . . alive! I saw His face looking at me with love.

'Three days before, I had burned the Bible, and yet He was not angry. I was suddenly changed . . . I saw Him as Christ, the living One, the Saviour of the world. I fell on my knees and knew a wonderful peace, which I had never found anywhere before. That was the happiness I had been seeking for such a long time.'

When I first heard about Sadhu Singh, the stories seemed to grow, until it was impossible to separate fact from fiction. Then he came to Holland and was asked by some people who were active in mission work to come to a weekend conference at Lunteren. I was so excited about the possibility of hearing him that I went to the conference grounds, although I knew it was booked to capacity.

With a rucksack and a blanket under my arm, I arrived at the entrance to the camp house. A tall student by the name of van Hoogstraten was giving out cards for the rooms. When he came to me I said, 'I don't have a reservation, but I can sleep out in the field. I would just like to attend the meetings with the Sadhu.'

The student smiled at my determination and said, 'Miss ten Boom, there's a room for you. You're welcome here.'

This same young student later became a missionary, and died in a Japanese prison camp during World War II. The kindness he showed me was one of his characteristics, and years later he was a blessing to his prison guards. One of his daughters, Connie, later became my first companion for seven years, as I toured the world.

That weekend, as I listened to the Sadhu, I was amazed but disturbed. He told of the visions he had seen – of how he really saw Jesus – at a time when he didn't believe. We had all read about the Apostle Paul's experiences on the road to Damascus, but here was a man who claimed to have had this experience himself.

One boy ventured to ask the question we all wanted to know, 'Please, sir, how did Jesus look?'

He put his hand before his eyes and said, 'Oh, His eyes, His eyes . . . they are so beautiful.' Since then I have longed to see Jesus' eyes.

Nobody moved or spoke. The Sadhu's face was the most Christlike face I've ever seen. It made me happy and sad at the same time.

After the meeting I needed to think, and so I started to

walk through the heather by myself, trying to understand all I had heard, questioning my own relationship with God.

As I was walking, I was deep in my own thoughts and almost ran into the Sadhu, who was going for a stroll, too. I worked up my courage to ask him some questions, but soon found he was very easy to talk to. He put me completely at ease.

'Please, Mr Sadhu, tell me what is wrong with me? I'm a child of God, I have received Jesus as my Saviour and I know that my sins are forgiven. I know He is with me for He has said, "I am with you always 'til the end of the world." But what's wrong with me? I've never seen a vision or experienced a miracle.'

The Sadhu smiled at me. 'Sometimes people come to me to see a miracle. When they come now I'll send them to Corrie ten Boom. That I know Jesus is alive and with me is no miracle . . . these eyes have seen Him. But you, who have never seen Him, know His presence. Isn't that a miracle of the Holy Spirit? Look in your Bible at what Jesus said to Thomas in John 20:29: '. . . Blessed are they who did not see, and yet believed.'

'Don't pray for visions; He gives you the assurance of His presence without visions.'

It was such a relief to me . . . it seemed as if the Lord had thrown a curtain aside and I could see the light. Yes, it's a tremendous thing that we can know the Lord is with us!

Paul has said, 'I know whom I have believed.'

And Peter . . . how beautifully he expressed it:

And though you have never seen Him, yet I know that you love Him. At present you trust Him without being able to see Him, and even now He brings you a joy that words cannot express and which has in it a hint of the glories of Heaven; and all the time you are receiving the result of your faith in Him – the salvation of your own souls.

I Peter 1:8, 9 PHILLIPS

Sharing

When I went home after that conference I couldn't wait to

tell what I had experienced. It was early in the morning and
Tante Anna was still in bed. I woke her up and began to spill
out what had happened. I couldn't stop talking.

Betsie and the others heard me and came in, all of us
crowding on the bed. I tried to recall everything. I had
heard and finally, when I paused long enough for anyone
to comment, Tante Anna said, 'It's just as if you have seen
and heard one of the disciples of Jesus.'

Father said, 'Isn't it wonderful to have such joy here on
earth? It's a little foretaste of heaven. Yes, the best is
yet to be.'

Father often said that after we had shared some particularly
rich occurrence.

Years later when Father entered a door of a prison, he said,
'Remember, Corrie, the best is yet to be.' After ten days
Father's spirit stepped out of that prison and into paradise.

The best had arrived.

9

Love and a Sound Mind

It was 1909. The world around us was bursting with change; an American explorer, Robert Peary, had reached the North Pole; the doomed *Lusitania*, one of the largest and most modern ocean liners, was steaming luxuriously across the Atlantic; in Russia the Tsar was beginning a programme of persecution against the Jews, while in Palestine a young man, David Ben Gurion, was dreaming of a return of God's chosen people to their ancient land.

The early part of the twentieth century was preparing the way for a surge of science and an upheaval of society. In Holland, however, our attention was upon the birth of a baby princess, Juliana, heiress to the throne.

In man's never-ending quest for man-made peace, the leaders of the world were gathering in The Hague, Holland, to make another attempt to form an international body, where nations might try to solve their disputes.

Nollie, Willem, Betsie, and I were young people intensely involved in our own pursuits, and yet revolving around each other.

Nollie was a naturally gifted teacher; eventually it became her profession. At one time she taught in Haarlem under a headmaster who was a very narrow-minded, disagreeable man. It was so painful to see our sweet, fun-loving Nollie become depressed on Sunday evening as she thought of the next day, when she would have to face her school superior again. Her face would get longer and longer, but she knew the children loved her so she continued as a first-grade teacher.

Eventually she went to another school in Amsterdam, and this took her away from home for the first time. She met Flip van Woerden, also a teacher, and they were married. The Lord gave her seven children, and she had a better chance to use her motherly gifts than in the classes at school.

My dear, studious brother, Willem, with his precise beard and inquiring mind, provided an intellectual stimulus to our conversations and home-life. Although Willem was the natural heir to Father's business, he did not have the inclination toward watchmaking, preferring to study theology instead. Father never pushed his children into work which they didn't want, and consequently Willem did not feel that he was disappointing Father by not following in his footsteps.

We all loved music, but Willem had only one favourite composer – Bach. We learned to sing Bach chorales just as most children learn nursery songs. Nollie sang soprano, Willem, bass, and I, alto. How fortunate we were to have a brother, because Bach with a ladies' trio would have been rather frothy!

Willem did not have any girl friends, so when he told his friends at the university that he had asked Tine to marry him, Karel, his good friend, said, 'I never thought you would marry! You never looked at any girl.'

When he had been married ten years Willem was called to be a minister for the Jews. He went to Dresden, Germany, and studied in the Delitcheanum. His thesis was written on racial anti-Semitism, a subject which may not have pleased some of his professors. He wrote that the severest pogrom in the entire history of the world could come in Germany. The amazing fact is that this study was presented by Willem in the year 1930, three years before the birth of Hitler's Third Reich.

I admired my brother very much, and sometimes wondered why God hadn't made me an intellectual. Perhaps He could use my simple way of thinking in some way, I thought – but I certainly didn't know how!

When I looked at Betsie, it was usually accompanied by a sigh. Bestie had beautiful curls, my hair was straight. Betsie was neat and lovely, I was put together as an afterthought.

How I loved Betsie, who was seven years older than I. She was not able to work hard, because she was weakened by severe anaemia, but she managed to accomplish so much.

Betsie could turn a drab room into a place of charm; she could transform a dull happening into a rollicking, amusing story. We were introduced to art at an early age, and Betsie could make an art exhibit a tremendous treat, when she was the guide.

We were so rich in art in Holland, and very conscious of our heritage from the masters of the past. When Betsie took me to the Frans Hals museum in Haarlem, she would point out the beauty of each masterpiece.

'Look, Corrie, at the way Hals paints the faces of his subjects. Aren't they marvellous? And look at their hands – have you ever seen anything more beautiful?'

She would explain to me the exceptional talents of Rembrandt, showing me how he expressed the character of those he painted. Betsie could weave stories through a visit to an art exhibit in such an exciting way that I couldn't wait for the next chapter. It added to the richness of my childhood and the quality of my appreciation for classical art and music.

Betsie didn't promote herself; she remained in the background, always helping and ready with good advice and a sense of humour. Sometimes she assisted Father with his weekly paper, which he wrote for watchmakers, turning an ordinary report on a visit to a factory into an original, humorous story.

The church of our childhood and later years was the *Grote Kerk*, or St Bavo's, the grand old cathedral which played such an important part in our lives. In the late afternoon there was a service called the 'everyday church' which was supposed to last about half an hour. Usually not more than twenty persons attended, but the ministers were obligated to conduct the service for the faithful few. Since it is human nature to forget a job you do not like, sometimes the ministers did not appear.

When I was in my late teens and early twenties, my cousin, Uncle Arnold's son took his father's job and was usher, or caretaker, of St Bavo's. He often telephoned me and said,

'Corrie, no pastor turned up for the service this afternoon. Please come and help us out.'

I remember once when that request came I had a particularly full day at the house and in the shop, and my head was blank of any message I could bring to the small gathering of people. I ran to the kitchen where Betsie was cooking, hoping she would have a suggestion.

'Betsie, what in the world can I tell the people at the cathedral?'

Her answer came without hesitation; it was as if she had prepared it all day. While she told me the sermon, she brushed my coat, fixed my hair, and looked critically at my appearance.

'Keep your coat on, Corrie; your dress isn't too clean. Take Psalm 23 as your subject – "The Lord is my Shepherd." Sheep can be very stupid, you know. Sometimes they don't see food behind their backs. We need the Lord just as much as sheep need a shepherd.'

Betsie told me the whole outline of the sermon while she accompanied me to the door.

'I'll pray for you . . . I'm sure God will bless the message.'

I was halfway through the little alley, and turned to see her still standing in the doorway.

'Betsie, I can't think . . . what hymns should I give them to sing?'

'Just ask them for their favourites.'

There was a blessing in the cathedral that day, while in the kitchen of our house, Betsie prayed.

She was tidy about her person, her possessions, and her thoughts. I remember years later I passed her cell in the German prison in Holland where we were political prisoners of the Nazi regime. The Red Cross had just sent a food package to the prisoners, and on the little corner shelf stood that food in neat rows. Over a stool was a handkerchief and a bottle with two tulips, a present from the judge with whom Betsie had prayed after the hearing. In those stark surroundings was an atmosphere of cleanliness and order, which was the stamp of Betsie's personality.

Although we had our individual interests, we loved a family project together. Mama and Papa's twenty-fifth anniversary was our chance to plan a real celebration. Nollie had been working as a teacher, and she had to supply the finances for the party. She had saved as much as she could in order to rent the hall of the YMCA. We planned the entertainment, but that was free – except for the personal price of courage I had to pay to perform before all the guests.

Willem came as Johann Sebastian Bach, playing his part with a dignified flourish. He was a musician, and I probably thought it was easy for him. Nollie, who loved to dress up, was Sarah Bernhardt. (Why hadn't I learned those social graces?)

The evening of the party Mother was flushed with excitement; I thought she had never looked more beautiful. Father escorted her to the YMCA as if he were taking the Queen herself to a royal ball. Dozens of friends from the rich to the servant class were at the party; merchants on the street; clients whose clocks Father repaired and wound; people to whom Mother had brought soup and comfort – all swarmed into the hall to bring their love and congratulations to the popular watchmaker and his wife.

When the party was almost over, I finally mustered the nerve to contribute my part to the entertainment. I was introduced with a flourish by Willem and stepped forward in a borrowed Salvation Army uniform. I can't remember whether the uniform fitted, or if I sang in tune, but I do know that an edge was taken off my shyness in my first public appearance.

The four of us had pooled our money to buy a silver serviette ring for Father and Mother, which Willem had engraved with a Hebrew inscription. It said: THE LORD IS GOOD. HIS MERCY IS FROM ETERNITY AND HIS FAITHFULNESS FROM GENERATION TO GENERATION.

The Lord was faithful in giving me the strength to sing in front of all those people. I don't think I dreamed when I was seventeen that I would be called to speak before thousands some day. His faithfulness is certainly 'from generation to generation'.

Ethics, Dogmatics and Bath-tubs

In 1910 a Bible school opened in Haarlem. When I saw the programme I was so excited. There was so much I wanted to learn. I plunged into this new enterprise, taking seven different subjects at one time. For two years I struggled with ethics, dogmatics, church history, Old Testament, New Testament, story of the Old Testament, and story of the New Testament. Such an undertaking might not be so difficult for a clever student – but that I wasn't.

During this time Mother suffered a slight stroke. Although she became weaker physically, her gentle spirit and positive attitude were an encouragement to all of us.

As my work load at home increased, it became more of a chore to keep up with my studies. Finally the day of judgment arrived – examinations. The first part was practical application; we had to give lessons and answer questions from students. I passed this quite well, and was full of confidence when I appeared before the group of ministers who were to give me the second part of the examination.

The ministers gathered to interrogate me in a room which should have held no terror for me. It was a large conference room opening off a familiar corridor in St Bavo's. Dot and I had played in that room as children, but when I saw the rather formidable-looking gentlemen sitting on both sides of the massive table my courage began to wither. The fireplace on one side of the room was large enough for me to walk into, but I realized I was no longer a child hiding in the cloak-room so the principal wouldn't see me.

The president of the church asked me the first question. 'Miss ten Boom, what did you study for ethics?'

'I followed the teaching of Mr Johnson for two years . . .' I began, but got no further.

St Bavo's was usually chilly, but the icicles seemed to form on the ceiling. Pastor Williamson, the president, lifted his eyebrows and stared at me. He and Pastor Johnson had been theological students at the same university, and their disagreements were well known among the faculty.

'You studied nothing else?' Pastor Williamson asked disdainfully.

It was tense. I was tense. Suddenly I couldn't remember a thing. Out of seven different subjects I managed to get seven failing grades!

Willem, why didn't I have your brains?

When I returned home with the news of my defeat, Betsie was one of the first to console me. However, I didn't think she gave me the sympathy I deserved because she said, 'You must do it again.' Something about the way she said it made me repress my objections.

'When you have failed an examination, Corrie, you know your whole life that you have failed; when you do it again, then you know your whole life that you have succeeded and have the diploma.'

Eight years later I took the examination again and passed.

The important lesson I learned from my Bible-school experience was that from these organized studies we learn the wisdom of the wise, but not much of the 'foolishness of God'.

The best learning I had came from teaching. I could serve the church by giving catechism lessons, and preparing people who were to take their confirmation. In the Dutch Reformed Church you do this when you are eighteen years or older. I was also licensed to give Bible lessons in the non-Christian schools. Parents who sent their children to secular schools could elect to have their children take these lessons.

I learned to listen to the Holy Spirit when I prepared for the lessons, and when I talked with the children and young people, my 'lessons' were more of a conversation with them than telling what I knew. It was a joy to learn in this way much of the reality of the Gospel. Talking over my experiences with Father and the others was an added training. Besides this important result of that fruitful time, there was the new experience that I received a small amount of money for this and decided to save that special income for a very special project.

When I was growing up there was one luxury I wanted:

a flush toilet. Of course we had toilets, one upstairs and one downstairs, but they were the accommodations which necessitated a once-a-month service from the workers in the city sanitation department. As I saved my salary from the Bible teaching, it was with great anticipation of supplying the Beje with two porcelain pleasures.

Next – a luxury of pure ecstasy – I saved to buy a bathtub! Each room in the house had a bowl to use for washing, but we were very frugal with precious heat during the winter, and there were many mornings when we broke the ice to splash our faces.

When my 'bath-tub fund' was large enough to buy the splendid fixture, it was a thrilling day at the Beje. The bath-tub was equipped with a gas water heater, so that it no longer was necessary to be polar bears to get clean. We had a platform built under the tub so the water would drain out.

Somehow all of those hours struggling over ethics, dogmatics, and all the rest of the subjects which enabled me to teach were worth it to achieve such a magnificent material goal. How I enjoyed that tub!

Patriotism and Prayer

Discussing the truths of the Bible was as natural to our family as talking about sports or current events. It was remarkable how Father found so many contrasting people for his Bible-study groups. It was this willingness to share his time with others which made him so rich with friends.

For three years we had a prayer meeting every Saturday night in Heemstede, a neighbouring village. Father, Betsie and I went on the tram-car to the meeting, in hot weather and cold, rain or snow; it was a regular part of our life.

In 1914, war swirled around our little country. Each nation had been trying to increase its own wealth and power for decades, and the threat of a clash was becoming a reality. Only five years had passed since The Hague Peace Conference, and yet all the great powers seemed to believe that threats and force were the tactics to use to get what they wanted. The world was engulfed in a terrifying game of fear.

From the time the Austrian crown prince, Archduke Francis Ferdinand, and his wife were assassinated, one after another of the countries of the world issued declarations of war.

Father continued to pray for the Queen and the government of Holland, as he always had. We were very patriotic and loyal to Queen Wilhelmina and her prime minister, Abraham Kuyper, who was also a prominent theologian.

A division of purpose developed in our weekly prayer group. 'Casper, it's not right to pray for those in government,' some of the people said. 'The world is evil – Satan is prince of this world and we should only look at the Kingdom of God.'

But Father said, 'As Christians we are in the world, but not of the world. We must not give over our country to the enemy, because then we would be disobeying 1 Timothy 2 which says, "First of all, then, I urge that entreaties and prayers, petitions and thanksgivings, be made on behalf of all men, for kings and all who are in authority, in order that we may lead a tranquil and quiet life in all godliness and dignity"' (vs. 1, 2).

As the weeks and months of World War I went on, the pietists became more uncomfortable as Father, Betsie, and I continued to pray for our government. The difference in these basic beliefs drove the group apart. The others began to draw more and more into their spiritual shells, until we could no longer meet together for prayer.

Beyond This World

Father was not quarrelsome about his biblical beliefs, but he stood fast in theological debates, especially with Tante Jans. They used to have some rather lively discussions, which Mother and I didn't enjoy.

Father was a Calvinist and I heard him speak frequently about predestination. I never quite understood what he meant, and one time I asked him, 'What is predestination?'

He answered, 'The ground on which I build my faith is not in me, but in the faithfulness of God.'

That was an answer I enjoyed, and I repeated it many times in the years to follow.

One of the main points of dissension between Father and Tante Jans came over faith and works. In the Book of Philippians it is written: 'So then, my beloved, just as you have always obeyed, not as in my presence only, but now much more in my absence, work out your salvation with fear and trembling; for it is God who is at work in you, both to will and to work for His good pleasure' (2:12, 13).

Father talked more about 'it is God who is at work in you . . .' and Tante Jans emphasized 'work out your salvation'. I believe the fear she had of death may have been the result of never quite believing she had worked hard enough for God.

The Great Journey

One of the great human mysteries I shared with Father was why Tante Jans, a powerful evangelist, a woman with a zeal to teach and write about the Lord Jesus, had such a dread of dying. When the time came when we knew she didn't have much longer on earth, we didn't know how she would react.

Father loved Tante Jans, as we all did, in spite of her crusty manner and argumentative personality.

'Jans,' Father patted her wrinkled hand gently, smiling into the no-longer stern face, 'are you ready to make the great journey? The doctor has said that it can't be too long before you have to leave us.'

Tante Jans's face lit up. 'Jesus said, "I give my sheep everlasting life." That's good . . . I can't do anything more . . . I'm safe in the hands of the Good Shepherd who gave His life for us. He prepared a mansion in the house of the Father for me.'

When the hour of death arrived, God took away her fear.

On the day of her burial the house was full of people who told how she had been used by the Lord to bring them to Him. We told them about the joy she had, and that the fear of death had vanished the moment she knew she had to die. A friend of hers, a nurse, said, 'I'm so glad to hear that. I often wonder if in the hour of death the devil will take away my assurance of salvation. I've seen so many Christian people die in agony, attacked by fear, although I knew they were children of God.'

Another nurse, who had also come to honour her friend, gave some good advice. 'Just tell the Lord that you have this fear . . . then pray that when the hour of death comes for you, Jesus will protect you against any attack of the enemy and that He will give you a clear experience of His presence. He said, "I am with you always 'til the end of the world." This prayer will be answered. I've seen many people dying, too. All who prayed this prayer beforehand died in great peace and assurance of Jesus' presence and salvation. I could see it on their faces.'

When the second aunt in our family died, it made me think more about time and eternity. We are citizens of heaven – our outlook goes beyond this world. I know the truth of the Bible, when it says that God doesn't give us a spirit of fear, but of power, of love and a sound mind.

Her Silent Love

One morning I was talking to Father about a chance to make some attractive magazine advertisements for our business, when I heard the sound of a crash. I ran into the kitchen and saw Mother slumped by the sink, a large kettle had fallen on the floor. Her left arm hung limply at her side, as she struggled to hold onto the counter.

'Mama, sit down, dear.' I helped her to a chair and ran to get Father.

'Hurry . . . something's wrong with Mother.'

Father rushed in and put his arms around her. She looked up and whispered in a voice which was barely audible, 'Oh, Cas, we've been so happy together.'

She thought she was going to die right then. We supported her carefully and guided her to her room. When the doctor had examined her, he comforted us by saying that strokes could be dangerous, but frequently were not so serious. 'One of my patients had a stroke and after that went to

Switzerland three times. Your mother can live another eight or ten years.'

Mother never fully recovered the use of her body after her next stroke, and for the remainder of her earthly life, her speech was limited to one word: 'Corrie.' With a word, the nod of her head, the opening or closing of her eyes, we saw a display of love which enriched all of us.

We developed a method of communication in which we would try to guess her thoughts, and she would answer with a motion of her head.

It was such a joy to be with her – and my own attitude improved during the three years God allowed Mother to be with us after her most severe stroke. I began to understand what the verse in Romans meant which says, 'For I consider that the sufferings of this present time are not worthy to be compared with the glory that is to be revealed to us' (Romans 8:18).

God's glory shone through Mother.

10

Reach Out

Europe was devastated at the end of World War I; there was danger of starvation in war-torn countries, and yet there was also a resurgence of hope in the world. 'Make the world safe for democracy' was the slogan of the Allies. The humanitarian compassion of the United States and the victor nations in sending supplies and food prevented millions from going hungry.

In Holland, we were thankful that we were spared from the terrible conflict, but we wanted to reach out with help for those who weren't so fortunate. What could the ten Boom family do?

Germany was a wounded country; many of its children were undernourished and suffering from severe malnutrition. We began to think of ways to provide homes for these children in Holland, building them up with good food and care, before returning them to their own homes. Since Father knew many watchmakers, he discussed with me how we could organize an outreach for children of watchmakers in Germany.

Father was chairman of the international watchmakers, a position he had earned not only because of the respect others in the profession had for him, but also because he was willing to work and keep his promises. After the war, he spent many hours contacting watchmakers all over Holland to ask them to take a German child into their homes for a time.

'Why don't you take one yourself, Father?' I asked.

But Father was more realistic. 'Just wait, Corrie. Many have promised to take children but not everyone will be faithful. We cannot depend on everyone. There will be children for whom I have no home and we can take them.'

When the day came for the children to arrive, Father, Betsie, and I went to the railway station to see that each child went with the proper family. What a scene it was. The children stood on the side, shy, wistful, frightened, and the adults waited expectantly to find out which ones were to be a part of their households. One by one names were called, and someone would step forward to welcome the poor little things. An attempt had been made to match children with families who had girls and boys of the same age. I had to struggle to hold back my tears. Our little Dutch children were so ruddy-cheeked and sturdy beside the pale, undernourished Germans.

Soon everyone was accounted for – well, almost everyone. I had been watching one little girl pushing herself into the corner of the waiting room, as if she hoped to become a part of the woodwork. As each name was called, she tried to make herself less noticeable.

'Father, look at that girl – don't you have anyone left on your list for her?'

'Let's see . . . no, I don't believe so. We shall take her home with us.'

My mind began to buzz. She could go to Willem's former room. (He had been married in 1916 to Tine, our doctor's sister.) I must see about some clothes for her – and perhaps we still had some dolls left in the attic.

Then we saw another one. A bedraggled little boy was waiting dejectedly for someone to claim him. Father checked his records, and found out that the mother had become ill in the house where he was supposed to go. So we took Willy, too.

'Come along, my young friends,' Father said. 'You need a good meal and a warm bed.'

He reached down and held out his hands to two skinny little children, one about ten and the other a year or two younger. What a sight they made. Four spindly legs raced to keep up with Father's stride as we returned home.

Willy was a street urchin from Berlin. The ten Boom

home, modest as it was, must have appeared like a palace to him. When the children sat down to the table and Tante Anna brought them soup, they both picked up their bowls and began to slurp, the excess making rivulets down their dirty chins.

'Corrie, these two must have a bath,' Betsie announced, although the need was obvious to anyone who could see or smell.

Willy only spoke German, but the word *bath* must have a universal meaning for little boys, because he looked first at Betsie and then at me. There was sheer panic in his eyes.

Father sensed immediately that Willy thought these two funny ladies were going to subject him to the indignity of washing.

'Come along, sir, I will show you the most magnificent invention of our time!'

I'm sure Willy didn't understand what he was saying, but the tone of his voice and the flourish with which he directed him to the bathroom must have assured him that there was a marvellous treat in store.

After we tucked the children between clean sheets, Betsie, Father, and I went to Mother's room to tell her about the additions to our household. She couldn't understand German, but in the following weeks it was such an inspiration to us to see how she managed to love and help those German children. She could quiet a quarrel with the shake of her head or ease a hurt with outstretched hands.

'Isn't it wonderful,' Betsie said, 'to have children in the house? And what a blessing it is to have Willy. Father has been so outnumbered by females.'

The next challenge soon arrived in the person of Mrs Treckmann and her two little girls. We had known her through our association with the YMCA, and when she wrote from Germany that she was in desperate need of help, and that her children were suffering from malnutrition, we started to make up more beds at once.

Mrs Treckmann was more undernourished than her girls, Ruth and Martha. Her face was gaunt and lined with the strain of hardship, which war writes on the bodies and spirits of human beings. *Oh, Lord,* I thought, *don't ever put us through that in Holland. I don't think I would have the personal strength to watch my own family suffer.*

For the weeks their mother was with us in the house, the two little girls were rather difficult to handle. Ruth would throw temper tantrums, which threatened not only the wood panelling on my bedroom door, as she kicked it uncontrollably, but also the peace of our house which was always active – but not with voices of discord. Her mother responded to these outbursts with several solid slaps across her face, which added to Ruth's rebellion.

Through Mrs Treckmann's actions we came in contact with the German way of discipline. Slapping for the slightest reason produced rather negative results, for Ruth responded with more tantrums.

In some way, without words, Mother taught Mrs Treckmann that sometimes a beating on the bottom side of the anatomy was healthy, but slapping was not wise.

Mrs Treckmann finally returned to Germany, but we kept Ruth and Martha, along with Willy and Katy for quite a while. The first time Ruth began her door-kicking, attention-getting tantrums, we ignored her as if she were nothing more than a little fly buzzing around our deaf ears.

No slapping was required. Ruth and Martha became two of the nicest little ladies we ever had.

It was many years later that I received a letter from Ruth. She wrote that she had read some of my books, and remembered the time she was in our house. 'What a naughty girl I was, and what love I experienced in your home!' she wrote. 'My husband and I pray that we can pass on the love we have received to people who need it. The Lord is our strength. How good to know that.'

It was twenty-eight years later and I was in Germany. Another World War had engulfed the nations, and by this time I knew from horrible first-hand experience what it was to see my family and thousands of others suffer, even more than those in the First World War.

After a meeting in West Berlin I saw a neatly dressed gentleman smiling at me. Something about him jogged my memory. Of course – the little street boy with his slang and naughty eyes!

'Tante Corrie, do you remember me? I'm Willy, who lived with your family many years ago.'

There was a new light in his eyes, and I wasn't surprised when he told me what had happened to him.

'I had never heard anyone pray in a house before. I knew that people went into the big cathedrals and said prayers, but when I lived with the ten Booms I heard praying before and after meals, and other times during the day. Many years later I accepted the Lord Jesus as my Saviour, but I believe it was because you had planted those seeds of love in that skinny, frightened boy who came out of the slums of Berlin.'

The Saddest Day

The children from Germany stayed for a while, building their bodies and healing their spirits, before returning to their homeland. Those were growing years for all of us, but weakening years for Mother. Three years after Mother's severe stroke – times in which her love and patience spoke louder than any sermon – her physical life slipped away from us. Father saw the woman he had loved for so many years, the wife who gave him such strength, leave for her home in heaven.

She had taught us so much. She never pushed Father toward greater success in his business; she sustained him with her encouragement, no matter what trials he had. When money was scarce, she stretched what we had; when we met defeats, she taught us to try again.

Father looked at the woman he loved so much, knowing that she was with Jesus, and that she was free of pain for the first time in many years.

'This is the saddest day of my life,' he said. 'Thank You, Lord, for giving her to me.'

Father's loss was acute, but he did not engulf himself in self-pity. He knew where Mother was and he also knew that the Lord's work had to go on in this world.

11

In and Out of the Watchmaker's Shop

Five . . . six . . . seven . . . eight . . . the chiming clocks in the shop told me it was eight o'clock in the morning. What a wonderful way to start the day . . . with the graceful Frisian clock singing the hour, the sonorous grandfather clock vibrating its bass melody, and a dozen or more pendulums joining the chorus. I hummed a little tune under my breath as I poked the fire under the coffee-pot, and brought one slice of white bread, and one of brown bread, out for Father's breakfast. He would descend the narrow staircase in exactly ten minutes. You could regulate your watch by his arrival in the dining room each morning.

This was the day Father wound the clocks in the homes of his wealthy clients. His breakfast must be prompt, for he was as disciplined as the timepieces he treated.

8:10 A.M. *'Goede morgen*, Corrie. You have been busy already, I believe.'

He looked at the sacks lined up against the cupboards, and knew that I had been up preparing meals for the day: meat, vegetables, potatoes, and stewed fruit started cooking before breakfast. I would begin the food in boiling water, and then remove it from the stove for a special long-cooking method. Each pot would be wrapped in sixteen newspaper pages and then enclosed in a towel, sealing in the heat. It was a very effective and efficient way to cook and store food.

After breakfast and prayers, Father would go to our astronomical clock and check his pocket watch. The clock

was impressive, taller than Father, with an accuracy which
demanded synchronization with the Naval Observatory clock
in Amsterdam. Neither cold nor heat affected the astronomical clock.

'Mmmm . . . two seconds fast,' Father commented. He
adjusted his own timepiece precisely in preparation for the
work of the day.

His bicycle was dusted, his hat adjusted, and off he went,
pedalling intensely down the narrow Haarlem streets, until
he reached the homes of his clients in the suburbs of the
city. He was an aristocrat and a servant, a gentleman of
dignity and a confidant of the most lowly. Class distinction
was very strong in Holland, but to him every human being
was someone of value.

As he whirred through the streets he waved to many
townspeople, endangering the security of his hat in the
wind. When he arrived at the first house, breathless, but
prompt, he would go to the back door, ring the bell, and
greet the servant girl who answered his summons.

'Hannah, how delightful to see your shining face this
morning.' he would say with a manner as gallant as one
approaching royalty.

'Oh, Mister ten Boom, I'm so happy to see you. I've been
reading the Book of John – just as you told me – and I have
so many questions.'

'Good, Hannah. I shall come to the kitchen for coffee at 11
o'clock. Perhaps some of the other servants will want to have
a little talk, too.'

Father made everyone feel important, and in a home where
there were twelve or fourteen servants, a downstairs maid or
cook's helper might not have too much feeling of self-worth.
Many of them looked forward all week to the arrival of the
watchmaker.

His clients were people of means, many of them in the
import business or owners of sugar-cane plantations in
Indonesia. The mistress of one mansion asked him which
dancing school he attended, in order to learn how to bow
in such a courtly manner.

Dancing school! Imagine such a thing. Father answered, 'I

never learned to dance, nor did I attend such a school. My father taught me manners.'

Formal training had not been a part of Father's background. He left school when he was fourteen years old to become Grandfather's helper in the workshop. He attended night school for a time, but his training was not of a highly intellectual level. He was self-taught, especially from theological books and magazines. Sometimes when Willem explained to his fellow students at the university Father's answer to a problem, he would be asked, 'Where did your father study theology?'

Father's horizon was wide, and he talked with even his most outstanding customers with wisdom and insight. He was equally at home in the kitchen and in the beautiful sitting rooms. He understood all these people because of the love in his heart, received through the Holy Spirit. (See Romans 5:5.)

Among the customers whose clocks he had to wind, was a distinguished pastor and philosopher, Dominee de Sopper. Father often asked him probing questions. After some months, the Dominee offered to give a course in philosophy in our home; although Father's beliefs didn't agree with this scholar's liberal views, the disputes between them didn't spoil their warm friendship.

For several winters this pastor, who later became professor of philosophy at the University of Leiden, had a weekly study group in our house. There were agnostics, atheists, fundamentalists, and liberals in this group, all with a quest for knowledge and none able to escape Casper ten Boom's direct answers to complex problems. 'The Bible says . . .' he would say when the arguments became involved.

Father had nothing against philosophy, for he believed in a philosophy of living based upon the Word of God. However, he would express his differences when others would base their beliefs in such men as Kant and Hegel. Kant, the eighteenth-century German philospher, had introduced a way of thinking which influenced many in the intellectual community. He did not believe in absolute right and wrong, and questioned whether people could accept things which were beyond their five senses. This would rule out spiritual realities or biblical truths. Hegel pursued the philosophy of relative thinking, which led to the basic political and economic ideas of Karl Marx and Adolf Hitler.

Without formal educational training, Father could debate with the most brilliant from the Book he knew so well. He baffled some, converted others, and had the honest respect of all in that unusual study group.

Out of the Frying Pan

When Father returned home after making his clock-winding rounds, I was anxious to hear what had happened.

'What did Mrs van der Vliet say today? Did you see Pastor de Sopper? What about the cook at the de Boks' – has she been reading the Bible we sent?'

'Oh, Corrie, Corrie,' Father laughed, 'let's wait until after supper. The thought of the food you prepared this morning sustained me for the last five miles.'

My job for many years was to assist Tante Anna in the housekeeping, cooking, cleaning, and nursing. Betsie worked with father in the shop as a book-keeper, and I pursued the household tasks. I loved housekeeping; I found it challenging and creative. For instance, I tried to beat my own time records in washing and ironing. On Monday my goal was to have the clothes folded and put away by 4 o'clock. If I could make it by 3:30 or 3:45, I would reward myself with an extra fifteen minutes to half an hour of reading. I learned to bake bread, churn butter, and stretch a little to make a lot.

The division of labour at the ten Booms was suddenly changed by a flu epidemic in Holland. All the members of the family became ill. When Betsie was sick, I had to do her work in the shop; this was something I had never done before. I felt as if I had two left hands. It was a different world: meeting people, remembering their particular likes and dislikes, seeing in facts and figures the precarious balance of the family business.

When Betsie was well again, I made a suggestion. 'Why

don't we exchange jobs for a few months, so I can learn more about shop-keeping? I'm so terribly ignorant of what goes on in the business.'

And so we switched. It was 1920; Willem and Tine had their own family, Nollie and Flip had been married a year, and the little German children had returned home. Time for a change.

I loved the work in the shop. The only thing I thought unpractical was that when a customer brought in a broken watch I always had to ask Father, or one of our watch-makers in the workshop, to look at what repairs were needed or broken parts replaced.

'Father, I believe it would be useful if I learned watch repairing – will you teach me the trade of watch-making?'

Immediately Father agreed. He had a great trust in my abilities.

'Of course I can teach you – and after some time I will send you to Switzerland to work as an apprentice in a factory. I hope you will become a better watch-maker than I am.'

Dear Father, he was one of the best watch-makers in all of Holland; he wrote a book about the exact regulation of watches; he edited a weekly watch-maker's paper; he had been a pupil of Howu, one of the world's best clock-makers in his time. How could Father expect me to become better than he?

Tante Anna overheard his remarks and said, 'Cas, I must warn you – Corrie will never give her full time to her trade. She always tries to do six things at a time.'

Tante Anna was right. She was a woman with singleness of purpose: the comfort of our family. It must have been difficult for her to cope with the many directions of my attention, those ambitions of my heart which ignored the circumstances of our lives. I knew I was the youngest child of a respected businessman who did not have much money, and I was happy and content as such a person. But I believed there was more for me to do.

'Dear Lord,' I would pray in the privacy of my little room, 'can You use me in some way?'

Blessed Money and Cursed Money

It only took a week for Betsie and me to know that changing jobs was right for both of us. Betsie, with her natural flair for beauty and order, added a new spark to the household. Cupboards were rearranged more efficiently, flowers appeared on the table and in window-boxes; even the meals seemed to have more imagination.

I loved the store and workshop. It had a very special atmosphere, and gradually I began to overcome my shyness and insecurity in meeting people, and enjoyed selling the watches and clocks. There were many ups and downs in the watch-making business, but Father seemed to have a keen understanding of the economic situation of our times. In his weekly paper, *Christiaan Huygens*, he wrote information and suggestions for others in the business. Since he read all other papers about his trade in German, English, and French, he could adequately fill his paper with important news about trade and business.

However, when it came to making money in his own shop, it wasn't always so simple. He loved his work, but he was not a moneymaker.

Once we were faced with a real financial crisis. A large bill had to be paid, and there simply wasn't enough money. One day a very well-dressed gentleman came into the shop and was looking at some very expensive watches. I stayed in the workshop and prayed, with one ear tuned to the conversation in the front room.

'Mmm . . . this is a fine watch, Mr ten Boom,' the customer said, turning a very costly timepiece over in his hands. 'This is just what I've been looking for.'

I held my breath as I saw the affluent customer reach into his inner pocket and pull out a thick wad of notes. Praise the Lord – cash! (I saw myself paying the overdue bill, and being relieved of the burden I had been carrying for the past few weeks.)

The blessed customer looked at the watch admiringly and commented, 'I had a good watch-maker here in Haarlem . . . his name was van Houten. Perhaps you knew him.'

Father nodded his head. He knew almost everyone in Haarlem, especially colleagues.

'Van Houten died and his son took over the business. However, I bought a watch from him which didn't go at all. I sent it back three times, but it was just a lemon. That's why I decided to find another watch-maker.'

'Will you show me that watch, please,' Father said. The man took a large watch out of his pocket and gave it to Father.

'Now, let me see,' Father said, opening the back of the watch. He adjusted something and returned it to the customer. 'There, that was a very little mistake. It will be fine now. Sir, I trust the young watch-maker . . . he is just as good as his father. I think you can encourage him by buying the new watch from him.'

'But, ten Boom!' the customer objected.

'This young man has had a difficult time in the trade without his father. If you have a problem with one of his watches, come to me, I'll help you out. Now, I shall give you back your money and you return my watch'.

I was horrified. I saw Father take back the watch and give the money to the customer. Then he opened the door for him and bowed deeply in his old-fashioned way.

My heart was where my feet should be as I emerged from the shelter of the workshop.

'Papa! How could you?'

I was so shocked by the enormity of what I had seen and heard, that I reverted to a childhood term.

'Corrie, you know that I brought the Gospel at the burial of Mr Van Houten.'

Of course I remembered. It was Father's job to speak at the burials of the watch-makers in Haarlem. He was greatly loved by his colleagues and was also a very good speaker; he always used the occasion to talk about the Lord Jesus.

Father often said that people were touched by eternity when they have seen someone dying. That is an opportunity we should use to tell about Him who is willing to give eternal life.

'Corrie, what do you think that young man would have said

when he heard that one of his good customers had gone to Mr ten Boom? Do you think that the name of the Lord would be honoured? There is blessed money and cursed money. Trust the Lord. He owns the cattle on a thousand hills and He will take care of us.'

I felt ashamed and knew that Father was right. I wondered if I could ever have that kind of trust. I remembered myself as a child, when I had to go to school for the first time. My fingers were tight on the railing again, not wanting to go the direction God wanted, only to follow my own stubborn path. Could I really trust Him – with an unpaid bill?

'Yes, Father,' I answered quietly. Who was I answering? My earthly father or my Father in heaven?

The Trivial Things

As I continued working with Father, we both realized that our characters were formed by our job. Watch repairing is a training in patience. How Father helped me when I had difficulties in the work!

'And who in the whole world should I help with more joy than my own daughter?' he often said.

The workshop was opened every morning with prayer and Bible reading. If there were problems, we prayed over them together. Father practised what Paul advised: '. . . whatever happens, make sure that your everyday life is worthy of the Gospel of Christ' (Philippians 1:27 PHILLIPS).

These simple things kept morale high, but also it was such a joy to experience Jesus' victory. He is a Friend who never leaves us alone.

When my hand was not steady and I had to do a very exacting piece of work like putting a frail part of a watch – the balance, for instance – into the movement, I prayed, 'Lord Jesus, will You lay Your hand on my hand?' He always did, and our joined hands worked securely. Jesus never fails us for a moment.

I experienced the miracle that the highest potential of God's love and power is available to us in the trivial things of everyday life.

12

All Is Well . . . Until It Rains

I felt a little strange among the people in that room. Most of
the women at the meeting of the Christian Union of the Lady
Friends of the Young Girl were very dignified, wearing their
beautiful black dresses with high collars and long sleeves.
What was I doing here? I thought. I was suddenly very
conscious of my rather low-necked, short-sleeve blouse,
which was appropriate for the watchmaker's workshop, but
a bit out of place for a gathering of the *Union des Amies de
la Jeune Fille*.

When one lady began to make her speech, I forgot about
myself and listened, as she expressed great warmth and
love for girls who needed help and guidance during a time
in their lives when there were possibilities for extremes in
good or bad.

In Holland Sunday-school classes ended when one was
twelve or thirteen years old, and YWCA groups were designed
for girls eighteen or older. In those crucial and formative years
between the two age groups there was nothing organized for
them in the Christian world.

Suddenly I felt a finger poking my back and a whispering
voice said, 'That's work for you, Corrie ten Boom.'

I turned around and looked into the kind eyes of Mrs
Bechtold, a dear old lady who had been a friend of Tante
Jans.

'No time,' I answered, thinking of the house, the shop,
the Bible studies in schools. Oh, dear, I was much, much
too busy!

'Talk it over with the Lord,' Mrs Bechtold said.

That was exactly what I did when I went to bed that evening.

Do it

The next day I told Betsie about the meeting and how the Lord had laid it upon my heart to do something about girls in their early teen years. She began to make plans – we had no money, no experience – but we started.

Betsie had taught Sunday school for many years, so it was not difficult for her to get long lists of names of former pupils. She began to talk to her girls about our plans, and in her quiet way she was a tremendous motivator. The first thing we did was to start the Church Walk Club. The youth church on the Bakenessegracht started at 10 o'clock Sunday morning, so we met the girls on a bridge at 8:30, had a long walk to the dunes, played there for a while, and then went to church together.

This was a beginning, but we realized that Sunday was not enough. We talked it over with the children, and decided that on Wednesday evening we would gather at our usual meeting place on the bridge, and walk to Bloemendaal, where some of the wealthy women had said we could use their parks and gardens for games. The grounds of some of those estates were like forest preserves, and it was such a privilege to be able to enjoy them so freely. After each time of fun we would have a talk about the Lord with the girls.

The club grew and grew as girls brought their friends. It began to get around that Tante Kees (my nickname) was 'not such a bad sort' – for an adult, that is!

Betsie and I soon realized that we had a serious need for more girls' club leaders. While Betsie gathered names and addresses of former Sunday-school pupils, I found my place for selecting prospects was in the shop. When a young lady bought a watch, or brought one in for repairs, I would find myself looking at her and thinking, 'Now I wonder if she's a Christian.' As I stood behind the counter and she was sitting in front on a chair, I would start to talk about juvenile delinquency, the need of the Gospel's reaching the whole world, particularly girls twelve to eighteen years of age.

When one of these young ladies seemed interested, I invited her to our leaders' club. Within a short time we had forty leaders. Soon some of them dropped out when they realized their responsibilities, but when the chaff left the wheat remained, and we had an enthusiastic, able group of young women.

Once a week the leaders got together, and everyone had to teach the others the games she knew. I instructed them in giving a Bible message with a short story, and a thought they could use that week. Whenever questions came up, we talked them over together to find the answer. We brought up our problems in our prayers, and didn't depend upon our own resources to work a miracle.

These leaders got together a list of former Sunday-school girls and told them about the clubs, where to meet on the bridge, and the name of the park or garden where they would have their game and talk club.

What a beginning we had! It was dynamic – until the rainy month of August started and the entire HMC (*Haarlemse Meisjes Clubs* or Haarlem Girls' Clubs) consisted of dripping-wet leaders who waited in vain on the bridge for the girls who didn't come. We had too many fair-weather girls! We could have given up at that point, but most of us believed if the Lord had directed us into this work, that He wanted us to go on! We were dampened but not drowned!

What we needed was a roof over our heads, and we found a room in a house on the Bakenessegracht. It was close to the Beje, and when supper was over, it only took me a few minutes to run to a meeting. On some Wednesday evenings we had a room jammed with girls, and at other times the place was empty. It was during the 'empty' time that our leaders' training club became our leaders' prayer group; we asked the Lord to give us a club-house instead of just a club-room.

Every city has its famous benefactors and in Haarlem the name of *Teyler* was well known. Stories of his wealth, the organizations he had endowed, and his reputation as a promoter of Dutch art were renowned. One of the many houses owned by Mr Teyler had a very large room with many smaller ones around it; from a family viewpoint, it was not a practical home. We asked the steward of the property if we could rent the house – and because we were going to use it for good moral purposes, our offer was quickly accepted. What an answer to our prayers!

We had the time of our lives! As we planned together with the girls, they all expressed their different areas of interest. One of the girls, for instance, wanted to learn English. The next week we had an English class started in one of the smaller rooms. The leader of that class was one of our customers in the shop.

The one thing which we couldn't do in the Teyler house was the vigorous physical activity which some girls wanted. So for one evening a week we rented a gymnastic hall in Haarlem with all of the equipment we needed. There we started the athletic clubs for the more adventurous.

God blessed the work. Yes, we made mistakes, but in spite of our blunders, the clubs grew in numbers and in strength.

As a result of my association with those women who had given me that first inspiration, we were made a part of the Christian Union of the Lady Friends of the Young Girl, with international headquarters in Switzerland. Our board of directors consisted of dignified ladies, most of them from the upper strata of society, and very strict in their opinions. However, they had a healthy sense of humour and astonishing flexibility, considering their background.

One of the areas of real challenge for the board was a young spinster with exploding ideas. Her name was Corrie ten Boom. A doctor's wife, Mrs Burkens, was given the job of 'controlling' Corrie, and protecting the larger group from adventures which were considered too dangerous.

Taboo!

Everything went very well with the board, until I came up with an idea which was revolutionary. I wanted to start a club with boys and girls together! Such a thing was unheard-of for a Christian organization; boys belonged in

boys' clubs, and girls in girls' clubs, especially during the
time of puberty.

Dating had no place in the Christian society; however, a
boy and a girl would meet each other in the streets, in secret.
After all, I knew a little bit about that – and I will never forget
Tante Jans's written tracts after she saw girls flirting in the
Bartel jorisstraat: *'Fonge Meisjes, Scharrelt Niet!'* ('Young
Girls, Don't Flirt!')

The reason we considered having a club for both boys and
girls was because the girls themselves were having such fun
together, that we began to be concerned that we were raising
a spinster society. The leaders' group thought if we started a
co-ed club, that girls would feel free to invite a boy-friend to
the club meeting, and wouldn't have to resort to seeing him
in secrecy.

I'll never forget the board meeting when I announced that
we were starting such a group.

'Corrie, what would some of the parents think?'

'It's never been done before!'

'Corrie, you really surprise us!'

I think I really surprised myself. I pleaded and argued that
this was such a good opportunity for real fellowship between
the sexes. The only possibility for boys and girls to be with
each other was to either meet in the streets, or in the case
of bad weather, to meet in the pubs.

I won the battle. However, the board left me with one
restriction: for one entire year nobody was allowed to tell
about our experiment. At the end of that critical first year,
if we didn't have any real problems, we were allowed more
publicity. So we started the *Vriendenkring* (The Club of
Friends). It may not have been a very clever title, but it was
a very popular club. The secrecy of its beginning increased
its popularity.

Each evening programme of the Friends' Club was unique.
My first question was, 'Well, what will we do this evening?'
Sometimes they discussed rowing on the Spaarne River, but
more often the topics centred around politics or the service
of the Lord. Somehow young people do not seem to have the
same aversion to these topics as their elders.

We had young men of many persuasions; some were communists, while others loved our country and our Queen. Many were faithful church members; others were agnostics or atheists. We had no requirements for joining the clubs, and if they didn't like the short Bible talks, they didn't have to listen.

Once the mixed club decided to climb the tower of the cathedral. I'll never forget how I felt as we climbed the highest steps on the outside of the tower and came into the middle of the pinnacle. I looked down upon the *grote markt*, which blossomed with the wares of the farmers and merchants three times a week, and probably wondered what it would be like to land in a bin of onions!

It was the first and last time I ever gathered courage for such an experiment. Going down was almost a greater nightmare than climbing up, and I may have considered (if I had time) the reason why the Lord was putting me through such a test of courage.

Boys and girls found each other in the club, and marriage feasts were high points for all of us. Some were married in churches but later told me, 'We have forgotten what the minister said, but the things you taught us in the club feast, we understood much better and have remembered them.'

Family Leadership

I had an area of concern about the mixed clubs, and that was my own feeling of inadequacy. I knew that the clubhouse needed a director, a substitute father and mother, and I certainly was not equipped for either position. We prayed about it, and out of the *Vriendenkring* came just the right couple.

Wim was a tailor from a family of tailors. His father, brother, and Wim's girl-friend, Fie, worked together in their business. They were such a joy to be around – they loved life and especially liked to celebrate with music. The first days of each week they devoted all of their time to developing their musical interests. The walls of their small tailor's shop were covered with musical instruments, such as violins, guitars, and mandolins – even the little nine-year-old daughter joined in the family orchestra.

I had to take one of Father's suits in for alteration one Monday morning, and was invited to sit down and listen to their concert. I was their only audience on that day and after almost an hour, I said, 'How long do your concerts last?'

'Oh, we play from eight in the morning until eleven at night most of the time on the first four days of the week.'

I wasn't used to this lack of work schedule. 'But what about your tailoring business?' I asked.

'Most of the time we start on Thursday . . . sometimes earlier, sometimes later. That depends on . . .'

Their mother finished the sentence, '. . . how much we have to eat in the house!'

My business sense was aroused. 'Do your customers agree with this long waiting time when they have ordered a suit or a dress?'

'They don't have to wait long,' Wirn answered. 'When we work, all four of us work together. Fie works with us, too.' He looked at her with love and pride. 'Soon, Tante Corrie, we'll get married and then we are going to live in her room.'

I knew Fie's room; it was just an attic in a large apartment house. Not a very pleasant place to begin married life, I thought.

'Well, the room is cheap,' Wim said when he saw my concerned face.

'Wim . . . Fie . . . I have an idea. Let's talk about it.'

Fie was not only a member of our Friends' Club, she was also a perfect leader of several of the girls' clubs. That Monday morning, in the tailor's shop temporarily turned concert hall, we began to dream. If Wim and Fie could live in the big clubhouse and be the directing couple for the HMC, not only would some of *their* immediate problems be solved, but also it would establish a permanent chaperone on the premises, which would quiet some of the criticisms we had heard.

Wim and Fie moved in and faithfully directed our clubhouse for many years. They became known as 'Uncle Wim and Aunt Fie', and later their baby daughter became the youngest member of the HMC.

All of my spare time was devoted to the clubs. Father and I experienced ups and downs in the watch-making business, but each evening I always had one or two clubs to attend. When I came home, Betsie and Father were always longing to hear what I had experienced. They were our prayer partners, and we knew that the Beje was home base for prayer support for all the work in the clubs. How we rejoiced together when people who came to the clubs gave their first *yes* to Jesus!

About forty years later I returned to Holland after tramping around the world; in a church one day I met a man who came to me and asked, 'Don't you know me? In your *Vriendenkring* I found the Lord. He has never failed me.'

Another time a minister saw me in his church and said from the pulpit, 'In your club, Corrie, I learned to appreciate the Bible as the living Word of God.'

I praised the Lord and chuckled to myself – it was certainly worth the year of being 'on trial', and that terrifying climb up the cathedral tower to hear testimonies like that!

13

The Red Cap Club

The quiet years of the early 1920s in our home were punctuated by the sound of Tante Anna's fading alto voice, singing the great old hymns of the church. As the once-vigorous body became weaker, she stayed in bed most of the time, memorizing verse after verse from her worn hymnal. She knew most of the songs slightly, but now learned all the words from the first to the last line. 'I've never had time to memorize,' she said, 'and it's such a joy.'

She knew that her time on earth was limited, but she seemed determined to enter heaven with a song on her lips.

When a day in the shop had been particularly difficult, or someone had come to the house burdened with heavy sorrow, it was an encouragement to hear from the little bedroom upstairs the beautiful words:

> He leadeth me, O blessed thought!
> O words with heavenly comfort fraught!
> What e'er I do, where e'er I be,
> Still 'tis God's hand that leadeth me.

After a short, severe illness, God led Tante Anna to her new home in heaven. Father, Betsie, and I sat at the big oval table, once so crowded with all the ten Booms, and talked about the past.

'It's a new life now, Corrie; we must remember the past, but live in anticipation of the future.'

Who could be despondent around Father? His positive attitude enlivened the dullest day. I looked at the empty chairs, and began to dream a bit. Mother had always encouraged us in our dreams. I recalled the time Betsie and I had gone to her with an idea we had.

'Mama, when we grow up we want to help children of missionaries. So many of them can't stay with their parents on the mission field, and then they are sent back to Holland to live in those big places where missionary children have their home.'

We had recently visited one of those houses, and although the leaders were kind, we felt so sorry for the boys and girls who had to sacrifice because their parents were obeying God by serving in other countries.

I remember how Mother brightened at the thought. She had just left the hospital after a minor operation, and told us about a talk she had with the head nurse.

'My nurse had been a missionary for years and when she heard that I had three daughters she said, "Mrs ten Boom, I think you should keep one daughter at home, one should be a deaconess in our hospital, and one you should give to the missions."'

My eyes grew big at the thought. Which one was I to be?

'What was your answer, Mama?'

'I told the nurse – I would not know if I could give a daughter of mine for the mission field!'

Mother explained the reason for her strong feelings. She continued her story: 'My own mother was in Indonesia when she was a little child. Her parents lived there, and both died on the same day. There were three small children left without parents. A black woman took them all to her home, and cared for them for two years before they could find a ship with a captain who was willing to take the three orphans to Holland on his ship, without grown-ups to supervise them. The kind Negroes who kept my mother and her brother and sister were very good to them, but my mother's childhood was very primitive. If you wish to serve the Lord by educating missionary children, I believe it would be a very worth-while pursuit, Corrie.'

That story and my dream soon leaped into reality. The meanderings of my mind were interrupted by Willem's familiar voice downstairs. 'Is anybody at home?'

He told us he had something important to tell us, so Betsie, Father, and I gathered in the parlour. Willem began by saying, 'As you know, I'm a board member of the Salatiga Dutch East Indies mission.'

Oh, dear, was Willem going to go to the mission field?

But that wasn't it at all. His request, I admit, was a strange 'coincidence' – coming at that particular time.

'There are three children of missionaries,' Willem continued, 'who need to have a home on short notice. Their parents must leave for the mission field. They're very clever children, two girls and a boy. Now we can find a home for the boy, but not for the girls. They all need to study, but there isn't much money.'

(That was a familiar phrase in our house.)

'This is a faith mission,' Willem explained. 'When the finances are good the parents can pay; but if there is nothing, then the foster parents must live by faith like the missionaries. I thought perhaps it could be something for you.'

'We'll pray about it, Willem,' Father replied, pulling on his beard, as he did when he was deep in thought.

Willem knew that he couldn't press Father into a decision before prayer; that was the way decisions were made in our family. However, after supper and prayer I cleared the dishes from the table, as Betsie poured milk into the steaming cups of coffee and Father lit a cigar.

'One girl could sleep in Tante Bep's room,' I suggested.

'So, you are already arranging the house,' Father chuckled. 'If you two agree, I will not refuse. However . . .' and Father paused, perhaps beginning to think of the foolishness of a man in his sixties with two unmarried daughters taking the responsibility of raising young children. '. . . let's not decide too quickly about this.'

The next day the mission director visited us.

'Mr ten Boom . . . ladies,' and he bowed gallantly to us, 'the board of the missions met last night and thanked the Lord that you are willing to take the two girls.'

Father smiled. 'Who told you that? Of course, if you have already thanked God, we cannot refuse. When can the children come that we may see them?'

'Tomorrow.'

Betsie and I began to rearrange closets, prepare beds, and plan meals before any of us had a chance to question our decision. It was quite clear to us that the Lord meant us to take the girls, but we hadn't counted on the added surprise in the missionary package.

The next day three children came: Puck, a spirited little girl of eleven, Hans, a twelve-year-old with great intelligence, and Hardy, their fourteen-year-old brother. We loved them from the beginning, responding immediately to their bright minds and willingness to adapt to a new way of life. When they were small, they were educated in Indonesia, where their parents served on the mission field; but when they grew older they were sent back to their home country to boarding school, or to live with families. Naturally, the children preferred families to the schools, so they were eager to please.

We showed Puck and Hans to their rooms, and they began to unpack their few belongings from the little cloth satchels they brought with them. Hardy stayed in the kitchen, looking down at the floor.

'Come along, Hardy, it's time for us to leave,' the mission director said.

'Sir,' Hardy said softly, looking from Father to the director, 'can't I stay in this house with the bearded old man? I had to say good-bye to Mum and Dad; I don't want to say good-bye to Hans and Puck, too.'

Father said, 'Of course you are staying, young man. You don't think I can run this household full of women all alone, do you?'

And then we were six.

Our quiet, thin little three-storey house was suddenly stretching its walls and echoing the activity of three children. The side door swung in and out like the pendulum on one of our clocks, and it was a good sound. Father seemed to increase his productivity with all the chatter and singing going on around him; the entire tempo of our lives picked up.

Betsie and I discussed the division of labour, and it was settled that she would take care of their clothing and food, and I would be responsible for sports and music. I could combine that with my club work. The first thing I did when the children came was to sell my bicycle. I decided to walk a great deal with them, and as long as we didn't have enough money for bicycles for everyone, I intended to train myself and the children to walk where we had to go.

The Alpina watch company had sent us little red caps – the type worn by the Swiss yodellers – and I gave each of the children one of these. The first time we all ventured out on a walk, the conductor of the street car saw us and said, 'Well, here comes Corrie and her Red Cap Club.'

We bobbed along the streets of Haarlem, and out to the dunes for our hikes, but it wasn't long before there were more red caps added to our little 'club'.

Along Comes Lessie

Just as we had the children of the watch-makers come to live with us after the first World War, we inherited another girl who had been promised a home in Holland, and then had been rejected. Lessie was a missionary's daughter, who was on a boat ready to sail from Indonesia to Holland, when a telegram came from the uncle she was going to visit, saying that she was not welcome. Her mother was so upset because Lessie needed a time in Holland to begin the training school for teachers, and all the arrangements had been made.

The parents of Hans and Puck were at the ship – bidding Lessie good-bye – when the telegram arrived. 'Send her to the Beje,' they said. 'They always have room, but if they don't, they'll make it.'

Consequently we received a letter announcing the arrival of Lessie within two days. There was no time to write our answer; in fact, there was no alternative.

'We have no room for more beds,' Betsie said. Her precise nature of housekeeping was straining with the increasingly crowded and cluttered conditions. However, she didn't complain, she moved things, rearranged furniture, and we made do.

'I can sleep in the tower – the place where the suitcases are kept,' Hardy said.

A plan was already forming in my mind. 'No, we'll put two beds on top of each other in my room.' I invented a type of bunk beds with our old bedsteads.

When Lessie arrived, hurt because she had been refused by her one relative, she was welcomed by us with open arms.

Within a short time the Lord chose to send us two more girls. We experienced that with men there are impossible situations and circumstances, but with God all things are possible.

Our Red Cap Club added more caps, and we began to look like a troop of yodellers!

All the girls went into the training school for teachers, and Hardy went to another school, just for boys. Poor Hardy, he was surrounded by girls, and I'm sure he must have felt over-whelmed at times. He began to disappear for several hours at a time, and one day Betsie marched into the kitchen with a frown on her gentle face.

'Do you know what Hardy is doing?'

Oh, dear. I began to imagine all sorts of evil things, none of which seemed to suit Hardy's basic good character.

'He's going to Charlie Chaplin movies!' Betsie announced indignantly.

'To the movies? You don't say!'

None of us had ever been to the movies, but somehow I didn't hold as scandalous a view of this new invention as Betsie did. We didn't forbid Hardy from this pursuit, but we tried to make the activities for the children so attractive that they weren't too interested in such things.

I loved the physical activities with my foster children. When we walked together, we talked together, and it was more valuable than any 'lectures' we might give. We had such great fun on our hikes. Once we walked with one of my clubs from Haarlem to Amsterdam, which was a distance of seventeen kilometres (about ten miles). We carried our lunch and sang whenever our spirits began to droop a bit. My foster children were the most enthusiastic.

We had gymnastic lessons, too, although I wasn't a very good pupil myself. My feet never seemed to do what my mind instructed them. We all worked out on the gymnastic bars, with a succession of teachers who taught their individual type of body movements; the German method taught a different style from the French, and both were contrary to the Swedish gymnastics. I learned to do a bird's nest on the bars, but I was certainly an awkward bird compared with my club girls.

In the middle of a gymnastic lesson, I would blow my whistle and we would have a Bible lesson which would last from two to five minutes. The lessons were usually in the form of stories that the children could remember – stories which emphasized a Bible truth.

For instance, I told the story about the old monk. 'There was an old monk who sang a Christmas song every Christmas Eve for his brothers in the monastery, and for visitors who would come from the village for the special services. His voice was very ugly, but he loved the Lord and sang from his heart. Once the director of the cloister said, "I'm sorry, Brother Don, we have a new monk who has such a beautiful voice . . . he will sing this Christmas."

'The man sang so beautifully that everyone was happy.

'But that night an angel came to the superior and said, "Why didn't you have a Christmas Eve song?"

'The superior was very surprised. "We had a beautiful song, didn't you hear it?"

'The angel shook his head sadly, "It may have been very inspiring to you, but we didn't hear it in heaven."

'You see, the old monk with the raspy voice had a personal relationship with the Lord Jesus, but the young monk was singing for his own benefit, not the Lord's.'

'That's a good story, Tante Kees,' Puck panted while trying to do a back-bend and talk at the same time. (She called me by the nickname that all the club girls used.) 'Is that in the Bible?'

'No, Puck, but the Bible does say, "but if any one loves

God, he is known by Him" (1 Corinthians 8:3). Do you think that God knew the young monk?'

The girls were in a training school for teachers, and the quick little Bible studies in story form came in very handy for them.

One day they told us about a student in their class who cried a lot. Hans was especially concerned about her, and at supper time, while everyone was around the oval table, she brought up the subject.

'Remember me telling you about Miep, the girl in our class who cries a lot? Well, I talked to her today during recess and found out that she lives with a cousin. Her parents are in Belgium. She can't seem to eat. Anyhow, her cousin told her that she had to finish her meal before she could leave for school, so she's almost always late. She's miserable with her cousin and doesn't want to go back.'

'Please, Tante Betsie, Tante Kees, take Miep into our house,' Puck said. ' She's really so sweet but so unhappy. We can sleep two in a bed.'

The next day, Betsie went to visit the cousin and his wife. They were good people, but had very little insight about raising a teenager. They agreed that we should have Miep in our house for a time.

When Miep arrived, Betsie gave her a real welcome. 'Look, Miep, no one here has to eat who doesn't want to . . . here is the bread; whenever you are hungry, you can help yourself and make a sandwich.'

Miep soon became a happy, relaxed girl, full of humour and a good, normal appetite.

With seven children in the house now, the Beje was an active, noisy place. In the evenings Father sat in the living room, surrounded by his second family, busily writing his weekly paper. He went about his work oblivious to the din surrounding him, looking up occasionally to smile at one of the children.

The girls were always in a hurry to get to one of their clubs, or to do their studying. They tried to shorten the devotions at night, but Father, called *Opa*, by the children, was aware of their methods.

Puck said once,'Opa, let's just read Psalm 117 tonight.'

'Well, now, Puck, I just think I'll read Psalm 119.'

A visitor commented to Father that he was astonished at all the noise and laughter in our house. Father said, 'Our children are such good kids . . . why they never quarrel and are always ready to help each other. They're just angels.'

I sighed and went upstairs to talk to Puck, who had been sent to her room for the 'angelic' way she had said, 'I hate Lessie!'

She was sitting on the corner of her bed, curled up in that defiant position children take when they know they're going to be punished.

'Puck, don't you know that Jesus says hatred is murder in God's eyes. He told us that we must love our enemies,' I said.

'Well, I can't love Lessie!'

'In Romans 5:5 Paul says, ". . . the love of God has been poured out within our hearts through the Holy Spirit who was given to us." If you give room in your heart for the Holy Spirit, He will give you His love, a part of the fruit of the Spirit – and that love never fails.'

Puck looked up, a trace of tears in her eyes, 'But, Tante Kees, what must I do? Such hateful thoughts come in my heart.'

'John says, "If we confess our sins, he is faithful and just to forgive us our sins, and to cleanse us from all unrighteousness" [1 John 1:9 AV]. Jesus will cleanse your heart with His blood, and then He will fill you with His love. Shall we go to Him now and tell Him everything?'

Puck relaxed. All the tension in her taut muscles left, and she lowered her head as we prayed together. Puck and Lessie became the greatest of friends. Years later Puck was in a concentration camp in Indonesia, placed there by the Japanese during World War II. The guards were very cruel, and how she needed the Holy Spirit to give her love for her enemies! She was married then and her husband, Fritz, was in a concentration camp in the Philippines. When she was released she only weighed 79 pounds. Fritz survived the years of imprisonment, and was an emaciated 106 pounds when he was freed.

Puck told me after the war, 'I always thought if I came out alive, "I wonder if my parents in Holland will have the strength to stand the hardships of the war – but I know that Opa and Tante Betsie and Tante Kees will be there." That gave me a feeling of security. When I was beaten, I thought of you and Opa, and remembered what you had taught me about love for my enemies.'

Puck's parents were still alive when she came back after the war. Opa and Tante Betsie were no longer there, but what they had taught Puck lasted. '. . . the righteous shall be in everlasting remembrance' (Psalm 112:6 av).

Although Betsie and I never married, we received such love from all of our children and were able to give them so much of our love! However, a house full of teenagers was not uncomplicated. There were many things to talk over with the Lord daily. Sometimes there was not much money. When they needed new shoes they had to wait until the finances were available. Cardboard or newspapers temporarily stuffed in the soles were frequent emergency measures.

We shared our sorrows and joys with all of them. When I sold an expensive clock or watch I came to the living room, stood in the door, and made an impressive announcement.

'Ladies – and the two gentlemen present – I wish to inform all of you gathered for this important occasion that Mrs van der Hoeven has just purchased the gold Alpina, and paid cash for it!'

Cheers. Hurrahs.

'Now I can get my shoes.'

'And I my petticoat.'

When the situation was serious, we prayed about it, and didn't forget afterward to thank God together. We lived as a real family.

Betsie was wonderful in contacting the parents; she wrote them every week. When one of the girls got a new dress, she took a snapshot, and sent it to the parents together with a piece of material.

Marijke was the only girl who had difficulties in school. She was studying to be a kindergarten teacher and loved children, but was terrified of examinations. Once she failed, and it was difficult to persuade her to go back the next time.

She adored Opa – as all the children did. The evening before the crucial day of the examination, he was writing his weekly paper and concentrating so intently that it was almost impossible to stir him, except with something very tempting.

He laid down his pen when Puck brought in the tea. She had made cookies, and everyone had to pay attention to such a treat.

'I'm not going to the examination tomorrow,' Marijke stated.

'Why not?' Father asked, immediately concerned over one of his children.

'I'll fail again.'

Father smiled. 'Listen, Marijke, you have done your best and possibly you can't do it alone. But Paul said, "I can do all things through Christ who strengthens me." Do you think He will give you strength if you trust Him?'

'Paul never had to go to examinations,' Hardy remarked with the complete assurance of a teenage boy who knows all the answers.

'I think his questioning from Felix was a bit tougher than an exam for a kindergarten teacher,' Lessie answered, pleased with herself for making this comparison. (We had been studying the Book of Acts.)

'Can you really pray for everything? Even something as little as an examination?' Marijke asked with renewed interest.

Father leaned back in his chair, warming his hands with the steaming tea, relishing the chance to discuss the Scriptures. 'Paul says in Philippians 1:27, "Whatever happens make sure that your everyday life is worthy of the Gospel of Jesus Christ." When you belong to the Lord, there's not one single thing you have to conquer in your own strength. The hairs of your head are numbered; can anything be more trivial than that?'

'But, Opa,' Puck said, 'yesterday I didn't learn French because I was busy making cookies. That was more fun than

dull old French. So this morning I prayed that I wouldn't be
called on. But God didn't help me. I did get called on – and
what a mess I made of the French words!'

'I'm not surprised,' Father chuckled. 'If you didn't learn,
you can't expect the Lord to help you.'

Hardy added, with a sudden burst of understanding which
made me very pleased with him, 'I've found out that if I want
to pray for something that is wrong, I simply can't.'

It was years later that I had to learn another lesson about
prayers for something that was not 100 per cent right.

It was in 1945, shortly after the war, that I went to
Switzerland. I had spoken there in many meetings, but
also I visited my former watchmaker friends from whom
I had learned my trade many years before. I bought some
watches while I was there. In Holland, there was still a severe
shortage of imported articles and to buy Swiss watches was
rather complicated.

When I put my watches in my suitcase, I smiled because of
the methods we had learned in the time of the underground
work when we saved Jewish people and hid articles in our
luggage. Surely nobody should be able to find my three
watches!

Before I went to the train, I prayed the way I always do
when I start a trip.

'Lord, protect us against accidents; bless the engineer of
the train and give him wisdom; make us a blessing for our
fellow travellers, and Lord . . . give us success in smuggling
. . . in smug . . .' (I wanted to say, 'In smuggling my watches,'
but I couldn't.)

The moment I started to pray for it, I knew it was a sin.
Smuggling to avoid paying money is the same as stealing.
I didn't smuggle my watches and I experienced again that
prayer can be a discipline. Praying for something that is
wrong is not possible.

As the girls grew older and discovered that boys were more
than just a nuisance, it became an increasing challenge to
answer their questions. The walks we had together brought

a closeness and ease of communication, in spite of our difference in age. Usually we walked on Sunday afternoon, since our week was filled with work and school. I remember when we walked from Haarlem to the dunes near Zandvoort, the sun warm on our faces, and the sand inviting us to sunbathe, we would frequently lie on our backs and talk about . . . well, just the things girls talk about.

'Tante Kees, were you ever engaged to be married?'

'Tante Kees, do you long to have a husband? Do you find it difficult to be single?'

Once they started the girls could ask questions as rapidly as a second hand could move in an accurate timepiece.

'You rascals . . . this is a very important subject to talk about, when you are beginning your lives as young women.' I had no sadness or regret, only joy in telling the story of Karel.

'There was a time in my life when I expected to marry a boy who loved me and whom I loved. He was going to be a minister, and was from a big family where several members were clergymen. They had the usual problems that ministers have with finances.

'His mother did not approve of our getting married. She wanted him to marry a rich girl.

'How I struggled with myself at that time! When he introduced me to the wealthy girl he was going to marry, I had the feeling that my heart would never survive such a blow.'

'What did you do, Tante Kees?'

'I went to my room and talked it over with the Lord. From what I can remember it was something like this: "I want, Lord, to belong to You with my body, soul, and mind. I claim Your victory, Lord Jesus, over that wound which is hurting me. Let Your victory be demonstrated also in my sex life."

'I didn't quite analyse what I needed, but the joy is that with the Lord, it is not necessary to give Him a clear diagnosis before He knows the cure.'

'Did you have an immediate victory?'

'No, there was still a battle – rather severe – but then the Lord healed me and the pain didn't come back. The Lord gave and continues to give me a very happy life. I have the love of all of you – and I love you. My life isn't dull at all. The best thing is that when Jesus restores such a loss, He gives a fulfilment that is a little bit of heaven – a peace that passes all understanding. From our side it is only necessary to surrender.'

After I had told this, Puck said, 'Now I understand more what Opa said yesterday: "Our times are in His hands."'

He Brings You Safely Home

It was the middle of May 1940. By that time the children were all away in their different jobs or married. It was a time of fear and confusion in our land.

Hitler and Goering had ordered a heavy bombing of Rotterdam – and we were bewildered! The Dutch experienced the first large-scale airborne attack in the history of warfare.

We were completely unprepared for such an ordeal. On the morning of May 14, 1940, a German staff officer crossed the bridge at Rotterdam with a white flag in his hand, and demanded the surrender of the city. He warned that unless it capitulated, it would be bombed.

While surrender negotiations were actually under way, the bombers appeared and wiped out the heart of our great city. Over 800 persons, mostly civilians, were massacred; several thousand were wounded, and 78,000 homeless. Rotterdam surrendered and then the Dutch armed forces did the same. It was then our dear Queen Wilhemina and the government members fled to London.

The German juggernaut was on the move. An army of tanks larger in size, concentration, and striking ability than any tank force yet mobilized, started through the Ardennes Forest from the German frontier. We read that these tanks stretched three columns wide, for a hundred miles behind the Rhine, and broke through the French armies headed for the English Channel.

Our Hans was married by then and had two children, and another one on the way. Her husband was a teacher, and they lived in Rotterdam during that terrible bombardment.

They fled to a small suburb of Rotterdam, where her third baby was born in a cellar. For a year they lived in that cellar, which formed a bomb shelter.

Hans told me in later years that over and over again she repeated to her children, 'Opa taught us, "When Jesus takes your hand, He keeps you tight. When Jesus keeps you tight, He leads you through your whole life. When Jesus leads you through your life, He brings you safely home."'

14

Even the Least of Them . . .

In addition to the work in the business, the club work, and
the care for our children, I continued with the Bible lessons
in the schools. One of these classes was for children who had
learning difficulties. It was such a joy to know that the Holy
Spirit doesn't need a high IQ in a person in order to reveal
Himself. Even people of normal or superior intelligence need
the Lord to understand the spiritual truths which are only
spiritually discerned.

God gave me a great love for the 'exceptional children'. I
remember going to these schools and telling Bible stories,
and being rewarded when their faces lit up with sweet and
simple happiness.

Sometimes I asked them questions to see if they understood what I told them. Once a feeble-minded girl answered
a question of mine which might have baffled a person of
normal intelligence. I asked, 'What is a prophet and what
is a priest?'

She said, 'They are both messengers between God and
man.'

I continued, 'Then they are the same – a prophet and a
priest?'

She thought a while and then answered, 'No, a prophet
has his back to God and his face to us – and a priest has his
face to God and his back to us.'

I wasn't sure if she had learned that by heart, so I asked
her, 'Well, what was I today?'

She said, 'You were both – you told us about God and

you were a prophet. Then you prayed. You didn't pray for yourself, but you prayed for us – then you were a priest.'

That was a backward child who answered in that manner! When you bring the Gospel, it is the Holy Spirit who works.

I tried to teach these children other things with much less success; one time I started to instruct them about the stars. I brought some white beans to school and laid them on the table in the form of constellations. I showed them Orion, and they looked at the formation of the beans, and all of them knew it very well. Then one evening I took them outside and said, 'Look, children, there is Orion . . . see it?'

They just shook their heads. 'No, Tante Corrie, they are white beans in the sky.'

They never understood what I told them about the stars, but the truths of the Lord they seemed to understand well.

Whenever you come in contact with feeble-minded people, please tell them that Jesus loves them. They often understand God's love better than people who have problems because of their intellectual doubt.

Paul wrote in 1 Corinthians 1:20, 21: 'For consider, what have the philosopher, the writer and the critic of this world to show for all their wisdom? Has not God made the wisdom of this world look foolish? For it was after the world in its wisdom had failed to know God, that He in His Wisdom chose to save all who would believe by the "simple-mindedness" of the Gospel message.'

Some Are Forgotten

Father shared my concern, my outreach for the debilitated and the disturbed. Once he heard from a servant girl about a woman in a mental hospital who never received a visit from anyone.

Father, Betsie, and I prayed for this woman and then I made the trip to the hospital. It took me some hours to go there, and when I finally found the woman I discovered that she was clear in her thinking, although a bit mentally disturbed. Also her body was sick, and she couldn't leave her bed.

'May I introduce myself? I'm Corrie ten Boom. I've come to visit you,' I said.

She looked up at me with tears of joy in her eyes.

'Did God send you?'

'Yes, I'm sure He did . . . and I'm glad, too, because I would like you to be my friend. Will you?'

'Oh, yes,' she said eagerly. 'Will you please visit me sometimes? Can you tell me about Jesus?'

I thought for a moment. How much did this woman know? What Bible story could help her? I prayed for inspiration, and then told her about the good shepherd who brought the lost sheep home.

We became real friends, in spite of being such an unequal combination! There I was, a healthy, normal girl, and she was an older woman with a confused mind. I truly believe the Lord brought us together.

Often in the midst of a very busy workday, with the watch repairs stacked on the counter waiting to be done, Father would say to me, 'Why don't you visit Alida today? She's come into my mind . . . perhaps she is lonely.'

Dear Papa! It meant more work for him, because a visit to this friend of mine took at least four hours of the day.

On one visit we talked at some length about heaven. Two days later the nurse at the hospital called me on the phone. 'Alida has died suddenly. Can you give us the address of her relatives?'

I know that tears came to my eyes, but I could thank the Lord that she was now with Him in the beautiful heaven we had so recently talked about. 'I'm sorry,' I told the nurse, 'I don't know anything about Alida's relatives.'

'But you were such a close friend,' she replied.

'I asked her once if she had sisters and brothers. She told me that years ago they had brought her to the hospital. She had never heard from them again. She didn't know if they were alive, and if so, where they lived.'

Father said that evening, 'Corrie, I believe that this friendship, and the time you gave that poor woman has shown God's loving kindness for the despised and lost more than any other work you have done. I'm sure it was important in God's eyes.'

Just a Boy Named Henk

Henk was a boy who was a member of my Bible class for mentally retarded. He came from a family with eleven children, and it was difficult for his poor tired mother to give him much attention.

It was from this simple little boy that I saw again how the Holy Spirit reveals Himself in such a marvellous way to low-IQ people.

Once I visited Henk at home, and his mother received me with such a thankful manner. 'Henk talks so much about the stories you tell in his Bible class. He never remembers anything about any other class, but when he comes from your class he talks to his brothers and sisters about it.'

'Is Henk at home?'

'He's in his room upstairs . . . in the corner of the attic. He's there most of the time . . . he's really my easiest boy. We know he'll never become a professor or anything important, but he does work for a salary – he's in a government workshop where he makes clothes-pegs the whole day. Dear Henk, he's so satisfied, but when he's at home the house is so full of noise that he goes to his attic room.'

I went upstairs and found Henk on his knees in front of a chair. Before him was an old dirty picture of Jesus on the cross. I stopped at the door to listen, for Henk was singing. His voice was soft and hoarse.

Out of my bondage, sorrow and night, Jesus, I come, Jesus, I come;
Into Thy freedom, gladness and light, Jesus, I come to Thee.
Out of the depths of ruin untold, into the peace of Thy sheltering fold,
Ever Thy glorious face to behold, Jesus, I come to Thee.

I've heard Bach played by Schweitzer, and anthems sung

by gigantic choirs, but at that moment I felt as if I were in a cathedral with angels surrounding me. I tiptoed back downstairs without disturbing him, praising God again for the love He brings into the lives of 'even the least of them'.

Some time later I heard that Henk's mother had gone into his attic room and found him before the chair, with the picture of Jesus in his hand. Henk was home with the Lord. When I heard about his death I wondered if he had been singing, 'Jesus, I come to Thee' at that last moment.

Thirty Years Later

It was after World War II and I was working in East Germany, teaching the Gospel in a huge cathedral. I went into a counselling area to talk with people individually; there were many more who needed help waiting outside in another room. I heard a very noisy discussion, everyone seemed to be talking too loudly at the same time. Suddenly everything was quiet and I heard an unusually tender, beautiful voice singing. It was Henk's hymn in German: 'Out of my bondage, sorrow and night, Jesus, I come.'

I opened the door into the room where the inquirers were waiting and saw a child of about fourteen years of age. Her face was like an angel, and there was something so moving about her that many in the room were crying. The girl's mother stood beside her and held her hand.

When they came into the inquiry room, I found out that the girl's name was Elsa, and I realized immediately that she was not a normal child.

'Where did you learn that song, Elsa?' I asked her gently.

'In prison . . . a man taught it to me, and I sang it every day.'

'Why was Elsa in prison?' I asked her mother.

'My husband is a communist. Elsa is mentally retarded. She loves the Lord Jesus and speaks about Him frequently, but her father is an atheist and a leader in his party, so he had no difficulty putting Elsa in prison. A short while ago we got her out . . . it was so terribly cold in that jail that the guards themselves helped me get Elsa out. They heard and enjoyed her singing, and Elsa was always ready to tell them about her Lord.'

My lips quivered as I held Elsa's hands, and I remembered so many things . . . the Bible studies in Holland . . . Henk in his attic room . . . and what Father had often said to me. 'Corrie, what you do among these people is of little importance in the eyes of men, but I'm sure in God's eyes it is the most valuable work of all.'

Chapter 15

Leaders and Blunders

I loved the activity – the challenge – the excitement of seeing lives changed. The need in the young people was obvious as the clubs multiplied rapidly.

Once a month we had representatives of every club gather to give suggestions and form plans. We had so many interest groups: handcrafts, sewing, piano, harmonium, choir. As a few girls with other talents expressed the need for another group, we would find a leader and begin another club.

I led the music group myself. Music has always been an important part of my life, and it was such a joy for me to work with these girls. Our club had eight members; seven girls worked at a table on harmony and the study of music, while one went to the piano or organ. Consequently, each member had the lengthy chance of five or ten minutes behind the keyboard.

My, what mistakes I made in that club! If I had taught them watch repair, I would have known exactly what I was doing; but the times that I sent a substitute leader my lack of real skill in music was glaringly evident! My substitute was Ann, a lady who had many diplomas from the music academy. When she took my organ and piano club, her trained ears suffered – to put it mildly. Dear Ann, I learned so much from her! She never refused to help me. In her humble and shy way, she lovingly told me of some of the horrible mistakes in instruction I had made. However, she didn't have a critical spirit, and was able to correct me in such a loving manner. This was a gift which set such an example for me.

I loved this music club, but the few-minutes' message was the important part of the evening for me. These short talks about the Lord weren't deep theological studies, but stories from the Bible and about the lives of other Christians. They were brief on purpose; some of the club members expected this part of the evening, but it wasn't really their cup of tea. They seemed to endure it for the sake of the fun in the clubs.

We had a theme for everything we did: It was 'Him in the Midst of the Clubs'. This is exactly what we did – put the message in the middle of the meeting. We knew if we gave it at the beginning, some would avoid it by coming late; if we talked of our theme later in the evening, they left early.

However, many seeds fell upon fertile ground, and when club members began to open their hearts and ask questions about Jesus, we decided to start a Catechism Club. In this group, they could learn enough to become a member of the church. Some called it the Confirmation Club.

I especially loved the Heidelberg Catechism (not all of the fifty-two Sundays, but many of them). I translated the old-fashioned and complicated style of expression into everyday language that my girls could understand. It was amazing how they enjoyed it, and how much it became a part of them.

My teaching, however, did not always meet with enthusiasm from the pastors of the churches.

To become a member of the Dutch Reformed Church there was an examination by the pastor in the presence of elders and deacons. The first time I had just a few confirmands, so the pastor invited me to come together with the new members he had trained. It was an interesting experience.

First the pastor asked one of his pupils a simple question. 'Who was the first man in the world?'

Silence. Embarrassment.

He hinted by saying, 'It starts with *A*.'

She replied with a proud smile, 'That must be Abram.'

The pastor was so humiliated.

My pupils studied the Bible and the catechism very hard. The last few weeks before confirmation, they came several evenings to see me and to repeat what they had learned. One of my confirmands was asked, 'Do you know the name of one judge of Israel?'

Without hesitation the boy rattled off the names of Othniel, Ehud, Shamgar, Deborah, and the names of the other judges. The examining board was impressed.

One of my girls was asked to tell the story of one of the judges. She said that Gideon was a very shy and bashful man; and when the angel appeared to him, he told Gideon that because the Lord was with him, he was a mighty man of valour. However, she added, 'I would never have chosen him to become a hero. I think he was a sissy. But because the Lord was with him, he was mighty.'

Later I heard from the French nanny of the minister's little boy that the pastor came home and declared, 'I'll never examine Corrie ten Boom's confirmands and mine together again! I've seldom been so ashamed of the poor results of my teaching.'

Later it was more than embarrassment, it became a real collision. I was examining a girl for confirmation and refused to recommend her, because she didn't believe that Jesus had died on the cross. She was very unhappy over my decision and, said, 'I'm not religious like you, but I'd like to become a member of a church. I think it's dignified and I like that. Besides, my mum is going to give me a new dress for the occasion.'

I still refused and she went to the minister, who reversed my decision, and allowed her to become a church member. He said, 'I like the idea of a herd. Some are sheep, some are not – but that doesn't matter.'

That minister eventually left the pastorate to become a professor of theology at a university.

Leadership Training

As the clubs and the work increased, it became obvious that we must devote more time to leadership training. When we had our weekly meetings with our leaders, we took turns telling a story from the Bible while the rest of us criticized. The types of questions we asked were:

Was the Gospel clear?
How was her first sentence; did it attract attention?
Was there humour?
What help was there for the girls this week?
What importance did the story have for eternity?
Did she describe colours, movements?
Did she draw clear pictures with good illustrations?
Was it an inspiration for action, for faith, for endurance?

Problems were discussed and then there was prayer. All of us did the work because we loved it; we had so much fun ourselves, but we also understood why it was important. It was a humble little piece of building the Kingdom of God.

One of the problems we had was that we didn't have enough able leaders. Another serious one was that it was difficult to get rid of the wrong ones. The most impossible of all the leaders was *Kipslang*. The girls gave her that name because she told the Adam and Eve story by saying that the snake had legs like a chicken. After that her name became Kipslang (chicken-snake).

The girls roared with laughter during her story about Adam and Eve, and she cried with holy indignation over their ridicule. Weren't girls supposed to be serious when listening to a Bible story? Kipslang's club was always a sensation. Girls cried often because of her harsh remarks, and she usually answered by crying also. There was always noise and disorder in her club, and on one occasion the girls began to throw chairs at each other. It was quite out of control, but no other club was as popular because something was always happening there!

It was really remarkable: once we had ten clubs which all formed as a result of split-ups from Kipslang's club! Dear Kipslang – she was often a headache, but club work certainly prepared her for the future. When I last heard of her, she had been married three years, and had just given birth to her second set of twins.

Let's Go Camping

During the summer we arranged camps which brought girls and leaders closer together than all the weekly meetings. Most of the time we went to the *Bliscap* (an old word for *joy*), which was a simple log cabin with room for about sixty girls.

The campfires were high spots during our outings. There we talked about the Lord, sang hymns, and prayed. The girls were very strict about our campfire time – they were rascals and 'born after the fall', but they always said, 'At a campfire you look into the flames and listen to God.'

On the camps and conferences, one of the biggest dangers was the gossip. We made a camp law and one of the articles was: 'If you must tell something negative about someone else, first tell ten positive qualities about him.'

If a gossiping remark was made during a meal, we simply said, 'Pass the salt, if you please.'

Our foster children enjoyed the club and camp life with me. All of them were such a great help to us as leaders, and the love between us made it possible for me to depend upon them for so many tasks. It was always such a joy to have them together with the other club girls. Most of them had such good training that later they were able to do club work wherever they were, scattered over the world.

My girls learned some of the basic lessons of life and death at the camps. Toddy and Janny, sisters, had several real aunts in Holland with whom they spent a part of their vacations. Once in a camp with me, they received a phone call from an uncle that their most beloved aunt had died. They had known that her life was in danger for she was a haemophiliac. When she had a wound, the bleeding wouldn't stop, and upon the birth of her first baby she died. She was very young, and the girls were broken-hearted. It was the first time that someone they loved had been taken from them by death.

'Would you like to go to be with your uncle?' I asked.

'Yes, we would. We couldn't enjoy camp any more – perhaps we can help with the funeral.'

'Tomorrow I'll take you to the train. There's no connection tonight,' I explained.

I saw their sad young faces and suggested taking a walk over the heather fields. When we were alone, I let them talk and talk about their aunt. I have found this is one of the most important things to do for a person who is grieving – have him talk about the loved one who is gone. Toddy and Janny knew their aunt loved the Lord, and that she had known there was the danger of dying as soon as she had a wound.

I had my little New Testament in the pocket of my uniform and read from Romans 8:28. '. . . all things work together for good to them that love God . . .'

Also, 'These little troubles (which are really so transitory) are winning for us a permanent and glorious reward out of all proportion to our pain' (2 Corinthians 4:17 PHILLIPS).

Toddy and Janny confronted the reality and the glory of death that summer at camp. Some years later Toddy married her uncle, which may seem strange, but he was only nine years older than she. They had several children and a good life together.

Along the River Rhine

One trip (which was unforgettable) was a hiking and camping adventure the club girls had through Germany. All the girls (who could spare the time and money) met each week in our club-house to learn the German language. If someone knew a sentence which would be useful when travelling, she would express it to the group, and all the girls would write the sentence in Dutch and in German in their notebooks. Everyone had a little knowledge of the language before we started our trip. I told them the German words and they wrote them down phonetically.

The Rhine River was never so beautiful as it was that summer. I don't believe I've ever enjoyed a trip through a foreign land as much as I did when travelling with girls who had never been outside their country.

Many years later, one of the girls who went on our German trip became seriously ill. In her feverish state she talked about the only foreign country trip she had ever made; it had been the highlight of her life. However, just the recall of that trip didn't help her when she was treading the valley of the shadow of death. There she was not alone, because Jesus was her Saviour. She had given her heart to Him in one of the clubs. This was the most important purpose of our club work: to confront each person with Him, who is our only comfort in life and death.

Jesus is the real security in this world, even in the hour we have to leave it.

Blunder Boom

Sometimes I think my middle name is *Blunder*. I made some big mistakes, but I can say that our clubs became a success in spite of me. I loved my girls, and shared many of their joys and difficulties.

As the years passed, and some of our club girls grew older, or others wished to join, some of the teenagers didn't like to belong to a club where 'older people' came.

'We must make an age limit for our clubs,' some experienced club leaders suggested. 'Let's make it twenty-five years.'

I protested. I had some fine girls who had already passed that age, and I couldn't stand the idea of being forced to send them away.

'I don't think we should have any limit – let's just consider the ages eight to eighty. Why not?'

No one challenged me. When I had a fixed opinion, it was almost impossible to dissuade me; consequently, the age limit was never changed.

One blunder (which may have turned into a blessing) was when I chose a camp-site rather close to soldiers' quarters. In their free time, the men showed a great interest in the girls. Of course, the girls returned that interest. That's understandable.

One day during that camp we marched through the village at the moment the soldiers came off duty. The boys surrounded us on all sides. An officer who had been one of Tante Jans's protégés years before and had been a daily visitor at the Beje, saw our problem. He took his bicycle and rode beside our group, ordering all the soldiers away. Then he escorted us, until we reached the camp.

That officer was a blessing to me, but I'm not sure all the girls felt the same way. The camp-fires became quite a problem. When the girls gathered around the fire, we seemed to have soldiers growing out of the trees. It was very difficult to get any attention from the girls for our talks and singing. I appealed to the officer for help and he offered, 'Every evening I'll send you two trustworthy sergeants to serve as camp watchers. They'll report any soldier who comes within a quarter of a mile of your tents and camp-fire.'

After that two men joined our camp-fire every evening. They were never the same men, so the rotation system worked very well. They told us later that they enjoyed their 'girls' club watch', and there was never a lack of volunteers.

I've sometimes wondered if there was some seed of the Gospel sown in the hearts of those men. We never know. God can give a straight blow with a crooked stick. He blesses in spite of our blunders.

16

Safety Pins on Uniforms

We used every method we could think of to recruit girls for our clubs. We took lists from school or church; we talked to shopkeepers; we even placed notices in the newspapers. One of our girls, Annie, answered our advertisement when she was only eleven or twelve years old, and remained as a club girl for many years. The advertisement was simple, but it brought results. It read: DO YOU LIKE TO GO FOR WALKS? IF YOU WANT TO MEET OTHER GIRLS AND HAVE FUN, COME TO THE TEN BOOM SHOP AT BARTELJORISSTRAAT 19.

The gymnastics club was one of the most popular. I worked out with the girls under the guidance of capable teachers, but I certainly wasn't one of the best pupils. Far from it. My girls were much stronger than I, and how they helped me because of my vain efforts to do some of the exercises.

When the gymnastics club needed a slogan, one of the girls suggested that it should be: WE MAKE STRAIGHT WHAT IS CROOKED. What rascals! They looked at my legs, and then at my face to see if I understood what they meant. We had such great fun together. The teasing made for an easier relationship. We were friends, and when I blew my whistle, they all sat down to listen. Most of them knew very little about the Lord Jesus, and several of them freely admitted that they came for fun and not for spiritual matters.

One time I flopped on the floor after trying some new trick on the bars, and failing miserably. The girls did their best to help Tante Kees accomplish the simple exercises. I spied Greetje sitting cross-legged in the corner and moved wearily toward her. Then I saw that she was crying and I asked her if she wanted to tell me what was wrong.

'My older sister Betty is dying. I have learned so much here about Jesus, but I know she doesn't know anything about Him.'

'Tell her,' I said.

'But how, Tante Kees; I don't know as much as you do.'

'Tell her about the cross where Jesus died to carry the punishment that we earned. Tell Betty that Jesus loves her and has said, "Come to me all" – and that means Betty, too.'

Greetje began to cry harder, but it was her turn to work out on the bars, so she struggled to get up and wiped away the tears. After she was through she came back to me.

'Then what should I do?'

'Ask Betty if she knows that she is a sinner.'

'She knows that.'

'Tell her that every sinner may come to Jesus. She must ask forgiveness, and then He will make her heart clean. You know what I told you about that today. She must ask Jesus to come into that clean heart. Let her first say: "Thank You, Jesus, for dying for me."'

Greetje went back for another work-out. The third time we talked I said, 'Tell Betty that Jesus has said, "In my Father's house are many mansions . . . I go to prepare a place for everyone who belongs to me." When Betty gives her heart to Jesus, she surely belongs to Him.'

For several gymnasium evenings, I taught Greetje more about the way to bring Betty to the Lord. After a few weeks, I was invited to come to their home. Greetje greeted me at the door and there was no sign of a distressed little girl. 'Tante Kees, come in . . . I want you to see Betty.'

Resting on a small bed against the wall was a pale young girl, smiling at me with the radiance only God can give. 'Jesus is in my heart . . . He has forgiven me my sins. Greetje told me all about it.'

Some days later that girl died, and again I had to speak at a burial. I praised the Lord that my work in gymnastics with the girls – even though awkward at times

– had been used to reach someone before it was too late.

Gradually the clubs began to take on some degree of organization. It was exciting to see that this wasn't the case of formation of an organization first, then imposing upon it the concept of girls' clubs – but of the need coming before the structured format.

Out of the gymnastics club, in particular, came the Girl Guide clubs in Holland. The uniforms, slogan, songs, and mottos were gradually added, but only as there was a necessity for them. We did discover, however, that there was a healthy difference between Boy Scouting and Girl Scouting.

One of our gymnast teachers was a scout leader. I asked him what activities he had with the boys that week, and he showed me some games and taught me some knots. *Oh, well*, I thought, *we can do that*. The next day I taught the knots and played games with my Girl Guides. *This is easy* ! *I'll just ask him each week what he does and copy those activities*.

The next week he told me that he had fastened a strong rope on a tree at the top of a dune, and strung the rope to another tree some distance away. The boys had to climb along that rope from one end to the other. I listened to this idea, but that day it dawned on my stupid mind that Boy Scouting and Girl Scouting were two different things!

The End of the World?

One evening I was meeting with a group of pioneers (the older Girl Guides), when Max, one of our faithful members, ran into the room, late and breathless, her voice high with alarm.

'Tante Kees, there's something wrong with the stars! They're running all over the sky, as if they want to see what is happening on the other side of the horizon.'

The girls, excitable creatures that they were, jumped up and ran outside. 'Why, those are meteors,' I said. 'Let's go to the Kenaupark and watch from there . . . we can see better.'

We ran to the Kenaupark where our beautiful cherry tree

The Bride of Haarlem was, and watched the exciting display of shooting stars.

Pietje said, 'I'm scared . . . is it the end of the world?'

'Girls, those are not stars, but meteors, perhaps broken off from other planets. As soon as they enter the earth's atmosphere they are heated, and become luminous like a streak of light.

'Pietje, this isn't a sign of the end of the world, although Jesus has told us that when He comes one of the signs of the time will be terrifying things happening in the heavens. Jesus told us to look for these signs. Peter makes it very practical when he tells us, "Because, my dear friends, you have a hope like this before you, I urge you to make certain that such a Day would find you at peace with God and man, clean and blameless in His sight" (2 Peter 3:14 PHILLIPS).

We returned to the club-house, and were seated again in our circle on the floor as the questions began to tumble out. It was an exciting time of sharing, and I was thankful for the shooting stars.

I told about the many signs that Jesus mentioned, and that Luke 21:32 tells us that the generation that will see all these signs shall not pass away, until they are all fulfilled.

Jap was one of the girls who was a deep thinker. 'I wonder, Tante Kees, if we are living in the generation when all the signs will be fulfilled, and Christ will return. We should keep our triangle within the circle and not forget it!'

(The triangle represented the three stages of development: social, intellectual, and physical; the circle meant the spiritual development. We emphasized that when the triangle was within the circle, we were in the proper position in our lives as children of God.)

Milly was puzzled; this was only her second time in our club, and she was hearing us speak of spiritual matters which confused her. 'What does that mean, about the triangle and the circle,' she said. 'Are you speaking in a secret language?'

For the first time Mien spoke up. 'It means . . . stop trying to work things out for yourself, and ask God to do it. I tried hard, but it didn't help . . . now I have asked Him to manage me.'

On Parade

There was one outstanding yearly occasion where my father took a direct part in working with my girls. This was the important Holland holiday on the Queen's birthday.

On August 31, Queen Wilhelmina's birthday, there was a great celebration, with parades and speeches, picnics and fairs. It was an old-fashioned Fourth of July done up in Dutch style. Father, as one of Haarlem's leading citizens, organized the activities of the day, and sat on the platform with the mayor.

Since Father was the chairman of the parade committee, my Girl Guides always had a very prominent place in the line-up. We could display our flag, with the triangle inside the circle, and take that opportunity to explain to anyone who asked what the significance was of our symbol.

On one parade route we marched with an elaborate horse-drawn carriage, resplendent with liveried coachmen. It was so elegant that I couldn't resist poking my head out of the coach window and making a funny face. Father, however, was always dignified, in spite of his prankish daughter.

After Wilhelmina was replaced by her daughter, Juliana, as Queen, the date for the celebration was changed to April 30. Since the following day was May Day, the occasion for the international communist parade, we always arranged for all the banners to be removed so that the Communists couldn't take advantage of our decorations.

Going International

The club work and Girl Guide activities grew each year, until some members of the YMCA in America heard of these efforts and invited me to an international conference in Riga, Latvia. Little Latvia was an independent country then, still able to practise religious freedom. After the communists seized Latvia in 1940, Christian practices were stamped out.

It was in the 1930s when I went to Latvia. On the way to the conference grounds, I was invited to be the guest of two old ladies in their home. Their country had been torn by wars and revolutions, and had changed nationalities several times. During a revolution, the house of the old women had been raided, many of their valuable possessions were destroyed, including their antique wall clock. It had been repaired many times, but never was able to strike the hours. The chain for the weight was hopelessly tangled, and I worked on the clock for quite some time, although I am a repairer of watches, not clocks. It was frustrating, so I talked over the problem with the Lord and He gave me the solution. I can still see the two ladies standing hand in hand, tears of joy on their faces, when they heard their clock strike again. That night, when one of them heard the clock, she awakened the other and whispered, 'Father's clock is striking.'

How glad I was that I was a watchmaker and could bring some happiness into their lonely lives.

At the conference I learned that I had a lot to learn! I heard about the leadership of Girl Guides in other countries, and felt like a real beginner. The spiritual training, however, was a bit of a disappointment. There was a lot of talk about 'character building', until finally I asked, 'Don't you think that we miss the purpose, when we tell the girls to be good citizens, but fail to bring them to Jesus Christ?'

To my amazement they changed the programme because of that question. The talk about evangelization in the clubs had been planned for the last day, but it was re-scheduled for the second day.

When I returned home, we decided to improve our image somewhat and have better uniforms. We made dark-blue uniforms, but if the girls didn't have enough money for that, we said that any navy-blue dress was adequate.

With my own home-made uniform, an orange ribbon substituted for the official Girl Guide's scarf, I went to my second international conference on a mountain near Vienna, Austria. There I met the top leaders of the Girl Guide movement in England, and they were very proper. Once we had an official roll call and I couldn't find my belt. I grabbed a belt from another dress and put that around my waist. We were making a horse-shoe march in formation and a Dutch Girl Guide whispered to me in agony when she passed me, 'You have two belts – one is hanging on your back.'

Suddenly I felt very shabby; I compared my dress with the smart uniforms, perfect to the smallest detail. I began to feel like Alice in Wonderland when she grew into a giant. There I was with two belts, and that glaring orange ribbon fastened to my front with a safety pin.

One of the Girl Guide officers said to me, 'I'm glad that I had the chance to meet you and talk on top of this mountain, but if I meet you in such a uniform in London, I will act as if I have never seen you before.'

After that experience I realized that this enterprise was too serious to remain amateurish. When I returned to Holland, we asked some prominent and talented women to help us form a national board of directors. We studied hand-books from other areas and held many conferences. Since there were groups of women interested in this work from many different places in Holland, we chose a central meeting place – the railway station in Amsterdam. We could work in the quiet first-class waiting room until the moment our trains left.

But I became concerned about the direction of the Girl Guides. Coming in contact with leaders from other parts of the country, we discovered that 'religious instruction' was not acceptable. It was considered propaganda for a religion. We could have clubs for Christian girls with Christian leaders, but our aim to reach the other girls was made impossible. It seemed that all the club work, Bible studies, conferences, camps, were just preparation for something more. Consequently, a new Christian movement was born.

De Nederlandse Meisjesclubs (Netherlands Girls' Clubs) grew out of the Girl Guide movement, but added the missing dimension. After a few years, the outreach of these clubs burst beyond the borders of Holland and we had six thousand members in the Netherlands East Indies, and eight hundred in the West Indies. Because of our symbol, the name of our club members was *Triangle Girls*.

The first article of our club law was impressed upon many young minds. It was: SEEK YOUR STRENGTH THROUGH PRAYER.

Years later, in a time when camping and parades, conferences and singing, were beautiful memories of peaceful times, I was in a prison cell. Every sound was magnified in the deadly silence of those cubicles; I realized there was a girl crying next door. I called to her and said, 'Don't cry, be strong . . . we'll be free soon.'

The answer shocked me.

'Tante Kees . . . oh, Tante Kees . . . is that you? I'm Annie.'

I recognized her voice. She was one of my faithful club girls, who had been arrested after my family and I had been taken to prison. My heart almost stopped. That poor girl was the last person I expected to be strong in such a terrible spot. I called to her through the barriers of the prison walls. 'Annie, do you remember the first article of our club law? "Seek your strength through prayer."'

She stopped crying.

17

Opposition!

Opposition to lives which are yielded to Jesus Christ takes many forms, some dramatic, some subtle. Satan is a clever angel of light, but sometimes he chooses supernatural ways to frighten us into inactivity.

During a time at camp with the girls, I was singing outside of the cabin after lights-out. The song had the words: 'Don't be afraid for whatever is coming, your heavenly Father takes care of you.'

Suddenly I heard horrible noises around me. It seemed as if among the trees some sort of beings were trying to make me stop. The noises grew and subsided, sending shivers through my body with their weird tones. While I sang, I pleaded with the Lord: 'Cover me and protect me with Your blood, Lord Jesus . . . give me the strength to go on singing and speak through me to reach all these girls.'

The noises remained and got louder and more ugly, but I didn't stop. I knew that I stood on the front line of battle, but through Jesus, it was victory ground, not defeat or retreat. As soon as I had finished the song, the noises stopped, just as abruptly as they began.

I went to bed and thanked the Lord for His victory. The next morning I asked the girls if they had heard anything unusual the previous night. They answered that they had never heard me sing so beautifully. Nobody heard anything else.

He Never Fails

Many of the girls in the clubs stand out in my memory. Peggy, for instance, was a member of the gym club who was not able to pay her dues, although it was only a *dubbeltje* (two cents). Unfortunately, we found that she stole from the club money, which was kept in a small box on the window-sill at the clubhouse. I was concerned about Peggy, so I marked a quarter and left it on the window-sill. When it disappeared, I called Peggy aside and asked to see her handbag. There was the marked quarter.

Peggy had accepted the Lord as her Saviour, but she was still bound to her past and background – a family of so-called down-and outers. I told her, 'Peggy, a child of God is tempted, but the difference from those who are not Christians is that God gives with the temptation a way of escape. He says, "Confess your sins, God is faithful and just to forgive . . ."'

Peggy understood, and right then confessed what she had done. From that time on, we elected her treasurer of our club and there was never a cent lost. Peggy really meant business when she gave her *yes* to Jesus; she trusted Him, and I did, too – that is why I could trust her. She never failed because Jesus never failed.

The Only Comfort

Pietje was a hunchback, one of our best-liked club girls. Although it was a long time ago, I remember her reactions to the Bible stories. One day we were discussing Exodus 20:5, where God speaks to the Jewish people about the sins of the fathers continuing upon the children, grandchildren, and great-grandchildren. Pietje began to cry, and when I noticed her, I took her into another room to talk over her troubles.

Pietje's face was very dark as she said, 'I am a hunchback and that was the punishment for my father who has been an alcoholic.'

'But Pietje, did you hear the following verse: "And showing mercy unto thousands of them that love me, and keep my commandments." When your father begins to love God he will experience His mercy. You love the Lord, and although you are a hunchback, you are a happy girl, because you experience the mercy and peace in your heart because Jesus lives in you.'

When Pietje was in a Bible-study group we read Romans 8:34 and I asked, 'Who is our Judge?' They answered, 'Jesus!' and I said, 'Who is our Advocate?' The answer came from Pietje, 'Jesus!' Then she almost shouted, 'What a joy! Judge and Advocate is the same! Jesus prays for us, so there is nothing to fear.'

One day they sent for me to come quickly because Pietje was in a large ward of a hospital, and they told me she was dying. I knew that she had accepted Jesus as her Saviour. As I stood beside her bed I said, 'It's such a comfort to know Jesus is our Judge, also our Advocate. How He loves you!'

At that moment I saw the transformation on her face from pain to peace. 'Pietje, can you hear me?' I said.

She didn't open her eyes. I couldn't reach her any more; I prayed with her, laying my hand on her feverish head, and asking the good Shepherd to take His lamb in His arms and carry her straight through the valley of the shadow of death into the house of the Father with many mansions.

When I said, '*Amen*', Pietje opened her eyes for the last time and smiled.

Pietje was still very fresh in my mind and heart when I met the next day with leaders and board members of the YWCA. We talked about club experiences, and then one lady said, 'I don't like the method of your clubs in Haarlem. All that preaching you do! I don't think it's right. I believe in Christian surroundings, and bringing girls into a Christian atmosphere – that will attract far more girls than just Bible talks will. I preach by my behaviour rather than by what I say.'

My answer was, 'Romans 10:14 says, ". . . How shall they believe in Him whom they have not heard? And how shall they hear without a preacher?"'

I'm glad that we told Pietje about our Judge and Advocate Jesus in the time we could still reach her. In the twenty-five years that we did club work, there were at least forty girls who died. Accidents, illnesses, even a murder, were the causes. When I stood at the death-bed of a club girl, I was so thankful that I had redeemed the time when she was still able to listen to the Gospel. Illness, pain, even drugs, during the last part of a person's life may make it impossible for him to hear.

When Pietje died, I was the speaker at her burial. Father had conducted so many burial services for his colleagues that he was able to help me in so many ways. His straightforward testimony was not always appreciated, but when death entered a family, Father was a welcome comforter. When someone dies, people are confronted with eternity and there is the right opportunity to speak about the security of eternal life that only Jesus can give.

Father gave me some practical advice for those sad occasions:

'When your time comes to speak, Corrie, don't hesitate. Many people are moved and nervous, so look for a place where everyone can hear and see you. Step forward without hesitation. Relatives and friends who are left behind must be challenged to repent of their sins and receive Jesus as their Saviour.'

Yes, opposition comes in strange places and through unusual vehicles: supernatural sounds from the darkness of a forest and even superficial attitudes from the self-righteous.

Doubt

Opposition also came from within. Has there been doubt in my heart? Has there been dryness in my prayer life? Yes, indeed, there has been.

There was a time when I needed a major operation. For some strange reason, I persuaded the surgeon not to give me a general anæsthetic, only a local. I didn't realize that this could be such a severe shock to my system. I didn't suffer pain during the operation, but I did have a great deal of tension. For several months afterwards I needed some painful treatments.

In that time my mind and spirit were very low; I couldn't pray; the Bible was uninteresting; church was dull. I remember that my prayers were very short. Most of the time I muttered, 'Lord, I can't reach You . . . I can't pray. Lord, I know that You can reach me. Keep me in Your care and help me to be able to pray again soon.'

The outward Corrie was the same. I did the club work as I had always done. I worked in the shop, met customers, and carried on all the activities of our busy lives. I don't know if anyone saw what a dark valley I was going through, for I held it inside. I didn't talk over my problems with my family and friends. After all, I thought, they have worries enough. Now I know how stupid that was.

Then a girl, Colly, came to me and asked if she could tell me her troubles. She was a bright girl from a good, hard-working family, and I liked her very much.

'Tante Kees,' she said with her head down, 'can you help me? For weeks I have been unable to pray. Do you think I'm lost? Do you think I'm no longer a child of God?'

'Colly, you're a child of God and you're not lost. Now sit down and I'll tell you something about myself. I know exactly how you feel, because I'm going through the same problem as you. For several weeks I haven't been able to pray . . . but even though the time has been dark, I know that Jesus is with me and He can reach me. Let's see if there is something in the Bible that can help both of us.'

We read Romans 8:26: 'The Spirit helps us in our infirmities, for we know not what we should pray, but the Spirit Himself makes intercession for us.'

Colly and I both realized that the Holy Spirit helps us with our daily problems and in our prayer problems. When we are totally inadequate, the Spirit is interceding with God the Father for us. The burden of guilt was taken from Colly and me, and together we thanked the Lord that He had forgiven us and restored our communication with Him.

Haarlemsche Meisjesclubs

The HMC (Haarlem Girls' Clubs) had a performance once each year in the concert hall, when each club demonstrated some of its skills and abilities. We opened the programme with all of the 250 to 300 girls marching onto the platform.

They sang a song, and I gave a five-minute talk to the people in the auditorium.

The mixed club (which had passed the 'year's trial' without any serious mishaps) provided the orchestra for the musical part of our entertainment. The first time this group had to play before all of those friends and relatives (about a thousand of them), they were frozen with stage fright. I walked over and picked up a violin and acted as if I were a real virtuoso, but making sure that no one in the audience saw that the bow was turned upside down and not touching the strings. As I 'played' the violin, the boys gained confidence and began to perform. The ones who were playing wind instruments probably had trouble stifling their laughter in order to make music.

Tears and laughter, opposition and support – the clubs taught those young men and women preparation for life.

When the war started, we had to close the HMC clubs. I will never forget the evening we were together for the last time. We saluted our flag, with tears running down our cheeks, and then folded it carefully, and hid it in a secret closet of the club-house.

As we sang the national hymn for the last time together, the girls had a very difficult time. 'Girls, we mustn't cry,' I said. 'We had great fun in the clubs, but it wasn't just for a good time that we have come together. We have learned the important facts of what makes us strong, even in times of disaster. The Lord Jesus gives us security even in the insecurity of wartime.'

I looked at those girls and wondered – would they draw on the Lord's strength in the days and years to come? What was in store for them in this world of ours which is filled with hatred and cruelty?

I was so grateful that the time in our clubs had not been wasted in just building 'good citizens', but that we had the opportunity to learn the vital message of Jesus' victory, which would give strength for the suffering which awaited many of us.

18

'. . . He Took My Hand'

War. It was early in the morning when we heard the bombs. We knew the sound of the explosions were coming from Schiphol, the airport near Haarlem. I ran to Betsie's room and found her sitting up in bed, pale and shaking. We put our arms around each other and trembled with each blast; the wavering red glow was so eerie in the darkness of our once-peaceful skies.

We were afraid, but had learned from childhood how to cast our burdens on the Lord. We prayed like frightened children, running to their father for help and protection.

'Lord, make us strong . . . give us strength to help others.'

'Lord, take away our fear. Give us trust.'

It was a crisis of fear in both of us, but Jesus gave us the victory over it. We were never so frightened as we were during that night, not even when war and occupation destroyed our whole family life, and everything we had known for more than a half a century. Was that night the Lord's way of inoculating us in preparation for the future?

In the five days of war that followed, many people came to the house; Father was a pillar of strength for all of them; he prayed with everyone who asked. Sometimes the shock of what was happening would engulf me, and while Father was bringing trust and peace to those in turmoil, I would go to the piano and play Bach. No other music gave me so much rest.

The darkest time during those five days was when our

royal family left, our Queen Wilhelmina for England and Crown
Princess Juliana for Canada. We knew then that our case was
hopeless.

There were not many times that I cried, but when I heard
about the royal family leaving the country, I was heartbroken
and wept. For the Dutch people the Queen was our security
– we loved her.

Then Holland surrendered. I walked in the street with
Father, and everyone was talking to everyone else. In
that moment there was a oneness which I had never seen
before. We were together in the great suffering, humiliation,
and defeat of our nation. Although my heart was aching
with misery, there was encouragement that people could
be so united.

In the millennium we will be like that: The whole world will
be covered with the knowledge of God as the waters cover
the bottom of the sea. The oneness will not be in misery, but
in our communion with the Lord.

The German army marched through the Barteljorisstraat:
tanks, cannons, cavalry, and hundreds and hundreds of soldiers. The narrow little street where Dot and I had played
games – the alley where I had seen the drunks when I was
only five, and prayed for 'all the people in the Smedestraat'
– the path we had taken on Sunday to St Bavo's – all were
filled with soldiers.

As the conquerors swept in, I noticed some of them were
red-faced, shame written in their expressions. After the war
a German told me, 'With every step I took in Holland, I felt
ashamed. I knew I was occupying a neutral nation.'

Churches were packed in those days; the Psalms, which
were written in times of great suffering, gained a new value.
Ministers who had never preached about the Second Coming
of Christ now chose their texts from the many places in the
Bible on that subject.

In the beginning, we saw little change in our daily life, but
gradually the enemy began to impose restrictions. At first
the curfew was ten o'clock, which was not difficult for us,
but later it was moved back to eight, then six. No one could
leave his house; there was absolute blackout, and every

window was covered with black paper as soon as the sun was down.

Telephones were cut off; food was rationed; and often after standing in long lines with our ration cards, we would find that the stores were empty.

One beautiful Sunday afternoon Betsie, Father, and I were walking through our park, south of Haarlem, when the Gestapo descended and took all of the young fathers around us, who were out walking with their families, leaving distraught wives and crying children behind.

All Dutch people have bicycles, and sometimes the Gestapo set up a bicycle blockade. Everyone who rode by was summoned to give up his vehicle. If you were fortunate enough to keep your bicycle, you learned to ride without tires, because they were confiscated and taken to Germany.

We were not even safe in church. Once during a service in the cathedral, the Germans guarded the doors so that nobody could move. Then they opened one door and ordered every man from eighteen to forty to come out. They were sent that same day to Germany – many of these men were never seen again.

The occupation – the underground movement to save Jews – the concentration camps – all of these are documented in *A Prisoner and Yet . . .*, and in my book and the movie, *The Hiding Place*.

For more than thirty years since World War II, I have been a tramp for the Lord in more than sixty countries on all the continents of this troubled world. Many people have asked me about my childhood, youth, and the years before *The Hiding Place*. A person doesn't spring into existence at the age of fifty; there are years of preparation, years of experience, which God uses in ways we may never know until we meet Him face to face.

However, from the perspective of over eighty years of living, I have had the marvellous opportunity to discover the sweetness of some of the fruit of His labour. Just recently I have heard from by letter or met in person some of my club 'girls'. (They are still girls to me!) It has been like a letter from the Lord.

Aukje

One of our faithful club girls was quiet Aukje. She was a peacemaker who could say few words, but make them count. When other girls were unruly and stubborn, I remember Aukje saying, 'Don't be so stupid. Why did we come to the club in the first place? Most of us want to have fun and learn something, so if you don't like it then leave and let the rest of us enjoy the club.'

To the point – but said with such kindness that most of the time the problems were overcome. When she was about seventeen, Aukje became a club leader herself and led a group of girls who learned handcrafts. She was so quiet and gentle that we didn't expect exciting results from her, but her love for the Lord was very clear.

When the ten Boom family was arrested Aukje came to our house, not knowing that it was a Gestapo trap. She was taken to the police station, and spent a week with our oldest Jewish underground girl, Mary, who had been in the hiding place, but was later arrested in the street.

Aukje talked to Mary about the Lord Jesus. She told her that Jesus had died on the cross for the sins of the whole world, and that He had said, 'Come to me, all who are heavy laden, I will give you rest.'

Mary said, 'I heard Grandpa ten Boom pray so often when I was in the Beje. He always said to me, "Mary, you are a Jew; you will not change that if you invite the Lord Jesus into your heart. On His divine side He was the Son of God, but on his human side He was a Jew."'

Mary received Jesus as her Saviour in that cell. Our quiet Aukje had a boldness for the Lord. She told me later that the moment Mary said her *yes* to Jesus in her prayer of accepting Him, the guards came into the cell and took her away. We heard later that she was sent to Poland where she died.

I heard nothing from Aukje for many years. What a surprise it was for me when she came to my room in Haarlem thirty years later. She told me that she was working in a small village where there was no minister; she preaches every Sunday for the little congregation. She said, 'What I learned in your clubs

I still use when I teach the children and have my Bible-study groups.'

Poes

Poes was an outgoing little rascal; wherever she was in a club there was laughing and fun. At camp she was the happy note, even when it was raining and spirits were low. When there were weaker girls who needed help in hikes or gymnastics, Poes was always ready to help.

I remember one time she was walking behind me, and was quite outspoken in her ideas about my legs. She said, 'If I had such legs, I should decide to march beside them.' She married an older boy and moved to South Africa. I met them there once after the war, but only briefly. He called himself an atheist, but did not object when Poes and I shared with him our love for the Lord Jesus. I promised to pray for him, but in later correspondence Poes never mentioned that he was interested in spiritual affairs.

Then a strange thing happened – one of those 'coincidences,' which are such a marvellous part of God's plan. Poes and her husband were walking in the streets of Johannesburg, when a boy asked them to buy a raffle ticket to raise money for a house for a boys' club. Poes said, 'Sure, I enjoyed clubs when I was a girl – I hope you have a lot of fun in your new cabin.'

Later she found out that they had the ticket which won the first prize in the raffle – it was a round-trip plane ride for two to the Netherlands! And so it happened that one day they stood in my room in Holland. What memories we shared! Poes told me she had become a member of a church, and Henk, her husband, listened with amusement as we talked about the clubs. He declared very strongly that he didn't believe in God. I knew I had only one chance to bring him the Gospel, so I said, 'Henk, I'll probably only have this one time to talk with you. There are two ways to live: you can go your way or God's way; you can accept Jesus Christ as your Saviour, and He will make you a child of God. Then you can bring Him all your sins, and ask and get forgiveness. He makes sure you're a child of God, and He will put your name in the book of life.'

After I prayed with them, Henk said, 'I believe it's time that I gave my heart to Jesus. I've seen much of Him in the life of Poes, and He must be a reality. I know I'm a sinner and you said that Jesus accepts sinners. So I'll tell Him all that I've done and I have been, and believe that He will make me a child of God.'

They returned to South Africa and Henk became a member of a lively church. Some months ago Henk died, but he said, 'Tell Tante Kees that God has used her to bring me to the Lord.'

God began working years before in a mischievous little girl, Poes, in a gymnastics club in a little Dutch town.

The Golden Tea Party

What would they be like? Would the years have changed them? What joys and sorrows, trials and triumphs would they have seen in the decades since we had last met?

I was as excited as that younger Corrie had been, when she introduced her club girls at the yearly performance in the Haarlem concert hall. Now in my eighties, I had returned to Holland for a visit, and had invited those women who had been in clubs in years past – and were still in the vicinity of Haarlem – to my house for tea.

No uniform with two belts and a safety pin this time! I wore my best red and white silk summer dress, and made sure that not one thing would mar my appearance.

They arrived at the front door at the same time. Some came on their big old-fashioned bicycles, some drove little cars, and others walked from the bus stop. There was no need for protocol, for they began to laugh and talk all at once.

What an afternoon we had! Each girl told a little of her story, ending on the same theme, which added so much joy to my heart.

Ariapja, whose nickname was *Jap*, bubbled with her enthusiasm about the club work. She told how she first became a part of our group and her mother had said, 'You may not have a uniform!'

So she went to her first camp feeling a bit ashamed, because she wasn't dressed like the rest of the girls. It was the most important issue in her life then. Hank, who had also come for tea that afternoon, was the one who gave Jap her uniform; that unselfish act was remembered by Jap all her life. When she went home she asked her mother if she could be a Girl Guide. Her mother told her that it was all right, if she didn't wear the uniform on Sunday.

Girl Guiding became Jap's life, and she told us that sunny afternoon in my living room in Holland that much she learned as a young girl in the clubs had prepared her for her total life experiences.

Stien had gone to one of my clubs when she was sixteen to learn the catechism. I had been her teacher, and after she was received into the Dutch Reformed church I said, 'Now, Stien, you must lead a club.'

After Stien had been one of our club leaders she took the initiative, and began a club for feeble-minded children. She told me later, 'You had taught me, Tante Kees, to love those less fortunate, and I truly did love those children.' For Stien, going to the clubs was the best part of her young life. Her home was never open to others, and she spent many evenings at the Beje. Fortunately, she had stayed at home on that fateful day in February 1944, when the Gestapo paid us an unwelcome visit.

Annie, who had answered a newspaper advertisement to join a club, said that she came for fun, and not for all those 'spiritual things'. And she did have fun! She joined the singing club, the English club, and the gymnastics club, and when she told about the latter, she reminded all of us about the club slogan. (I knew someone would bring that up – the rascals!) The gymnastics club slogan – WE MAKE STRAIGHT WHAT IS CROOKED – was not very good – too long to put on a programme. (I had to pretend not to notice the laughter every time it was mentioned.)

Annie told how she felt in love with the gym teacher. However, when his girl friend came Annie became very jealous, and out of spite sewed his pants together and put water in his shoes.

(Tea cups almost fell off laps when this story was recounted.)

As a punishment, I told Annie that she would not be allowed to go to the club for three weeks. She reminded me, however, that she returned in one week, proving that Tante Kees's discipline was sometimes a little lax.

When Annie was seventeen, she was at the camp at Bliscap, feeling very low. She had just split up with her current boyfriend, and thought it was the end of the world. She remembered that we were sitting outside, looking at the stars, and I had told her, 'When you're in need and don't know the answer, tell the Lord about it. He has your past, present, and future in His hands.' It was then that Annie accepted Jesus Christ as her Saviour; she said that every time she was in need in years to come she remembered that moment.

'I know the Lord is willing to take your life in His hands when you're small,' Annie said.

Nellie was born in Germany, and didn't come to Holland until she was fourteen years old. She came into the clubs when she was eighteen, not as a believer in Jesus Christ, but found Him during one of the camps. When Nellie remembered the outstanding experiences of her club time, she talked about the camp-fires – the time of deep discussions together. She thought a while when we asked what club work had prepared her for. Then she remembered one of the articles in the club law, which was to 'give help' to others. She said that even today people know there is help in her home. 'Let's go over to Nell's – she always has the soup on . . .'

As the girls began to share more and more of their memories and their later life experiences, one story after another spilled out. Reina told how she loved the circle and the club song. It was difficult for Ellen de Kroon, my secretary, and Carole Carlson to contain themselves as we all stood up and joined hands to repeat our motto, and sing our song after almost forty years of separation! The voices may have changed a bit, but the fervour was still there!

Reina said she had come from a Christian family, but the

club work had inspired in her the personal desire to bring the Gospel to other girls.

'Did you know,' she said, looking around the room, 'that the last time the Girl Guides wore their uniforms was at my wedding?'

Hank was in at the start of the clubs, and remembered the first camp experience she had. One of the girls had trouble with sleep-walking, and she told how Tante Kees had been so concerned about her, and had walked her gently back to bed. However, it was also discovered that the so-called sleep-walker had a sweet tooth, for the following morning the chocolate bars, which had been left out for camp-fire treats, had been strangely consumed by someone in her sleep.

Julie had been rather quiet, but finally began to bring the conversation back to the present. 'I want so much to give our young people some of the love, the experiences, the strength in knowing the Lord, that we learned in your clubs, Tante Kees. Our children have so much – and yet they're so poor. They're so free today – much more so than we were – and yet they face many more dangers from the world.'

It became very still in the room. Everyone had her own thoughts about children, grandchildren – our youth, who face the 'wars and rumours of wars' that exist in a world racing towards self-destruction.

I looked through my small living room into the dining room, where Papa's portrait hangs. I could see him at the oval table, head bowed, praying: 'Lord, bless the Queen; we thank You for this beautiful Lord's Day, and for the promise of Your soon coming. Thank You for this food, and for this family. In the Name of Jesus Christ, *Amen.*'

How grateful I am to have lived in my Father's House! Yes, Lord, I thank You for this family. I looked at my friends, gathered for an afternoon of tea and memories, and thanked the Lord for the family of believers all over this globe. How the love of God stretched in and out of the watch-maker's shop to all parts of the world – to mansions in California and hospitals in Kenya, from queens to prison guards.

As the 'golden tea party' ended, and the club girls left, we broke some of our Dutch restraint and hugged each other.

Many of them had suffered much through the years, and yet they had remained strong in the Lord. I realized that all we do through our own strength has to be cleansed, but what we do through the Lord has value for time and eternity.

This is no time to look back. What challenges we have today! I remember what Father often said:

> *When Jesus takes your hand He keeps you tight. When Jesus keeps you tight He leads you through life. When Jesus leads you through life He brings you safely home.*

THE HIDING PLACE

The Hiding Place

**Corrie ten Boom with
John and Elizabeth Sherrill**

Hodder & Stoughton
LONDON SYDNEY AUCKLAND

Preface

When we were doing the research for *God's Smuggler*, a name kept cropping up: Corrie ten Boom. This Dutch lady – in her mid-seventies when we first began to hear of her – was Brother Andrew's favorite traveling companion. Brother Andrew is a missionary behind the Iron Curtain; his fascinating stories about her in Vietnam, where she had earned that most honorable title 'Double-old Grandmother' – and in a dozen other Communist countries – came to mind so often that we finally had to hold up our hands to stop his flow of reminiscence. 'We could never fit her into the book,' we said. 'She sounds like a book in herself.' It's the sort of thing you say. Not meaning anything.

It was in May, 1968, that we attended a church service in Germany. A man was speaking about his experiences in a Nazi concentration camp. His face told the story more eloquently than his words: pain-haunted eyes, shaking hands that could not forget. He was followed at the lectern by a white-haired woman, broad of frame and sensible of shoe, with a face that radiated love, peace, joy. But – the story that these two people were relating was the same! She too had been in a concentration camp, seen the same savagery, suffered the same losses. His response was easy to understand. But hers?

We stayed behind to talk with her. And as we did, we realized that we were meeting Andrew's Corrie. Cornelia ten Boom's worldwide ministry of comfort and counsel had begun there in the concentration camp where she had found, as the prophet Isaiah promised, 'a hiding place from the wind, a covert from the tempest . . . the shadow of a great rock in a weary land'.

On subsequent visits we got to know this amazing woman well. Together we visited the crooked little Dutch house – one room wide – where till her fifties she lived the uneventful life of a spinster watchmaker, little dreaming as she cared for her older sister and their elderly father that a world of high adventure lay just around the corner. We went to the garden in south Holland where young Corrie gave her heart away forever. To the big brick house in Haarlem where Pickwick served real coffee in the middle of the war . . .

And all the while we had the extraordinary feeling that we were not looking into the past but into the future. As though these people and places were speaking to us not about things that had already happened but about the world that lay ahead of us in the 1970s. Already we found ourselves actually putting into practice how-to's we learned from her about:

- handling separation
- getting along with less
- security in the midst of insecurity
- forgiveness
- how God can use weakness
- dealing with difficult people
- facing death
- how to love your enemies
- what to do when evil wins

We commented to her about the practicalness of everything she recalled, how her memories seemed to throw a spotlight on problems and decisions we faced here and now. 'But,' she said, 'this is what the past is for! Every experience God gives us, every person He puts in our lives is the perfect preparation for the future that only He can see.'

Every experience, every person . . . Father, who did the finest watch repairs in Holland and then forgot to send the bill. Mama, whose body became a prison, but whose spirit soared free. Betsie, who could make a party out of three potatoes and some twice-used tea leaves. As we looked into the twinkling blue eyes of this undefeatable woman, we wished that these people were part of our own lives.

And then, of course, we realized that they could be . . .

John and Elizabeth Sherrill

July, 1971
Chappaqua, New York

1

The One Hundredth Birthday Party

I jumped out of bed that morning with one question in my mind
– sun or fog? Usually it was fog in January in Holland, dank,
chill, and gray. But occasionally – on a rare and magic day –
a white winter sun broke through. I leaned as far as I could
from the single window in my bedroom: it was always hard
to see the sky from the Beje. Blank brick walls looked back
at me, the backs of other ancient buildings in this crowded
center of old Haarlem. But up there where my neck craned
to see, above the crazy roofs and crooked chimneys, was a
square of pale pearl sky. It was going to be a sunny day for
the party!

I attempted a little waltz as I took my new dress from the
tipsy old wardrobe against the wall. Father's bedroom was
directly under mine but at seventy-seven he slept soundly.
That was one advantage to growing old, I thought, as I
worked my arms into the sleeves and surveyed the effect
in the mirror on the wardrobe door. Although some Dutch
women in 1937 were wearing their skirts knee-length, mine
was still a cautious three inches above my shoes.

You're not growing younger yourself, I reminded my
reflection. Maybe it was the new dress that made me
look more critically at myself than usual: forty-five years
old, unmarried, waistline long since vanished.

My sister Betsie, though seven years older than I, still
had that slender grace that made people turn and look after
her in the street. Heaven knows it wasn't her clothes;
our little watch shop had never made much money. But

when Betsie put on a dress something wonderful happened to it.

On me – until Betsie caught up with them – hems sagged, stockings tore, and collars twisted. But today, I thought, standing back from the mirror as far as I could in the small room, the effect of dark maroon was very smart.

Far below me down on the street, the doorbell rang. Callers? Before 7:00 in the morning? I opened my bedroom door and plunged down the steep twisting stairway. These stairs were an afterthought in this curious old house. Actually it was two houses. The one in front was a typical tiny old-Haarlem structure, three stories high, two rooms deep, and only one room wide. At some unknown point in its long history its rear wall had been knocked through to join it with the even thinner, steeper house in back of it – which had only three rooms, one on top of the other – and this narrow corkscrew staircase squeezed between the two.

Quick as I was, Betsie was at the door ahead of me. An enormous spray of flowers filled the doorway. As Betsie took them, a small delivery boy appeared. 'Nice day for the party, Miss,' he said, trying to peer past the flowers as though coffee and cake might already be set out. He would be coming to the party later, as indeed, it seemed, would all of Haarlem.

Betsie and I searched the bouquet for the card. 'Pickwick!' we shouted together.

Pickwick was an enormously wealthy customer who not only bought the very finest watches but often came upstairs to the family part of the house above the shop. His real name was Herman Sluring; Pickwick was the name Betsie and I used between ourselves because he looked so incredibly like the illustrator's drawing in our copy of Dickens. Herman Sluring was without doubt the ugliest man in Haarlem. Short, immensely fat, head bald as a Holland cheese, he was so wall-eyed that you were never quite sure whether he was looking at you or someone else – and as kind and generous as he was fearsome to look at.

The flowers had come to the side door, the door the family used, opening onto a tiny alleyway, and Betsie and I carried them from the little hall into the shop. First was the workroom where watches and clocks were repaired. There was the high bench over which Father had bent for so many years, doing the delicate, painstaking work that was known as the finest in Holland. And there in the center of the room was my bench, and next to mine Hans the apprentice's, and against the wall old Christoffels'.

Beyond the workroom was the customers' part of the shop with its glass case full of watches. All the wall clocks were striking 7:00 as Betsie and I carried the flowers in and looked for the most artistic spot to put them. Ever since childhood I had loved to step into this room where a hundred ticking voices welcomed me. It was still dark inside because the shutters had not been drawn back from the windows on the street. I unlocked the street door and stepped out into the Barteljorisstraat. The other shops up and down the narrow street were shuttered and silent: the optician's next door, the dress shop, the baker's, Weil's Furriers across the street.

I folded back our shutters and stood for a minute admiring the window display that Betsie and I had at last agreed upon. This window was always a great source of debate between us, I wanting to display as much of our stock as could be squeezed onto the shelf, and Betsie maintaining that two or three beautiful watches, with perhaps a piece of silk or satin swirled beneath, was more elegant and more inviting. But this time the window satisfied us both: it held a collection of clocks and pocketwatches all at least a hundred years old, borrowed for the occasion from friends and antique dealers all over the city. For today was the shop's one hundredth birthday. It was on this day in January 1837 that Father's father had placed in this window a sign: TEN BOOM. WATCHES.

For the last ten minutes, with a heavenly disregard for the precisions of passing time, the church bells of Haarlem had been pealing out 7:00 o'clock, and now half a block away in the town square, the great bell of St Bavo's solemnly donged seven times. I lingered in the street to count them, though it was cold in the January dawn. Of course everyone in Haarlem had radios now, but I could remember when the life of the city had run on St Bavo time, and only trainmen and others who needed to know the exact hour had come here to read the 'astronomical clock.' Father would take the train to Amsterdam each week to bring back the time from the Naval Observatory and it was a source of pride to him that the astronomical clock was never more than two seconds off in the seven days. There it stood now, as I stepped back into the shop, still tall and gleaming on its concrete block, but shorn now of eminence.

The doorbell on the alley was ringing again; more flowers. So it went on for an hour, large bouquets and small ones, elaborate set pieces and home-grown plants in clay pots. For although the party was for the shop, the affection of a city was for Father. 'Haarlem's Grand Old Man' they called him and they were setting about to prove it. When the shop and the workroom would not hold another bouquet, Betsie and I started carrying them upstairs to the two rooms above the shop. Though it was twenty years since her death, these were still 'Tante Jans's rooms.' Tante Jans was Mother's older sister and her presence lingered in the massive dark furniture she had left behind her. Betsie set down a pot of greenhouse-grown tulips and stepped back with a little cry of pleasure.

'Corrie, just look how much brighter!'

Poor Betsie. The Beje was so closed in by the houses around that the window plants she started each spring never grew tall enough to bloom.

At 7:45 Hans, the apprentice, arrived and at 8:00 Toos, our saleslady-bookkeeper. Toos was a sour-faced, scowling individual whose ill-temper had made it impossible for her to keep a job until – ten years ago – she had come to work for Father. Father's gentle courtesy had disarmed and mellowed her and, though she would have died sooner than admit it, she loved him as fiercely as she disliked the rest of the world. We left Hans and Toos to answer the doorbell and went upstairs to get breakfast.

Only three places at the table, I thought, as I set out the plates. The dining room was in the house at the rear, five steps higher than the shop but lower than Tante Jans's rooms. To me this room with its single window looking into the alley was the heart of the home. This table, with a blanket thrown over it, had made me a tent or a pirate's cove when I was small. I'd done my homework here as a schoolchild. Here Mama read aloud from Dickens on winter evenings while the coal whistled in the brick hearth and cast a red glow over the tile proclaiming, 'Jesus is Victor.'

We used only a corner of the table now, Father, Betsie and I, but to me the rest of the family was always there. There was Mama's chair, and the three aunts' places over there (not only Tante Jans but Mama's other two sisters had also lived with us). Next to me had sat my other sister, Nollie, and Willem, the only boy in the family, there beside Father.

Nollie and Willem had had homes of their own many years now, and Mama and the aunts were dead, but still I seemed to see them here. Of course their chairs hadn't stayed empty long. Father could never bear a house without children and whenever he heard of a child in need of a home a new face would appear at the table. Somehow, out of his watch shop that never made money he fed and dressed and cared for eleven more children after his own four were grown. But now these, too, had grown up and married or gone off to work, and so I laid three plates on the table.

Betsie brought the coffee in from the tiny kitchen, which was little more than a closet off the dining room, and took bread from the drawer in the sideboard. She was setting them on the table when we heard Father's step coming down the staircase. He went a little slowly now on the winding stairs; but still as punctual as one of his own watches, he entered the dining room, as he had every morning since I could remember, at 8:10.

'Father!' I said kissing him and savoring the aroma of cigars that always clung to his long beard, 'a sunny day for the party!'

Father's hair and beard were now as white as the best tablecloth Betsie had laid for this special day. But his blue eyes behind the thick round spectacles were as mild and merry as ever, and he gazed from one of us to the other with frank delight.

'Corrie, dear! My dear Betsie! How gay and lovely you both look!'

He bowed his head as he sat down, said the blessing over bread, and then went on eagerly, 'Your mother – how she would have loved these new styles and seeing you both looking so pretty!'

Betsie and I looked hard into our coffee to keep from laughing. These 'new styles' were the despair of our young nieces, who were always trying to get us into brighter colors, shorter skirts, and lower necklines. But conservative though we were, it was true that Mama had never had anything even as bright as my deep maroon dress or Betsie's dark blue one. In Mama's day married women – and unmarried ones 'of a certain age' – wore black from the chin to the ground. I had never seen Mama and the aunts in any other color.

'How Mama would have loved everything about today!' Betsie said. 'Remember how she loved "occasions"?'

Mama could have coffee on the stove and a cake in the oven as fast as most people could say, 'best wishes.' And since she knew almost everyone in Haarlem, especially the poor, sick and neglected, there was almost no day in the year that was not for somebody, as she would say with eyes shining, 'a very special occasion!'

And so we sat over our coffee, as one should on anniversaries, and looked back – back to the time when Mama was alive, and beyond. Back to the time when Father was a small boy growing up in this same house. 'I was born right in this room,' he said, as though he had not told us a hundred times. 'Only of course it wasn't the dining room then, but a bedroom. And the bed was in a kind of cupboard set into the wall with no windows and no light or air of any kind. I was the first baby who lived. I don't know how many there were before me, but they all died. Mother had tuberculosis you see, and they didn't know about contaminated air or keeping babies away from sick people.'

It was a day for memories. A day for calling up the past. How could we have guessed as we sat there – two middle-aged spinsters and an old man – that in place of memories we were about to be given adventure such as we had never dreamed of? Adventure and anguish, horror and heaven were just around the corner, and we did not know.

Oh Father! Betsie! If I had known would I have gone ahead? Could I have done the things I did?

But how could I know? How could I imagine this white-haired man, called Opa – Grandfather – by all the children of Haarlem, how could I imagine this man thrown by strangers into a grave without a name?

And Betsie, with her high lace collar and her gift for making beauty all around her, how could I picture this dearest person on earth to me standing naked before a roomful of men? In that room on that day, such thoughts were not even thinkable.

Father stood up and took the big brass-hinged Bible from its shelf as Toos and Hans rapped on the door and came in. Scripture reading at 8:30 each morning for all who were in the house was another of the fixed points around which life in the Beje revolved. Father opened the big volume and Betsie and I held our breaths. Surely, today of all days, when there was still so much to do, it would not be a whole chapter! But he was turning to the Gospel of Luke where we'd left off yesterday – such long chapters in Luke too. With his finger at the place, Father looked up.

'Where is Christoffels?' he said.

Christoffels was the third and only other employee in the shop, a bent, wizened little man who looked older than Father though actually he was ten years younger. I remembered the day six or seven years earlier when he had first come into the shop, so ragged and woebegone that I'd assumed that he was one of the beggars who had the Beje marked as a sure meal. I was about to send him up to the kitchen where Betsie kept a pot of soup simmering when he announced with great dignity that he was considering permanent employment and was offering his services first to us.

It turned out that Christoffels belonged to an almost vanished trade, the itinerant clockmender who trudged on foot throughout the land, regulating and repairing the tall pendulum clocks that were the pride of every Dutch farmhouse. But if I was surprised at the grand manner of this shabby little man I was even more astonished when Father hired him on the spot.

'They're the finest clockmen anywhere,' he told me later,

'these wandering clocksmiths. There's not a repair job they haven't handled with just the tools in their sack.'

And so it had proved through the years as people from all over Haarlem brought their clocks to him. What he did with his wages we never knew; he had remained as tattered and threadbare as ever. Father hinted as much as he dared – for next to his shabbiness Christoffels' most notable quality was his pride – and then gave it up.

And now, for the first time ever, Christoffels was late.

Father polished his glasses with his napkin and started to read, his deep voice lingering lovingly over the words. He had reached the bottom of the pages when we heard Christoffels' shuffling steps on the stairs. The door opened and all of us gasped. Christoffels was resplendent in a new black suit, new checkered vest, a snowy white shirt, flowered tie, and stiff starched collar. I tore my eyes from the spectacle as swiftly as I could, for Christoffels' expression forbade us to notice anything out of the ordinary.

'Christoffels, my dear associate,' Father murmured in his formal, old-fashioned way, 'what joy to see you on this – er – auspicious day.' And hastily he resumed his Bible reading.

Before he reached the end of the chapter the doorbells were ringing, both the shop bell on the street and the family bell in the alley. Betsie ran to make more coffee and put her taartjes in the oven while Toos and I hurried to the doors. It seemed that everyone in Haarlem wanted to be first to shake Father's hand. Before long a steady stream of guests was winding up the narrow staircase to Tante Jans's rooms where he sat almost lost in a thicket of flowers. I was helping one of the older guests up the steep stairs when Betsie seized my arm.

'Corrie! We're going to need Nollie's cups right away! How can we—?'

'I'll go get them!'

Our sister Nollie and her husband were coming that afternoon as soon as their six children got home from school. I dashed down the stairs, took my coat and my bicycle from inside the alley door, and was wheeling it over the threshold when Betsie's voice reached me, soft but firm.

'Corrie, your new dress!'

And so I whirled back up the stairs to my room, changed into my oldest skirt and set out over the bumpy brick streets. I always loved to bike to Nollie's house. She and her husband lived about a mile and a half from the Beje, outside the cramped old center of the city. The streets there were broader and straighter; even the sky seemed bigger. Across the town square I pedaled, over the canal on the Grote Hout bridge and along the Wagenweg, reveling in the thin winter sunshine. Nollie lived on Bos en Hoven Straat, a block of identical attached houses with white curtains and potted plants in the windows.

How could I foresee as I zipped around the corner, that one summer day, when the hyacinths in the commercial bulb flats nearby were ripe and brown, I would brake my bicycle here and stand with my heart thudding in my throat, daring to go no closer for fear of what was taking place behind Nollie's starched curtains?

Today I careened onto the sidewalk and burst through the door with never a knock. 'Nollie, the Beje's jammed already! You ought to see! We need the cups right now!'

Nollie came out of the kitchen, her round pretty face flushed with baking. 'They're all packed by the door. Oh I wish I could go back with you – but I've got batches of cookies still to bake and I promised Flip and the children I'd wait for them.'

'You're – *all* coming, aren't you?'

'Yes, Corrie, Peter will be there.' Nollie was loading the cups into the bicycle bags. As a dutiful aunt I tried to love all my nieces and nephews equally. But Peter . . . well, was Peter. At thirteen he was a musical prodigy and a rascal and the pride of my life.

'He's even written a special song in honor of the day,' Nollie said. 'Here now, you'll have to carry this bagful in your hand, so be careful.'

The Beje was more crowded than ever when I got back, the alley so jammed with bicycles I had to leave mine at the corner. The mayor of Haarlem was there in his tailcoat and gold watch chain. And the postman and the trolley motorman and half a dozen policemen from the Haarlem Police Headquarters just around the corner.

After lunch the children started coming and, as children always did, they went straight to Father. The older ones sat on the floor around him, the smallest ones climbed into his lap. For in addition to his twinkling eyes and long cigar-sweet beard, Father ticked. Watches lying on a shelf run differently from watches carried about, and so Father always wore the ones he was regulating. His suit jackets had four huge inside pockets, each fitted with hooks for a dozen watches, so that wherever he went the hum of hundreds of little wheels went gaily with him. Now with a child on each knee and ten more crowded close, he drew from another pocket his heavy cross-shaped winding key, each of the four ends shaped for a different size clock. With a flick of his finger he made it spin, gleaming, glinting . . .

Betsie stopped in the doorway with a tray of cakes. 'He doesn't know there's anyone else in the room,' she said.

I was carrying a stack of soiled plates down the stairs when a little shriek below told me that Pickwick had arrived. We used to forget, we who loved him, what a shock the first sight of him could be to a stranger. I hurried down to the door, introduced him hastily to the wife of an Amsterdam wholesaler, and got him upstairs. He sank his ponderous bulk into a chair beside Father, fixed one eye on me, the other on the ceiling, and said, 'Five lumps, please.'

Poor Pickwick! He loved children as much as Father did, but while children took to Father on sight, Pickwick had to win them. He had one trick, though, that never failed. I brought him his cup of coffee, thick with sugar, and watched him look around in mock consternation. 'But my dear Cornelia!' he cried. 'There's no table to set it on!' He glanced out of one wide-set eye to make sure the children were watching. 'Well, it's a lucky thing I brought my own!' And with that he set cup and saucer on his own protruding paunch. I had never known a child who could resist it; soon a respectful circle had gathered round him.

A little later Nollie and her family arrived. 'Tante Corrie!' Peter greeted me innocently. 'You don't *look* one hundred

years old!' And before I could swat him he was sitting at
Tante Jans's upright piano filling the old house with melody.
People called out requests – popular songs, selections from
Bach chorales, hymns – and soon the whole room was joining
in the choruses.

How many of us were there, that happy afternoon, who
were soon to meet under very different circumstances! Peter,
the policemen, dear ugly Pickwick, all of us were there except
my brother Willem and his family. I wondered why they should
be so late. Willem and his wife and children lived in the town
of Hilversum, thirty miles away: still, they should have been
here by now.

Suddenly the music stopped and Peter from his perch on
the piano bench hissed across the room, 'Opa! Here's the
competition!'

I glanced out the window. Turning into the alley were Mr
and Mrs Kan, owners of the other watch shop on the street.
By Haarlem standards they were newcomers, having opened
their store only in 1910 and so been on the Barteljorisstraat
a mere twenty-seven years. But since they sold a good many
more watches than we did, I considered Peter's comment
factual enough.

Father, however, was distressed. 'Not competitors, Peter!'
he said reprovingly. 'Colleagues!' And lifting children quickly
off his knees, he got up and hurried to the head of the stairs
to greet the Kans.

Father treated Mr Kan's frequent visits to the shop below
as social calls from a cherished friend. 'Can't you see what
he's doing?' I would rage after Mr Kan had gone.

'He's finding out how much we're charging so he can
undersell us!' Mr Kan's display window always featured in
bold figures prices exactly five guilders below our own.

And Father's face would light up with a kind of pleased
surprise as it always did on those rare occasions when he
thought about the business side of watchmaking. 'But Corrie,
people will save money when they buy from him!' And then
he would always add, 'I wonder how he does it.'

Father was as innocent of business know-how as his father
had been before him. He would work for days on a difficult

repair problem and then forget to send a bill. The more rare and expensive a watch, the less he was able to think of it in terms of money. 'A man should pay for the privilege of working on such a watch!' he would say.

As for merchandising methods, for the first eighty years of the shop's history the shutters on the streets had been closed each evening promptly at 6:00. It was not until I myself had come into the business twenty years ago that I had noticed the throngs of strollers crowding the narrow sidewalks each evening and had seen how the other stores kept their windows lighted and open. When I pointed this out to Father he was as delighted as though I had made a profound discovery. 'And if people see the watches it might make them want to buy one! Corrie, my dear, how very clever you are!'

Mr Kan was making his way toward me now, full of cake and compliments. Guilty for the jealous thoughts I harbored I took advantage of the crowd and made my escape downstairs. The workroom and shop were even more crowded with well-wishers than the upstairs rooms. Hans was passing cakes in the back room, as was Toos in the front, wearing the nearest thing to a smile that her perpetually down-drawn lips would permit. As for Christoffels, he had simply and astonishingly expanded. It was impossible to recognize that stooped and shabby little man in the glorious figure at the door, greeting newcomers with a formal welcome followed by a relentless tour of the shop. Quite obviously it was the greatest day of his life.

All through the short winter afternoon they kept coming, the people who counted themselves Father's friends. Young and old, poor and rich, scholarly gentlemen and illiterate servant girls – only to Father did it seem that they were all alike. That was Father's secret: not that he overlooked the differences in people; that he didn't know they were there.

And still Willem was not here. I said goodbye to some guests at the door and stood for a moment gazing up and down the Barteljorisstraat. Although it was only 4:00 in the afternoon the lights in the shops were coming on against the January dusk. I still had a great deal of little-sister worship for this big brother, five years older than I, an ordained minister and the only ten Boom who had ever been to college. Willem saw things, I felt. He knew what was going on in the world.

Oftentimes, indeed, I wished that Willem did not see quite so well, for much that he saw was frightening. A full ten years ago, way back in 1927, Willem had written in his doctoral thesis, done in Germany, that a terrible evil was taking root in that land. Right at the university, he said, seeds were being planted of a contempt for human life such as the world had never seen. The few who had read his paper had laughed.

Now of course, well, people weren't laughing about Germany. Most of the good clocks came from there, and recently several firms with whom we had dealt for years were simply and mysteriously 'out of business.' Willem believed it was part of a deliberate and large-scale move against Jews; every one of the closed businesses was Jewish. As head of the Dutch Reformed Church's program to reach Jews, Willem kept in touch with these things.

Dear Willem, I thought, as I stepped back inside and closed the door, he was about as good a salesman of the church as Father was of watches. If he'd converted a single Jew in twenty years I hadn't heard about it. Willem didn't try to change people, just to serve them. He had scrimped and saved enough money to build a home for elderly Jews in Hilversum – for the elderly of all faiths, in fact, for Willem was against any system of segregation. But in the last few months the home had been deluged with younger arrivals – all Jews and all from Germany. Willem and his family had given up their own living quarters and were sleeping in a corridor. And still the frightened, homeless people kept coming, and with them tales of a mounting madness.

I went up to the kitchen where Nollie had just brewed a fresh pot of coffee, picked it up, and continued with it upstairs to Tante Jans's rooms. 'What does he want?' I asked a group of men gathered around the cake table as I set down the pot. 'This man in Germany, does he want war?' I knew it was poor talk for a party, but somehow thoughts of Willem always set my mind on hard subjects.

A chill of silence fell over the table and spread swiftly around the room.

'What does it matter?' a voice broke into it. 'Let the big countries fight it out. It won't affect us.'

'That's right!' from a watch salesman. 'The Germans let us alone in the Great War. It's to their advantage to keep us neutral.'

'Easy for you to talk,' cried a man from whom we bought clock parts. 'Your stock comes from Switzerland. What about us? What do I do if Germany goes to war? A war could put me out of business!'

And at that moment Willem entered the room. Behind him came Tine, his wife, and their four children. But every eye in the room had settled on the figure whose arm Willem held in his. It was a Jew in his early thirties in the typical broad-brimmed black hat and long black coat. What glued every eye to this man was his face. It had been burned. In front of his right ear dangled a gray and frizzled ringlet, like the hair of a very old man. The rest of his beard was gone, leaving only a raw and gaping wound.

'This is Herr Gutlieber,' Willem announced in German. 'He just arrived in Hilversum this morning. Herr Gutlieber, my father.'

'He got out of Germany on a milk truck,' Willem told us rapidly in Dutch. 'They stopped him on a street corner – teenaged boys in Munich – set fire to his beard.'

Father had risen from his chair and was eagerly shaking the newcomer's hand. I brought him a cup of coffee and a plate of Nollie's cookies. How grateful I was now for Father's insistence that his children speak German and English almost as soon as Dutch.

Herr Gutlieber sat down stiffly on the edge of a chair and fixed his eyes on the cup in his lap. I pulled up a chair beside him and talked some nonsense about the unusual January weather. And around us conversation began again, a hum of party talk rising and falling.

'Hoodlums!' I heard the watch salesman say. 'Young hooligans! It's the same in every country. The police'll catch up with 'em – you'll see. Germany's a civilized country.'

And so the shadow fell across us that winter afternoon in

1937, but it rested lightly. Nobody dreamed that this tiny cloud would grow until it blocked out the sky. And nobody dreamed that in this darkness each of us would be called to play a role: Father and Betsie and Mr Kan and Willem – even the funny old Beje with its unmatching floor levels and ancient angles.

In the evening after the last guest had gone I climbed the stairs to my room thinking only of the past. On my bed lay the new maroon dress; I had forgotten to put it back on. 'I never did care about clothes,' I thought. 'Even when I was young . . .'

Childhood scenes rushed back at me out of the night, strangely close and urgent. Today I know that such memories are the key not to the past, but to the future. I know that the experiences of our lives, when we let God use them, become the mysterious and perfect preparation for the work He will give us to do.

I didn't know it then – nor, indeed, that there was any new future to prepare for in a life as humdrum and predictable as mine. I only knew as I lay in my bed at the top of the house that certain moments from long ago stood out in focus against the blur of years. Oddly sharp and near they were, as though they were not yet finished, as though they had something more to say . . .

2

Full Table

It was 1898 and I was six years old. Betsie stood me in front of the wardrobe mirror and gave me a lecture.

'Just look at your shoes! You've missed every other button. And those old torn stockings your very first day at school? See how nice Nollie looks!'

Nollie and I shared this bedroom at the top of the Beje. I looked at my eight-year-old sister: sure enough, her high-buttoned shoes were neatly fastened. Reluctantly I pulled off mine while Betsie rummaged in the wardrobe.

At thirteen, Betsie seemed almost an adult to me. Of course Betsie had always seemed older because she couldn't run and roughhouse the way other children did. Betsie had been born with pernicious anemia. And so while the rest of us played tag or bowl-the-hoop or had skate races down frozen canals in winter, Betsie sat and did dull grown-up things like embroidery. But Nollie played as hard as anyone and wasn't much older than I and it didn't seem fair that she should always do everything right.

'Betsie,' she was saying earnestly, 'I'm *not* going to wear that great ugly hat to school just because Tante Jans paid for it. Last year it was that ugly gray one – and this year's is even worse!'

Betsie looked at her sympathetically. 'Well, but . . . you can't go to school without a hat. And you know we can't afford another one.'

'We don't have to!'

With an anxious glance at the door, Nollie dropped to her

knees, reached beneath the single bed which was all our tiny
room would hold, and drew out a little round hat box. Inside
nestled the smallest hat I had ever seen. It was of fur, with
a blue satin ribbon for under the chin.

'Oh, the darling thing!' Betsie lifted it reverently from the
box and held it up to the patch of light that struggled into
the room over the surrounding rooftops. 'Where did you
ever — '

'Mrs van Dyver gave it to me.' The van Dyvers owned
the millinery shop two doors down. 'She saw me looking at
it and later she brought it here, after Tante Jans picked out
. . . *that.*'

Nollie pointed to the top of the wardrobe. A deep-rimmed
brown bonnet with a cluster of lavender velvet roses proclaimed in every line the personage who had picked it out.
Tante Jans, Mama's older sister, had moved in with us when
her husband died to spend, as she put it, 'what few days
remain to me,' though she was still only in her early forties.

Her coming had greatly complicated life in the old house –
already crowded by the earlier arrivals of Mama's other two
sisters, Tante Bep and Tante Anna – since along with Tante
Jans had come quantities of furniture, all of it too large for the
little rooms at the Beje.

For her own use Tante Jans took the two second-story
rooms of the front house, directly over the watch shop and
workroom. In the first room she wrote the flaming Christian
tracts for which she was known all over Holland, and in the
second received the well-to-do ladies who supported this
work. Tante Jans believed that our welfare in the hereafter
depended on how much we could accomplish here on earth.
For sleep she partitioned off a cubicle from her writing room
just large enough to hold a bed. Death, she often said, was
waiting to snatch her from her work, and so she kept her
hours of repose as brief and businesslike as possible.

I could not remember life in the Beje before Tante Jans's
arrival, nor whose these two rooms had been before. Above
them was a narrow attic beneath the steep, sloping roof of
the first house. For as long as I could recall, this space had
been divided into four truly miniature rooms. The first one,

looking out over the Barteljorisstraat – and the only one with a real window – was Tante Bep's. Behind it, strung like railroad compartments off a narrow aisle, were Tante Anna's, Betsie's, and our brother Willem's. Five steps up from these rooms, in the second house behind, was Nollie's and my small room, beneath ours Mama's and Father's room, and beneath theirs the dining room with the kitchen tacked like an afterthought to the side of it.

If Tante Jans's share in this crowded house was remarkably large, it never seemed so to any of us living there. The world just naturally made place for Tante Jans. All day long the horse-drawn trolley clopped and clanged past our house to stop at the Grote Markt, the central town square half a block away. At least that was where it stopped for other people. When Tante Jans wished to go somewhere she stationed herself on the sidewalk directly in front of the watch-shop door and as the horses thundered close, held up a single gloved finger. It looked to me more possible to stop the sun in the sky than to halt the charge of that trolley before its appointed place. But it stopped for Tante Jans, brakes squealing, horses nearly falling over one another, and the driver tipped his tall hat as she swept aboard.

And this was the commanding eye past which Nollie had to get the little fur hat. Tante Jans had bought most of the clothing for us three girls since coming to live with us, but her gifts had a price. To Tante Jans, the clothes in fashion when she was young represented God's final say on human apparel; all change since then came from the style-book of the devil. Indeed, one of her best-known pamphlets exposed him as the inventor of the mutton sleeve and the bicycle skirt.

'I know!' I said now as the buttonhook in Betsie's swift fingers sped up my shoes, 'you could fit the fur hat right inside the bonnet! Then when you get outside, take the bonnet off!'

'Corrie!' Nollie was genuinely shocked. 'That wouldn't be honest!' And with a baleful glance at the big brown hat she picked up the little fur one and started after Betsie round the stairs down to breakfast.

I picked up my own hat – the despised gray one from last

year – and trailed after them, one hand clinging to the center post. Let Tante Jans see the silly hat then. I didn't care. I never could understand all the fuss over clothes.

What I did understand, what was awful and alarming, was that this was the day I was to start school. To leave this old house above the watch shop, leave Mama and Father and the aunts, in fact leave behind everything that was certain and well-loved. I gripped the post so tight that my palm squeaked as I circled around. The elementary school was only a block and a half away, it was true, and Nollie had gone there two years without difficulty. But Nollie was different from me; she was pretty and well-behaved and always had her handkerchief.

And then, as I rounded the final curve, the solution came to me, so clear and simple that I laughed out loud. I just wouldn't go to school! I'd stay here and help Tante Anna with the cooking and Mama would teach me to read and I'd never go into that strange ugly building at all. Relief and comfort flooded me and I took the last three steps in a bound.

'Shhh!' Betsie and Nollie were waiting for me outside the dining room door. 'For heaven's sake, Corrie, don't do anything to get Tante Jans started wrong,' Betsie said. 'I'm sure,' she added doubtfully, 'that Father and Mama and Tante Anna will like Nollie's hat.'

'Tante Bep won't,' I said.

'She never likes anything,' Nollie said, 'so she doesn't count.'

Tante Bep, with her perpetual, disapproving scowl, was the oldest of the aunts and the one we children liked least. For thirty years she had worked as a governess in wealthy families and she continually compared our behavior with that of the young ladies and gentlemen she was used to.

Betsie pointed to the Frisian clock on the stairwall, and with a finger on her lips silently opened the dining room door. It was 8:12: breakfast had already begun.

'Two minutes late!' cried Willem triumphantly.

'The Waller children were never late,' said Tante Bep.

'But they're here!' said Father. 'And the room is brighter!'

The three of us hardly heard: Tante Jan's chair was empty.

'Is Tante Jans staying in bed today?' asked Betsie hopefully as we hung our hats on their pegs.

'She's making herself a tonic in the kitchen,' said Mama. She leaned forward to pour our coffee and lowered her voice. 'We must all be specially considerate of dear Jans today. This is the day her husband's sister died some years ago – or was it his cousin?'

'I thought it was his aunt,' said Tante Anna.

'It was a cousin and it was a mercy,' said Tante Bep.

'At any rate,' Mama hurried on, 'you know how these anniversaries upset dear Jans, so we must all try to make it up to her.'

Betsie cut three slices from the round loaf of bread while I looked around the table trying to decide which adult would be most enthusiastic about my decision to stay at home. Father, I knew, put an almost religious importance on education. He himself had had to stop school early to go to work in the watch shop, and though he had gone on to teach himself history, theology, and literature in five languages, he always regretted the missed schooling. He would want me to go – and whatever Father wanted, Mama wanted too.

Tante Anna then? She'd often told me she couldn't manage without me to run errands up and down the steep stairs. Since Mama was not strong, Tante Anna did most of the heavy housework for our family of nine. She was the youngest of the four sisters, with a spirit as generous as Mama's own. There was a myth in our family, firmly believed in by all, that Tante Anna received wages for this work – and indeed every Saturday Father faithfully paid her one guilder. But by Wednesday when the greengrocer came he often had to ask for it back, and she always had it, unspent and waiting. Yes, she would be my ally in this business.

'Tante Anna,' I began, 'I've been thinking about you working so hard all day when I'm in school and — '

A deep dramatic intake of breath made us all look up. Tante Jans was standing in the kitchen doorway, a tumbler of thick brown liquid in her hand. When she had filled her chest with air she closed her eyes, lifted the glass to her lips and drained it down. Then with a sigh she let out the breath, set the glass on the sideboard and sat down.

'And yet,' she said, as though we had been discussing the subject, 'what do doctors know? Dr Blinker prescribed this tonic – but what can medicine really do? What good does anything do when one's Day arrives?'

I glanced round the table; no one was smiling. Tante Jans's preoccupation with death might have been funny, but it wasn't. Young as I was I knew that fear is never funny.

'And yet, Jans,' Father remonstrated gently, 'medicine has prolonged many a life.'

'It didn't help Zusje! And she had the finest doctors in Rotterdam. It was this very day when she was taken – and she was no older than I am now, and got up and dressed for breakfast that day, just as I have.'

She was launching into a minute-by-minute account of Zusje's final day when her eyes lit on the peg from which dangled Nollie's new hat.

'A fur muff?' she demanded, each word bristling with suspicion. 'At this time of year!'

'It isn't a muff, Tante Jans,' said Nollie in a small voice.

'And is it possible to learn what it is?'

'It's a hat, Tante Jans,' Betsie answered for her, 'a surprise from Mrs van Dyver. Wasn't it nice of — '

'Oh no. Nollie's hat has a brim, as a well-brought-up girl's should. I know. I bought – and paid – for it myself.'

There were flames in Tante Jan's eyes, tears in Nollie's when Mama came to the rescue. 'I'm not at *all* sure this cheese is fresh!' She sniffed at the big pot of yellow cheese in the center of the table and pushed it across to Father. 'What do you think, Casper?'

Father, who was incapable of practicing deceit or even recognizing it, took a long and earnest sniff. 'I'm sure it's perfectly fine, my dear! Fresh as the day it came. Mr Steerwijk's cheese is always — ' Catching Mama's look he stared from her to Jans in confusion. 'Oh-er-ah, Jans – ah, what do you think?'

Tante Jans seized the pot and glared into it with righteous zeal. If there was one subject which engaged her energies even more completely than modern clothing it was spoiled food. At last, almost reluctantly it seemed to me, she approved the cheese, but the hat was forgotten. She had plunged into the sad story of an acquaintance 'my very age' who had died after eating a questionable fish, when the shop people arrived and Father took down the heavy Bible from its shelf.

There were only two employees in the watch shop in 1898, the clock man and Father's young apprentice-errand boy. When Mama had poured their coffee, Father put on his rimless spectacles and began to read:

'Thy word is a lamp unto my feet, and a light unto my path . . . Thou art my hiding place and my shield: I hope in thy word . . .'

What kind of hiding place, I wondered idly as I watched Father's brown beard rise and fall with the words. What was there to hide from?

It was a long, long psalm; beside me Nollie began to squirm. When at last Father closed the big volume, she, Willem, and Betsie were on their feet in an instant and snatching up their hats. Next minute they had raced down the last five stairs and out the alley door.

More slowly the two shopworkers got up and followed them down the stairs to the shop's rear entrance. Only then did the five adults notice me still seated at the table.

'Corrie!' cried Mama. 'Have you forgotten you're a big girl now? Today you go to school too! Hurry, or you must cross the street alone!'

'I'm not going.'

There was a short, startled silence, broken by everybody at once.

'When I was a girl — ' Tante Jans began.

'Mrs Waller's children — ' from Tante Bep.

But Father's deep voice drowned them out. 'Of course she's not going alone! Nollie was excited today and forgot to wait, that's all. Corrie is going with me.'

And with that he took my hat from its peg, wrapped my hand in his and led me from the room. My hand in Father's!

That meant the windmill on the Spaarne, or swans on the canal. But this time he was taking me where I didn't want to go! There was a railing along the bottom five steps: I grabbed it with my free hand and held on. Skilled watchmaker's fingers closed over mine and gently unwound them. Howling and struggling I was led away from the world I knew into a bigger, stranger, harder one . . .

Mondays, Father took the train to Amsterdam to get the time from the Naval Observatory. Now that I had started school it was only in the summer that I could go with him. I would race downstairs to the shop, scrubbed, buttoned, and pronounced passable by Betsie. Father would be giving last-minute instructions to the apprentice. 'Mrs Staal will be in this morning to pick up her watch. This clock goes to the Bakker's in Bloemendaal.'

And then we would be off to the station, hand in hand, I lengthening my strides and he shortening his to keep in step. The train trip to Amsterdam took only half an hour, but it was a wonderful ride. First the close-wedged buildings of old Haarlem gave way to separate houses with little plots of land around them. The spaces between houses grew wider. And then we were in the country, the flat Dutch farmland stretching to the horizon, ruler-straight canals sweeping past the window. At last, Amsterdam, even bigger than Haarlem, with its bewilderment of strange streets and canals.

Father always arrived a couple of hours before the time signal in order to visit the wholesalers who supplied him with watches and parts. Many of these were Jews, and these were the visits we both liked best. After the briefest possible discussion of business, Father would draw a small Bible from his traveling case; the wholesaler, whose beard would be even longer and fuller than Father's, would snatch a book or a scroll out of a drawer, clap a prayer cap onto his head; and the two of them would be off, arguing, comparing, interrupting, contradicting – reveling in each other's company.

And then, just when I had decided that this time I had really been forgotten, the wholesaler would look up, catch sight of me as though for the first time, and strike his forehead with the heel of his hand.

'A guest! A guest in my gates and I have offered her no refreshment!' And springing up he would rummage under shelves and into cupboards and before long I would be holding on my lap a plate of the most delicious treats in the world – honey cakes and date cakes and a king of confection of nuts, fruits, and sugar. Desserts were rare in the Beje, sticky delights like these unknown.

By five minutes before noon we were always back at the train station, standing at a point on the platform from which we had a good view of the tower of the Naval Observatory. On the top of the tower where it could be seen by all the ships in the harbor was a tall shaft with two movable arms. At the stroke of 12:00 noon each day the arms dropped. Father would stand at his vantage point on the platform almost on tiptoe with the joy of precision, holding his pocket watch and a pad and pencil. There! Four seconds fast. Within an hour the 'astronomical clock' in the shop in Haarlem would be accurate to the second.

On the train trip home we no longer gazed out the window. Instead we talked – about different things as the years passed. Betsie's graduation from secondary school in spite of the months missed with illness. Whether Willem, when he graduated, would get the scholarship that would let him go on to the university. Betsie starting work as Father's bookkeeper in the shop.

Oftentimes I would use the trip home to bring up things that were troubling me, since anything I asked at home was promptly answered by the aunts. Once – I must have been ten or eleven – I asked Father about a poem we had read at school the winter before. One line had described 'a young man whose face was not shadowed by sex-sin.' I had been far too shy to ask the teacher what it meant, and Mama had blushed scarlet when I consulted her. In those days just after the turn of the century sex was never discussed, even at home.

So the line held stuck in my head. 'Sex,' I was pretty sure, meant whether you were a boy or a girl, and 'sin' made Tante Jans very angry, but what the two together meant I could not imagine. And so, seated next to Father in the train compartment, I suddenly asked, 'Father, what is sex-sin?'

He turned to look at me, as he always did when answering a question, but to my surprise he said nothing. At last he stood up, lifted his traveling case from the rack over our heads, and set it on the floor.

'Will you carry it off the train, Corrie?' he said.

I stood up and tugged at it. It was crammed with the watches and spare parts he had purchased that morning.

'It's too heavy,' I said.

'Yes,' he said. 'And it would be a pretty poor father who would ask his little girl to carry such a load. It's the same way, Corrie, with knowledge. Some knowledge is too heavy for children. When you are older and stronger you can bear it. For now you must trust me to carry it for you.'

And I was satisfied. More than satisfied – wonderfully at peace. There were answers to this and all my hard questions – for now I was content to leave them in my father's keeping.

Evenings at the Beje there was always company and music. Guests would bring their flutes or violins and, as each member of the family sang or played an instrument, we made quite an orchestra gathered around the upright piano in Tante Jans's front room.

The only evenings when we did not make our own music was when there was a concert in town. We could not afford tickets but there was a stage door at the side of the concert hall through which sounds came clearly. There in the alley outside this door we and scores of other Haarlem music lovers followed every note. Mama and Betsie were not strong enough to stand so many hours, but some of us from the Beje would be there, in rain and snow and frost, and while from inside we would hear coughs and stirrings, there was never a rustle in the listeners at the door.

Best of all was when there were concerts at the cathedral, because a relative was sexton there. Just inside his small private entrance a wooden bench ran along the wall. Here we sat, our backs chilled by the ancient stone, our ears and hearts warmed by the music.

The great golden organ was one that Mozart had played, and some of its notes seemed to come from heaven itself. Indeed, I was sure that heaven was like St Bavo's, and probably about the same size. Hell, I knew, was a hot place, so heaven must be like this cold, dank, holy building, where smoke rose like incense from the footwarmers of the paying customers. In heaven, I fervently believed, everybody had footwarmers. Even in the summer the chill never left the marble grave slabs on the floor. But when the organist touched the keys we scarcely noticed – and when he played Bach, not at all.

I was following Mama and Nollie up a dark, straight flight of stairs where cobwebs clutched at our hair and mice scuttled away ahead of us. The building was less than a block from the Beje, and probably a century newer, but here was no Tante Anna to wax and scrub.

We were going to see one of the many poor families in the neighborhood whom Mama had adopted. It never occurred to any of us children that we ourselves were poor; 'the poor' were people you took baskets to. Mama was always cooking up nourishing broths and porridges for forgotten old men and pale young mothers – on days, that is, when she herself was strong enough to stand at the stove.

The night before, a baby had died, and with a basket of her own fresh bread Mama was making the prescribed call on the family. She toiled painfully up the railless stairs, stopping often for breath. At the top a door opened into a single room that was obviously cooking, eating, and sleeping quarters all at once. There were already many visitors, most of them standing for lack of chairs. Mama went at once to the young mother, but I stood frozen on the threshold. Just to the right of the door, so still in the homemade crib, was the baby.

It was strange that a society which hid the facts of sex from children made no effort to shield them from death. I stood staring at the tiny unmoving form with my heart thudding strangely against my ribs. Nollie, always braver than I, stretched out her hand and touched the ivory-white cheek. I longed to do it too, but hung back, afraid. For a while curiosity and terror struggled in me. At last I put one finger on the small curled hand.

It was cold.

Cold as we walked back to the Beje, cold as I washed for supper, cold even in the snug gas-lit dining room. Between me and each familiar face around the table crept those small icy fingers. For all Tante Jans's talk about it, death had been only a word. Now I knew that it could really happen – if to the baby, then to Mama, to Father, to Betsie!

Still shivering with that cold, I followed Nollie up to our room and crept into bed beside her. At last we heard Father's footsteps winding up the stairs. It was the best moment in every day, when he came up to tuck us in. We never fell asleep until he had arranged the blankets in his special way and laid his hand for a moment on each head. Then we tried not to move even a toe.

But that night as he stepped through the door I burst into tears. 'I need you!' I sobbed. 'You can't die! You can't!'

Beside me on the bed Nollie sat up. 'We went to see Mrs Hoog,' she explained. 'Corrie didn't eat her supper or anything.'

Father sat down on the edge of the narrow bed. 'Corrie,' he began gently, 'when you and I go to Amsterdam – when do I give you your ticket?'

I sniffed a few times, considering this.

'Why, just before we get on the train.'

'Exactly. And our wise Father in heaven knows when we're going to need things, too. Don't run out ahead of Him, Corrie. When the time comes that some of us will have to die, you will look into your heart and find the strength you need – just in time.'

3

Karel

I first met Karel at one of the 'occasions' for which Mama was famous. Afterward I never could remember whether it was a birthday, a wedding anniversary, a new baby – Mama could make a party out of anything. Willem introduced him as a friend from Leiden and he shook hands with us one by one. I took that long strong hand, looked up into those deep brown eyes and fell irretrievably in love.

As soon as everyone had coffee I sat down just to gaze at him. He seemed quite unaware of me, but that was only natural. I was a child of fourteen, while he and Willem were already university men, sprouting straggly beards and breathing out cigar smoke with their conversation.

It was enough, I felt, to be in the same room with Karel. As for being unnoticed, I was thoroughly used to that. Nollie was the one boys noticed, though like so many pretty girls, she seemed not to care. When a boy asked for a lock of her hair – the standard method in those days of declaring passion – she would pull a few strands from the ancient gray carpet in our bedroom, tie them with a sentimental blue ribbon, and make me the messenger. The carpet was quite threadbare by now, the school full of broken hearts.

I, on the other hand, fell in love with each boy in my class in turn, in a kind of hopeless, regular rhythm. But since I was not pretty, and far too bashful to express my feelings, a whole generation of boys was growing up unaware of the girl in seat thirty-two.

Karel, though, I thought as I watched him spooning sugar

into his cup, was different. I was going to love Karel forever.

It was two years before I saw Karel again. That was the winter, 1908, that Nollie and I made a trip to the university at Leiden to pay Willem a visit. Willem's sparsely furnished room was on the fourth floor of a private home. He gathered both Nollie and me into a bear-hug and then ran to the window.

'Here,' he said, taking in from the sill a cream bun he had been keeping cold there. 'I bought this for you. You'd better eat it quick before my starving friends arrive.'

We sat on the edge of Willem's bed gulping down the precious bun; I suspected that to buy it Willem had had to go without lunch. A second later the door slammed open and in burst four of his friends – tall, deep-voiced young men in coats with twice-turned collars and threadbare cuffs. Among them was Karel.

I swallowed the last bite of cream bun, wiped my hands on the back of my skirt and stood up. Willem introduced Nollie and me around. But when he came to Karel, Karel interrupted.

'We know each other already.' He bowed ever so slightly. 'Do you remember? We met at a party at your home.' I glanced from Karel to Nollie – but no, he was looking straight at me. My heart poured out a rapturous reply, but my mouth was still filled with the sticky remains of bun and it never reached my lips. Soon the young men were seated at our feet on the floor, all talking eagerly and at once.

Perched beside me on the bed, Nollie joined in as naturally as though visiting a university was an everyday event for us. For one thing, she looked the part: at eighteen she was already in long skirts, while I was acutely conscious of the six inches of thick black school-girl stockings between the hem of my dress and the top of my shoes.

Also, Nollie had things to talk about: the year before she had started Normal School. She didn't really want to be a teacher, but in those days universities did not offer scholarships to girls and Normal Schools were inexpensive. And so she chatted easily and knowledgeably about things of interest to students – this new theory of relativity by a man called

Einstein, and whether Admiral Peary would really reach the North Pole.

'And you, Corrie. Will you go on to be a teacher, too?'

Sitting on the floor at my feet, Karel was smiling at me. I felt a blush rise beneath my high collar.

'Next year, I mean,' he persisted. 'This is your final year in secondary school, isn't it?'

'Yes. I mean – no. I'll stay home with Mama and Tante Anna.'

It came out so short and flat. Why did I say so little when I wanted to say so very much? . . .

That spring I finished school and took over the work of the household. It had always been planned that I would do this, but now there was an added reason. Tante Bep had tuberculosis.

The disease was regarded as incurable: the only known treatment was rest at a sanatorium and that was only for the rich. And so for many months Tante Bep lay in her little closet of a room, coughing away her life.

To keep down the risk of infection, only Tante Anna went in or out. Around the clock she nursed her older sister, many nights getting no sleep at all, and so the cooking and washing and cleaning for the family fell to me. I loved the work, and except for Tante Bep would have been completely happy. But over everything lay her shadow: not only the illness, but her whole disgruntled and disappointed life.

Often I would catch a glimpse inside when I handed in a tray or Tante Anna passed one out. There were the few pathetic mementos of thirty years in other people's homes. Perfume bottles – empty many years – because well-bred families always gave the governess perfume for Christmas. Some faded Daguerrotypes of children who by now must have children and grandchildren of their own. Then the door would shut. But I would linger in that narrow passage under the eaves, yearning to say something, to heal something. Wanting to love her better.

I spoke once about my feelings to Mama. She too was more and more often in bed. Always before when pain from the gallstones had got too bad she'd had an operation. But a small stroke after the last one made further surgery impossible, and many days, making up a tray for Tante Bep, I carried one upstairs to Mama also.

This time when I brought in her lunch she was writing letters. When Mama wasn't supplying the neighborhood with caps and baby dresses from her flying needles, she was composing cheery messages for shut-ins all over Haarlem. The fact that she herself had been shut-in much of her life never seemed to occur to her. 'Here's a poor man, Corrie,' she cried as I came in, 'who's been cooped up in a single room for three years. Just think, shut away from the sky!'

I glanced out Mama's single window at the brick wall three feet away. 'Mama,' I said as I set the tray on the bed and sat down beside it, 'can't we do something for Tante Bep? I mean, isn't it sad that she has to spend her last days here where she hates it, instead of where she was so happy? The Wallers' or someplace?'

Mama laid down her pen and looked at me. 'Corrie,' she said at last, 'Bep has been just as happy here with us – no more and no less – than she was anywhere else.'

I stared at her, not understanding.

'Do you know when she started praising the Wallers so highly?' Mama went on. 'The day she left them. As long as she was there, she had nothing but complaints. The Wallers couldn't compare with the van Hooks where she'd been before. But at the van Hooks she'd actually been miserable. Happiness isn't something that depends on our surroundings, Corrie. It's something we make inside ourselves.'

Tante Bep's death affected her sisters in characteristic fashion. Mama and Tante Anna redoubled their cooking and sewing for the needy in the neighborhood, as though realizing how brief was anyone's lifetime of service. As for Tante Jans, her own particular specter moved very close. 'My own sister,' she would exclaim at odd moments of the day. 'Why, it might as well have been me!'

A year or so after Tante Bep's death, a new doctor took over Dr Blinker's house calls. The new man's name was Jan van Veen and with him came his young sister and nurse, Tine van Veen. With him also came a new gadget for taking blood pressure. We had no idea what this meant but everyone in the household submitted to having the strip of cloth wrapped around his arm and air pumped into it.

Tante Jans, who loved medical praphernalia of every kind, took a tremendous fancy to the new doctor and from then on consulted him as often as her finances would permit. And so it was Dr van Veen, a couple of years later, who first discovered that Tante Jans had diabetes.

In those day this was a death sentence as surely as tuberculosis had been. For days the household was numb with the shock of it. After all these years of fearing even the idea, here was the dread thing itself. Tante Jans went straight to bed on hearing the news.

But inaction went poorly with her vigorous personality and one morning to everyone's surprise she appeared for breakfast in the dining room precisely at 8:10 with the announcement that doctors were often wrong. 'All these tests and tubes,' said Tate Jans, who believed in them implicitly, 'what do they really prove?'

And from then on she threw herself more forcefully than ever into writing, speaking, forming clubs, and launching projects. Holland in 1914, like the rest of Europe, was mobilizing for war, and the streets of Haarlem were suddenly filled with young men in uniform. From her windows overlooking the Barteljorisstraat, Tante Jans watched them idling by, gazing aimlessly into the shop windows, most of them young, penniless, and lonesome. And she conceived the idea of a soldiers' center.

It was a novel idea for its day and Tante Jans threw all the passion of her nature into it. The horse-drawn trolley on the Barteljorisstraat had recently been replaced with a big new electric one. But it still squealed to a stop, spitting sparks from rails and wire, when Tante Jans stood imperiously before the Beje. She would sweep aboard, her long black skirts in one hand, in the other a list of the well-to-do ladies who were about to become patronesses of the new venture. Only those of us who know her best were aware, beneath all the activity, of the monstrous fear which drove her on.

And meanwhile her disease posed financial problems. Each week a fresh test had to be made to determine the sugar-content of her blood, and this was a complicated and expensive process requiring either Dr van Veen or his sister to come to the house.

At last Tine van Veen taught me to run the weekly test myself. There were several steps involved, the most crucial being to heat the final compound to exactly the right temperature. It was hard to make the old coal-burning range in our dark kitchen do anything very precisely, but I finally learned how and from then on each Friday mixed the chemicals and conducted the test myself. If the mixture remained clear when heated, all was well. It was only if it turned black that I was to notify Dr van Veen.

It was that spring that Willem came home for his final holiday before ordination. He had graduated from the university two years before and was now in his last months of theological school. One warm evening during his visit we were all sitting around the dining room table. Father with thirty watches spread out before him was marking in a little notebook in his precise, beautiful script: 'two seconds lost,' 'five seconds gained,' while Willem read aloud from a history of the Dutch Reformation.

All at once the bell in the alley rang. Outside the dining room window a mirror faced the alley door so that we could see who was there before going down to open it. I glanced into it and sprang up from the table.

'Corrie!' said Betsie reprovingly. 'Your skirt!'

I could never remember that I was wearing long skirts now, and Betsie spent many evenings mending the rips I put in them when I moved too fast. Now I took all five steps in a bound. For at the door, a bouquet of daffodils in her hands, was Tine van Veen. Whether it was the soft spring night that put it in my mind, or Willem's dramatic, pulpit-trained voice, I suddenly knew that the meeting of these two people had to be a very special moment.

'For your mother, Corrie,' Tine said, holding out the flowers as I opened the door. 'I hope she's — '

'No, no, you carry the flowers. You look beautiful with them!' And without even taking her coat I pushed the startled girl up the stairs ahead of me.

I prodded her through the dining room door, almost treading on her heels to see Willem's reaction. I knew exactly how it would be. My life was lived just then in romantic novels; I borrowed them from the library in English, Dutch, and German, often reading ones I liked in all three languages, and I had played this scene when hero meets heroine a thousand times.

Willem rose slowly to his feet, his eyes never leaving Tine's. Father stood up too. 'Miss van Veen,' Father said in his old-fashioned manner, 'allow me to present to you our son, Willem. Willem, this is the young lady of whose talent and kindness you have heard us speak.'

I doubt if either one heard the introduction. They were staring at each other as though there were not another soul in the room or in the world.

Willem and Tine were married two months after his ordination. During all the weeks of getting ready, one thought stood out in my mind: Karel will be there. The wedding day dawned cool and sparkling. My eyes picked Karel immediately from the crowd in front of the church, dressed in top hat and tails as were all the male guests, but incomparably the handsomest there.

As for me, I felt that a transformation had taken place since he had seen me last. The difference between my twenty-one years and his twenty-six was not, after all, as big as it had once been.

But more than that, I felt – no, not beautiful. Even on such a romantic day as this I could not persuade myself of that. I knew that my jaw was too square, my legs too long, my hands too large. But I earnestly believed – and all the books agreed – that I would look beautiful to the man who loved me.

Betsie had done my hair that morning, laboring for an hour with the curling iron until it was piled high on my head – and so far, for a wonder, it had stayed. She'd made my silk dress too, as she'd made one for each of the women in the family, working by lamplight in the evenings because the shop was open six days a week and she would not sew on Sundays.

Now looking around me I decided that our homemade outfits were as stylish as any there. Nobody would guess, I thought as the gentle press toward the door began, that Father had given up his cigars and Tante Jans the coal fire in her rooms in order to buy the silk that swished so elegantly with us now.

'Corrie?'

In front of me stood Karel, tall black hat in his hands, his eyes searching my face as though he were not quite sure.

'Yes, it's me!' I said laughing up at him. It's me, Karel, and it's you, and it's the moment I've been dreaming of!

'But you're so – so grown up. Forgive me, Corrie, of course you are! It's just that I've always thought of you as the little girl with the enormous blue eyes.' He stared at me a little longer and then added softly, 'And now the little girl is a lady, and a lovely one.'

Suddenly the organ music swelling from the open door was for us, the arm he offered me was the moon, and my gloved hand resting upon it the only thing that kept me from soaring right over the peaked rooftops of Haarlem.

It was a windy, rainy Friday morning in January when my eyes told me what at first my brain refused to grasp. The liquid in the glass beaker on the kitchen stove was a muddy, sullen black.

I leaned against the old wooden sink and shut my eyes. 'Please God, let me have made a mistake!' I went over in my mind the different steps, looked at the vials of chemicals, the measuring spoons. No. All just the same as I'd always done.

It was this wretched room then – it was always dark in this little cupboard of a kitchen. With a pot holder I snatched up the beaker and ran to the window in the dining room.

Black. Black as fear itself.

Still clutching the beaker I pounded down the five steps

and through the rear door of the shop. Father, his jeweler's glass in his eye, was bent over the shoulder of the newest apprentice, deftly selecting an infinitesimal part from the array before them on the workbench.

I looked through the glass in the door to the shop, but Betsie, behind her little cashier's desk, was talking to a customer. Not a customer, I corrected myself, a nuisance – I knew the woman. She came here for advice on watches and then bought them at that new place, Kan's, across the street. Neither Father nor Betsie seemed to care that this was happening more and more.

As the woman left I burst through the door with the telltale beaker.

'Betsie!' I cried. 'Oh Betsie, it's black! How are we going to tell her? What are we going to do?'

Betsie came swiftly from behind the desk and put her arms around me. Behind me Father came into the shop. His eyes travelled from the beaker to Betsie to me.

'And you did it exactly right, Corrie? In every detail?'

'I'm afraid so, Father.'

'And I am sure of it, my dear. But we must have the doctor's verdict too.'

'I'll take it at once,' I said.

And so I poured the ugly liquid into a small bottle and ran with it over the slippery, rain-washed streets of Haarlem.

There was a new nurse at Dr van Veen's and I spent a miserable, silent half-hour in the waiting room. At last his patient left and Dr van Veen took the bottle into his small laboratory.

'There is no mistake, Corrie,' he said as he emerged. 'Your aunt has three weeks at the very most.'

We held a family conference in the watch shop when I got back: Mama, Tante Anna, Father, Betsie, and me (Nollie did not get home from her teaching job until evening). We agreed that Tante Jans must know at once.

'We will tell her together,' Father decided, 'though I will speak the necessary words. And perhaps,' he said, his face brightening, 'perhaps she will take heart from all she has accomplished. She puts great store on accomplishment, Jans does, and who knows but that she is right!'

And so the little procession filed up the steps to Tante Jans's rooms. 'Come in,' she called to Father's knock, and added as she always did, 'and close the door before I catch my death of drafts.'

She was sitting at her round mahogany table, working on yet another appeal for her soldiers' center. As she saw the number of people entering the room, she laid down her pen. She looked from one face to another, until she came to mine and gave a little grasp of comprehension. This was Friday morning, and I had not yet come up with the results of the test.

'My dear sister-in-law,' Father began gently, 'there is a joyous journey which each of God's children sooner or later set out on. And, Jans, some must go to their Father empty-handed, but you will run to Him with hands full!'

'All your clubs . . .,' Tante Anna ventured.

'Your writings . . .,' Mama added.

'The funds you've raised . . .,' said Betsie.

'Your talks . . .,' I began.

But our well-meant words were useless. In front of us the proud face crumpled; Tante Jans put her hands over her eyes and began to cry. 'Empty, empty!' she choked at last through her tears. 'How can we bring anything to God? What does He care for our little tricks and trinkets?'

And then as we listened in disbelief she lowered her hands and with tears still coursing down her face whispered, 'Dear Jesus, I thank You that we must come with empty hands. I thank You that You have done all – all – on the Cross, and that all we need in life or death is to be sure of this.'

Mama threw her arms around her and they clung together. But I stood rooted to the spot, knowing that I had seen a mystery.

It was Father's train ticket, given at the moment itself.

With a flourish of her handkerchief and a forceful clearing of her nose, Tante Jans let us know that the moment for sentiment had passed.

'If I had a moment's privacy,' she said, 'I might get some work accomplished.'

She glanced at Father, and into those stern eyes crept the

nearest thing to a twinkle I had ever seen. 'Not that the work matters, Casper. Not that it matters at all. But,' she dismissed us crisply, 'I'm not going to leave an untidy desk behind for someone else to clean up.'

It was four months after Tante Jans's funeral that the long-awaited invitation came to Willem's First Sermon. After less than a year as assistant to a minister in Uithuizen, he had been given a church of his own in Brabant, the beautiful rural southern part of Holland. And in the Dutch Reformed Church, a minister's first sermon in his first church was the most solemn, joyous, emotional occasion that an unemotional people could conceive. Family and friends would come from great distances and stay for days.

From his own assistant pastorate Karel wrote that he would be there and looked forward to seeing us all again. I endowed that word 'all' with special meaning and pressed dresses and packed trunks in a delirium of anticipation.

It was one of Mama's bad times. She huddled in the corner of our train compartment, the hand that gripped Father's whitening at the knuckles each time the train lurched or swayed. But while the rest of us gazed out at long rows of poplars in their bright June green, Mama's eyes never left the sky. What to us was a trip through the country, to her was a feast of clouds and light and infinite blue distances.

Both the village of Made and the congregation of Willem's church had declined in recent years. But the church building itself, dating back to better days, was large, and so was Willem and Tine's house across the street. Indeed by Beje standards it was enormous; for the first few nights the ceiling seemed so far overhead that I could not sleep. Uncles and cousins and friends arrived each day, but no matter how many people moved in, the rooms always looked to me half empty.

Three days after we got there I answered the front door knocker and there stood Karel, coal dust from the train trip still speckling his shoulders. He tossed his brown carpetbag past me into the hall, seized my hand, and drew me out into the June sunshine. 'It's a lovely day in the country, Corrie!' he cried. 'Come walking!'

From then on it seemed taken for granted that Karel and I would go walking each day. Each time we wandered a little farther down the country lanes that wound in every direction away from the village, the dirt beneath our feet so different from the brick streets of Haarlem. It was hard to believe, at such moments, that the rest of Europe was locked in the bloodiest war in history. Even across the ocean the madness seemed to be spreading: the papers said America would enter.

Here in neutral Holland one sunlit June day followed another. Only a few people – like Willem – insisted that the war was Holland's tragedy too. His first sermon was on this theme. Europe and the world were changing, he said: no matter which side won, a way of life was gone forever. I looked around at his congregation of sturdy villagers and farmers and saw that they did not care for such ideas.

After the sermon, friends and more distant family started home. But Karel lingered on. Our walks lasted longer. Often we talked about Karel's future, and suddenly we were speaking not about what Karel was going to do, but about what *we* were going to do. We imagined that we had a huge old manse like this one to decorate, and rejoiced to discover that we had the same ideas about furniture, flowers, even the same favorite colors. Only about children did we disagree: Karel wanted four, while I held out stubbornly for six.

And all this while the word 'marriage' was never spoken.

One day when Karel was in the village, Willem came out of the kitchen with two cups of coffee in his hands. Tine with a cup of her own was just behind him.

'Corrie,' Willem said, handing me the coffee and speaking as though with effort, 'has Karel led you to believe that he is — '

'Serious?' Tine finished the sentence for him.

The hateful blush that I could never control set my cheeks burning. 'I . . . no . . . we . . . why?'

Willem's face reddened too. 'Because, Corrie, this is something that can never be. You don't know Karel's family. They've wanted one thing since he was a small child. They've sacrificed for it, planned for it, built their whole lives around it. Karel is to . . . "marry well" is the way I think they put it.'

The big barren parlor seemed suddenly emptier still. 'But – what about what Karel wants? He's not a small child now!'

Willem fixed his sober, deep-set eyes on mine. 'He will do it, Corrie. I don't say he wants it. To him it's just a fact of life like any other. When we'd talk about girls we liked – at the university – he'd always say at the end, "Of course I could never marry her. It would kill my mother".'

The hot coffee scalded my mouth but I gulped it down and made my escape to the garden. I hated that gloomy old house and sometimes I almost hated Willem for always seeing the dark, hard side of things. Here in the garden it was different. There wasn't a bush, hardly a flower, that Karel and I hadn't looked at together, that didn't have a bit of our feeling for each other still clinging to it. Willem might know more than I did about theology and war and politics – but when it came to romance! Things like money, social prestige, family expectations, why, in the books they vanished like rainclouds, every time . . .

Karel left Made a week or so later, and his last words made my heart soar. Only months afterward did I remember how strangely he spoke them, the urgency, almost desperation in his voice. We were standing in the driveway of the manse waiting for the horse and cart which Made still regarded as the only dependable conveyance when there was a train to be caught. We had said goodbye after breakfast and if part of me was disappointed that he still had not proposed, another part of me was content just to be beside him. Now suddenly in the driveway he seized both my hands.

'Corrie, write to me!' he said, but not gaily. Pleadingly. 'Write me about the Beje! I want to know everything. I want every detail of that ugly, beautiful, crumbling old house! Write about your father, Corrie! Write how he forgets to send the bills. Oh Corrie, it's the happiest home in Holland!'

And so it was, indeed, when Father, Mama, Betsie, Nollie, Tante Anna, and I returned. It had always been a happy place, but now each little event seemed to glow because I could share it with Karel. Every meal I cooked was an offering to him, each shining pot a poem, every sweep of the broom an act of love.

His letters did not come as often as mine went singing to him, but I put this down to his work. The minister he was assisting, he wrote, had turned the parish calling over to him: it was a wealthy congregation and large contributors expected frequent and unhurried visits from the clergy.

As time went by his letters came more seldom. I made up for it with mine and went humming my way through the summer and fall. One glorious, nippy November day when all of Holland was singing with me, the doorbell rang. I was washing the lunch dishes in the kitchen, but I ran through the dining room and down the steps before the rest of the family could stir.

I flung open the alley door and there was Karel.

Beside him was a young woman.

She stood smiling at me. I took in the hat with its sweeping feather, the ermine collar, the white-gloved hand resting, on his arm. Then a blur seemed to move over the scene, for Karel was saying. 'Corrie, I want you to meet my fiancée.'

I must have said something. I must have led them up to Tante Jans's front room that we now used as a parlor. I only recall how my family came to the rescue, talking, shaking hands, taking coats, finding chairs, so that I would not have to do or say anything. Mama broke even her own record for making coffee. Tante Anna passed cakes. Betsie engaged the young woman in a discussion of winter fashions and Father pinned Karel in a corner with questions of the most international and impersonal nature. What did he make of the news that President Wilson was sending American troops to France?

Somehow the half-hour passed. Somehow I managed to shake her hand, then Karel's hand, and to wish them every happiness. Betsie took them down to the door. Before it clicked shut I was fleeing up the stairs to my own room at the top of the house where the tears could come.

How long I lay on my bed sobbing for the one love of my

life I do not know. Later, I heard Father's footsteps coming up the stairs. For a moment I was a little girl again waiting for him to tuck the blankets tight. But this was a hurt that no blanket could shut out, and suddenly I was afraid of what Father would say. Afraid he would say, 'There'll be someone else soon,' and that forever afterward this untruth would lie between us. For in some deep part of me I knew already that there would not – soon or ever – be anyone else.

The sweet cigar-smell came into the room with Father. And of course he did not say the false, idle words.

'Corrie,' he began instead, 'do you know what hurts so very much? It's love. Love is the strongest force in the world, and when it is blocked that means pain.

'There are two things we can do when this happens. We can kill the love so that it stops hurting. But then of course part of us dies, too. Or, Corrie, we can ask God to open up another route for that love to travel.

'God loves Karel – even more than you do – and if you ask Him, He will give you His love for this man, a love nothing can prevent, nothing destroy. Whenever we cannot love in the old, human way, Corrie, God can give us the perfect way.'

I did not know, as I listened to Father's footsteps winding back down the stairs, that he had given me more than the key to this hard moment. I did not know that he had put into my hands the secret that would open far darker rooms than this – places where there was not, on a human level, anything to love at all.

I was still in kindergarten in these matters of love. My task just then was to give up my feeling for Karel without giving up the joy and wonder that had grown with it. And so, that very hour, lying there on my bed, I whispered the enormous prayer:

'Lord, I give to You the way I feel about Karel, my thoughts about our future – oh, You know! Everything! Give me Your way of seeing Karel instead. Help me to love him that way. That much.'

And even as I said the words I fell asleep.

4

The Watch Shop

I was standing on a chair washing the big window in the dining room, waving now and then to passersby in the alley, while in the kitchen Mama peeled potatoes for lunch. It was 1918; the dreadful war was finally over: even in the way people walked you could sense a new hope in the air.

It wasn't like Mama, I thought, to let the water keep running that way; she never wasted anything.

'Corrie.'

Her voice was low, almost a whisper.

'Yes, Mama?'

'Corrie,' she said again.

And then I heard the water spilling out of the sink onto the floor. I jumped down from the chair and ran into the kitchen. Mama stood with her hand on the faucet, staring strangely at me while the water splashed from the sink over her feet.

'What is it, Mama!' I cried, reaching for the faucet. I pried her fingers loose, shut off the water, and drew her away from the puddle on the floor.

'Corrie,' she said again.

'Mama, you're ill! We've got to get you to bed!'

'Corrie.'

I put an arm beneath her shoulder and guided her through the dining room and up the stairs. At my cry Tante Anna came running down them and caught Mama's other arm. Together we got her onto her bed and then I raced down to the shop for Father and Betsie.

For an hour the four of us watched the effect of the

cerebral hemorrhage spread slowly over her body. The paralysis seemed to affect her hands first, traveling from them along her arms and then down into her legs. Dr van Veen, for whom the apprentice had gone running, could do no more than we.

Mama's consciousness was the last thing to go, her eyes remaining open and alert, looking lovingly at each one of us until very slowly they closed and we were sure she was gone forever. Dr van Veen, however, said that this was only a coma, very deep, from which she could slip either into death or back to life.

For two months Mama lay unconscious on that bed, the five of us, with Nollie on the evening shift, taking turns at her side. And then one morning, as unexpectedly as the stroke had come, her eyes opened and she looked around her. Eventually she regained the use of her arms and legs enough to be able to move about with assistance, though her hands would never again hold her crochet hook or knitting needles.

We moved her out of the tiny bedroom facing the brick wall, down to Tante Jans's front room where she could watch the busy life of the Barteljorisstraat. Her mind, it was soon clear, was as active as ever, but the power of speech did not return – with the exception of three words. Mama could say 'yes,' 'no,' and – perhaps because it was the last one she had pronounced – 'Corrie.' And so Mama called everybody 'Corrie.'

To communicate, she and I invented a little game, something like Twenty Questions. 'Corrie,' she would say.

'What is it, Mama? You're thinking of someone!'

'Yes.'

'Someone in the family.'

'No.'

'Somebody you saw on the street?'

'Yes.'

'Was it an old friend.'

'Yes.'

'A man?'

'No.'

A woman Mama had known for a long time. 'Mama, I'll bet
it's somebody's birthday!' And I would call out names until I
heard her delighted, 'Yes!' Then I would write a little note
saying that Mama had seen the person and wished her a
happy birthday. At the close I always put the pen in her
stiffened fingers so she could sign it. An angular scrawl was
all that was left of her beautiful curling signature, but it was
soon recognized and loved all over Haarlem.

It was astonishing, really, the quality of life she was able to
lead in that crippled body, and watching her during the three
years of her paralysis, I made another discovery about love.

Mama's love had always been the kind that acted itself out
with soup pot and sewing basket. But now that these things
were taken away, the love seemed as whole as before. She
sat in her chair at the window and loved us. She loved the
people she saw in the street – and beyond: her love took in
the city, the land of Holland, the world. And so I learned that
love is larger than the walls which shut it in.

More and more often, Nollie's conversation at the dinner table
had been about a young fellow teacher at the school where she
taught, Flip van Woerden. By the time Mr van Woerden paid
the formal call on Father, Father had rehearsed and polished
his little speech of blessing a dozen times.

The night before the wedding, as Betsie and I lifted her
into bed, Mama suddenly burst into tears. With Twenty
Questions we discovered that no, she was not unhappy about
the marriage; yes, she liked Flip very much. It was that the
solemn mother-daughter talk promised over the years for
this night, the entire sex education which our taciturn society
provided, was now not possible.

In the end, that night, it was Tante Anna who mounted
the stairs to Nollie's room, eyes wide and cheeks aflame.
Years before, Nollie had moved from our room at the top
of the stairs down to Tante Bep's little nook, and there she
and Tante Anna were closeted for the prescribed half-hour.
There could have been no one in all Holland less informed
about marriage than Tante Anna, but this was ritual: the
older woman counseling the younger one down through the

centuries – one could no more have got married without it than one could have dispensed with the ring.

Nollie was radiant, the following day, in her long white dress. But it was Mama I could not take my eyes off. Dressed in black as always, she was nevertheless suddenly young and girlish, eyes sparkling with joy at this greatest Occasion the ten Booms had ever held. Betsie and I took her into the church early and I was sure that most of the van Woerden family and friends never dreamed that the gracious and smiling lady in the first pew could neither walk alone nor speak.

It was not until Nollie and Flip came down the aisle together that I thought for the very first time of my own dreams of such a moment with Karel. I glanced at Betsie, sitting so tall and lovely on the other side of Mama. Betsie had always known that, because of her health, she could not have children, and for that reason had decided long ago never to marry. Now I was twenty-seven. Betsie in her mid-thirties, and I knew that this was the way it was going to be: Betsie and I the unmarried daughters living at home in the Beje.

It was a happy thought, not a sad one. And that was the moment when I knew for sure that God had accepted the faltering gift of my emotions made four years ago. For with the thought of Karel – all shining round with love as thoughts of him had been since I was fourteen – came not the slightest trace of hurt. 'Bless Karel, Lord Jesus,' I murmured under my breath. 'And bless her. Keep them close to one another and to You.' And that was a prayer, I knew for sure, that could not have sprung unaided from Corrie ten Boom.

But the great miracle of the day came later. To close the service we had chosen Mama's favorite hymn, 'Fairest Lord Jesus.' And now as I stood singing it I heard, behind me in the pew, Mama's voice singing too. Word after word, verse after verse, she joined in, Mama who could not speak four words, singing the beautiful lines without a stammer. Her voice, which had been so high and clear was hoarse and cracked, but to me it was the voice of an angel.

All the way through she sang, while I stared straight ahead, not daring to turn around for fear of breaking the spell. When at last everyone sat down, Mama's eyes, Betsie's, and mine were brimming with tears.

At first we hoped it was the beginning of Mama's recovery. But the words she had sung she was not able to say, nor did she ever sing again. It had been an isolated moment, a gift to us from God. His own very special wedding present. Four weeks later, asleep with a smile on her lips, Mama slipped away from us forever.

It was in late November that year that a common cold made a big difference. Betsie began to sniff and sneeze and Father decided that she must not sit behind the cashier's table where the shop door let in the raw winter air.

But Christmas was coming, the shop's busiest time: with Betsie bundled up in bed, I took to running down to the shop as often as I could to wait on customers and wrap packages and save Father clambering up and down from his tall workbench a dozen times an hour.

Tante Anna insisted she could cook and look after Betsie. And so I settled in behind Betsie's table, writing down sales and repair charges, recording cash spent for parts and supplies, and leafing through past records in growing disbelief.

But – there was no system here anywhere! No way to tell whether a bill had been paid or not, whether the price we were asking was high or low, no way in fact to tell if we were making money or losing it.

I hurried down the street to the bookseller one wintry afternoon, bought a whole new set of ledgers, and started in to impose method on madness. Many nights after the door was locked and the shutters closed I sat on in the flickering gaslight, poring over old inventories and wholesalers' statements.

Or I would question Father. 'How much did you charge Mr Hoek for that repair work last month?'

Father would look at me blankly. 'Why . . . ah . . . my dear . . . I can't really . . .'

'It was a Vacheron, Father, an old one. You had to send all the way to Switzerland for the parts and here's their bill and — '

His face lit up. 'Of course I remember! A beautiful watch, Corrie! A joy to work on. Very old, only he'd let dust get into it. A fine watch must be kept clean, my dear!'

'But how much did you charge, Father?'

I developed a system of billing and, increasingly, my columns of figures began to correspond to actual transactions. And increasingly, I discovered that I loved it. I had always felt happy in this little shop with its tiny voices and shelves of small shining faces. But now I discovered that I liked the business side of it too, liked catalogues and stock listings, liked the whole busy, energetic world of trade.

Every now and then when I remembered that Betsie's cold had settled in her chest and threatened, as hers always did, to turn into pneumonia, I would reproach myself for being anything but distressed at the present arrangement. And at night when I would hear the hard, racking cough from her bedroom below I would pray with all my heart for her to be better at once.

And then one evening two days before Christmas, when I had closed up the shop for the night and was locking the hallway door, Betsie came bursting in from the alley with her arms full of flowers. Her eyes when she saw me there were like a guilty child's.

'For Christmas, Corrie!' she pleaded. 'We have to have flowers for Christmas!'

'Betsie ten Boom!' I exploded. 'How long has this been going on? No wonder you're not getting better!'

'I've stayed in bed most of the time, honestly — ' she stopped while great coughs shook her. 'I've only got up for really important things.'

I put her to bed and then prowled the rooms with new-opened eyes, looking for Betsie's 'important things.' How little I had really noticed about the house! Betsie had wrought changes everywhere. I marched back up to her room and confronted her with the evidence. 'Was it important, Betsie, to rearrange all the dishes in the corner cupboard?'

She looked up at me and her face went red. 'Yes, it was,' she said defiantly. 'You just put them in any old way.'

'And the door to Tante Jans's rooms? Someone's been using paint remover on it, and sandpaper too – and that's hard work!'

'But there's beautiful wood underneath. I just know it! For years I've wanted to get that old varnish off and see. Oh Corrie,' she said, her voice suddenly small and contrite, 'I know it's horrid and selfish of me when you've had to be in the shop day after day. And I will take better care of myself so you won't have to do it much longer; but, oh, it's been so glorious being here all day, pretending I was in charge, you know, planning what I'd do . . .'

And so it was out. We had divided the work backwards. It was astonishing, once we'd made the swap, how well everything went. The house had been clean under my care; under Betsie's it glowed. She saw beauty in wood, in pattern, in color, and helped us to see it too. The small food budget which had barely survived my visits to the butcher and disappeared altogether at the bakery, stretched under Betsie's management to include all kinds of delicious things that had never been on our table before. 'Just wait till you see what's for dessert this noon!' she'd tell us at the breakfast table, and all morning in the shop the question would shimmer in the back of our minds.

The soup kettle and the coffee pot on the back of the stove, which I never seemed to find time for, were simmering again the first week Betsie took over, and soon a stream of postmen and police, derelict old men and shivering young errand boys were pausing inside our alley door to stamp their feet and cup their hands around hot mugs, just as they'd done when Mama was in charge.

And meanwhile, in the shop, I was finding a joy in work that I'd never dreamed of. I soon knew that I wanted to do more than wait on customers and keep the accounts. I wanted to learn watch repair itself.

Father eagerly took on the job of teaching me. I eventually learned the moving and stationary parts, the chemistry of oils and solutions, tool and grindwheel and magnifying techniques. But Father's patience, his almost mystic rapport with the harmonies of watchworks, these were not things that could be taught.

Wristwatches had become fashionable and I enrolled in a school which specialized in this kind of work. Three years after Mama's death I became the first licensed woman watchmaker in Holland.

And so was established the pattern our lives were to follow for over twenty years. When Father had put the Bible back on its shelf after breakfast he and I would go down the stairs to the shop while Betsie stirred the soup pot and plotted magic with three potatoes and a pound of mutton. With my eye on income-and-outlay the shop was doing better and soon we were able to hire a saleslady to preside over the front room while Father and I worked in back.

There was a constant procession through this little back room. Sometimes it was a customer; most often it was simply a visitor – from a laborer with wooden klompen on his feet to a fleet owner – all bringing their problems to Father. Quite unabashedly, in the sight of customers in the front room and the employees working with us, he would bow his head and pray for the answer.

He prayed over the work, too. There weren't many repair problems he hadn't encountered. But occasionally one would come along that baffled even him. And then I would hear him say: 'Lord, You turn the wheels of the galaxies. You know what makes the planets spin and You know what makes this watch run . . .'

The specifics of the prayer were always different, for Father – who loved science – was an avid reader of a dozen university journals. Through the years he took his stopped watches to 'the One who set the atoms dancing,' or 'Who keeps the great currents circling through the sea.' The answers to these prayers seemed often to come in the middle of the night: many mornings I would climb onto my stool to find the watch that we had left in a hundred despairing pieces fitted together and ticking merrily.

One thing in the shop I never learned to do as well as Betsie, and that was to care about each person who stepped through the door. Often when a customer entered I would slip out the rear door and up to Betsie in the kitchen. 'Betsie! Who is the woman with the Alpina lapel-watch on a blue velvet band – stout, around fifty?'

'That's Mrs van den Keukel. Her brother came back from Indonesia with malaria and she's been nursing him. Corrie,' as I sped back down the stairs, 'ask her how Mrs Rinker's baby is!'

And Mrs van den Keukel, leaving the shop a few minutes later would comment mistakenly to her husband, 'That Corrie ten Boom is just like her sister!'

Even before Tante Anna's death in the late 1920s, the empty beds in the Beje were beginning to fill up with the succession of foster children who for over ten years kept the old walls ringing with laughter and Betsie busy letting down hems and pants cuffs.

And meanwhile Willem and Nollie were having families – Willem and Tine four children, Nollie and Flip six. Willem had long since left the parish ministry, where his habit of speaking the hard truth had made a succession of congregations unhappy, and had started his nursing home in Hilversum, thirty miles from Haarlem.

Nollie's family we saw more often, as their school – of which Flip was now principal – was right in Haarlem. It was a rare day when one or another of their six was not at the Beje to visit Opa at his workbench or peer into Tante Betsie's mixing bowl or race up and down the winding stairs with the foster children.

Indeed it was at the Beje that we first discovered young Peter's musical gift. It happened around our radio. We had first heard this modern wonder at a friend's house. 'A whole orchestra,' we kept repeating to each other – somehow that seemed especially difficult to produce inside a box. We began to put pennies aside toward a radio of our own.

Long before the sum was raised Father came down with the hepatitis that almost cost his life: during the long stay in the hospital his beard turned snow white. The day he returned home – a week after his seventieth birthday – a little committee paid us a visit. They represented shopkeepers, street sweepers, a factory owner, a canal bargeman – all people who had realized during Father's illness what he meant to them. They had pooled their resources and bought him a radio.

It was a large table model with an ornate shell-shaped speaker and it brought us many years of joy. Every Sunday Betsie would scour the papers, British, French, and German as well as our own, since the radio brought in stations from all over Europe, and plan the week's program of concerts and recitals.

It was one Sunday afternoon when Nollie and her family were visiting that Peter suddenly spoke up in the middle of a Brahms concerto.

'It's funny they put a bad piano on the radio.'

'Sshhh,' said Nollie, but, 'What do you mean, Peter?' asked Father.

'One of the notes is wrong.'

The rest of us exchanged glances: what could an eight-year-old know? But Father led the boy to Tante Jans's old upright. 'Which note, Peter?'

Peter struck the keys up the scale till he reached B above middle C. 'This one,' he said.

And then everyone in the room heard it too: the B on the concert grand was flat.

I spent the rest of the afternoon sitting beside Peter on the piano bench giving him simple musical quizzes, uncovering a phenomenal musical memory and perfect pitch. Peter became my music student until – in about six months – he had learnt everything I knew and went on to more expert teachers.

The radio brought another change to our lives, one that Father at first resisted. Every hour, over the BBC, we could hear the striking hours of Big Ben. And with his stopwatch in his hand corrected to the astronomical clock in the shop, Father conceded that the first stroke of the English clock time after time coincided with the hour.

Father remained, however, mistrustful of this English time. He knew several Englishmen – and they were invariably late. As soon as he was strong enough to travel by train again, he resumed his weekly trips to Amsterdam to get Naval Observatory time.

But as the months passed and Big Ben and the Observatory continued in perfect agreement, he went less regularly, and finally not at all. The astronomical clock in any case was so jarred and jiggled by the constant rattle of automobile traffic in the narrow street outside that it was no longer the precision instrument it had been. The ultimate ignominy came the day Father set the astronomical clock by the radio.

In spite of this and other changes, life for the three of us – Father, Betsie, and me – stayed essentially the same. Our foster children grew up and went away to jobs or to marry, but they were often in the house for visits. The Hundredth Anniversary came and went; the following day Father and I were back at our workbenches as always.

Even the people we passed on our daily walks were perfectly predictable Though it was years now since his illness, Father still walked unsteadily and I still went with him on his daily stroll through the downtown streets. We took our walk always at the same time, after the midday dinner and before the shop reopened at two, and always over the same route. And since other Haarlemers were just as regular in their habits, we knew exactly whom we would meet.

Many of those we nodded to were old friends or customers, others we knew only from this daily encounter – the woman sweeping her steps on Koningstraat, the man who read the *World Shipping News* at the trolley stop on the Grote Markt. And our favorite, the man we called The Bulldog. This was not only because we never saw him without two large bulldogs on the end of a leash but because, with his wrinkled, jowly face and short bowlegs he looked exactly like one of his own pets. His obvious affection for the animals was what touched us: as they went along he constantly muttered and fussed at them. Father and The Bulldog always tipped their hats to one another ceremoniously as we passed.

And while Haarlem and the rest of Holland strolled and bowed and swept its steps, the neighbor on our east geared for war. We knew what was happening – there was no way to keep from knowing. Often in the evening, turning the dial on the radio, we would pick up a voice from Germany. The voice did not talk, or even shout. It screamed. Oddly, it was even-tempered Betsie who reacted most strongly, hurtling from her chair and flinging herself at the radio to shut off the sound.

And yet, in the interludes, we forgot. Or, when Willem was visiting and would not let us forget, or when letters to Jewish suppliers in Germany came back marked 'Address Unknown,' we still managed to believe that it was primarily a German problem. 'How long are they going to stand for it?' we said. 'They won't put up with that man for long.'

Only once did the changes taking place in Germany reach inside the little shop on the Barteljorisstraat, and that was in the person of a young German watchmaker. Germans frequently came to work under Father for a while, for his reputation reached even beyond Holland. So when this tall good-looking young man appeared with apprentice papers from a good firm in Berlin, Father hired him without hesitation. Otto told us proudly that he belonged to the Hitler Youth. Indeed it was a puzzle to us why he had come to Holland, for he found nothing but fault with Dutch people and products. 'The world will see what Germans can do,' he often said.

His first morning at work he came upstairs for coffee and Bible reading with the other employees; after that he sat alone down in the shop. When we asked him why, he said that though he had not understood the Dutch words, he had seen that Father was reading from the Old Testament which, he informed us, was the Jews' 'Book of Lies.'

I was shocked, but Father was only sorrowful. 'He has been taught wrong,' he told me. 'By watching us, seeing that we love this Book and are truthful people, he will realize his error.'

It was several weeks later that Betsie opened the door from the hallway and beckoned to Father and me. Upstairs on Tante Jans's tall mahogany chair sat the lady who ran the rooming house where Otto lived. Changing the bed sheets that morning, she said, she had found something under his pillow. And she drew from her market satchel a knife with a curving ten-inch blade.

Again, Father put the best interpretation on it. 'The boy is probably frightened, alone in a strange country. He probably bought it to protect himself.'

It was true enough that Otto was alone. He spoke no Dutch, nor made any effort to learn, and besides Father, Betsie, and me, few people in this working-class part of the city spoke German. We repeated our invitation to join us upstairs in the evenings, but whether he did not care for our choice of radio programs, or because the evening ended as the morning began, with prayer and Bible reading, he seldom did.

In the end, Father did fire Otto – the first employee he had ever discharged in more than sixty years in business. And it was not the knife or the anti-Semitism that finally brought it about, but Otto's treatment of the old clock mender, Christoffels.

From the very first I had been baffled by his brusqueness with the old man. It wasn't anything he did – not in our presence anyway – but what he didn't do. No standing back to let the older man go first, no helping on with a coat, no picking up a dropped tool. It was hard to pin down. One Sunday when Father, Betsie, and I were having dinner at Hilversum I commented on what I had concluded was simple thoughtlessness.

Willem shook his head. 'It's very deliberate,' he said. 'It's because Christoffels is old. The old have no value to the State. They're also harder to train in the new ways of thinking. Germany is systematically teaching disrespect for old age.'

We stared at him, trying to grasp such a concept. 'Surely you are mistaken, Willem!' Father said. 'Otto is extremely courteous to me – unusually so. And I'm a great deal older than Christoffels.'

'You're different. You're the boss. That's another part of the system: respect for authority. It is the old and the weak who are to be eliminated.'

We rode the train home in stunned silence – and we starting watching Otto more closely. But how could we know, how in the Holland of 1939 could we have guessed, that it was not in the shop where we could observe him but in the streets and alleys outside that Otto was subjecting Christoffels to a very real, small persecution. 'Accidental' collisions and trippings, a shove, a heel ground into a toe, were making the old clockman's journeys to and from work times of terror.

The erect and shabby little man was too proud to report any of this to us. It was not until the icy February morning that Christoffels stumbled into the dining room with a bleeding cheek and a torn coat that the truth came out. Even then, Christoffels said nothing. But running down to the street to pick up his hat, I encountered Otto surrounded by an indignant little cluster of people who had seen what happened. Rounding the corner into the alley, the young man had deliberately forced the older one into the side of the building and ground his face against the rough bricks.

Father tried to reason with Otto as he let him go, to show him why such behavior was wrong. Otto did not answer. In silence he collected the few tools he had brought with him and in silence left the shop. It was only at the door that he turned to look at us, a look of the most utter contempt I had ever seen.

5

Invasion

The slender hands of the clock on the stair wall pointed to 9:25 as we left the dining room that night. That in itself was unusual in our orderly lives. Father was eighty years old now, and promptly at 8:45 each evening – an hour sooner than formerly – he would open the Bible, the signal for prayers, read one chapter, ask God's blessing on us through the night, and by 9:15 be climbing the stairs to his bedroom. Tonight, however, the Prime Minister was to address the nation at 9:30. One question ached through all of Holland like a long-held breath: Would there be war?

We circled up the steps to Tante Jans's rooms and Father went to warm up the big table radio. We did not so often spend the evenings up here listening to music now. England, France and Germany were at war; their stations carried mostly war reports or code messages and many frequencies were jammed. Even Dutch stations carried mostly war news, and that we could hear just as well on the small portable radio we kept now in the dining room, a gift from Pickwick the Christmas before.

This, though, was to be a major broadcast; somehow we all felt it merited the large old set with its elaborate speaker. We sat now, waiting for 9:30, tense and upright in the high-backed wooden chairs, avoiding as if by a kind of premonition the cushioned and comfortable seats.

Then the Prime Minister's voice was speaking to us, sonorous and soothing. There would be no war. He had had assurances from high sources on both sides. Holland's neutrality would be respected. It would be the Great War all over again. There was nothing to fear. Dutchmen were urged to remain calm and to —

The voice stopped. Betsie and I looked up, astonished. Father had snapped off the set and in his blue eyes was a fire we had never seen before.

'It is wrong to give people hope when there is no hope,' he said. 'It is wrong to base faith upon wishes. There will be war. The Germans will attack and we will fall.'

He stamped out his cigar stub in the ashtray beside the radio and with it, it seemed, the anger too, for his voice grew gentle again. 'Oh, my dears, I am sorry for all Dutchmen now who do not know the power of God. For we will be beaten. But He will not.' He kissed us both goodnight and in a moment we heard the steps of an old man climbing the stairs to bed.

Betsie and I sat rooted to our chairs. Father, so skilled at finding good in every situation, so slow to believe evil. If Father saw war and defeat, then there was no other possibility at all.

I sat bolt upright in my bed. What was that? There! There it was again! A brilliant flash followed a second later by an explosion which shook the bed. I scrambled over the covers to the window and leaned out. The patch of sky above the chimney tops glowed orange-red.

I felt for my bathrobe and thrust my arms through the sleeves as I whirled down the stairs. At Father's room I pressed my ear against the door. Between bomb bursts I heard the regular rhythm of his breathing.

I dived down a few more steps and into Tante Jans's rooms. Betsie had long since moved into Tante Jans's little sleeping cubicle where she would be nearer the kitchen and the doorbell. She was sitting up in the bed. I groped toward her in the darkness and we threw our arms round each other.

Together we said it aloud:

'War.'

It was five hours after the Prime Minister's speech. How long we clung together, listening, I do not know. The bombing seemed mostly to be coming from the direction of the airport.

At last we tiptoed uncertainly out to Tante Jans's front room. The glowing sky lit the room with a strange brilliance. The chairs, the mahogany bookcase, the old upright piano, all pulsed with an eerie light.

Betsie and I knelt down by the piano bench. For what seemed hours we prayed for our country, for the dead and injured tonight, for the Queen. And then, incredibly, Betsie began to pray for the Germans, up there in the planes, caught in the fist of the giant evil loose in Germany. I looked at my sister kneeling beside me in the light of burning Holland. 'Oh Lord,' I whispered, 'listen to Betsie, not me, because I cannot pray for those men at all.'

And it was then that I had the dream. It couldn't have been a real dream because I was not asleep. But a scene was suddenly and unreasonably in my mind. I saw the Grote Markt, half a block away, as clearly as though I were standing there, saw the town hall and St Bavo's and the fish mart with its stair-stepped façade.

Then as I watched, a kind of odd, old farm wagon – old fashioned and out of place in the middle of a city – came lumbering across the square pulled by four enormous black horses. To my surprise I saw that I myself was sitting in the wagon. And Father too! And Betsie! There were many others, some strangers, some friends. I recognized Pickwick and Toos, Willem and young Peter. All together we were slowly being drawn across the square behind those horses. We couldn't get off the wagon, that was the terrible thing. It was taking us away – far away, I felt – but we didn't want to go . . .

'Betsie!' I cried, jumping up, pressing my hands to my eyes. 'Betsie, I've had such an awful dream!'

I felt her arm around my shoulder. 'We'll go down to the kitchen where the light won't show, and we'll make a pot of coffee.'

The booming of the bombs was less frequent and farther away as Betsie put on the water. Closer by was the wail of fire alarms and the beep of the hose trucks. Over coffee, standing at the stove, I told Betsie what I had seen.

'Am I imagining things because I'm frightened? But it

wasn't like that! It was real. Oh Betsie, was it a kind of vision?'

Betsie's finger traced a pattern on the wooden sink worn smooth by generations of ten Booms. 'I don't know,' she said softly. 'But if God has shown us bad times ahead, it's enough for me that He knows about them. That's why He sometimes shows us things, you know – to tell us that this too is in His hands.'

For five days Holland held out against the invader. We kept the shop open, not because anyone was interested in watches, but because people wanted to see Father. Some wanted him to pray for husbands and sons stationed at the borders of the country. Others, it seemed to me, came just to see him sitting there behind his workbench as he had for sixty years and to hear in the ticking clocks a world of order and reason.

I never opened my workbench at all but joined Betsie making coffee and carrying it down. We brought down the portable radio, too, and set it up on the display case. Radio was Haarlem's eyes and ears and very pulse-rate, for after that first night, although we often heard planes overhead, the bombing never came so close again.

The first morning over the radio came instructions that ground-floor windows must be taped. Up and down the Barteljorisstraat shopowners were out on the sidewalk; there was an unaccustomed neighborhood feel as advice, rolls of adhesive, and tales of the night's terror passed from door to door. One store owner, an outspoken anti-Semite, was helping Weil the Jewish furrier put up boards where a pane of glass had shaken loose. The optician next door to us, a silent, withdrawn individual came over and taped the top of our display window where Betsie and I could not reach.

A few nights later the radio carried the news we dreaded: the Queen had left. I had not cried the night of the invasion but I cried now, for our country was lost. In the morning the radio announced tanks advancing over the border.

And suddenly all of Haarlem was in the streets. Even Father, whose daily stroll was as predictable as his own clock chimes, broke his routine to go walking at the unheard-of hour of 10:00 A.M. It was as though we wanted to face what was coming together, the whole city united, as though each would draw strength from each other Hollander.

And so the three of us walked, jostled by the crowd, over the bridge on the Spaarne, all the way to the great wild cherry tree whose blossoms each spring formed such a white glory that it was called the Bride of Haarlem. A few faded petals clung now to the new-leafed branches, but most of the Bride's flowers had fallen, forming a wilted carpet beneath us.

A window down the street flew open.

'We've surrendered!'

The procession in the street stopped short. Each told his neighbor what we had all heard for ourselves. A boy of maybe fifteen turned to us with tears rolling down his cheeks. 'I would have fought! I wouldn't ever have given up!' Father stooped down to pick up a small bruised petal from the brick pavement; tenderly he inserted it in his buttonhole.

'That is good, my son,' he told the youngster. 'For Holland's battle has just begun.'

But during the first months of occupation, life was not so very unbearable. The hardest thing to get used to was the German uniform everywhere, German trucks and tanks in the street, German spoken in the shops. Soldiers frequently visited our store, for they were getting good wages and watches were among the first things they bought. Toward us they took a superior tone as though we were not-quite-bright children. But among themselves, as I listened to them excitedly discussing their purchases, they seemed like young men anywhere off on a holiday. Most of them selected women's watches for mothers and sweethearts back home.

Indeed, the shop never made so much money as during that first year of the war. With no new shipments coming in, people bought up everything we had in stock, even the *winkeldochters*, the 'shop-daughters,' merchandise that had lain around so long it seemed part of the furniture. We even sold the green marble mantle clock with the twin brass cupids.

The curfew too, at first, was no hardship for us, since it

was originally set at 10:00 P.M., long after we were indoors in any case. What we did object to were the identity cards each citizen was issued. These small folders containing photograph and fingerprints had to be produced on demand. A soldier or a policeman – the Haarlem police were now under the direct control of the German Commandant – might stop a citizen at any time and ask to see his card; it had to be carried in a pouch about the neck. We were issued ration cards too, but at least that first year, the coupons represented food and merchandise actually available in the stores. Each week the newspapers announced what the current coupons could be exchanged for.

That was another thing it was hard to adjust to – newspapers that no longer carried news. Long glowing reports of the successes of the German army on its various fronts. Eulogies of German leaders, denunciations of traitors and saboteurs, appeals for the unity of the 'Nordic peoples.' But not news that we could trust.

And so we depended again on the radio. Early in the occupation, Haarlemers were ordered to turn in all private sets. Realizing it would look strange if our household produced none at all, we decided to turn in the portable and hide the larger, more powerful instrument in one of the many hollow spaces beneath the old twisting staircase.

Both suggestions were Peter's. He was sixteen at the time of the invasion and shared with other Dutch teenagers the restless energy of anger and impotence. Peter installed the table radio beneath a curve in the stairs just above Father's room and expertly replaced the old boards, while I carried the smaller one down to the big Vroom en Dreesman department store where the radio collection was being made. The army clerk looked at me across the counter.

'Is this the only radio you own?'

'Yes.'

He consulted a list in front of him. 'Ten Boom, Casper, Ten Boom, Elizabeth, at the same address. Do either of them own a radio?'

I had known from childhood that the earth opened and the heavens rained fire upon liars, but I met his gaze.

'No.'

Only as I walked out of the building did I begin to tremble. Not because for the first time in my life I had told a conscious lie. But because it had been so dreadfully easy.

But we had saved our radio. Every night Betsie or I would remove the stair tread and crouch over the radio, the volume barely audible, while the other one thumped the piano in Tante Jans's room as hard as she could, to hear the news from England. And at first the news over the radio and the news in our captive press was much the same. The German offensive was everywhere victorious. Month after month the Free Dutch broadcasts could only urge us to wait, to have courage, to believe in the counter-offensive which must surely some day be mounted.

The Germans had repaired the bomb damage to the airport and were using it now as a base for air raids against England. Night after night we lay in bed listening to the growl of engines heading west. Occasionally English planes retaliated and then the German fighters might intercept them right over Haarlem.

One night I tossed for an hour while dogfights raged overhead, streaking my patch of sky with fire. At last I heard Betsie stirring in the kitchen and ran down to join her.

She was making tea. She brought it into the dining room where we had covered the windows with heavy black paper and set out the best cups. Somewhere in the night there was an explosion; the dishes in the cupboard rattled. For an hour we sipped our tea and talked, until the sound of planes died away and the sky was silent. I said good-night to Betsie at the door to Tante Jans's rooms and groped my way up the dark stairs to my own. The fiery light was gone from the sky. I felt for my bed: there was the pillow. Then in the darkness my hand closed over something hard. Sharp too! I felt blood trickle along a finger.

It was a jagged piece of metal, ten inches long.

'Betsie!'

I raced down the stairs with the shrapnel shard in my hand. We went back to the dining room and stared at it in the light while Betsie bandaged my hand. 'On your pillow,' she kept saying.

'Betsie, if I hadn't heard you in the kitchen — '

But Betsie put a finger on my mouth. 'Don't say it, Corrie! There are no "if's" in God's world. And no places that are safer than other places. The center of His will is our only safety – O Corrie, let us pray that we may always know it!'

The true horror of occupation came over us only slowly. During the first year of German rule there were only minor attacks on Jews in Holland. A rock through the window of a Jewish-owned store. An ugly word scrawled on the wall of a synagogue. It was as though they were trying us, testing the temper of the country. How many Dutchmen would go along with them?

And the answer, to our shame, was many. The National Socialist Bond, the quisling organization of Holland, grew larger and bolder with each month of occupation. Some joined the NSB simply for the benefits: more food, more clothing coupons, the best jobs and housing. But others became NSBers out of conviction. Nazism was a disease to which the Dutch too were susceptible, and those with an anti-Semitic bias fell sick of it first.

On our daily walk Father and I saw the symptoms spread. A sign in a shop window: JEWS WILL NOT BE SERVED. At the entrance to a public park: NO JEWS. On the door of the library. In front of restaurants, theaters, even the concert hall whose alley we knew so much better than its seats.

A synagogue burned down and the fire trucks came. But only to keep the flames from spreading to the buildings on either side.

One noon as Father and I followed our familiar route, the sidewalks were bright with yellow stars sewn to coats and jacket fronts. Men, women, and children wore the six-pointed star with the word *Jood* ('Jew') in the center. We were surprised, as we walked, at how many of the people we had passed each day were Jews. The man who read the *World Shipping News* in the Grote Markt wore a star on his neatly pressed business suit. So did The Bulldog, his jowly face more deeply lined than ever, his voice as he fussed at his dogs, sharp with strain.

Worst were the disappearances. A watch, repaired and ready, hanging on its hook in the back of the shop, month after month. A house in Nollie's block mysteriously deserted, grass growing in the rose garden. One day Mr Kan's shop up the street did not open. Father knocked on his door as we passed that noon, to see if someone were ill, but there was no answer. The shop remained shuttered, the windows above dark and silent for several weeks. Then, although the shop stayed closed, an NSB family moved into the apartment above.

We never knew whether these people had been spirited away by the Gestapo or gone into hiding before this could happen. Certainly public arrests, with no attempt to conceal what was happening, were becoming more frequent. One day as Father and I were returning from our walk we found the Grote Markt cordoned off by a double ring of police and soldiers. A truck was parked in front of the fish mart; into the back were climbing men, women, and children, all wearing the yellow star. There was no reason we could see why this particular place at this particular time had been chosen.

'Father! Those poor people!' I cried.

The police line opened, the truck moved through. We watched till it turned the corner.

'Those poor people,' Father echoed. But to my surprise I saw that he was looking at the soldiers now forming into ranks to march away. 'I pity the poor Germans, Corrie. They have touched the apple of God's eye.'

We talked often, Father, Betsie and I, about what we could do if a chance should come to help some of our Jewish friends. We knew that Willem had found hiding places at the beginning of the occupation for the German Jews who had been living in his house. Lately he had also moved some of the younger Dutch Jews away from the nursing home. 'Not my old people,' he would say. 'Surely they will not touch my old people.'

Willem had addresses. He knew of farms in rural areas

where there were few occupying troops. Willem would be the one to ask.

It was a drizzly November morning in 1941, a year and a half after the invasion, as I stepped outside to fold back the shutters, that I saw a group of four German soldiers coming down the Barteljorisstraat. They were wearing combat helmets low over their ears, rifles strapped to their shoulders. I shrank back into the doorway and watched. They were checking shop numbers as they walked. At Weil's Furriers directly across the street the group stopped. One of the soldiers unstrapped his gun and with the butt banged on the door. He was drawing it back for another blow when the door opened and all four pushed inside.

I dashed back through our shop and up to the dining room where Betsie was setting out three places. 'Betsie! Hurry! Something awful is happening at Weil's!' We reached the front door again in time to see Mr Weil backing out of his shop, the muzzle of a gun pressed against his stomach. When he had prodded Mr Weil a short way down the sidewalk, the soldier went back into the store and slammed the door. Not an arrest, then.

Inside, we could hear glass breaking. Soldiers began carrying out armloads of furs. A crowd was gathering in spite of the early morning hour. Mr Weil had not moved from the spot on the sidewalk where the soldier had left him.

A window over his head opened and a small shower of clothes rained down on him – pajamas, shirts, underwear. Slowly, mechanically, the old furrier stooped and began to gather up his clothing. Betsie and I ran across the street to help him.

'Your wife!' Betsie whispered urgently. 'Where is Mrs Weil?'

The man only blinked at her.

'You must come inside!' I said, snatching socks and handkerchiefs from the sidewalk. 'Quick. with us!'

And we propelled the bewildered old man across to the Beje. Father was in the dining room when we reached it and greeted Mr Weil without the slightest sign of surprise. His natural manner seemed to relax the furrier a bit. His wife, he said, was visiting a sister in Amsterdam.

'We must find a telephone and warn her not to come home!' Betsie said.

Like most private telephones ours had been disconnected early in the occupation. There were public phones at several places in the city, but of course messages went to a public reception center at the other end. Was it right to connect a family in Amsterdam with the trouble here? And if Mrs Weil could not come home, where was she to go? Where were the Weils to live? Certainly not with the sister where they could so easily be traced. Father and Betsie and I exchanged glances. Almost with a single breath we said, 'Willem.'

Again it was not the kind of matter that could be relayed through the public phone system. Someone had to go, and I was the obvious choice. Dutch trains were dirty and overcrowded under the occupation; the trip that should have taken under an hour took nearly three. Willem was not there when I finally reached the big nursing home just after noon, but Tine and their twenty-two-year-old son Kik were. I told them what had happened on the Barteljorisstraat and gave them the Amsterdam address.

'Tell Mr Weil to be ready as soon as it's dark,' Kik said.

But it was nearly 9:00 P.M. – the new curfew hour – before Kik rapped at the alley door. Tucking Mr Weil's clothing bundle beneath his arm, he led the man away into the night.

It was more than two weeks before I saw Kik again to ask him what had happened. He smiled at me, the broad, slow smile I had loved since he was a child.

'If you're going to work with the underground, Tante Corrie, you must learn not to ask questions.'

That was all we ever learned of the Weils. But Kik's words went round and round in my head. 'The underground . . . If you're going to work with the underground.' Was Kik working with this secret and illegal group? Was Willem?

We knew of course that there was an underground in Holland – or suspected it. Most cases of sabotage were not reported in our controlled press, but rumors abounded. A factory had been blown up. A train carrying political prisoners had been stopped and seven, or seventeen, or seventy, had made it away. The rumors tended to get more spectacular with each repetition. But always they featured things we believed were wrong in the sight of God? Stealing, lying, murder. Was this what God wanted in times like these? How should a Christian act when evil was in power?

It was about a month after the raid on the fur shop that Father and I, on our usual walk, saw something so very unusual that we both stopped in mid-stride. Walking toward us along the sidewalk, as so many hundreds of times before, came The Bulldog with his rolling short-legged gait. The bright yellow star had now ceased to look extraordinary, so what – and then I knew what was wrong. The dogs. The dogs were not with him!

He passed without seeming to see us. With one accord Father and I turned around and walked after him. He turned a number of corners while we grew more and more embarrassed at following him without any real excuse. Although Father and he had tipped their hats to each other for years, we had never spoken and did not even know his name.

At last the man stopped in front of a small secondhand shop, took out a ring of keys, and let himself in. We looked through the window at the cluttered interior. Only a glance showed us that this was more than the usual hodgepodge of bric-a-brac and hollow-seated chairs. Someone who loved beautiful things had chosen everything here. 'We must bring Betsie!' I said.

A little bell over the door jingled as we stepped in. Astonishing to see The Bulldog hatless and indoors, unlocking a cash drawer at the rear of the store.

'Permit an introduction, Sir,' Father began. 'I am Casper ten Boom and this is my daughter, Cornelia.'

The Bulldog shook hands and again I noticed the deep creases in the sagging cheeks. 'Harry de Vries,' he said.

'Mr de Vries, we've so often admired your – er – affection for your bulldogs. We hope they are well?'

The squat little man stared from one of us to the other. Slowly the heavy-rimmed eyes filled with tears. 'Are they well?' he repeated. 'I believe they are well. I hope that they are well. They are dead.'

'Dead!' we said together.

'I put the medicine in their bowl with my own hands and I petted them to sleep. My babies. My little ones. If you could only have seen them eat! I waited, you know, till we had enough coupons for meat. They used to have meat all the time.'

We stared at him dumbly. 'Was it,' I ventured at last, 'was it because of the rationing?'

With a gesture of his hands the little man invited us into a small room in back of the shop and gave us chairs. 'Miss ten Boom, I am a Jew. Who knows when they will come to take me away? My wife too – although she is a Gentile – is in danger because of her marriage.'

The Bulldog raised his chin so high his jowls stretched taut. 'It is not for ourselves we mind. We are Christians, Cato and I. When we die we will see Jesus, and this is all that matters.

'But I said to Cato, "What about the dogs? If we are taken away who will feed them? Who will remember their water and their walk? They will wait and we will not come and they will not understand." No! This way my mind is at ease.'

'My dear friend!' Father grasped The Bulldog's hand in both of his. 'Now that these dear companions may no longer walk with you, will you not do my daughter and me the great honor of accompanying us?'

But this The Bulldog would not do. 'It would put you in danger,' he kept saying. He did, however, accept an invitation to come to visit us. 'After dark, after dark,' he said.

And so one evening the following week Mr de Vries came to the alley door of the Beje bringing his sweet, shy wife, Cato, and soon she and Harry were almost nightly visitors in Tante Jans's front room.

The Bulldog's chief delight at the Beje, after talking with Father, were the tomes of Jewish theology now housed in Tante Jans's big mahogany case. For he had become a Christian forty years earlier, without ceasing in the least to be a loyal Jew. 'A completed Jew!' he would tell us smilingly. 'A follower of the one perfect Jew.'

The books belonged to the rabbi of Haarlem. He had brought them to Father more than a year before: 'Just in case I should not be able to care for them – ah – indefinitely.' He had waved a bit apologetically at the procession of small boys behind him, each staggering under the weight of several huge volumes. 'My little hobby. Book collecting. And yet, old friend, books do not age as you and I do. They will speak still when we are gone, to generations we will never see. Yes, the books must survive.'

The rabbi had been one of the first to vanish from Haarlem.

How often it is a small, almost unconscious event that marks a turning point. As arrests of Jews in the street became more frequent, I had begun picking up and delivering work for our Jewish customers myself so that they would not have to venture into the center of town. And so one evening in the early spring of 1942 I was in the home of a doctor and his wife. They were a very old Dutch family: the portraits on the walls could have been a textbook of Holland's history.

The Heemstras and I were talking about the things that were discussed whenever a group of people got together in those days, rationing and the news from England, when down the stairs piped a childish voice.

'Daddy! You didn't tuck us in!'

Dr Heemstra was on his feet in an instant. With an apology to his wife and me he hurried upstairs and in a minute we heard a game of hide-and-seek going and the shrill laughter of two children.

That was all. Nothing had changed. Mrs Heemstra continued with her recipe for stretching the tea ration with rose leaves. And yet everything was changed. For in that instant, reality broke through the numbness that had grown in me since the invasion. At any minute there might be a rap on this door. These children, this mother and father, might be ordered to the back of a truck.

Dr Heemstra came back to the living room and the

conversation rambled on. But under the words a prayer was forming in my heart.

'Lord Jesus, I offer myself for Your people. In any way. Any place. Any time.'

And then an extraordinary thing happened.

Even as I prayed, that waking dream passed again before my eyes. I saw again those four black horses and the Grote Markt. As I had on the night of the invasion I scanned the passengers drawn so unwillingly behind them. Father, Betsie, Willem, myself – leaving Haarlem, leaving all that was sure and safe – going where?

6

The Secret Room

It was Sunday, May 10, 1942, exactly two years after the fall of Holland. The sunny spring skies, the flowers in the lamppost boxes, did not at all reflect the city's mood. German soldiers wandered aimlessly through the streets, some looking as if they had not yet recovered from a hard Saturday night, some already on the lookout for girls, a few hunting for a place to worship.

Each month the occupation seemed to grow harsher, restrictions more numerous. The latest heartache for Dutchmen was an edict making it a crime to sing the 'Wilhelmus,' our national anthem.

Father, Betsie, and I were on our way to the Dutch Reformed church in Velsen, a small town not far from Haarlem, where Peter had won the post of organist in competition against forty older and more experienced musicians. The organ at Velsen was one of the finest in the country; though the train seemed slower each time, we went frequently.

Peter was already playing, invisible in the tall organ loft, when we squeezed into the crowded pew. That was one thing the occupation had done for Holland: churches were packed.

After hymns and prayers came the sermon, a good one today, I thought. I wished Peter would pay closer attention. He regarded sermons as interesting only to venerable relics like his mother and me. I had reached fifty that spring, to Peter the age at which life had definitely passed by. I would beg him to remember that death and ultimate issues could come for any of us at any age – especially these days – but he would reply charmingly that he was too fine a musician to die young.

The closing prayers were said. And then, electrically, the whole church sat at attention. Without preamble, every stop pulled out to full volume, Peter was playing the 'Wilhelmus'!

Father, at eighty-two, was the first one on his feet. Now everyone was standing. From somewhere in back of us a voice sang out the words. Another joined in, and another. Then we were all singing together, the full voice of Holland singing her forbidden anthem. We sang at the top of our lungs, sang our oneness, our hope, our love for Queen and country. On this anniversary of defeat it seemed almost for a moment that we were victors.

Afterward we waited for Peter at the small side door of the church. It was a long time before he was free to come away with us, so many people wanted to embrace him, to shake his hand and thump his back. Clearly he was enormously pleased with himself.

But now that the moment had passed I was, as usual, angry with him. The Gestapo was certain to hear about it, perhaps already had: their eyes and ears were everywhere. I thought of Nollie, home fixing Sunday dinner for us all. I thought of Peter's brothers and sisters. And Flip – what if he lost the principalship of the school for this? And for what had Peter risked so much? Not for people's lives but for a gesture. For a moment's meaningless defiance.

At Bos en Hoven Straat, however, Peter was a hero as one by one his family made us describe again what had happened. The only members of the household who felt as I did were the two Jewish women staying at Nollie's. One of these was an elderly Austrian lady whom Willem had sent into hiding here. 'Katrien,' as the family had rechristened her, was posing as the van Woerdens' housemaid – although Nollie confided to me that she had yet so much as to make her own bed. Probably she did not know how, as she came from a wealthy and aristocratic family.

The other woman was a young, blonde, blue-eyed Dutch

Jew with flawless false identity papers supplied by the Dutch national underground itself. The papers were so good and Annaliese looked so unlike the Nazi stereotype of a Jew, that she went freely in and out of the house, shopping and helping out at the school, giving herself out to be a friend of the family whose husband had died in the bombing of Rotterdam. Katrien and Annaliese could not understand any more than I could Peter's deliberately doing something which would attract the attention of the authorities.

I spent an anxious afternoon, tensing at the sound of every motor, for only the police, Germans and NSBers had automobiles nowadays. But the time came to go home to the Beje and still nothing had happened.

I worried two more days, then decided either Peter had not been reported or that the Gestapo had more important things to occupy them. It was Wednesday morning just as Father and I were unlocking our workbenches that Peter's little sister Cocky burst into the shop.

'Opa! Tante Corrie! They came for Peter! They took him away!'

'Who? Where?'

But she didn't know and it was three days before the family learned that he had been taken to the federal prison in Amsterdam.

It was 7:55 in the evening, just a few minutes before the new curfew hour of 8:00. Peter had been in prison for two weeks. Father and Betsie and I were seated around the dining room table, Father replacing watches in their pockets and Betsie doing needlework, our big, black, slightly-Persian cat curled contentedly in her lap. A knock on the alley door made me glance in the window mirror. There in the bright spring twilight stood a woman. She carried a small suitcase and – odd for the time of year – wore a fur coat, gloves, and a heavy veil.

I ran down and opened the door. 'Can I come in?' she asked. Her voice was high-pitched in fear.

'Of course.' I stepped back. The woman looked over her shoulder before moving into the little hallway.

'My name is Kleermaker. I'm a Jew.'

'How do you do?' I reached out to take her bag, but she held onto it. 'Won't you come upstairs?'

Father and Betsie stood up as we entered the dining room. 'Mrs Kleermaker, my father and my sister.'

'I was about to make some tea!' cried Betsie. 'You're just in time to join us!'

Father drew out a chair from the table and Mrs Kleermaker sat down, still gripping the suitcase. The 'tea' consisted of old leaves which had been crushed and reused so often they did little more than color the water. But Mrs Kleermaker accepted it gratefully, plunging into the story of how her husband had been arrested some months before, her son gone into hiding. Yesterday the S.D. – the political police who worked under the Gestapo – had ordered her to close the family clothing store. She was afraid now to go back to the apartment above it. She had heard that we had befriended a man on this street . . .

'In this household,' Father said, 'God's people are always welcome.'

'We have four empty beds upstairs,' said Betsie. 'Your problem will be choosing which one to sleep in!' Then to my astonishment she added, 'First though, give me a hand with the tea things.'

I could hardly believe my ears. Betsie never let anyone help in her kitchen: 'I'm just a fussy old maid,' she'd say.

But Mrs Kleermaker had jumped to her feet with pathetic eagerness and was already stacking plates and cups . . .

Just two nights later the same scene was repeated. The time was again just before 8:00 on another bright May evening. Again there was a furtive knock at the side door. This time an elderly couple was standing outside.

'Come in!'

It was the same story: the same tight-clutched possessions, the same fearful glance and tentative tread. The story of neighbors arrested, the fear that tomorrow their turn would come.

That night after prayer-time the six of us faced our

dilemma. 'This location is too dangerous,' I told our three guests. 'We're half a block from the main police headquarters. And yet I don't know where else to suggest.'

Clearly it was time to visit Willem again. So the next day I repeated the difficult trip to Hilversum. 'Willem,' I said. 'we have three Jews staying right at the Beje. Can you get places for them in the country?'

Willem pressed his fingers to his eyes and I noticed suddenly how much white was in his beard. 'It's getting harder,' he said. 'Harder every month. They're feeling the food shortage now even on the farms. I still have addresses, yes, a few. But they won't take anyone without a ration card.'

'Without a ration card! But, Jews aren't issued ration cards!'

'I know.' Willem turned to stare out the window. For the first time I wondered how he and Tine were feeding the elderly men and women in their care.

'I know,' he repeated. 'And ration cards can't be counterfeited. They're changed too often and they're too easy to spot. Identity cards are different. I know several printers who do them. Of course you need a photographer.'

A photographer? Printers? What was Willem talking about? 'Willem, if people need ration cards and there aren't any counterfeit ones, what do they do?'

Willem turned slowly from the window. He seemed to have forgotten me and my particular problem. 'Ration cards?' He gestured vaguely. 'You steal them.'

I stared at this Dutch Reformed clergyman. 'Then, Willem, could you steal . . . I mean . . . could you get three stolen cards?'

'No, Corrie! I'm watched! Don't you understand that? Every move I make is watched!'

He put an arm around my shoulder and went on more kindly. 'Even if I can continue working for a while, it will be far better for you to develop your own sources. The less connection with me – the less connection with anyone else – the better.'

Joggling home on the crowded train I turned Willem's words

over and over in my mind. 'Your own sources.' That sounded
so – so professional. How was I going to find a source of
stolen ration cards? Who in the world did I know . . .

And at that moment a name appeared in my mind.

Fred Koornstra.

Fred was the man who used to read the electric meter
at the Beje. The Koornstras had a retarded daughter,
now a grown woman, who attended the 'church' I had
been conducting for the feeble-minded for some twenty
years. And now Fred had a new job working for the Food
Office. Wasn't it in the department where ration books were
issued?

That evening after supper I bumped over the brick streets
to the Koornstra house. The tires on my faithful old bicycle
had finally given out and I had joined the hundreds clattering
about town on metal wheel rims. Each bump reminded me
jarringly of my fifty years.

Fred, a bald man with a military bearing, came to the door
and stared at me blankly when I said I wanted to talk to
him about the Sunday service. He invited me in, closed the
door, and said, 'Now Corrie, what is it you really came to see
me about?'

('Lord,' I prayed silently, 'if it is not safe to confide in Fred,
stop this conversation now before it is too late.')

'I must first tell you that we've had some unexpected
company at the Beje. First it was a single woman, then a
couple, when I got back this afternoon, another couple.' I
paused for just an instant. 'They are Jews.'

Fred's expression did not change.

'We can provide safe places for these people but they must
provide something too. Ration cards.'

Fred's eyes smiled. 'So. Now I know why you came
here.'

'Fred, is there any way you can give out extra cards? More
than you report?'

'None at all, Corrie. Those cards have to be accounted for
a dozen ways. They're checked and double-checked.'

The hope that had begun to mount in me tumbled. But Fred
was frowning.

'Unless — ' he began.

'Unless?'

'Unless there should be a hold-up. The Food Office in Utrecht was robbed last month – but the men were caught.'

He was silent a while. 'If it happened at noon,' he said slowly, 'when just the record clerk and I are there . . . and if they found us tied and gagged . . .' He snapped his fingers. 'And I know just the man who might do it! Do you remember the — '

'Don't!' I said, remembering Willem's warning. 'Don't tell me who. And don't tell me how. Just get the cards if you possibly can.'

Fred stared at me a moment. 'How many do you need?'

I opened my mouth to say, 'Five.' But the number that unexpectedly and astonishingly came out instead was, 'One hundred.'

When Fred opened the door to me just a week later, I gasped at the sight of him. Both eyes were a greenish purple, his lower lip cut and swollen.

'My friend took very naturally to the part,' was all he would say.

But he had the cards. On the table in a brown manila envelope were one hundred passports to safety. Fred had already torn the 'continuing coupon' from each one. This final coupon was presented at the Food Office the last day of each month in exchange for the next month's card. With these coupons Fred could 'legally' continue to issue us one hundred cards.

We agreed that it would be risky for me to keep coming to his house each month. What if he were to come to the Beje instead, dressed in his old meterman uniform?

The meter in the Beje was in the back hall at the foot of the stairs. When I got home that afternoon I pried up the tread of the bottom step, as Peter had done higher to hide the radio, and found a hollow space inside. Peter would be proud of me I thought as I worked – and was flooded by a wave of lonesomeness for that brave and cocksure boy. But even he would have to admit, I concluded as I stepped back at last to admire the completed hideaway, that a watchmaker's hand and eye were worth something. The hinge was hidden deep in the wood, the ancient riser undisturbed. I was ridiculously pleased with it.

We had our first test of the system on July 1. Fred was to come in through the shop as he always had, carrying the cards beneath his shirt. He would come at 5:30, when Betsie would have the back hall free of callers. To my horror at 5:25 the shop door opened and in stepped a policeman.

He was a tall man with close-cropped orange-red hair whom I knew by name – Rolf van Vliet – but little else. He had come to the Hundredth Birthday Party, but so had half the force. Certainly he was not one of Betsie's 'regulars' for winter morning coffee.

Rolf had brought in a watch that needed cleaning, and he seemed in a mood to talk. My throat had gone dry, but Father chatted cheerfully as he took off the back of Rolf's watch and examined it. What were we going to do? There was no way to warn Fred Koornstra. Promptly at 5:30 the door of the shop opened and in he walked, dressed in his blue workclothes. It seemed to me that his chest was too thick by a foot at least.

With magnificent aplomb Fred nodded to Father, the policeman, and me. 'Good evening.' Courteous but a little bored.

He strode through the door at the rear of the shop and shut it behind him. My ears strained to hear him lift the secret lid. There! Surely Rolf must have heard it too.

The door behind us opened again. So great was Fred's control that he had not ducked out the alleyway exit, but came strolling back through the shop.

'Good evening,' he said again.

'Evening.'

He reached the street door and was gone. We had got away with it this time, but somehow, some way, we were going to have to work out a warning system.

For meanwhile, in the weeks since Mrs Kleermaker's unexpected visit, a great deal had happened at the Beje. Supplied with ration cards, Mrs Kleermaker and the elderly couple and the next arrivals and the next had found homes in safer locations. But still the hunted people kept coming, and the needs were often more complicated than ration cards and addresses. If a Jewish woman became pregnant where could she go to have her baby? If a Jew in hiding died, how could he be buried?

'Develop your own sources,' Willem had said. And from the moment Fred Koornstra's name had popped into my mind, an uncanny realization had been growing in me. We were friends with half of Haarlem! We knew nurses in the maternity hospital. We knew clerks in the Records Office. We knew someone in every business and service in the city.

We didn't know, of course, the political views of all these people. But – and here I felt a strange leaping of my heart – God did! My job was simply to follow His leading one step at a time holding every decision up to Him in prayer. I knew I was not clever or subtle or sophisticated; if the Beje was becoming a meeting place for need and supply, it was through some strategy far higher than mine.

A few nights after Fred's first 'meterman' visit the alley bell rang long after curfew. I sped downstairs expecting another sad and stammering refugee. Betsie and I had already made up beds for four new overnight guests that evening: a Jewish woman and her three small children.

But to my surprise, close against the wall of the dark alley, stood Kik. 'Get your bicycle,' he ordered with his usual young abruptness. 'And put on a sweater. I have some people I want you to meet.'

'Now? After curfew?' But I knew it was useless to ask questions. Kik's bicycle was tireless too, the wheel rims swathed in cloth. He wrapped mine also to keep down the clatter, and soon we were pedalling through the blacked-out streets of Haarlem at a speed that would have scared me even in daylight.

'Put a hand on my shoulder,' Kik whispered. 'I know the way.'

We crossed dark side streets, crested bridges, wheeled round invisible corners. At last we crossed a broad canal and I knew we had reached the fashionable suburb of Aerdenhout.

We turned into a driveway beneath shadowy trees. To my astonishment Kik picked up my bicycle and carried both his and mine up the front steps. A serving girl with starched white apron and ruffled cap opened the door. The entrance hall was jammed with bicycles.

Then I saw him. One eye smiling at me, the other at the door, his vast stomach hastening ahead of him. Pickwick!

He led Kik and me into the drawing room where, sipping coffee and chatting in small groups, was the most distinguished-looking group of men and women I had ever seen. But all my attention, that first moment, was on the inexpressibly fragrant aroma in that room. Surely, was it possible they were drinking real coffee?

Pickwick drew me a cup from the silver urn on the sideboard. It was coffee. After two years, rich, black, pungent Dutch coffee. He poured himself a cup too, dropping in his usual five lumps of sugar as though rationing had never been invented. Another starched and ruffled maid was passing a tray heaped high with cakes.

Gobbling and gulping I trailed about the room after Pickwick, shaking the hands of the people he singled out. They were strange introductions for no names were mentioned, only, occasionally, an address, and 'Ask for Mrs Smit.' When I had met my fourth Smit, Kik explained with a grin, 'It's the only last name in the underground.'

So this was really and truly the underground! But – where were these people from? I had never laid eyes on any of them. A second later I realized with a shiver down my spine that I was meeting the national group.

Their chief work, I gleaned from bits of conversation, was liaison work with England and the Free Dutch forces fighting elsewhere on the continent. They also maintained the underground route through which downed Allied plane crews reached the North Sea coast.

But they were instantly sympathetic with my efforts to help Haarlem's Jews. I blushed to my hair roots to hear Pickwick describe me as 'the head of an operation here in this city.' A hollow space under the stairs and some haphazard friendships were not an operation. The others here were obviously competent, disciplined, and professional.

But they greeted me with grave courtesy, murmuring what they had to offer as we shook hands. False identity papers. The use of a car with official government plates. Signature forgery.

In a far corner of the room Pickwick introduced me to a frail-appearing little man with a wispy goatee. 'Our host informs me,' the little man began formally, 'that your headquarters building lacks a secret room. This is a danger for all, those you are helping as well as yourselves and those who work with you. With your permission I will pay you a visit in the coming week . . .'

Years later I learned that he was one of the most famous architects in Europe. I knew him only as Mr Smit.

Just before Kik and I started our dash back to the Beje, Pickwick slipped an arm through mine. 'My dear, I have good news. I understand that Peter is about to be released.' . . .

So he was, three days later, thinner, paler, and not a whit daunted by his two months in a concrete cell. Nollie, Tine and Betsie used up a month's sugar ration baking cakes for his welcome-home party.

And one morning soon afterward the first customer in the shop was a small thin-bearded man named Smit. Father took his jeweler's glass from his eye. If there was one thing he loved better than making a new acquaintance, it wa discovering a link with an old one.

'Smit,' he said eagerly. 'I know several Smits in Amsterdam. Are you by any chance related to the family who — '

'Father,' I interrupted, 'this is the man I told you about. He's come to, ah, inspect the house.'

'A building inspector? Then you must be the Smit with offices in the Grote Hout Straat. I wonder that I haven't — '

'Father!' I pleaded, 'he's not a building inspector, and his name is not Smit.'

'Not Smit?'

Together Mr Smit and I attempted to explain, but Father simply could not understand a person's being called by a

name not his own. As I led Mr Smit into the back hall we
heard him musing to himself, 'I once knew a Smit on Koning
Straat . . .'

Mr Smit examined and approved the hiding place for
ration cards beneath the bottom step. He also pronounced
acceptable the warning system we had worked out. This was
a triangle-shaped wooden sign advertising 'Alpina Watches'
which I had placed in the dining room window. As long as
the sign was in place, it was safe to enter.

But when I showed him a cubby hole behind the corner
cupboard in the dining room, he shook his head. Some ancient
redesigning of the house had left a crawl space in that corner
and we'd been secreting jewelry, silver coins, and other
valuables there since the start of the occupation. Not only
the rabbi had brought us his library but other Jewish families
had brought their treasures to the Beje for safe-keeping. The
space was large enough that we had believed a person could
crawl in there if necessary, but Mr Smit dismissed it without
a second glance.

'First place they'd look. Don't bother to change it though.
It's only silver. We're interested in saving people, not
things.'

He started up the narrow corkscrew stairs, and as he
mounted so did his spirits. He paused in delight at the
odd-placed landings, pounded on the crooked walls, and
laughed aloud as the floor levels of the two old houses
continued out of phase.

'What an impossibility!' he said in an awestruck voice. 'What
an improbable, unbelievable, unpredictable impossibility! Miss
ten Boom, if all houses were constructed like this one, you
would see before you a less worried man.'

At last, at the very top of the stairs, he entered my room
and gave a little cry of delight. 'This is it!' he exclaimed.

'You want your hiding place as high as possible,' he went
on eagerly. 'Gives you the best chance to reach it while the
search is on below. He leaned out the window, craning his
thin neck, the little faun's beard pointing this way and that.

'But . . . this is my bedroom . . .'

Mr Smit paid no attention. He was already measuring. He

moved the heavy, wobbly old wardrobe away from the wall
with surprising ease and pulled my bed into the center of the
room. 'This is where the false wall will go!' Excitedly he drew
out a pencil and drew a line along the floor thirty inches from
the back wall. He stood up and gazed at it moodily.

'That's as big as I dare,' he said. 'It will take a cot mattress,
though. Oh yes. Easily!'

I tried again to protest, but Mr Smit had forgotten I existed.
Over the next few days he and his workmen were in and out of
our house constantly. They never knocked. At each visit each
man carried in something. Tools in a folded newspaper. A few
bricks in a briefcase. 'Wood!' he exclaimed when I ventured to
wonder if a wooden wall would not be easier to build. 'Wood
sounds hollow. Hear it in a minute. No, no. Brick's the only
thing for false walls.'

After the wall was up, the plasterer came, then the
carpenter, finally the painter. Six days after he had begun,
Mr Smit called Father, Betsie, and me to see.

We stood in the doorway and gaped. The smell of fresh
paint was everywhere. But surely nothing in this room was
newly painted! All four walls had that streaked and grimy
look that old rooms got in coal-burning Haarlem. The ancient
molding ran unbroken around the ceiling, chipped and peeling
here and there, obviously undisturbed for a hundred and fifty
years. Old water stains streaked the back wall, a wall that
even I who had lived half a century in this room, could
scarcely believe was not the original, but set back a precious
two-and-a-half feet from the true wall of the building.

Built-in bookshelves ran along this false wall, old, sagging
shelves whose blistered wood bore the same water stains as
the wall behind them. Down in the far lefthand corner, beneath
the bottom shelf, a sliding panel, two feet high and two wide,
opened into the secret room.

Mr Smit stooped and silently pulled this panel up. On hands
and knees Betsie and I crawled into the narrow room behind
it. Once inside we could stand up, sit, or even stretch out one
at a time on the single mattress. A concealed vent, cunningly
let into the real wall, allowed air to enter from outside.

'Keep a water jug there,' said Mr Smit, crawling in behind

us. 'Change the water once a week. Hardtack and vitamins keep indefinitely. Anytime there is anyone in the house whose presence is unofficial, all possessions except the clothes actually on his back must be stored in here.'

Dropping to our knees again we crawled single file out into my bedroom. 'Move back into this room,' he told me. 'Everything exactly as before.'

With his fist he struck the wall above the bookshelves.

'The Gestapo could search for a year,' he said. 'They'll never find this one.'

7

Eusie

Peter was home, yet he was not safe, any more than any healthy young male was safe. In Germany the munitions factories were desperate for workers. Without warning soldiers would suddenly surround a block of buildings and sweep through them, herding every male between sixteen and thirty into trucks for transport. This method of lightning search and seizure was called 'the razzia,' and every family with young men lived in dread of it.

Flip and Nollie had rearranged their kitchen to give them an emergency hiding place as soon as the razzias started. There was a small potato cellar beneath the kitchen floor: they enlarged the trapdoor letting into it, put a large rug on top of it and moved the kitchen table to stand on this spot.

Since Mr Smit's work at the Beje I realized that this hole under the kitchen floor was a totally inadequate hiding place. Too low in the house for one thing, and probably as Mr Smit would say, 'the first place they'd look.' However, it was not a sustained search by trained people it was intended for, but a swoop by soldiers, a place to get out of sight for half an hour. And for that, I thought, it was probably sufficient . . .

It was Flip's birthday when the razzia came to that quiet residential street of identical attached homes. Father, Betsie, and I had come early with a quarter-pound of real English tea from Pickwick.

Nollie, Annaliese, and the two older girls were not yet back when we arrived. A shipment of men's shoes had been announced by one of the department stores and Nollie had determined to get Flip a pair 'if I have to stand in line all day.'

We were chatting in the kitchen with Cocky and Katrien when all at once Peter and his older brother, Bob, raced into the room, their faces white. 'Soldiers! Quick! They're two doors down and coming this way!'

They jerked the table back, snatched away the rug and tugged open the trapdoor. Bob lowered himself first, lying down flat, and Peter tumbled in on top of him. We dropped the door shut, yanked the rug over it and pulled the table back in place. With trembling hands Betsie, Cocky, and I threw a long tablecloth over it and started laying five places for tea.

There was a crash in the hall as the front door burst open and a smaller crash close by as Cocky dropped a teacup. Two uniformed Germans ran into the kitchen, rifles leveled.

'Stay where you are. Do not move.'

We heard boots storming up the stairs. The soldiers glanced around disgustedly at this room filled with women and one old man. If they had looked closer at Katrien she would surely have given herself away: her face was a mask of terror. But they had other things on their minds.

'Where are your men?' the shorter soldier asked Cocky in clumsy, thick-accented Dutch.

'These are my aunts,' she said, 'and this is my grandfather. My father is at his school, and my mother is shopping, and — '

'I didn't ask about the whole tribe!' the man exploded in German. Then in Dutch: 'Where are your brothers?'

Cocky stared at him a second, then dropped her eyes. My heart stood still. I knew how Nollie had trained her children – but surely, surely now of all times a lie was permissible!

'Do you have brothers?' the officer asked again.

'Yes,' Cocky said softly. 'We have three.'

'How old are they?'

'Twenty-one, nineteen, and eighteen.'

Upstairs we heard the sounds of doors opening and shutting, the scrape of furniture dragged from walls.

'Where are they now?' the soldier persisted.

Cocky leaned down and began gathering up the broken

bits of cup. The man jerked her upright. 'Where are your brothers?'

The oldest one is at the Theological College. He doesn't get home most nights because — '

'What about the other two?'

Cocky did not miss a breath.

'Why, they're under the table.'

Motioning us all away from it with his gun, the soldier seized a corner of the cloth. At a nod from him the taller man crouched with his rifle cocked. Then he flung back the cloth.

At last the pent-up tension exploded: Cocky burst into spasms of high hysterical laughter. The soldiers whirled around. Was this girl laughing at them?

'Don't take us for fools!' the short one snarled. Furiously he strode from the room and minutes later the entire squad trooped out – not, unfortunately, before the silent soldier had spied and pocketed our precious packet of tea.

It was a strange dinner party that evening, veering as it did from heartfelt thanksgiving to the nearest thing to a bitter argument our close-knit family had ever had. Nollie stuck by Cocky, insisting she would have answered the same way. 'God honors truth-telling with perfect protection!'

Peter and Bob, from the viewpoint of the trapdoor, weren't so sure. And neither was I. I had never had Nollie's bravery – no, nor her faith either. But I could spot illogic. 'And it isn't logical to *say* the truth and *do* a lie! What about Annaliese's false papers – and that maid's uniform on Katrien?'

'"Set a watch, O Lord, before my mouth,"' Nollie quoted. '"Keep the door of my lips." Psalm One Hundred Forty-one!' she finished triumphantly.

'All right, what about the radio? I had to lie with my lips to keep that!'

'And yet whatever came from your lips, Corrie, I am sure it was spoken in love!' Father's kindly voice reproached my flushed face.

Love. How did one show it? How could God Himself show truth and love at the same time in a world like this?

By dying. The answer stood out for me sharper and chiller

than it ever had before that night: the shape of a Cross etched on the history of the world.

It was getting harder and harder to find safe homes in the country for the scores of Jews who were passing through our underground station by early 1943. Even with ration cards and forged papers there were not enough places for them all. Sooner or later we knew we were going to have to start hiding people here in the city. How sad that the very first should have been the dearest of all.

It was in the middle of a busy morning in the shop when Betsie slipped through the workshop door. 'Harry and Cato are here!' she said.

We were surprised. Harry had never come to the Beje in the daytime because he feared his yellow star would cause awkwardness for us. Father and I hurried behind Betsie up the stairs.

Harry de Vries related the familiar story. The visit the evening before from an NSB quisling. The announcement that the shop was confiscated. Who cared if Harry were a Christian? Any Jew can convert to avoid trouble, the NSBer said. This morning the appearance of a uniformed German to make it official: the shop was closed 'in the interest of national security.'

'But – if I am a security risk,' said poor Harry, 'surely they will not stop with taking my store.'

Doubtless they would not. But just then there was absolutely no available place outside the city. In fact the only underground address we had at the moment was the home of a woman named De Boer, not four blocks from the Beje.

That afternoon I knocked on Mrs De Boer's door. She was a dumpy woman dressed in a blue cotton smock and bedroom slippers. We supplied Mrs De Boer with ration cards and had arranged an emergency appendectomy from there. She showed me the living quarters in her attic. Eighteen Jews were staying there, most of them in their early twenties. 'They've been cooped up too long,' she said. 'They sing and dance and make all sorts of noise.'

'If you think one more couple is too much . . .'

'No. No . . . how can I turn them away? Bring them tonight. We'll manage.'

And so Harry and Cato began their life at Mrs De Boer's, living in one of the narrow dormers in the attic. Betsie went every day to take them some homemade bread, a bit of tea, a slice of sausage. But Betsie's main concern was not for the morale of Harry and Cato, it was for their very lives.

'They're in danger, you know,' she told Father and me. 'It's true that these young people are at the bursting point. This afternoon they were making such a commotion I could hear them down on the street!'

There were other concerns that bitter gray winter. Though there was little snow, the cold came early and stayed late, and fuel was scarce. Here and there in the parks and along the canals trees began to disappear as people cut them down to heat cookstoves and fireplaces.

The damp unheated rooms were hardest on the very young and the very old. One morning Christoffels did not appear for Bible reading in the dining room, nor later in the workshop. His landlady found him dead in his bed, the water in his washbasin frozen solid. We buried the old clockmaker in the splendid suit and vest he had worn to the Hundredth Birthday Party, six years and another lifetime ago.

Spring came slowly. We celebrated my fifty-first birthday with a little party in the de Vrieses' alcove home.

It was one week later, April 22, that Cato arrived alone at the Beje. Inside the door she burst into tears. 'Those foolish young people went crazy! Last night eight of them left the house. Naturally they were stopped and arrested – the boys hadn't even bothered to cut their sideburns. The Gestapo didn't have any trouble getting information out of them.'

The house had been raided, she said, at 4:00 that morning. Cato was released when they discovered she was not Jewish. 'But everyone else – Harry, Mrs De Boer too – oh what will become of them!'

For the next three days Cato was at the Haarlem police station from early morning until curfew, pestering Dutch and Germans alike to let her see her husband. When they sent

her away, she stepped across the street and waited silently
on the sidewalk.

Friday just before the noon closing when the shop was
crowded a policeman pushed open the street door, hesitated,
then continued back into the rear room. It was Rolf van Vliet,
the officer who had been here when our ration cards were
first delivered. He took off his cap and I noticed again that
startling orange-red hair.

'This watch is still not keeping time,' Rolf said. He took
off his wristwatch, placed it on my workbench, and leaned
forward. Was he saying something? It was all I could do to
hear. 'Harry de Vries will be taken to Amsterdam tomorrow.
If you want to see him, come promptly at three this afternoon.'
And then, 'Do you see? The second hand still hesitates at the
top of the dial.'

At three that afternoon Cato and I stepped through the tall
double doors of the police station. The policeman on duty at
the guard post was Rolf himself.

'Come with me,' he said gruffly. He led us through a door
and along a high-ceilinged corridor. At a locked metal gate he
stopped. 'Wait here,' Rolf said.

Someone on the other side opened the gate and Rolf passed
through. He was gone several minutes. Then the door opened
again and we were face to face with Harry. Rolf stood back as
Harry took Cato into his arms.

'You have only a few seconds,' whispered Rolf.

They drew apart, looking into each other's eyes.

'I'm sorry,' said Rolf. 'He'll have to go back.'

Harry kissed his wife. Then he took my hand and shook
it solemnly. Tears filled our eyes. For the first time Harry
spoke 'I shall use this place – wherever they're taking us,'
he said. 'It will be my witness stand for Jesus.'

Rolf took Harry by the elbow.

'We will pray for you many times every day, Harry!' I cried
as the gate swung shut.

An instinct which I shared with no one told me that this
was the last time I would ever see our friend The Bulldog.

That night we held a meeting about Rolf: Betsie and I and the dozen or so teenage boys and girls who acted as messengers for this work. If Rolf had risked his own safety to tell us about Harry's transport, perhaps he should work with us.

'Lord Jesus,' I said aloud, 'this could be a danger for all of us and for Rolf too.' But even with the words came a flood of assurance about this man. How long, I wondered, would we be led by this Gift of Knowledge.

I assigned one of our younger boys to follow Rolf home from work next day and learn where he lived. The older boys, the ones susceptible to the factory draft, we sent out only after dark now, and then most often dressed as girls.

The following week I visited Rolf at home. 'You have no idea how much it meant to see Harry,' I said when I was safe inside. 'How can we repay this kindness?'

Rolf ran his hands through his bright hair. 'Well, there is a way. The cleaning woman at the jail has a teenage son and they've almost picked him up twice. She's desperate to find another place for him to live.'

'Perhaps I can help,' I said. 'Do you think she could find that her watch needs repairing?'

The next day Toos came to the door of Tante Jans's room where I was talking with two new volunteers for our work. More and more I was leaving the watch shop to her and Father as our underground 'operation' required more time. 'There's a funny looking little woman downstairs,' Toos said. 'She says her name is Mietje. She says to tell you "Rolf sent her."'

I met Mietje in the dining room. The hand that I shook was ridged and leathery from years of scrubbing floors. A tuft of hair grew from her chin. 'I understand,' I said, 'that you have a son you're very proud of.'

'Oh yes!' Mietje's face lit up at the mention of him.

I took the bulky old alarm clock she had brought with her. 'Come for your clock tomorrow afternoon and I'll hope to have good news.'

That night we listened to our messengers' reports. The long, cruel winter had opened up places at several addresses. There was a place on a nearby tulip farm, but the farmer had decided he must be paid for the risk he was taking. We would have to provide a fee – in silver rijksdaalders, not paper money

– plus an additional ration card. It didn't happen often that a 'host' would require money for his services; when one did we paid gladly.

When Mietje appeared the following morning I took a small banknote from my purse and tore off a corner. 'This is for your son,' I said. 'Tonight he is to go to the Gravenstenenbrug. There is a tree stump right next to the bridge – they cut down the tree last winter. He is to wait beside it, looking into the canal. A man will come up and ask if he has change for a bankbill. Your son is to match the missing corner, and then follow this man without asking questions.'

Betsie came into the dining room as Mietje was grasping my hand in her two sandpaper ones. 'I'll make it up to you! Somehow, some day, I'll find a way to repay you!'

Betsie and I exchanged smiles. How could this simple little soul help with the kind of need we faced?

And so the work grew. As each new need arose, a new answer was found, too. Through Pickwick, for example, we met the man at the central telephone exchange whose department handled orders to connect and disconnect lines. With a little rewiring and juggling of numbers, he soon had our instrument in operation.

What a day it was when the old wall phone in the rear hall jangled joyously for the first time in three years! And how we needed it! For by now there were eighty Dutchmen – elderly women and middle-aged men along with our teenagers – working in 'God's underground' as we sometimes laughingly called ourselves. Most of these people never saw one another; we kept face-to-face contacts as few as possible. But all knew the Beje. It was headquarters, the center of a spreading web: the knot where all threads crossed.

But if the telephone was a boon, it was also a fresh risk – as was each added worker and connection. We set the phone's ring as low as we could and still hear it; but who might happen to be passing through the hall when it rang?

For that matter how long would curious eyes up and down the street continue to believe that one small watch shop was quite as busy as it appeared? It was true that repair work was in demand: plenty of legitimate customers still passed in and out. But there was altogether too much coming and going, especially in the early evening. The curfew was now 7:00 P.M., which in spring and summer left no night-time hours at all in which workers could move legally through the streets.

It was an hour and a half before that time on the first of June, 1943, and I was thinking of all this as I sat impatiently behind my workbench. Six workers still not back and so many loose ends to tie up before 7:00. For one thing, being the first of the month, Fred Koornstra should be arriving with the new ration cards. The hundred cards which had seemed such an extravagant request a year ago were now far too few for our needs and Fred was only one of our suppliers, some of the stolen cards coming from as far away as Delft. How long can we go on this way? I wondered. How long can we continue to count on this strange protection?

My thoughts were interrupted by the side entrance bell. Betsie and I reached it at the same instant. In the alley stood a young Jewish woman cradling a tiny blanketed bundle in her arms. Behind her I recognized an intern from the maternity hospital.

The baby, he told us in the hallway, had come prematurely. He had kept mother and child in the hospital longer than permitted already because she had nowhere else to go.

Betsie held out her arms for the baby and at that moment Fred Koornstra opened the door from the shop. He blinked a moment at seeing people in the hall, then turned with great deliberation to the meter on the wall. The young doctor, seeing what he took to be an actual meterman, turned as white as his own collar. I longed to reassure both him and Fred, but knew that the fewer of the group who knew one another the safer it was for all. The poor intern gulped a hasty goodbye while Betsie and I got mother and baby up to the dining room and closed the door on Fred and his work.

Betsie poured a bowl of the soup she had cooked for supper from a much-boiled bone. The baby began a thin high wail; I rocked it while the mother ate. Here was a new danger, a tiny fugitive too young to know the folly of making a noise. We had had many Jewish children over a night or several nights at the Beje and even the youngest had developed the uncanny silence of small hunted things. But at two weeks this one had yet to discover how unwelcoming was its world: we would need a place for them far removed from other houses.

And the very next morning into the shop walked the perfect solution. He was a clergyman friend of ours, pastor in a small town outside of Haarlem, and his home was set back from the street in a large wooded park.

'Good morning, Pastor,' I said, the pieces of the puzzle falling together in my mind. 'Can we help you?'

I looked at the watch he had brought in for repair. It required a very hard-to-find spare part. 'But for you, Pastor, we will do our very best. And now I have something I want to confess.'

The pastor's eyes clouded. 'Confess?'

I drew him out the back door of the shop and up the stairs to the dining room.

'I confess that I too am searching for something.' The pastor's face was now wrinkled with a frown. 'Would you be willing to take a Jewish mother and her baby into your home? They will almost certainly be arrested otherwise.'

Color drained from the man's face. He took a step back from me. 'Miss ten Boom! I do hope you're not involved with any of this illegal concealment and undercover business. It's just not safe! Think of your father! And your sister – she's never been strong!'

On impulse I told the pastor to wait and ran upstairs. Betsie had put the newcomers in Willem's old room, the farthest from windows on the street. I asked the mother's permission to borrow the infant: the little thing weighed hardly anything in my arms.

Back in the dining room I pulled back the coverlet from the baby's face.

There was a long silence. The man bent forward, his hand in spite of himself reaching for the tiny fist curled round the blanket. For a moment I saw compassion and fear struggle in his face. Then he straightened. 'No. Definitely not. We could lose our lives for that Jewish child!'

Unseen by either of us, Father had appeared in the doorway. 'Give the child to me, Corrie,' he said.

Father held the baby close, his white beard brushing its cheek, looking into the little face with eyes as blue and innocent as the baby's own. At last he looked up at the pastor. 'You say we could lose our lives for this child. I would consider that the greatest honor that could come to my family.'

The pastor turned sharply on his heels and walked out of the room.

So we had to accept a bad solution to our problem. On the edge of Haarlem was a truck farm which hid refugees for short periods of time. It was not a good location, since the Gestapo had been there already. But there was nowhere else available on short notice. Two workers took the woman and child there that afternoon.

A few weeks later we heard that the farm had been raided. When the Gestapo came to the barn where the woman was hidden, not the baby but the mother began to shriek with hysteria. She, the baby, and her protectors were all taken. We never learned what happened to them.

Although we had a friend at the telephone exchange, we could never be sure that our line was not tapped. So we developed a system for coding our underground messages in terms of watches.

'We have a woman's watch here that needs repairing. But I can't find a mainspring. Do you know who might have one?' (We have a Jewish woman in need of a hiding place and we can't find one among our regular contacts.)

'I have a watch here with a face that's causing difficulty. One of the numbers has worked loose and it's holding back the hand. Do you know anyone who does this kind of repair work?' (We have a Jew here whose features are especially Semitic. Do you know anyone who would be willing to take an extra risk?)

'I'm sorry, but the child's watch you left with us is not repairable. Do you have the receipt?' (A Jewish child has died in one of our houses. We need a burial permit.)

One morning in the middle of June the telephone rang with this message. 'We have a man's watch here that's giving us trouble. We can't find anyone to repair it. For one thing, the face is very old-fashioned . . .'

So, a Jew whose features gave him away. This was the hardest kind of person to place. 'Send the watch over and I'll see what we can do in our own shop,' I said.

Promptly at 7:00 that evening the side doorbell rang. I glanced at the mirror in the window of the dining room where we were still sitting over tea of rose leaves and cherry stems. Even from the side of his head I could tell that this was our old-fashioned watch. His form, his clothes, his very stance were music-hall-comedy Jewish.

I ran down to the door. 'Do come in.'

The smiling slender man in his early thirties, with his protruding ears, balding head, and miniscule glasses, gave an elaborate bow. I liked him instantly.

Once the door was closed he took out a pipe. 'The very first thing I must ask,' he said, 'is whether or not I should leave behind my good friend the pipe? Meyer Mossel and his pipe are not easily separated. But for you, kind lady, should the smell get into your drapes, I would gladly say goodbye to my friend nicotine.'

I laughed. Of all the Jews who had come to our house this was the first to enter gaily and with a question about our own comfort.

'Of course you must keep your pipe!' I said. 'My father smokes a cigar – when he can get one these days.'

'Ah! These days!' Meyer Mossel raised his arms and shoulders in an enormous shrug. 'What do you expect, when the barbarians have overrun the camp?'

I took him up to the dining room. There were seven seated at the table, a Jewish couple waiting placement and three underground workers in addition to Father and Betsie. Meyer Mossel's eyes went straight to Father.

'But,' he cried. 'One of the Patriarchs!'

It was exactly the right thing to say to Father. 'But,' he returned with equal good humor, 'a brother of the Chosen People!'

'Can you recite the One Hundred and Sixty-sixth Psalm, Opa?' Meyer said.

Father beamed. Of course there is no Psalm 166; the Psalter stops with 150. It must be a joke, and nothing could please Father better than a scriptural joke. 'The Hundred and Sixty-sixth Psalm?'

'Shall I recite it for you?' Meyer asked.

Father gave a bow of assent and Meyer plunged into verse.

'But that's Psalm One Hundred!' Father interrupted. And then his face lit up. Of course! Psalm 66 started with the identical words. Meyer had asked for the One Hundredth *and* the Sixty-sixth Psalm. For the rest of the evening I could hear Father chuckling, 'Psalm One Hundred and Sixty-six!'

At 8:45 Father took the old brass-bound Bible from its shelf. He opened to the reading in Jeremiah where we had left off the night before, then with sudden inspiration passed the Bible across the table to Meyer.

'I would consider it an honor if you would read for us tonight,' Father said.

Lifting the Book lovingly, Meyer rose to his feet. From a pocket came a small prayer cap, and then, from deep in his throat, half-sung, half-pleaded, came the words of the ancient prophet, so feelingly and achingly that we seemed to hear the cry of the Exile itself.

Meyer Mossel, he told us afterward, had been cantor in the synagogue in Amsterdam. For all his lightheartedness he had suffered much. Most of his family had been arrested; his wife and children were in hiding on a farm in the north which had declined to accept Meyer – 'for obvious reasons,' he said with a grimace at his own unmistakable features.

And gradually it dawned on all of us that this endearing man was at the Beje to stay. It was certainly not an ideal place, but for Meyer nothing could be ideal right now.

'At least,' I told him one evening, 'your name doesn't have to give you away too.' Ever since the days when Willem was studying church history, I had remembered the fourth-century church father, Eusebius.

'I think we'll call you Eusebius,' I decided. We were sitting in Tante Jans's front room with Kik and some other young men who had made us a delivery of forged travel-permits too late to get home by curfew.

Meyer leaned back and stared at the ceiling pensively. He took his pipe out of his mouth. 'Eusebius Mossel,' he said, tasting the words. 'No, it doesn't sound quite right. Eusebius Gentile Mossel.'

We all laughed. 'Don't be a goose,' Betsie said. 'You must change both names!'

Kik looked slyly at Father. 'Opa! How about Smit? That seems a popular name these days.'

'It does seem so!' said Father, not catching the joke. 'Extraordinarily popular!'

And Eusebius Smit it became.

Changing Meyer's name was easy – at once he became 'Eusie.' But getting Eusie to eat non-kosher food was something else. The problem of course was that we were grateful for food of any kind: we stood in line for hours, this third year of the occupation, to get whatever was available.

One day the paper announced that coupon number four was good for pork sausage. It was the first meat we'd had in weeks. Lovingly Betsie prepared the feast, saving every drop of fat for flavoring other foods later.

'Eusie,' Betsie said as she carried the steaming casserole of pork and potatoes to the table, 'the day has come.'

Eusie knocked the ashes out of his pipe and considered his plight out loud. He, who had always eaten kosher, he, the oldest son of an oldest son of a respected family, in fact, he Meyer Mossel Eusebius Smit, was seriously being asked to eat pork.

Betsie placed a helping of sausage and potato before him. 'Bon appetit.'

The tantalizing odor reached our meat-starved palates. Eusie wet his lips with his tongue. 'Of course,' he said, 'there's a provision for this in the Talmud.' He speared the meat with his fork, bit hungrily and rolled his eyes heavenward in pure pleasure. 'And I'm going to start hunting for it, too,' he said, 'just as soon as dinner's over.'

As if Eusie's arrival had broken down a last hesitation,

within a week there were three new permanent additions to the household. First there was Jop, our current apprentice, whose daily trip from his parents' home in the suburbs had twice nearly ended in seizure for the factory transport. The second time it happened his parents asked if he could stay at the Beje and we agreed. The other two were Henk, a young lawyer, and Leendert, a schoolteacher. Leendert made an especially important contribution to the secret life of the Beje. He installed our electric warning system.

By now I had learned to make the nighttime trip out to Pickwick's almost as skillfully as could Kik. One evening when I had gratefully accepted a cup of coffee, my wall-eyed friend sat me down for a lecture.

'Cornelia,' he said, settling his bulk on a velvet chair too small for him, 'I understand you have no alarm system in your house. This is purest folly. Also I am given to believe that you are not carrying on regular drills for your guests.'

I was always amazed at how well Pickwick knew what went on at the Beje.

'You know that a raid may come any day,' Pickwick continued. 'I don't see how you can avoid one. Scores of people in and out – and an NSB agent living over Kan's up the street.

'Your secret room is no good to you if people can't get to it in time. I know this Leendert. He's a good man and a very passable electrician. Get him to put a buzzer in every room with a door or a window on the street. Then hold practice drills until your people can disappear into that room without a trace in less than a minute. I'll send someone to get you started.'

Leendert did the electrical work that weekend. He installed a buzzer near the top of the stairs – loud enough to be heard all over the house but not outside. Then he placed buttons to sound the buzzer at every vantage point where trouble might first be spotted. One button went beneath the dining room windowsill, just below the mirror which gave onto the side door. Another went in the downstairs hall just inside that door and a third inside the front door on the Barteljorisstraat. He also put a button behind the counter in the shop and one in each workbench as well as beneath the windows in Tante Jans's rooms.

We were ready for our first trial run. The four unacknowledged members of our household were already climbing up to the secret room two times a day: in the morning to store their night clothes, bedding and toilet articles, and in the evening to put away their day things. Members of our group, too, who had to spend the night, kept raincoats, hats, anything they had brought with them, in that room. Altogether that made a good deal of traffic in and out of my small bedroom – smaller now indeed by nearly a yard. Many nights my last waking sight would be Eusie in long robe and tasseled nightcap, handling his day clothes through the secret panel.

But the purpose of the drills was to see how rapidly people could reach the room at any hour of the day or night without prior notice. A tall sallow-faced young man arrived from Pickwick one morning to teach me how to conduct the drills.

'Smit!' Father exclaimed when the man introduced himself. 'Truly it's most astonishing! We've had one Smit after another here lately. Now you bear a great resemblance to . . .'

Mr Smit disentangled himself gently from Father's genealogical inquiries and followed me upstairs.

'Mealtimes,' he said. 'That's a favorite hour for a raid. Also the middle of the night.' He strode from room to room pointing everywhere to evidence that more than three people lived in the house. 'Watch wastebaskets and ashtrays.'

He paused in a bedroom door. 'If the raid comes at night they must not only take their sheets and blankets but get the mattress turned. That's the S. D.'s favorite trick – feeling for a warm spot on a bed.'

Mr Smit stayed for lunch. There were eleven of us at the table that day, including a Jewish lady who had arrived the night before and a Gentile woman and her small daughter, members of our underground, who acted as 'escorts.' The three of them were leaving for a farm in Brabant right after lunch.

Betsie had just passed around a stew so artfully prepared you scarcely missed the meat when, without warning,

Mr Smit leaned back in his chair and pushed the button below the window.

Above us the buzzer sounded. People sprang to their feet, snatching up glasses and plates, scrambling for the stairs, while the cat clawed halfway up the curtain in consternation. Cries of 'Faster!' 'Not so loud!' and 'You're spilling it!' reached us as Father, Betsie, and I hastily rearranged table and chairs to look like a lunch for three in progress.

'No, leave my place,' Mr Smit instructed. 'Why shouldn't you have a guest for lunch? The lady and the little girl could have stayed too.'

At last we were seated again and silence reigned upstairs. The whole process had taken four minutes.

A little later we were all gathered again around the dining room table. Mr Smit set out before him the incriminating evidence he had found: two spoons and a piece of carrot on the stairs, pipe ashes in an 'unoccupied' bedroom. Everyone looked at Eusie who blushed to the tips of his large ears.

'Also those,' he pointed to the hats of mother and daughter still dangling from the pegs on the dining room wall. 'If you have to hide, stop and think what you arrived with. Besides which, you're all simply too slow.'

The next night I sounded the alarm again and this time we shaved a minute thirty-three seconds off our run. By our fifth trial we were down to two minutes. We never did achieve Pickwick's ideal of under a minute, but with practice we learned to jump up from whatever we were doing and get those who had to hide into the secret room in seventy seconds. Father, Toos, and I worked on 'stalling techniques' which we would use if the Gestapo came through the shop door; Betsie invented a similar strategy for the side door. With these delaying tactics we hoped we could gain a life-saving seventy ticks of a second hand.

Because the drills struck so close to the fear which haunted each of our guests – never spoken, always present – we tried to keep these times from becoming altogether serious. 'Like a game!' we'd tell each other: 'a race to beat our own record!' One of our group owned the bakery in the next street. Early in the month I would deposit a supply of sugar coupons with

him. Then when I decided it was time for a drill I would go
to him for a bag of cream puffs – an inexpressible treat in
those sweetless days – to be secreted in my workbench and
brought out as a reward for a successful practice.

Each time the order of cream puffs was larger. For by now,
in addition to the workers whom we wanted to initiate into
the system, we had three more permanent boarders: Thea
Dacosta, Meta Monsanto, and Mary Itallie.

Mary Itallie, at seventy-six the oldest of our guests, was
also the one who posed the greatest problem. The moment
Mary stepped through our door I heard the asthmatic wheezing which had made other hosts unwilling to take her in.

Since her ailment compromised the safety of the others,
we took up the problem in caucus. The seven most concerned
– Eusie, Jop, Henk, Leendert, Meta, Thea, and Mary
herself – joined Father, Betsie, and me in Tante Jans's
front room.

'There is no sense in pretending,' I began. 'Mary has a
difficulty – especially after climbing stairs – that could put
you all in danger.'

In the silence that followed, Mary's labored breathing
seemed especially loud.

'Can I speak?' Eusie asked.

'Of course.'

'It seems to me that we're all here in your house because
of some difficulty or other. We're the orphan children – the
ones nobody else wanted. Any one of us is jeopardizing all
the others. I vote that Mary stay.'

'Good,' said lawyer Henk, 'let's put it to the vote.'

Hands began rising but Mary was struggling to speak.
'Secret ballots,' she brought out at last. 'No one should be
embarrassed.'

Henk brought a sheet of paper from the desk in the
next room and tore it into nine small strips. 'You too,' he
said, handing ballots to Betsie, Father, and me. 'If we're
discovered, you suffer the same as us.'

He handed around pencils. 'Mark "No" if it's too great a
risk, "Yes" if you think she belongs here.'

For a moment pencils scratched, then Henk collected the

folded ballots. He opened them in silence, then reached over and dropped them into Mary's lap.

Nine little scraps of paper, nine times the word, 'Yes.'

And so our 'family' was formed. Others stayed with us a day or a week, but these seven remained, the nucleus of our happy household.

That it could have been happy, at such a time and in such circumstances, was largely a tribute to Betsie. Because our guests' physical lives were so very restricted, evenings under Betsie's direction became the door to the wide world. Sometimes we had concerts, with Leendert on the violin, and Thea, a truly accomplished musician, on the piano. Or Betsie would announce 'an evening of Vondel' (the Dutch Shakespeare), with each of us reading a part. One night a week she talked Eusie into giving Hebrew lessons, another night Meta taught Italian.

The evening's activity had to be kept brief because the city now had electricity only a short while each night, and candles had to be hoarded for emergencies. When the lamps flickered and dimmed we would wind back to the dining room where my bicycle was set up on its stand. One of us would climb onto it, the others taking chairs, and then while the rider pedaled furiously to make the headlight glow bright, someone would pick up the chapter from the night before. We changed cyclist and reader often as legs or voice grew tired, reading our way through histories, novels, plays.

Father always went upstairs after prayers at 9:15, but the rest of us lingered, reluctant to break the circle, sorry to see the evening end. 'Oh well,' Eusie would say hopefully as we started at last to our rooms, 'maybe there'll be a drill tonight! I haven't had a cream puff in nearly a week . . .'

8

Storm Clouds Gather

If evenings were pleasant, daytimes grew increasingly tense.
We were too big; the group was too large, the web too
widespread. For a year and a half now we had got away
with our double lives. Ostensibly we were still an elderly
watchmaker living with his two spinster daughters above
his tiny shop. In actuality the Beje was the center of an
underground ring that spread now to the farthest corners
of Holland. Here daily came dozens of workers, reports,
appeals. Sooner or later we were going to make a mistake.

It was mealtimes especially when I worried. There were
so many now for every meal that we had to set the chairs
diagonally around the dining room table. The cat loved this
arrangement. Eusie had given him the Hebrew name 'Maher
Shalal Hashbaz,' meaning appropriately enough, 'hastening to
the spoils, hurrying to the prey.' With the chairs set so close
M. S. Hashbaz could circle the entire table on our shoulders,
purring furiously, traveling round and round.

But I was uneasy at being so many. The dining room was
only five steps above street-level; a tall passerby could see
right in the window. We'd hung a white curtain across it
providing a kind of screen while letting in light. Still, only
when the heavy blackout shades were drawn at night did I
feel truly private.

At lunch one day, looking through the thin curtain I thought
I saw a figure standing just outside in the alley. When I
looked again a minute later it was still there. There was
no reason for anyone to linger there unless he was curious

about what went on in the Beje. I got up and parted the curtain an inch.

Standing a few feet away, seemingly immobilized by some terrible emotion was old Katrien from Nollie's house!

I bolted down the stairs, threw open the door, and pulled her inside. Although the August day was hot, the old lady's hands were cold as ice. 'Katrien! What are you doing here? Why were you just standing there?'

'She's gone mad?' she sobbed. 'Your sister's gone mad!'

'Nollie? Oh, what's happened!'

'They came!' she said. 'The S. D.! I don't know what they knew or who told them. Your sister and Annaliese were in the living room and I heard her!' The sobs broke out again. 'I heard her!'

'Heard what?' I nearly screamed.

'Heard what she told them! They pointed at Annaliese and said, "Is she a Jew?" And your sister said, "Yes."'

I felt my knees go weak. Annaliese, blonde, beautiful young Annaliese with the perfect papers. And she'd trusted us! Oh Nollie, Nollie, what has your rigid honesty done! 'And then?' I asked.

'I don't know. I ran out the back door. She's gone mad!'

I left Katrien in the dining room, wheeled my bicycle down the stairs and bumped as fast as I could the mile and a half to Nollie's. Today the sky did not seem larger above the Wagenweg. At the corner of Bos en Hoven Straat I leaned my bike against a lamppost and stood panting, my heart throbbing in my throat. Then, as casually as I was able, I strolled up the sidewalk toward the house. Except for a car parked at the street curb directly in front, everything looked deceptively normal. I walked past. Not a sound from behind the white curtains. Nothing to distinguish this house from the replicas of it on either side.

When I got to the corner I turned around. At that moment the door opened and Nollie came out. Behind her walked a man in a brown business suit. A minute later a second man appeared, half-pulling, half supporting Annaliese. The young woman's face was white as chalk; twice before they reached the car I thought she would faint. The car doors slammed, the motor roared, and they were gone.

I pedaled back to the Beje fighting back tears of anxiety. Nollie, we soon learned, had been taken to the police station around the corner, to one of the cells in back. But Annaliese had been sent to the old Jewish theater in Amsterdam from which Jews were transported to extermination camps in Germany and Poland.

It was Mietje, stooped, care-worn little Mietje whose offer of help we had discounted, who kept us in touch with Nollie. She was in wonderful spirits, Mietje said, singing hymns and songs in her high sweet soprano.

How could she sing when she had betrayed another human being! Meitje delivered the bread that Betsie baked for Nollie each morning, and the blue sweater Nollie asked for, her favorite, with flowers embroidered over the pocket.

Mietje relayed another message from Nollie, one especially for me: 'No ill will happen to Annaliese. God will not let them take her to Germany. He will not let her suffer because I obeyed Him.'

Six days after Nollie's arrest, the telephone rang. Pickwick's voice was on the other end. 'I wonder, my dear, if I could trouble you to deliver that watch yourself?'

A message, then, that he could not relay over the phone. I biked at once out to Aerdenhout, taking along a man's watch for safe measure.

Pickwick waited until we were in the drawing room with the door shut. 'The Jewish theater in Amsterdam was broken into last night. Forty Jews were rescued. One of them – a young woman – was most insistent that Nollie know: "Annaliese is free."'

He fixed me with one of his wide-set eyes. 'Do you understand this message?'

I nodded, too overcome with relief and joy to speak. How had Nollie known? How had she been so sure?

After ten days in the Haarlem jail, Nollie was transferred to the federal prison in Amsterdam.

Pickwick said that the German doctor in charge of the

prison hospital was a humane man who occasionally arranged a medical discharge. I went at once to Amsterdam to see him. But what could I say, I wondered, as I waited in the entrance hall of his home. How could I get into the good graces of this man?

Lolling about the foyer sniffing from time to time at my legs and hands, were three perfectly huge Doberman pinschers. I remembered the book we were reading aloud by bicycle lamp, *How to Win Friends and Influence People*. One of the techniques advocated by Dale Carnegie was: find the man's hobby. Hobby, dogs . . . I wonder . . .

At last the maid returned and showed me into a small sitting room. 'How smart of you, Doctor!' I said in German to the grizzle-haired man on the sofa.

'Smart?'

'Yes, to bring these lovely dogs with you. They must be good company when you have to be away from your family.'

The doctor's face brightened. 'You like dogs then?'

About the only dogs I had ever known were Harry de Vries' bulldogs. 'Bulls are my favorite. Do you like bulls?'

'People don't realize it,' the doctor said eagerly, 'but bulldogs are very affectionate.'

For perhaps ten minutes, while I racked my brain for everything I had ever heard or read on the subject, we talked about dogs. Then abruptly the doctor stood up. 'But I'm sure you haven't come here to talk about dogs. What's on your mind?'

I met his eye. 'I have a sister in prison here in Amsterdam. I was wondering if . . . I don't think she's well.'

The doctor smiled. 'So, you aren't interested in dogs at all.'

'I'm interested now,' I said, smiling too. 'But I'm far more interested in my sister.'

'What's her name?'

'Nollie van Woerden.'

The doctor went out of the room and came back with a brown notebook. 'Yes. One of the recent arrivals. Tell me something about her. What is she in prison for?'

Taking a chance, I told the doctor that Nollie's crime had

been hiding a Jew. I also told him that she was the mother of six children, who if left without aid could become a burden to the State. (I did not mention that the youngest of these children was now seventeen.)

'Well, we'll see.' He walked to the door of the sitting room. 'You must excuse me now.'

I was more encouraged than at any time since Nollie's arrest as I rode the train back to Haarlem. But days, then a week, then two weeks passed and there was no further news. I went back to Amsterdam. 'I've come to see how those Dobermans are,' I told the doctor.

He was not amused. 'You mustn't bother me. I know that you have not come to talk about dogs. You must give me time.'

So there was nothing to do but wait.

It was a bright September noon when seventeen of us were squeezed around the dining room table. All of a sudden Nils, seated across from me, turned pale. Nils, one of our workers, had come to report old Katrien safely arrived at a farm north of Alkmaar. Now Nils spoke in a low normal voice.

'Do not turn around. Someone is looking over the curtain.'

Over the curtain! But – that was impossible! He'd have to be ten feet high. The table fell silent.

'He's on a ladder, washing the window,' Nils said.

'I didn't order the windows washed,' said Betsie.

Whoever it was, we mustn't sit here in this frozen, guilty silence! Eusie had an inspiration. 'Happy Birthday!' he sang. 'Happy Birthday to you!' We all got the idea and joined in lustily. 'Happy Birthday, dear Opa . . .,' the song was still echoing through the Beje when I went out the side door and stood next to the ladder, looking up at the man holding bucket and sponge.

'What are you doing? We didn't want the windows washed. Especially not during the party!'

The man took a piece of paper from his hip pocket and consulted it. 'Isn't this Kuiper's?'

'They're across the street. But – anyhow, come in and help

us celebrate.' The man shook his head. He thanked me, but he had work to do. I watched him crossing the Barteljorisstraat with his ladder to Kuiper's candy store.

'Did it work?' a clamor of voices asked when I got back to the dining room. 'Do you think he was spying?'

I didn't answer. I didn't know.

That was the hardest. Never knowing. And one of the biggest unknowns was my own performance under questioning. As long as I was awake I felt fairly sure of myself. But if they should come at night . . . Over and over again the group worked with me – Nils, Henk, Leendert – bursting into my room without warning, shaking me awake, hurling questions at me.

The first time it happened I was sure the real raid had come. There was a terrific pounding on my door, then the beam of a flashlight in my eyes. 'Get up! On your feet!' I could not see the man who was speaking.

'Where are you hiding your nine Jews?'

'We have only six Jews now.'

There was an awful silence. The room light came on to show Rolf clutching his head with his hands. 'Oh no. Oh no,' he kept saying. 'It can't be that bad.'

'Think now,' said Henk just behind him. 'The Gestapo is trying to trap you. The answer is, "What Jews! We don't have Jews here."'

'Can I try again?'

'Not now,' said Rolf. 'You're wide-awake now.'

They tried again a few nights later. 'The Jews you're hiding, where do they come from?'

I sat up groggily. 'I don't know. They just come to the door.'

Rolf flung his hat to the floor. 'No, no, no!' he shouted. '"What Jews! There are no Jews!" Can't you learn?'

'I'll learn,' I promised. 'I'll do better.'

And sure enough the next time I woke a little more completely. Half a dozen shadowy forms filled the room. 'Where do you hide the ration cards?' a voice demanded.

Under the bottom stair, of course. But this time I would

not be trapped into saying so. A crafty reply occurred to me:
'In the Frisian clock on the stairwell!'

Kik sat down beside me on the bed and put an arm around
me. 'That was better, Tante Corrie,' he said. 'You tried, this
time. But remember – you *have* no cards except the three for
you, Opa, and Tante Betsie. There *is* no underground activity
here, you don't understand what they're talking about . . .'

Gradually, with repeated drills, I got better. Still, when
the time actually came, when they were real Gestapo agents
really trained in getting the truth from people, how would I
perform?

Willem's underground work brought him frequently to Haarlem.
There was an expression of something like despair mingled
now with the worry lines in his face. Twice soldiers had been
to the nursing home, and although he had managed to deceive
them about most of the Jews still in residence there, one sick
blind old woman had been taken away.

'Ninety-one!' Willem kept saying. 'She couldn't even walk
– they had to carry her to the car.'

So far, Willem's position as a minister had prevented direct
action against him and Tine, but he was watched, he said,
more closely than ever. To provide an official reason for
his visits to Haarlem he started conducting a weekly prayer
fellowship at the Beje each Wednesday morning.

But Willem could do nothing routinely – especially pray –
and soon the meeting was attended by dozens of Haarlemers
hungry for something to believe in, this fourth year of
the occupation. Most of those coming to the services had
no idea of the double life of the Beje. In a way they
posed a fresh danger as they passed workers and cou-
riers from other underground groups coming and going
on the narrow stairs. But in another way, we thought,
it might be an advantage to have these flocks of obviously innocent people in and out. That, at least, was our
hope.

We were sitting around the supper table after curfew one
night, three ten Booms, the seven 'permanent guests,' and

two Jews for whom we were seeking homes, when the shop doorbell chimed.

A customer after closing? And one bold enough to stand on the Barteljorisstraat after curfew? Taking the keys from my pocket I hurried down to the hall, unlocked the workshop door, and felt my way through the dark store. At the front door I listened a moment.

'Who's there?' I called.

'Do you remember me?'

A man's voice speaking German. 'Who is it?' I asked in the same language.

'An old friend, come for a visit. Open the door!'

I fumbled with the lock and drew the door gingerly back. It was a German soldier in uniform. Before I could reach the alarm button behind the door, he had pushed his way inside. Then he took off his hat and in the October twilight I recognized the young German watchmaker whom Father had discharged four years ago.

'Otto!' I cried.

'Captain Altschuler,' he corrected me. 'Our positions are slightly reversed, Miss ten Boom, are they not?'

I glanced at his insignia. He was not a captain or anything close to it, but I said nothing. He looked around the shop.

'Same stuffy little place,' he said. He reached for the wall switch, but I put my hand over it.

'No! We don't have blackout shades in the shop!'

'Well, let's go upstairs where we can talk over old times. That old clock cleaner still around?'

'Christoffels? He died in the fuel shortage last winter.'

Otto shrugged. 'Good riddance then! What about the pious old Bible reader?'

I was edging my way to the sales counter where another bell was located. 'Father is very well, thank you.'

'Well, aren't you going to invite me up to pay my respects?'

Why was he so eager to go upstairs? Had the wretched fellow come just to gloat, or did he suspect something? My finger found the button.

'What was that!' Otto whirled around suspiciously.

'What was what?'

'That sound! I heard a kind of buzzing.'

'I didn't hear anything.'

But Otto had started back through the workshop

'Wait!' I shouted. 'Let me get the front door locked and I'll go up with you! I – I want to see how long it takes them to recognize you.'

I dawdled at the door as long as I dared: definitely his suspicions were aroused. Then I followed him through the rear door into the hall. Not a sound from the dining room or the stairs. I dashed past him up the steps and rapped on the door.

'Father! Betsie!' I cried in what I hoped as a playful voice. 'I'll give you three – no, uh – six guesses who's standing here!'

'No guessing games!' Otto reached past me and flung open the door.

Father and Betsie looked up from their meal. The table was set for three, my unfinished plate on the other side. It was so perfect that even I, who had just seen twelve people eating here, could scarcely believe this was anything hut an innocent old man dining with his daughters. The 'Alpina' sign stood on the sideboard: they had remembered everything.

Uninvited, Otto pulled out a chair. 'Well!' he crowed. 'Things happened just like I said, didn't they?'

'So it would seem,' said Father mildly.

'Betsie,' I said, 'give Captain Altschuler some tea!'

Otto took a sip of the brew Betsie poured him and glared round the table at us. 'Where did you get real tea! No one else in Holland has tea.'

How stupid of me. The tea had come from Pickwick.

'If you must know,' I said, 'it comes from a German officer. But you mustn't ask any further questions.' I tried to imply clandestine dealings with a high occupation official.

Otto lingered another fifteen minutes. And then, feeling perhaps that he had underlined his victory sufficiently, sauntered out into the empty streets.

It was only after another half-hour that we dared give the all clear to nine cramped and shaky people.

*   *   *

The second week in October, during a particularly hectic morning with underground problems, the secret telephone number rang downstairs in the hall. I hurried down to pick it up; only Father, Betsie, or I ever answered it.

'Well!' said a voice. 'Aren't you coming to pick me up?'

It was Nollie.

'Nollie! When – How – Where are you?'

'At the train station in Amsterdam! Only I have no money for the trainfare.'

'Stay right there! Oh, Nollie, we're coming!'

I biked to Bos en Hoven Straat and then with Flip and the children who happened to be at home, hurried to the Haarlem station. We saw Nollie even before our train came to a stop in Amsterdam – her bright blue sweater like a patch of blue sky in the big dark shed.

Seven weeks in prison had left her pallid-faced, but as radiantly Nollie as ever. A prison doctor, she said, had pronounced her low blood pressure a serious condition, one that might leave her permanently disabled and her six children a burden to society. Her face wrinkled in puzzlement as she said it.

Christmas, 1943, was approaching. The light snow which had fallen was the only festive quality of the season. Every family it seemed had someone in jail, in a work camp, or in hiding. For once the religious side of the holidays was uppermost in every mind.

At the Beje, we had not only Christmas to celebrate but also Hanukkah, the Jewish 'Festival of Lights.' Betsie found a Hanukkah candlestand among the treasures stored with us behind the dining room cupboard and set it up on the upright piano. Each night we lighted one more candle as Eusie read the story of the Maccabees. Then we would sing, haunting, melancholy desert music. We were all very Jewish those evenings.

About the fifth night of the Festival, as we were gathered round the piano, the doorbell in the alley rang. I opened it to find Mrs Beukers, wife of the optician next door, standing in the snow. Mrs Beukers was as round and placid as her

husband was thin and worried, but tonight her plump face
was twisted with anxiety.

'Do you think,' she whispered, 'your Jews could sing a little
more softly? We can hear them right through the walls and –
well, there are all kinds of people on this street . . .'

Back in Tante Jans's rooms we considered this news in
consternation. If the Beukers family knew all about our affairs,
how many other people in Haarlem did too?

It wasn't long before we discovered that one who did was
the chief of police himself. One dark January morning when
it was trying to snow again, Toos burst into underground
'headquarters' in Tante's Jans's rear room clutching a letter in
her hand. The envelope bore the seal of the Haarlem police.

I tore it open. Inside, on the police chief's stationery, was
a handwritten note. I read it silently, then aloud.

'You will come to my office this afternoon at three o'clock.'

For twenty minutes we tried to analyze that note. Some
felt it was not a prelude to arrest. Why would the police
give you a chance to escape? Still, it was safest to prepare for search and imprisonment. Workers slipped out of
the house, one at a time. Boarders emptied wastebaskets
and picked up scraps of sewing in preparation for a quick
flight to the secret room. I burned incriminating papers
in the long-empty coal hearth in the dining room. The
cat caught the tension in the air and sulked beneath the
sideboard.

Then I took a bath, perhaps the last for months, and packed
a prison bag according to what Nollie and others had learned:
a Bible, a pencil, needle and thread, soap – or what we
called soap these days – toothbrush, and comb. I dressed
in my warmest clothes with several sets of underwear and
a second sweater beneath the top one. Just before 3:00 I
hugged Father and Betsie tight, and walked through the gray
slush to the Smedestraat.

The policeman on duty was an old acquaintance. He looked
at the letter, then at me with a curious expression. 'This way,'
he said.

He knocked at a door marked 'Chief.' The man who sat
behind the desk had red-gray hair combed forward over a

bald spot. A radio was playing. The chief reached over and twisted the volume knob not down but up.

'Miss ten Boom,' he said. 'Welcome.'

'How do you do, Sir.'

The chief had left his desk to shut the door behind me. 'Do sit down,' he said. 'I know all about you, you know. About your work.'

'The watchmaking you mean. You're probably thinking more about my father's work than my own.'

The chief smiled. 'No, I mean your 'other' work.'

'Ah, then you're referring to my work with retarded children? Yes. Let me tell you about that — '

'No, Miss ten Boom,' the chief lowered his voice. 'I am not talking about your work with retarded children. I'm talking about still another work, and I want you to know that some of us here are in sympathy.'

The chief was smiling broadly now. Tentatively I smiled back. 'Now, Miss ten Boom,' he went on, 'I have a request.'

The chief sat down on the edge of his desk and looked at me steadily. He dropped his voice until it was just audible. He was, he said, working with the underground himself. But an informer in the police department was leaking information to the Gestapo. 'There's no way for us to deal with this man but to kill him.'

A shudder went down my spine.

'What alternative have we?' the chief went on in a whisper. 'We can't arrest him — there are no prisons except those controlled by the Germans. But if he remains at large many others will die. That is why I wondered, Miss ten Boom, if in your work *you* might know of someone who could — '

'Kill him?'

'Yes.'

I leaned back. Was this all a trap to trick me into admitting the existence of a group, into naming names?

'Sir,' I said at last, seeing the chief's eyes flicker impatiently, 'I have always believed that it was my role to save life, not destroy it. I understand your dilemma, however, and I have a suggestion. Are you a praying man?'

'Aren't we all, these days?'

'Then let us pray together now that God will reach the heart of this man so that he does not continue to betray his countrymen.'

There was a long pause. Then the chief nodded. 'That I would very much like to do.'

And so there in the heart of the police station, with the radio blaring out the latest news of the German advance, we prayed. We prayed that this Dutchman would come to realize his worth in the sight of God and the worth of every other human being on earth.

At the end of the prayer the chief stood up. 'Thank you, Miss ten Boom.' He shook my hand. 'Thank you again. I know now that it was wrong to ask you.'

Still clutching my prison bag, I walked through the foyer and around the corner to the Beje.

Upstairs, people crowded around wanting to know everything. But I did not tell them. Not everything – I did not want Father and Betsie to know that we had been asked to kill. It would have been an unnecessary burden for them to bear.

The episode with the chief of police should have been encouraging. Apparently we had friends in high places. As a matter of fact the news had the opposite effect upon us. Here was one more illustration of how our secret was no secret at all. All of Haarlem seemed to know what we were up to.

We knew we should stop the work, but how could we? Who would keep open the network of supplies and information on which the safety of hundreds depended? If a hideaway had to be abandoned, as happened all the time, who would coordinate the move to another address? We had to go on, but we knew that disaster could not be long in coming.

As a matter of fact, it came first to Jop, the seventeen-year-old apprentice who had sought a safe home at the Beje.

Late one afternoon near the end of January, 1944, Rolf stepped stealthily into the workshop. He glanced at Jop. I nodded: Jop was party to everything that went on in the house.

'There's an underground home in Ede that is going to be raided this evening. Do you have anyone who can go?'

But I did not. Not a single courier or escort person was at the Beje this late in the day.

'I'll go,' Jop said.

I opened my mouth to protest that he was inexperienced, and liable to the factory transport himself if stopped on the street. Then I thought of the unsuspecting people at Ede. We had a wardrobe of girls' scarves and dresses upstairs . . .

'Then quickly, boy,' Rolf said. 'You must leave immediately.' He gave Jop the details and hurried away. In a few moments Jop reappeared, making a very pretty brunette in long coat and kerchief, a fur muff hiding his hands. Did the lad have some kind of premonition? To my astonishment he turned at the door and kissed me.

Jop was supposed to be back by the 7:00 P.M. curfew. Seven came and went. Perhaps he had been delayed and would return in the morning.

We did have a visitor early the next day but it was not Jop. I knew the minute Rolf stepped through the door that bad news was weighing him down.

'It's Jop, isn't it?'

'Yes.'

'What happened?'

Rolf had learned the story from the sergeant at the night desk. When Jop got to the address in Ede the Gestapo was already there. Jop had rung the bell; the door opened. Pretending to be the owner of the house, the S.D. man had invited Jop in.

'And Corrie,' Rolf said, 'we must face it. The Gestapo will get information out of Jop. They have already taken him to Amsterdam. How long will he be able to hold his tongue.

Once again we considered stopping the work. Once again we discovered we could not.

That night Father and Betsie and I prayed long after the others had gone to bed. We knew that in spite of daily mounting risks we had no choice but to move forward. This was evil's hour: we could not run away from it. Perhaps only when human effort had done its best and failed, would God's power alone be free to work.

9

The Raid

At the sound of someone in my room I opened my eyes painfully. It was Eusie, carrying up his bedding and night clothes to store in the secret room. Behind him came Mary and Thea with their bundles.

I shut my eyes again. It was the morning of February 28, 1944. For two days I had been in bed with influenza. My head throbbed, my joints were on fire. Every little sound, Mary's wheeze, the scrape of the secret panel, made me want to shriek. I heard Henk and Meta come in, then Eusie's laugh as he handed the day things out to the others through the low door.

Go away all of you! Leave me alone! I bit my lip to keep from saying it.

At last they collected their clothes and belongings and trooped out, closing the door behind them. Where was Leendert? Why hadn't he come up? Then I remembered that Leendert was away for a few days setting up electrical warning systems like ours in several of our host homes. I drifted back into a feverish sleep.

The next thing I knew, Betsie was standing at the foot of the bed, a steaming cup of herb tea in her hand. 'I'm sorry to wake you, Corrie. But there's a man down in the shop who insists he will talk only to you.'

'Who is he?'

'He says he's from Ermelo. I've never seen him before.'

I sat up shakily. 'That's all right. I have to get up anyway. Tomorrow the new ration cards come.'

I sipped the scalding tea, then struggled to my feet. There by the bed lay my prison bag, packed and ready as it had been since the summons from the chief of police. In fact I'd been adding to it. Besides the Bible, clothing, and toilet things, it now held vitamins, aspirins, iron pills for Betsie's anemia and much else. It had become a kind of talisman for me, a safeguard against the terrors of prison.

I got slowly into my clothes and stepped out onto the landing. The house seemed to reel around me. I crept down, clinging to the handrail. At the door to Tante Jans's rooms I was surprised to hear voices. I looked in. Of course, I'd forgotten. It was Wednesday morning, people were gathering for Willem's weekly service. I saw Nollie passing around 'occupation coffee' as we called the current brew of roots and dried figs. Peter was already at the piano, as he was most weeks to provide the music. I continued down around the stairs, passing new arrivals streaming up.

As I arrived, wobble-kneed, in the shop, a small sandy-haired man sprang forward to meet me. 'Miss ten Boom!'

'Yes?' There was an old Dutch expression: you can tell a man by the way he meets your eyes. This man seemed to concentrate somewhere between my nose and my chin. 'Is it about a watch?' I asked.

'No, Miss ten Boom, something far more serious!' His eyes seemed to make a circle around my face. 'My wife has just been arrested. We've been hiding Jews, you see. If she is questioned, all of our lives are in danger.'

'I don't know how *I* can help,' I said.

'I need six hundred guilders. There's a policeman at the station in Ermelo who can be bribed for that amount. I'm a poor man – and I've been told you have certain contacts.'

'Contacts?'

'Miss ten Boom! It's a matter of life and death! If I don't get it right away she'll be taken to Amsterdam and then it will be too late.'

Something about the man's behavior made me hesitate. And yet how could I risk being wrong? 'Come back in half an hour. I'll have the money,' I said.

For the first time the man's eyes met mine.

'I'll never forget this,' he said.

The amount was more than we had at the Beje so I sent Toos to the bank with instructions to hand the man the money, but not to volunteer any information.

Then I struggled back up the stairs. Where ten minutes earlier I'd been burning with fever, now I was shaking with cold. I stopped at Tante Jans's rooms just long enough to take a briefcase of papers from the desk. Then with apologies to Willem and the others I continued to my room. I undressed again, refilled the vaporizer where it was hissing on its small spirit-stove, and climbed back into bed. For a while I tried to concentrate on the names and addresses in the briefcase. Five cards needed this month in Zandvoort. None in Overveen. We would need eighteen in . . . The flu roared behind my eyes, the papers swam in front of me. The briefcase slipped from my hand and I was asleep.

In my fevered dream a buzzer kept ringing. On and on it went. Why wouldn't it stop? Feet were running, voices whispering, 'Hurry! Hurry!'

I sat bolt upright. People were running past my bed. I turned just in time to see Thea's heels disappear through the low door. Meta was behind her, then Henk.

But – I hadn't planned a drill for today! Who in the world – unless – unless it wasn't a drill. Eusie dashed past me, white-faced, his pipe rattling in the ashtray that he carried in shaking hands.

And at last it penetrated my numbed brain that the emergency had come. One, two, three people already in the secret room; four as Eusie's black shoes and scarlet socks disappeared. But Mary – where was Mary? The old woman appeared in the bedroom door, mouth open, gasping for air. I sprang from my bed and half-pulled, half-shoved her across the room.

I was sliding the secret panel down behind her when a slim white-haired man burst into the room. I recognized him from Pickwick's, someone high in the national Resistance. I'd no idea he was in the house. He dived after Mary. Five, six. Yes, that was right with Leendert away.

The man's legs vanished and I dropped the panel down and leapt back into bed. Below I heard doors slamming, heavy footsteps on the stairs. But it was another sound that turned my blood to water: the strangling, grating rasp of Mary's breathing.

'Lord Jesus!' I prayed. 'You have the power to heal! Heal Mary now!'

And then my eye fell on the briefcase, stuffed with names and addresses. I snatched it up, yanked up the sliding door again, flung the case inside, shoved the door down and pushed my prison bag up against it. I had just reached the bed again when the bedroom door flew open.

'What's your name?'

I sat up slowly and – I hoped – sleepily.

'What?'

'Your name!'

'Cornelia ten Boom.' The man was tall and heavy-set with a strange, pale face. He wore an ordinary blue business suit. He turned and shouted down the stairs, 'We've got one more up here, Willemse.'

He turned back to me. 'Get up! Get dressed!'

As I crawled out from under the covers, the man took a slip of paper from his pocket and consulted it. 'So you're the ring leader!' He looked at me with new interest. 'Tell me now, where are you hiding the Jews?'

'I don't know what you're talking about.'

The man laughed. 'And you don't know anything about an underground ring, either. We'll see about that!'

He had not taken his eyes off me, so I began to pull on my clothes over my pyjamas, ears straining for a sound from the secret room.

'Let me see your papers!'

I pulled out the little sack that I wore around my neck. When I took out my identification folder, a roll of bills fell out with it. The man stooped, snatched up the money from the floor, and stuffed it into his pocket. Then he took my papers and looked at them. For a moment the room was silent. Mary Itallie's wheeze – why wasn't I hearing it?

The man threw the papers back at me. 'Hurry up!'

But he was not in half the hurry I was to get away from that room. I buttoned my sweater all wrong in my haste and stuffed my feet into my shoes without bothering to tie them. Then I was about to reach for my prison bag.

Wait.

It stood where I had shoved it in my panic: directly in front of the secret panel. If I were to reach down under the shelf to get it now, with this man watching my every move, might not his attention be attracted to the last place on earth I wanted him to look?

It was the hardest thing I had ever done to turn and walk out of that room, leaving the bag behind.

I stumbled down the stairs, my knees shaking as much from fear as from flu. A uniformed soldier was stationed in front of Tante Jans's rooms; the door was shut. I wondered if the prayer meeting had ended, if Willem and Nollie and Peter had got away. Or were they all still in there? How many innocent people might be involved?

The man behind me gave me a little push and I hurried on down the stairs to the dining room. Father, Betsie, and Toos were sitting on chairs pulled back against the wall. Beside them sat three underground workers who must have arrived since I had gone upstairs. On the floor beneath the window, broken in three pieces, lay the 'Alpina' sign. Someone had managed to knock it from the sill.

A second Gestapo agent in plain clothes was pawing eagerly through a pile of silver rijksdaalders and jewelry heaped on the dining room table. It was the cache from the space behind the corner cupboard: it had been indeed the first place they looked.

'Here's the other one listed at the address,' said the man who had brought me down. 'My information says she's the leader of the whole outfit.'

The man at the table, the one called Willemse, glanced at me, then turned back to the loot in front of him. 'You know what to do, Kapteyn.'

Kapteyn seized me by the elbow and shoved me ahead of him down the remaining five steps and into the rear of the shop. Another soldier in uniform stood guard just inside this

door. Kapteyn prodded me through to the front room and
pushed me against the wall.

'Where are the Jews?'

'There aren't any Jews here.'

The man struck me hard across the face.

'Where do you hide the ration cards?'

'I don't know what you're — '

Kapteyn hit me again. I staggered up against the astronomical clock. Before I could recover he slapped me again,
then again, and again, stinging blows that jerked my head
backward.

'Where are the Jews?'

Another blow.

'Where is your secret room?'

I tasted blood in my mouth. My head spun, my ears rang
– I was losing consciousness. 'Lord Jesus,' I cried out,
'protect me!'

Kapteyn's hand stopped in midair.

'If you say that name again I'll kill you!'

But instead his arm slowly dropped to his side. 'If you won't
talk, the skinny one will.'

I stumbled ahead of him up the stairs. He pushed me into
one of the chairs against the dining room wall. Through a blur
I saw him lead Betsie from the room.

Above us hammer blows and splintering wood showed
where a squad of trained searchers was probing for the
secret room. Then down in the alley the doorbell rang. But
the sign! Didn't they see the 'Alpina' sign was gone and –
I glanced at the window and caught my breath. There on
the sill, the broken pieces fitted carefully together, sat the
wooden triangle.

Too late I looked up to see Willemse staring intently at
me. 'I thought so!' he said. 'It was a signal, wasn't it?'

He ran down the stairs. Above us the hammering and the
tramp of boots had stopped. I heard the alley door open and
Willemse's voice, smooth and ingratiating.

'Come in, won't you?'

'Have you heard! 'A woman's voice. 'They've got Oom
Herman!'

Pickwick? Not Pickwick!

'Oh' I heard Willemse say. 'Who was with him?' He pumped her as hard as he could, then placed her under arrest. Blinking with fright and confusion, the woman was seated with us along the wall. I recognized her only as a person who occasionally took messages for us about the city. I stared in anguish at the sign in the window announcing to the world that all was as usual at the Beje. Our home had been turned into a trap: how many more would fall into it before this day was over! And Pickwick! Had they really caught Pickwick!

Kapteyn appeared with Betsie in the dining room door. Her lips were swollen and puffy, a bruise was darkening on her cheek. She half fell into the chair next to mine.

'Oh Betsie! He hurt you!'

'Yes.' She dabbed at the blood on her mouth. 'I feel so sorry for him.'

Kapteyn whirled, his white face even paler. 'Prisoners will remain silent!' he shrieked. Two men were clumping down the stairs and into the dining room carrying something between them. They had discovered the old radio beneath the stairs.

'Law-abiding citizens, are you?' Kapteyn went on. 'You! The old man there. I see you believe in the Bible.' He jerked his thumb at the well-worn book on its shelf. 'Tell me, what does it say in there about obeying the government?'

'"Fear God,"' Father quoted, and on his lips on that room the words came as blessing and reassurance. '"Fear God and honor the Queen."'

Kapteyn stared at him. 'It doesn't say that. The Bible doesn't say that.'

'No,' Father admitted. 'It says, "Fear God, honor the King." But in our case, that is the Queen.'

'It's not King or Queen!' roared Kapteyn. 'We're the legal government now, and you're all lawbreakers!'

The doorbell rang again. Again there were the questions and the arrest. The young man – one of our workers – had barely been assigned a chair when again the bell sounded. It seemed to me that we had never had so many callers: the dining room was getting crowded. I felt sorriest for those who had come simply on social visits. An elderly retired missionary was brought in, jaw quivering with fear. At least, from the banging and thumping above, they had not yet discovered the secret room.

A new sound made me jump. The phone down in the hall was ringing.

'That's a telephone!' cried Willemse.

He glared around the room, then grabbing me by the wrist yanked me down the stairs behind him. He thrust the receiver up against my ear but kept his own hand on it.

'Answer!' he said with his lips.

'This is the ten Boom residence and shop,' I said as stiffly as I dared.

But the person on the other end did not catch the strangeness. 'Miss ten Boom, you're in terrible danger! They've arrested Herman Sluring! They know everything! You've got to be careful!' On and on the woman's voice babbled, the man at my side hearing everything.

She had scarcely hung up when the phone rang again. A man's voice, and again the message. 'Oom Herman's been taken to the police station. That means they're on to everything . . .'

At last, the third time I repeated my formal and untypical little greeting, there was a click at the other end. Willemse snatched the earpiece from my hand.

'Hello! Hello!' he shouted. He jiggled the cradle on the wall. The line had gone dead. He shoved me back up the stairs and into my chair again. 'Our friends wised up,' he told Kapteyn. 'But I heard enough.'

Apparently Betsie had received permission to leave her chair: she was slicing bread at the sideboard. I was surprised to realize it was already lunchtime. Betsie passed the bread around the room but I shook my head. The fever was raging again. My throat ached and my head throbbed.

A man appeared in the doorway. 'We've searched the whole place, Willemse,' he said. 'If there's a secret room here, the devil himself built it.'

Willemse looked from Betsie to Father to me. 'There's a secret room,' he said quietly. 'And people are using it or they would have admitted it. All right. We'll set a guard around the house till they've turned to mummies.'

In the hush of horror which followed there was a gentle pressure on my knees. Maher Shalal Hashbaz had jumped up into my lap to rub against me. I stroked the shining black fur. What would become of him now? I would not let myself think about the six people upstairs.

It had been half an hour since the doorbell had last rung. Whoever had caught my message over the phone must have spread the alarm. Word was out: no one else would walk into the trap at the Beje.

Apparently Willemse had come to the same conclusion because abruptly he ordered us on our feet and down to the hallway with our coats and hats. Father, Betsie, and me he held in the dining room till last. In front of us down the stairs came the people from Tante Jan's rooms. I held my breath scanning them. Apparently most of those at the prayer service had left before the raid. But by no means all. Here came Nollie, behind her, Peter. Last in the line came Willem.

The whole family then. Father, all four of his children, one grandchild. Kapteyn gave me a shove.

'Get moving.'

Father took his tall hat from the wall peg. Outside the dining room door he paused to pull up the weights on the old Frisian clock.

'We mustn't let the clock run down,' he said.

Father! Did you really think we would be back home when next the chain ran out?

The snow had gone from the streets; puddles of dirty water stood in the gutters as we marched through the alley and into the Smedestraat. The walk took only a minute, but by the time we got inside the double doors of the police station I was shaking with cold. I looked anxiously around the foyer for Rolf and the others we knew, but saw no one. A contingent of German soldiers seemed to be supplementing the regular police force.

We were herded along a corridor and through the heavy metal door where I had last seen Harry de Vries. At the end of this hall was a large room that had obviously been a gymnasium. Windows high in the walls were covered with wire mesh; rings and basketball hoops were roped to the ceiling. Now a desk stood in the center of the room with a German officer seated behind it. Tumbling mats had been spread out to cover part of the floor and I collapsed onto one of them.

For two hours the officer took down names, addresses, and other statistics. I counted those who had been arrested with us: thirty-five people from the raid on the Beje.

People from previous arrests were sitting or lying about on the mats too, some of them faces we knew. I looked for Pickwick but he was not among them. One of them, a fellow watchmaker who often came to the Beje on business, seemed especially distressed at what had happened to us. He came and sat down beside Father and me.

At last the officer left. For the first time since the alarm buzzer sounded we could talk among ourselves. I struggled to sit up. 'Quick!' I croaked. 'We've got to agree on what to say! Most of us can simply tell the truth but — ' My voice died in my throat. It seemed to my flu-addled brain that Peter was giving me the most ferocious frown I had ever seen.

'But if they learn that Uncle Willem was teaching this morning from the Old Testament, it could make trouble for him,' Peter finished for me.

He jerked his head to one side and I clambered unsteadily to my feet. 'Tante Corrie!' he hissed when we were on the other side of the room. 'That man, the watchmaker! He's a Gestapo plant.' He patted my head as though I were a sick child. 'Lie down again, Tante Corrie. Just for heaven's sake don't do any talking.'

I was waked by the heavy door of the gym slamming open. In strode Rolf.

'Let's have it quiet in here!' he shouted. He leaned close to Willem and said something I could not hear. 'Toilets are out back,' he continued in a loud voice. 'You can go one at a time under escort.'

Willem sat down beside me. 'He says we can flush incriminating documents if we shred them fine enough.' I fumbled through my coat pockets. There were several scraps of paper and a billfold containing a few paper rijksdaalders. I went over each item, trying to think how I could explain it in a court process. Beside the row of outdoor toilets was a basin with a tin cup on a chain. Gratefully I took a long drink – the first since the tea Betsie had brought me that morning.

Towards evening a policeman carried into the gym a large basket of fresh hot rolls. I could not swallow mine. Only the water tasted good to me, though I grew embarrassed at asking again and again to be taken outside.

When I got back the last time, a group had gathered around Father for evening prayers. Every day of my life had ended like this: that deep steady voice, that sure and eager confiding of us all to the care of God. The Bible lay at home on its shelf, but much of it was stored in his heart. His blue eyes seemed to be seeing beyond the locked and crowded room, beyond Haarlem, beyond earth itself, as he quoted from memory: 'Thou art my hiding place and my shield: I hope in thy word . . . Hold thou me up, and I shall be safe . . .'

None of us slept much. Each time someone left the room he had to step over a dozen others. At last light crept through the high, screened windows at the top of the room. The police again brought rolls. As the long morning wore on I dozed with my back up against the wall; the worst pain now seemed to be in my chest. It was noon when soldiers entered the room and ordered us on our feet. Hastily we struggled into our coats and filed again through the cold corridors.

In the Smedestraat a wall of people pressed against police barricades set across the street. As Betsie and I stepped out with Father between us, a murmur of horror greeted the sight of 'Haarlem's Grand Old Man' being led to prison. In front of the door stood a green city bus with soldiers occupying the rear seats. People were climbing aboard while friends and relatives in the crowd wept or simply stared. Betsie and I gripped Father's arms to start down the steps. Then we froze. Stumbling past us between two soldiers, hatless and coatless, came Pickwick. The top of his bald head was a welter of bruises, dried blood clung to the stubble on his chin. He did not look up as he was hauled onto the bus.

Father, Betsie, and I squeezed into a double seat near the front. Through the window I caught a glimpse of Tine standing in the crowd. It was one of those radiant winter days when the air seemed to shimmer with light. The bus shuddered and started up. Police cleared a path and we inched forward. I gazed hungrily out the window, holding onto Haarlem with my eyes. Now we were crossing the Grote Markt, the walls of the great cathedral glowing a thousand shades of gray in the crystal light. In a strange way it seemed to me that I had lived through this moment before.

Then I recalled.

The vision. The night of the invasion. I had seen it all. Willem, Nollie, Pickwick, Peter – all of us here – drawn against our wills across this square. It had all been in the dream – all of us leaving Haarlem, unable to turn back. Going where?

10

Scheveningen

Outside Haarlem the bus took the south road, paralleling the sea. On our right rose the low sandy hills of the dune country, soldiers silhouetted on the ridges. Clearly we were not being taken to Amsterdam.

A two-hour drive brought us instead into the streets of The Hague. The bus stopped in front of a new, functional building; word was whispered back that this was Gestapo headquarters for all of Holland. We were marched – all but Pickwick, who seemed unable to rise out of his seat – into a large room where the endless process of taking down names, addresses, and occupations began all over again.

On the other side of the high counter running the length of the room I was startled to see both Willemse and Kapteyn. As each of the prisoners from Haarlem reached the desk, one or the other would lean forward and speak to a man seated at a typewriter and there would be a clatter of sound from the machine.

Suddenly the chief interrogator's eye fell on Father. 'That old man!' he cried. 'Did he have to be arrested? You, old man!'

Willem led Father up to the desk. The Gestapo chief leaned forward. 'I'd like to send you home, old fellow,' he said. 'I'll take your word that you won't cause any more trouble.'

I could not see Father's face, only the erect carriage of his shoulders and the halo of white hair above them. But I heard his answer.

'If I go home today,' he said evenly and clearly, 'tomorrow I will open my door again to any man in need who knocks.'

The amiability drained from the other man's face. 'Get back in line!' he shouted. '*Schnell*! This court will tolerate no more delays!'

But delays seemed all that this court existed for. As we inched along the counter there were endless repetitions of questions, endless consulting of papers, endless coming and going of officials. Outside the windows the short winter day was fading. We had not eaten since the rolls and water at dawn.

Ahead of me in line, Betsie answered, 'Unmarried,' for the twentieth time that day.

'Number of children?' droned the interrogator.

'I'm unmarried,' Betsie repeated.

The man did not even look up from his papers. 'Number of children?' he snapped.

'No children,' said Betsie resignedly.

Toward nightfall a stout little man wearing the yellow star was led past us to the far end of the room. A sound of scuffling made us all look up. The wretched man was attempting to hold onto something clutched in his hands.

'It's mine!' he kept shouting. 'You can't take it! You can't take my purse!'

What madness possessed him? What good did he imagine money would do him now? But he continued to struggle, to the obvious glee of the men around him.

'Here Jew!' I heard one of them say. He lifted his booted foot and kicked the small man in the back of his knees. 'This is how we take things from a Jew.'

It made so much noise. That was all I could think as they continued to kick him. I clutched the counter to keep from falling myself as the sounds continued. Wildly, unreasonably, I hated the man being kicked, hated him for being so helpless and so hurt. At last I heard them drag him out.

Then all at once I was standing in front of the chief questioner. I looked up and met Kapteyn's eyes, just behind him.

'This woman was the ringleader,' he said.

Through the turmoil inside me I realized it was important for the other man to believe him. 'What Mr Kapteyn says is true,' I said. 'These others – they know nothing about it. It was all my — '

'Name?' the interrogator inquired imperturbably.

'Cornelia ten Boom, and I'm the — '

'Age?'

'Fifty-two. The rest of these people had nothing to do — '

'Occupation?'

'But I've told you a dozen times!' I burst out in desperation.

'Occupation?' he repeated.

It was dark night when we were marched at last out of the building. The green bus was gone. Instead we made out the bulk of a large canvas-roofed army truck. Two soldiers had to lift Father over the tailgate. There was no sign of Pickwick. Father, Betsie, and I found places to sit on a narrow bench that ran around the sides.

The truck had no springs and bounced roughly over the bomb-pitted streets of The Hague. I slipped my arm behind Father's back to keep him from striking the edge. Willem, standing near the back, whispered back what he could see of the blacked-out city. We had left the downtown section and seemed to be headed west toward the suburb of Scheveningen. That was our destination then, the federal penitentiary named after this seaside town.

The truck jerked to a halt; we heard a screech of iron. We bumped forward a few feet and stopped again. Behind us massive gates clanged shut.

We climbed down to find ourselves in an enormous courtyard surrounded by a high brick wall. The truck had backed up to a long low building; soldiers prodded us inside. I blinked in the white glare of bright ceiling lights.

'*Nasen gegen Mauer*!' – 'Noses to the wall!'

I felt a shove from behind and found myself staring at cracked plaster. I turned my eyes as far as I could, first left and then right. There was Willem. Two places away from him, Betsie. Next to me on the other side was Toos. All like me standing with their faces to the wall. Where was Father?

There was an endless wait while the scars on the wall before my eyes became faces, landscapes, animal shapes. Then somewhere to the right a door opened.

'Women prisoners follow me!'

The matron's voice sounded as metallic as the squealing door. As I stepped away from the wall I glanced swiftly round the room for Father. There he was – a few feet out from the wall, seated in a straight-backed chair. One of the guards must have brought it for him.

Already the matron was starting down the long corridor that I could see through the door. But I hung back, gazing desperately at Father, Willem, Peter, all our brave underground workers.

'Father!' I cried suddenly. 'God be with you!'

His head turned toward me. The harsh overhead light flashed from his glasses.

'And with you, my daughters,' he said.

I turned and followed the others. Behind me the door slammed closed. And with you! And with you! Oh Father, when will I see you next?

Betsie's hand slipped around mine. A strip of coconut-palm matting ran down the center of the wide hall. We stepped onto it off the damp concrete.

'Prisoners walk to the side.' It was the bored voice of the guard behind us. 'Prisoners must not step on the matting.'

Guiltily we stepped off the privileged path.

Ahead of us in the corridor was a desk, behind it a woman in uniform. As each prisoner reached this point she gave her name for the thousandth time that day and placed on the desk whatever she was wearing of value. Nollie, Betsie, and I unstrapped our beautiful wristwatches. As I handed mine to the officer, she pointed to the simple gold ring that had belonged to Mama. I wriggled it from my finger and laid it on the desk along with my wallet and paper guilders.

The procession down the corridor continued. The walls on both sides of us were lined with narrow metal doors. Now the column of women halted: the matron was fitting a key into one of them. We heard the thud of a bolt drawn back, the screech of hinges. The matron consulted a list in her hand, then called the name of a lady I didn't even know, one of those who had been at Willem's prayer meeting.

Was it possible that that had been only yesterday? Was this only Thursday night? Already the events at the Beje seemed part of another lifetime. The door banged shut; the column moved on. Another door unlocked, another human being closed behind it. No two from Haarlem in the same cell.

Among the very first names read from the list was Betsie's. She stepped through the door; before she could turn or say goodbye, it had closed. Two cells farther on, Nollie left me. The clang of those two doors rang in my ears as the slow march continued.

Now the corridor branched and we turned left. Then right, then left again, an endless world of steel and concrete.

'Ten Boom, Cornelia.'

Another door rasped open. The cell was deep and narrow, scarcely wider than the door. A woman lay on the single cot, three others on straw ticks on the floor. 'Give this one the cot,' the matron said. 'She's sick.'

And indeed, even as the door slammed behind me a spasm of coughing seized my chest and throat.

'We don't want a sick woman in here!' someone shouted. They were stumbling to their feet, backing as far from me as the narrow cubicle would allow.

'I'm . . . I'm so very sorry — ' I began, but another voice interrupted me.

'Don't be. It isn't your fault. Come on, Frau Mikes, give her the cot.' The young woman turned to me. 'Let me hang up your hat and coat.'

Gratefully I handed her my hat, which she added to a row of clothes hanging from hooks along one wall. But I kept my coat wrapped tight around me. The cot had been vacated and I moved shakily toward it, trying not to sneeze or breathe as I squeezed past my cellmates. I sank down on the narrow bed, then went into a fresh paroxysm of coughs as a cloud of choking black dust rose from the filthy straw mattress. At last the attack passed and I lay down. The sour straw smell filled my nostrils. I felt each slat of wood through the thin pallet.

'I will never be able to sleep on such a bed,' I thought,

and the next thing I knew it was morning and there was a clattering at the door. 'Food call,' my cellmates told me. I struggled to my feet. A square of metal had dropped open in the door, forming a small shelf. Onto this someone in the hall was placing tin plates filled with a steaming gruel.

'There's a new one here!' the woman called Frau Mikes called through the aperture. 'We get five portions!' Another tin plate was slammed onto the shelf. 'If you're not hungry,' Frau Mikes added, 'I'll help you with it.'

I picked up my plate, stared at the watery gray porridge and handed it silently to her. In a little while the plates were collected and the pass-through in the door slammed shut.

Later in the morning a key grated in the lock, the bolt banged, and the door opened long enough for the sanitary bucket to be passed out. The wash basin was also emptied and returned with clean water. The women picked up their straw pallets from the floor and piled them in a corner, raising a fresh storm of dust which started me coughing helplessly again.

Then a prison boredom – which I soon learned to fear above all else – settled over the cell. At first I attempted to relieve it by talking with the others, but though they were as courteous as people can be who are living literally on top of one another, they turned aside my questions and I never learned much about them.

The young woman who had spoken kindly to me the night before, I did discover, was a baroness, only seventeen years old. This young girl paced constantly, from morning until the overhead light bulb went off at night, six steps to the door, six steps back, dodging those sitting on the floor, back and forth like an animal in a cage.

Frau Mikes turned out to be an Austrian woman who had worked as a charwoman in an office building. She often cried for her canary. 'Poor little thing! What will become of him! They'll never think to feed him.'

This would start me thinking of our cat. Had Maher Shalal Hashbaz made his escape into the street – or was he starving inside the sealed house? I would picture him prowling among the chairlegs in the dining room, missing the shoulders he loved to walk on. I tried not to let my mind venture higher in the house, not to let it climb the stairs to see if Thea, Mary, Eusie – no! I could do nothing for them here in this cell. God knew they were there.

One of my cellmates had spent three years here in Scheveningen. She could hear the rattle of the meal cart long before the rest of us and tell by the footstep who was passing in the corridor. 'That's the trusty from medical supply. Someone's sick.' . . . 'This is the fourth time someone in 316 has gone for a hearing.'

Her world consisted of this cubicle and the corridor outside – and soon I began to see the wisdom of this narrowed vision, and why prisoners instinctively shied away from questions about their larger lives. For the first days of my imprisonment I stayed in a frenzy of anxiety about Father, Betsie, Willem, Pickwick. Was Father able to eat this food? Was Betsie's blanket as thin as this one?

But these thoughts led to such despair that I soon learned not to give in to them. In an effort to fix my mind on something I asked Frau Mikes to teach me the card game that she played hour after hour. She had made the cards herself with the squares of toilet paper that were issued two a day to each prisoner; all day she sat on a corner of the cot endlessly laying them out in front of her and gathering them up again.

I was a slow learner, since no cards of any kind had been played at the Beje. Now as I began to grasp the solitaire game I wondered what Father's resistance to them had been – surely nothing could be more innocent than this succession of shapes called clubs, spades, diamonds . . .

But as the days passed I began to discover a subtle danger. When the cards went well my spirits rose. It was an omen: someone from Haarlem had been released! But if I lost . . . Maybe someone was ill. The people in the secret room had been found . . .

At last I had to stop playing. In any case I was finding it hard to sit up so long. Increasingly I was spending the days as I did the nights, tossing on the thin straw pallet trying in vain to find a position in which all aches at once were eased. My head throbbed continually, pain shot up and down my arms, my cough brought up blood.

I was thrashing feverishly on the cot one morning when
the cell door opened and there stood the steel-voiced matron
I had seen the night I entered the cell two weeks before.

'Ten Boom, Cornelia.'

I struggled to my feet.

'Bring your hat and your coat and come with me.'

I looked around at the others for a hint as to what was
happening. 'You're going to the outside,' our prison expert
said. 'When you take your hat you always go outside.'

My coat I was wearing already, but I took my hat from its
hook and stepped out into the corridor. The matron relocked
the door then set off so rapidly that my heart hammered as
I trotted after her, careful to stay off the precious matting.
I stared yearningly at the locked doors on either side of us;
I could not remember behind which ones my sisters had
disappeared.

At last we stepped out into the broad, high-walled courtyard. Sky! For the first time in two weeks, blue sky! How
high the clouds were, how inexpressibly white and clean. I
remembered suddenly how much sky had meant to Mama.

'Quick!' snapped the matron.

I hurried to the shiny black automobile beside which she
was standing. She opened the rear door and I got in. Two
others were already in the back seat, a soldier and a woman
with a gaunt gray face. In front next to the driver slumped
a desperately ill-looking man whose head lolled strangely on
the seat back. As the car started up the woman beside me
lifted a blood-stained towel to her mouth and coughed into
it. I understood: the three of us were ill. Perhaps we were
going to a hospital!

The massive prison gate opened and we were in the
outside world, spinning along broad city streets. I stared
in wonderment through the window. People walking, looking
in store windows, stopping to talk with friends. Had I truly
been as free as that only two weeks ago?

The car parked before an office building; it took both the
soldier and the driver to get the sick man up three flights of
stairs. We entered a waiting room jammed with people and
sat down under the watchful eyes of the soldier. When nearly

an hour had passed I asked permission to use the lavatory. The soldier spoke to the trim white-uniformed nurse behind the reception desk.

'This way,' she said crisply. She took me down a short hall, stepped into the bathroom with me and shut the door. 'Quick! Is there any way I can help?'

I blinked at her. 'Yes. Oh yes! A Bible! Could you get me a Bible? And – a needle and thread! And a toothbrush! And soap!'

She bit her lip doubtfully. 'So many patients today – and the soldier – but I'll do what I can.' And she was gone.

But her kindness shone in the little room as brightly as the gleaming white tiles and shiny faucets. My heart soared as I scrubbed the grime off my neck and face.

A man's voice at the door: 'Come on! You've been in there long enough!'

Hastily I rinsed off the soap and followed the soldier back to the waiting room. The nurse was back at her desk, coolly efficient as before; she did not look up. After another long wait my name was called. The doctor asked me to cough, took my temperature and blood pressure, applied his stethoscope, and announced that I had pleurisy with effusion, pre-tubercular.

He wrote something on a sheet of paper. Then with one hand on the doorknob he laid the other for an instant on my shoulder. 'I hope,' he said in a low voice, 'that I am doing you a favor with this diagnosis.'

In the waiting room the soldier was on his feet ready for me. As I crossed the room the nurse rose briskly from her desk and swished past me. In my hand I felt a small knobby something wrapped in paper.

I slid it into my coat pocket as I followed the soldier down the stairs. The other woman was already back in the car; the sick man did not reappear. All during the return ride my hand kept straying to the object in my pocket, stroking it, tracing the outline. 'Oh Lord, it's so small, but still it could be – let it be a Bible!'

The high walls loomed ahead, the gate rang shut behind us. At last, at the end of the long echoing corridors, I reached my cell and drew the package from my pocket. My cellmates crowded round me as I unwrapped the newspaper with trembling hands. Even the baroness stopped her pacing to watch.

As two bars of precious prewar soap appeared, Frau Mikes clapped her hand over her mouth to suppress her yelp of triumph. No toothbrush or needle but – unheard-of wealth – a whole packet of safety pins! And, most wonderful of all, not indeed a whole Bible, but in four small booklets, the four Gospels.

I shared the soap and pins among the five of us but, though I offered to divide the books as well, they refused. 'They catch you with those,' the knowledgeable one said, 'and it's double sentence and *kalte kost* as well.' *Kalte kost* – the bread ration alone without the daily plate of hot food – was the punishment constantly held over our heads. If we made too much noise we'd have *kalte kost*. If we were slow with the bucket it would be *kalte kost*. But even *kalte kost* would be a small price to pay, I thought as I stretched my aching body on the foul straw, for the precious books I clutched between my hands.

It was two evenings later, near the time when the light bulb usually flickered off, that the cell door banged open and a guard strode in.

'Ten Boom, Cornelia,' she snapped. 'Get your things.'

I stared at her, an insane hope rising in me. 'You mean — '

'Silence! No talking!'

It did not take long to gather my 'things': my hat and an undervest that was drying after a vain attempt to get it clean in the much-used basin water. My coat with the precious contents of its pockets had never yet been off my back. Why such strict silence, I wondered. Why should I not be allowed even a goodbye to my cellmates? Would it be so very wrong for a guard to smile now and then, or give a few words of explanation?

I said farewell to the others with my eyes and followed the stiff-backed woman into the hall. She paused to lock the door, then marched off down the corridor. But – the wrong way! We were not heading toward the outside entrance at all, but deeper into the maze of prison passageways.

Still without a word she halted in front of another door and opened it with a key. I stepped inside. The door clanged behind me. The bolt slammed shut.

The cell was identical with the one I had just left, six steps long, two wide, a single cot at the back. But this one was empty. As the guard's footsteps died away down the corridor I leaned against the cold metal of the door. Alone. Alone behind these walls . . .

I must not let my thoughts run wildly; I must be very mature and very practical. Six steps. Sit down on the cot. This one reeked even worse than the other: the straw seemed to be fermenting. I reached for the blanket: someone had been sick on it. I thrust it away but it was too late. I dashed for the bucket near the door and leaned weakly over it.

At that moment the light bulb in the ceiling went out. I groped back to the cot and huddled there in the dark, setting my teeth against the stink of the bedding, wrapping my coat tighter about me. The cell was bitter cold, wind hammered against the wall. This must be near the outside edge of the prison: the wind had never shrieked so in the other one.

What had I done to be separated from people this way? Had they discovered the conversation with the nurse at the doctor's office? Or perhaps some of the prisoners from Haarlem had been interrogated and the truth about our group was known. Maybe my sentence was solitary confinement for years and years . . .

In the morning my fever was worse. I could not stand even long enough to get my food from the shelf in the door and after an hour or so the plate was taken away untouched.

Toward evening the pass-through dropped open again and the hunk of coarse prison bread appeared. By now I was desperate for food but less able to walk than ever. Whoever was in the hall must have seen the problem. A hand picked up the bread and hurled it toward me. It landed on the floor beside the cot where I clawed for it and gnawed it greedily.

For several days while the fever raged my supper was delivered in this manner. Mornings the door squealed open and a woman in a blue smock carried the plate of hot gruel to the cot. I was as starved for the sight of a human face as for the food and tried in a hoarse croak to start a conversation. But the woman, obviously a fellow prisoner, would only shake her head with a fearful glance toward the hall.

The door also opened once a day to let in the trusty from Medical Supply with a dose of some stinging yellow liquid from a very dirty bottle. The first time he entered the cell I clutched at his sleeve. 'Please!' I rasped. 'Have you seen an eighty-four-year-old man – white hair, a long beard? Casper ten Boom! You must have taken medicine to him!'

The man tugged loose. 'I don't know! I don't know anything!'

The cell door slammed back against the wall, framing the guard. 'Solitary prisoners are not permitted to talk! If you say another word to one of the work-duty prisoners it will be *kalte kost* for the duration of your sentence!' And the door banged behind the two of them.

This same trusty was also charged with recording my temperature each time he came. I had to take off my shirt and place the thermometer between my arm and the side of my body. It did not look to me like an accurate system: sure enough, by the end of the week an irritable voice called through the food slot, 'Get up and get the food yourself! Your fever's gone – you won't be waited on again!'

I felt sure that the fever had not gone, but there was nothing for it but to creep, trembling, to the door for my plate. When I had replaced it I would lie down again on the smelly straw, steeling myself for the bawling out I knew would come. 'Look at the great lady, back in bed again! Are you going to lie there all day long?' Why lying down was such a crime I could never understand. Nor indeed what one was supposed to accomplish if one got up . . .

Thoughts, now that I was alone, were a bigger problem than ever. I could no longer even pray for family and friends by name, so great was the fear and longing wrapped round each one. 'Those I love, Lord,' I would say. 'You know them. You see them. Oh – bless them all!'

Thoughts were enemies. That prison bag . . . how many times I opened it in my mind and pawed through all the things I had left behind. A fresh blouse. Aspirin, a whole bottle of them. Toothpaste with a kind of pepperminty taste, and —

Then I would catch myself. How ridiculous, such thoughts! If I had it to do again would I really put these little personal comforts ahead of human lives? Of course not. But in the dark nights, as the wind howled and the fever pulsed, I would draw that bag out of some dark corner of my mind and root through it once again. A towel to lay on this scratchy straw. An aspirin . . .

In only one way was this new cell an improvement over the first one. It had a window. Seven iron bars ran across it, four bars up and down. It was high in the wall, much too high to look out of, but through those twenty-eight squares I could see the sky.

All day I kept my eyes fixed on that bit of heaven. Sometimes clouds moved across the squares, white or pink or edged with gold, and when the wind was from the west I could hear the sea. Best of all, for nearly an hour each day, gradually lengthening as the spring sun rose higher, a shaft of checkered light streamed into the dark little room. As the weather turned warmer and I grew stronger I would stand up to catch the sunshine on my face and chest, moving along the wall with the moving light, climbing at last onto the cot to stand on tiptoe in the final rays.

As my health returned, I was able to use my eyes longer. I had been sustaining myself from my Scriptures a verse at a time; now like a starving man I gulped entire Gospels at a reading, seeing whole the magnificent drama of salvation.

And as I did, an incredible thought prickled the back of my neck. Was it possible that this – all of this that seemed so wasteful and so needless – this war, Scheveningen prison, this very cell, none of it was unforeseen or accidental? Could it be part of the pattern first revealed in the Gospels? Hadn't Jesus – and here my reading became intent indeed – hadn't Jesus been defeated as utterly and unarguably as our little group and our small plans had been?

But . . . if the Gospels were truly the pattern of God's activity, then defeat was only the beginning. I would look around at the bare little cell and wonder what conceivable victory could come from a place like this.

The prison expert in the first cell had taught me to make a kind of knife by rubbing a corset stay against the rough cement floor. It seemed to me strangely important not to lose track of time. And so with a sharp-honed stay I scratched a calendar on the wall behind the cot. As each long featureless day crawled to a close, I checked off another square. I also started a record of special dates beneath the calendar:

February 28, 1944	Arrest
February 29, 1944	Transport to Scheveningen
March 16, 1944	Beginning of Solitary
And now a new date:	
April 15, 1944	My Birthday in Prison

A birthday had to mean a party, but I searched in vain for a single cheerful object. At least in the other cell there had been bright bits of clothing: the baroness' red hat, Frau Mikes' yellow blouse. How I regretted now my own lack of taste in clothes.

At least I would have a song at my party! I chose one about the Bride of Haarlem tree – she would be in full bloom now. The child's song brought it all close: the bursting branches, the petals raining like snow on the brick sidewalk —

'Quiet in there!' A volley of blows sounded on my iron door. 'Solitary prisoners are to keep silent!'

I sat on the cot, opened the Gospel of John, and read until the ache in my heart went away.

Two days after my birthday I was taken for the first time to the big, echoing shower room. A grim-faced guard marched beside me, her scowl forbidding me to take pleasure in the expedition. But nothing could dim the wonder of stepping into that wide corridor after so many weeks of close confinement.

At the door to the shower room several women were waiting. Even in the strict silence this human closeness was joy and strength. I scanned the faces of those coming out, but neither Betsie nor Nollie was there, nor anyone else from Haarlem. And yet, I thought, they are all my sisters. How rich is anyone who can simply see human faces!

The shower too was glorious: warm clean water over my festering skin, streams of water through my matted hair. I went back to my cell with a new resolve: the next time I was permitted a shower I would take with me three of my Gospels. Solitary was teaching me that it was not possible to be rich alone.

And I was not alone much longer: into my solitary cell came a small busy black ant. I had almost put my foot where he was one morning as I carried my bucket to the door when I realized the honor being done me. I crouched down and admired the marvelous design of legs and body. I apologized for my size and promised I would not so thoughtlessly stride about again.

After a while he disappeared through a crack in the floor. But when my evening piece of bread appeared on the door shelf, I scattered some crumbs and to my joy he popped out almost at once. He picked up a heroic piece, struggled down the hole with it and came back for more. It was the beginning of a relationship.

Now in addition to the daily visit of the sun I had the company of this brave and handsome guest – in fact soon of a whole small committee. If I was washing out clothes in the basin or sharpening the point of my homemade knife when the ants appeared, I stopped at once to give them my full attention. It would have been unthinkable to squander two activities on the same bit of time!

One evening as I was crossing another long, long day from the calendar scratched on my wall, I heard shouts far down the corridor. They were answered closer by. Now noisy voices came from every direction. How unusual for the prisoners to be making a racket! Where were the guards?

The shelf in my door had not been closed since the bread came two hours ago. I pressed my ear to it and listened but it was hard to make sense of the tumult outside. Names were being passed from cell to cell. People were singing, others pounding on their doors. The guards must all be away!

'Please! Let's be quiet!' a voice nearby pleaded. 'Let's use this time before they get back!'

'What's happening?' I cried through the open slot. 'Where are the guards?'

'At the party,' the same voice answered me. 'It's Hitler's birthday.'

Then – these must be their own names people were shouting down the corridor. This was our chance to tell where we were, to get information.

'I'm Corrie ten Boom!' I called through the food shelf. 'My whole family is here somewhere! Oh, has anyone seen Casper ten Boom! Betsie ten Boom! Nollie van Woerden! Willem ten Boom!' I shouted names until I was hoarse and heard them repeated from mouth to mouth down the long corridor. I passed names too, to the right and left, as we worked out a kind of system.

After a while answers began to filter back. 'Mrs van der Elst is in Cell 228 . . .' 'Pietje's arm is much better . . .' Some of the messages I could hardly bear to relay: 'The hearing was very bad: he sits in the cell without speaking.' 'To my husband Joost: our baby died last week . . .'

Along with personal messages were rumors about the world outside, each more wildly optimistic than the last.

'There is a revolution in Germany!'

'The Allies have invaded Europe!'

'The war cannot last three weeks longer!'

At last some of the names I had shouted out began to return. 'Betsie ten Boom is in cell 312. She says to tell you that God is good.'

Oh, that was Betsie! That was every inch Betsie!

Then: 'Nollie van Woerden was in cell 318, but she was released more than a month ago.' Released! Oh, thank God! Toos, too, released!

News from the men's section was longer returning, but as it did my heart leapt higher and higher:

Peter van Woerden. Released!

Herman Sluring. Released!

Willem ten Boom. Released!

As far as I could discover, every single one taken in the

raid on the Beje – with the exception of Betsie and me – had been freed. Only about Father could I discover no news at all, although I called his name over and over into the murmuring hall. No one seemed to have seen him. No one seemed to know . . .

It was perhaps a week later that my cell door opened and a prison trusty tossed a package wrapped in brown paper onto the floor. I picked it up, hefted it, turned it over and over. The wrapping paper had been torn open and carelessly retied, but even through the disarray I could spot Nollie's loving touch. I sat on the cot and opened it.

There, familiar and welcoming as a visit from home, was the light blue embroidered sweater. As I put it on I seemed to feel Nollie's arms circling my shoulders. Also inside the package were cookies and vitamins, needle and thread, and a bright red towel. How Nollie understood the gray color-hunger of prison! She had even wrapped the cookies in gay red cellophane.

I was biting into the first one when an inspiration came to me. I dragged the cot out from the wall to stand under the naked overhead bulb. Climbing on it I fashioned a lampshade with the paper: a cheery red glow at once suffused the bleak little room.

I was rewrapping the cookies in the brown outer paper when my eyes fell on the address written in Nollie's careful hand, slanting upward toward the postage stamp. But – Nollie's handwriting did not slant . . . The stamp! Hadn't a message once come to the Beje under a stamp, penciled in the tiny square beneath? Laughing at my own overwrought imagination I moistened the paper in the basin water and worked the stamp gently free.

Words! There was definitely writing there – but so tiny I had to climb again onto the cot and hold the paper close to the shaded bulb.

'All the watches in your closet are safe.'

Safe. Then – then Eusie, and Henk, and Mary, and – they'd got out of the secret room! They'd escaped! They were free!

I burst into racking sobs, then heard heavy footsteps

bearing down the corridor. Hastily I jumped down from the cot and shoved it back to the wall. The pass-through clattered open.

'What's the commotion in here!'

'It's nothing. I – won't do it again.'

The slot in the door snapped shut. How had they managed it? How had they got past the soldiers? Never mind, dear Lord, You were there, and that was all that mattered . . .

The cell door opened to let in a German officer followed by the head matron herself. My eyes ran hungrily over the well-pressed uniform with its rows of brilliant-colored battle ribbons.

'Miss ten Boom,' the officer began in excellent Dutch, 'I have a few questions I believe you can help me with.'

The matron was carrying a small stool which she leapt to set down for the officer. I stared at her. Was this obsequious creature the terrible-voiced terror of the women's wing?

The officer sat down, motioning me to take the cot. There was something in that gesture that belonged to the world outside the prison. As he took out a small notebook and began to read names from it I was suddenly conscious of my rumpled clothes, my long, ragged fingernails.

To my relief I honestly did not know any of the names he read – now I understood the wisdom of the ubiquitous 'Mr Smit.' The officer stood up. 'Will you be feeling well enough to come for your hearing soon?'

Again that ordinary human manner. 'Yes – I – I hope so.' The officer stepped out into the hall, the matron bobbing and scurrying after him with the stool.

It was the third of May; I was sitting on my cot sewing. Since Nollie's package had been delivered I had a wonderful new occupation: one by one I was pulling the threads from the red towel and with them embroidering bright figures on the pajamas that I had only recently stopped wearing beneath my clothes. A window with ruffled curtains. A flower with an impossible number of petals and leaves. I had just started work on the head of a cat over the right pocket when the food shelf in the door banged open and shut with a single motion.

And there on the floor of the cell lay a letter.

I dropped the pajamas and sprang forward. Nollie's writing. Why should my hand tremble as I picked it up?

The letter had been opened by the censors – held by them too: the postmark was over a week old. But it was a letter, a letter from home – the very first one! Why this sudden fear?

I unfolded the paper. 'Corrie, can you be very brave?'

No! No, I couldn't be brave! I forced my eyes to read on.

'I have news that is very hard to write you. Father survived his arrest by only ten days. He is now with the Lord . . .'

I stood with the paper between my hands so long that the daily shaft of sunlight entered the cell and fell upon it. Father . . . Father . . . the letter glittered in the criss-cross light as I read the rest. Nollie had no details, not how or where he had died, not even where he was buried.

Footsteps were passing on the coconut matting. I ran to the door and pressed my face to the closed pass-through. 'Please! Oh please!'

The steps stopped. The shelf dropped open. 'What's the matter?'

'Please! I've had bad news – oh please, don't go away!'

'Wait a minute.' The footsteps retreated, then returned with a jangle of keys. The cell door opened.

'Here.' The young woman handed me a pill with a glass of water. 'It's a sedative.'

'This letter just came,' I explained. 'It says that my father – it says my father has died.'

The girl stared at me. 'Your father!' she said in astonished tones.

I realized how very old and decrepit I must look to this young person. She stood in the doorway a while, obviously embarrassed at my tears. 'Whatever happens,' she said at last, 'you brought it on yourself by breaking the laws!'

Dear Jesus, I whispered as the door slammed and her footsteps died away, how foolish of me to have called for human help when You are here. To think that Father sees

You now, face to face! To think that he and Mama are together again, walking those bright streets . . .

I pulled the cot from the wall and below the calendar scratched another date:

March 9, 1944 Father. Released.

11

The Lieutenant

I was walking with a guard – behind and a little to the right of
her so my feet would not touch the sacrosanct mat – down a
corridor I had not seen before. A turn to the right, a few steps
down, right again . . . what an endless labyrinth this prison
was. At last we stepped out into a small interior courtyard.
A drizzle of rain was falling. It was a chill raw morning in late
May: after three months in prison I had been called for my
first hearing.

Barred windows stared from tall buildings on three sides of
the courtyard, along the fourth was a high wall and against this
stood a row of small huts. So these were where the infamous
interrogations took place. My breath came short and hard as
I thought back to the reports I had passed on, the night of
Hitler's birthday.

'Lord Jesus, You were called to a hearing too. Show me
what to do.'

And then I saw something. Whoever used the fourth of
the huts had planted a row of tulips along the side. They
were wilted now, only tall stems and yellowing leaves, but
. . . 'Dear Lord, let me go to hut number four!'

The guard had paused to unstrap a long military cape
fastened to the shoulder of her uniform. Protected from
the rain, she crunched up the gravel path. Past the first
hut, the second, the third. She halted in front of the hut with
the flowerbed and rapped on the door.

'*Ja*! *Herrein*!' called a man's voice.

The guard pushed open the door, gave a straight-armed

salute and marched smartly off. The man wore a gun in a leather holster and a beribboned uniform. He removed his hat and I was staring into the face of the gentle-mannered man who had visited me in my cell.

'I am Lieutenant Rahms,' he said, stepping to the door to close it behind me. 'You're shivering! Here, let me get a fire going.'

He filled a pot-bellied stove from a small coal scuttle, for all the world a kindly German householder entertaining a guest. What if this were all a subtle trap? This kind, human manner – perhaps he had simply found it more effective than brutality in tricking the truth from affection-starved people. 'Oh Lord, let no weak gullibility on my part endanger another's life.'

'I hope,' the officer was saying, 'we won't have many more days this spring as cold as this one.' He drew out a chair for me to sit on.

Warily I accepted it. How strange after three months, to feel a chair-back behind me, chair-arms for my hands! The heat from the stove was quickly warming the little room. In spite of myself I began to relax. I ventured a timid comment about the tulips: 'So tall, they must have been beautiful.'

'Oh they were!' he seemed ridiculously pleased. 'The best I've ever grown. At home we always have Dutch bulbs.'

We talked about flowers for a while and then he said, 'I would like to help you, Miss ten Boom. But you must tell me everything. I may be able to do something, but only if you do not hide anything from me.'

So there it was already. All the friendliness, the kindly concern that I had half-believed in – all a device to elicit information. Well, why not? This man was a professional with a job to do. But I, too, in a small way, was a professional.

For an hour he questioned me, using every psychological trick that the young men of our group had drilled me in. In fact, I felt like a student who has crammed for a difficult exam and then is tested on only the most elementary material. It soon became clear that they believed the Beje had been a headquarters for raids on food ration offices around the country. Of all the illegal activities I had on my conscience, this was probably the one I knew least about. Other than receiving the stolen cards each month and passing them on, I knew no details of the operation. Apparently my real ignorance began to show; after a while Lieutenant Rahms stopped making notes of my hopelessly stupid answers.

'Your other activities, Miss ten Boom. What would you like to tell me about them?'

'Other activities? Oh, you mean – you want to know about my church for mentally retarded people!' And I plunged into an eager account of my efforts at preaching to the feeble-minded.

The lieutenant's eyebrows rose higher and higher. 'What a waste of time and energy?' he exploded at last. 'If you want converts, surely one normal person is worth all the half-wits in the world!'

I stared into the man's intelligent blue-gray eyes: true National-Socialist philosophy I thought, tulip bed or no. And then to my astonishment I heard my own voice saying boldly, 'May I tell you the truth, Lieutenant Rahms?'

'This hearing, Miss ten Boom, is predicated on the assumption that you will do me that honor.'

'The truth, Sir,' I said, swallowing, 'is that God's viewpoint is sometimes different from ours – so different that we could not even guess at it unless He had given us a Book which tells us such things.'

I knew it was madness to talk this way to a Nazi officer. But he said nothing so I plunged ahead. 'In the Bible I learn that God values us not for our strength or our brains but simply because He has made us. Who knows, in His eyes a half-wit may be worth more than a watchmaker. Or – a lieutenant.'

Lieutenant Rahms stood up abruptly. 'That will be all for today.' He walked swiftly to the door. 'Guard!'

I heard footsteps on the gravel path.

'The prisoner will return to her cell.'

Following the guard through the long cold corridors, I knew I had made a mistake. I had said too much. I had ruined whatever chance I had that this man might take an interest in my case.

And yet the following morning it was Lieutenant Rahms himself who unlocked my cell door and escorted me to the hearing. Apparently he did not know of the regulation that forbade prisoners to step on the mat, for he indicated that I was to walk ahead of him down the center of the hall. I avoided the eyes of the guards along the route, guilty as a well-trained dog discovered on the living room sofa.

In the courtyard this time a bright sun was shining.

'Today,' he said, 'we will stay outside. You are pale. You are not getting enough sun.'

Gratefully I followed him to the farthest corner of the little yard where the air was still and warm. We settled our backs against the wall. 'I could not sleep last night,' the lieutenant said, 'thinking about that Book where you have read such different ideas. What else does it say in there?'

On my closed eyelids the sun glimmered and blazed. 'It says,' I began slowly, 'that a Light has come into this world, so that we need no longer walk in the dark. Is there darkness in your life, Lieutenant?'

There was a very long silence.

'There is great darkness,' he said at last. 'I cannot bear the work I do here.'

Then all at once he was telling me about his wife and children in Bremen, about their garden, their dogs, their summer hiking vacations. 'Bremen was bombed again last week. Each morning I ask myself, are they still alive?'

'There is One Who has them always in His sight Lieutenant Rahms. Jesus is the Light the Bible shows to me, the Light that can shine even in such darkness as yours.'

The man pulled the visor of his hat lower over his eyes; the skull-and-crossbones glinted in the sunlight. When he spoke it was so low I could hardly hear. 'What can you know of darkness like mine . . .?'

Two more mornings the hearings continued. He had dropped all pretense of questioning me on my underground activities and seemed especially to enjoy hearing about my childhood. Mama, Father, the aunts – he wanted to hear stories about them again and again. He was incensed to learn that Father had died right here in Scheveningen; the documents on my case made no mention of it.

These documents did answer one question: the reason

for solitary confinement. 'Prisoner's condition contagious to others in cell.' I stared at the brief typed words where Lieutenant Rahm's finger rested. I thought of the long wind-haunted nights, the scowling guards, the rule of silence. 'But, if it wasn't punishment, why were they so angry with me? Why couldn't I talk?'

The lieutenant squared the edges of the papers in front of him. 'A prison is like any institution, Miss ten Boom, certain rules, certain ways of doing things — '

'But I'm not contagious now! I've been better for weeks and weeks, and my own sister is so close! Lieutenant Rahms, if I could only see Betsie! If I could just talk with her a few minutes!'

He lifted his eyes from the desk and I saw anguish in them. 'Miss ten Boom, it is possible that I appear to you a powerful person. I wear a uniform, I have a certain authority over those under me. But I am in prison, dear lady from Haarlem, a prison stronger than this one.'

It was the fourth and final hearing, and we had come back into the small hut for the signing of the *procès-verbal*. He gathered up the completed transcript and went out with it, leaving me alone. I was sorry to say goodbye to this man who was struggling so earnestly for truth. The hardest thing for him seemed to be that Christians should suffer. 'How can you believe in God now?' he'd ask. 'What kind of a God would have let that old man die here in Scheveningen?'

I got up from the chair and held my hands out to the squat little stove. I did not understand either why Father had died in such a place. I did not understand a great deal.

And suddenly I was thinking of Father's own answer to hard questions: 'Some knowledge is too heavy . . . you cannot bear it . . . your Father will carry it until you are able.' Yes! I would tell Lieutenant Rahms about the traincase – he always liked stories about Father.

But when the lieutenant returned to the room a guard from the women's wing was with him. 'Prisoner ten Boom has completed her hearings,' he said, 'and will return to her cell.'

The young woman snapped to attention. As I stepped through the door, Lieutenant Rahms leaned forward.

'Walk slowly,' he said, 'in Corridor F.'

Walk slowly? What did he mean? The guard strode down the long door-lined halls so swiftly that I had to trot to keep up with her. Ahead of us a prison trusty was unlocking the door to a cell. I trailed behind the guard as much as I dared, my heart thumping wildly. It would be Betsie's cell – I knew it!

Then I was abreast of the door. Betsie's back was to the corridor. I could see only the graceful upswept bun of her chestnut hair. The other women in the cell stared curiously into the corridor; her head remained bent over something in her lap. But I had seen the home Betsie had made in Scheveningen.

For unbelievably, against all logic, this cell was charming. My eyes seized only a few details as I inched reluctantly past. The straw pallets were rolled instead of piled in a heap, standing like little pillars along the walls, each with a lady's hat atop it. A headscarf had somehow been hung along the wall. The contents of several food packages were arranged on a small shelf; I could just hear Betsie saying, 'The red biscuit tin here in the center!' Even the coats hanging on their hooks were part of the welcome of that room, each sleeve draped over the shoulder of the coat next to it like a row of dancing children —

'*Schneller! Aber schnell!*'

I jumped and hurried after my escort. It had been a glimpse only, two seconds at the most, but I walked through the corridors of Scheveningen with Betsie's singing spirit at my side.

All morning I heard doors opening and closing. Now keys rattled outside my own: a very young guard in a very new uniform bounded in.

'Prisoner stand at attention!' she squeaked. I stared at her wide, blinking eyes; the girl was in mortal fear of something or someone.

Then a shadow filled the doorway and the tallest woman I had ever seen stepped into the cell. Her features were classically handsome, the face and height of a goddess – but one carved in marble. Not a flicker of feeling registered in her eyes.

'No sheets here either, I see,' she said in German to the guard. 'See that she has two by Friday. One to be changed every two weeks.'

The ice-cold eyes appraised me exactly as they had the bed. 'How many showers does the prisoner get?'

The guard wet her lips. 'About one a week, *Wacht-meisterin*.'

One a week! One shower a month was closer.

'She will go twice a week.'

Sheets! Regular showers! Were conditions going to be better? The new head matron took two strides into the cell; she did not need the cot to reach the overhead bulb. Rip! Off came my red-cellophane lampshade. She pointed to a box of soda crackers that had come in a second package from Nollie.

'No boxes in the cells!' cried the little guard in Dutch, as indignantly as though this had been a long-standing rule.

Not knowing what else to do I dumped the crackers out onto the cot. At the matron's unspoken command I emptied a bottle of vitamins and a sack of peppermint drops the same way.

Unlike the former head matron, who shrieked and scolded endlessly in her rusted-hinge voice, this woman worked in a terrifying silence. With a gesture she directed the guard to feel beneath the mattress. My heart wedged in my throat; my precious remaining Gospel was hidden there. The guard knelt and ran her hands the length of the cot. But whether she was too nervous to do a thorough job or whether there was a more mysterious explanation, she straightened up empty-handed.

And then they were gone.

I stood gazing numbly at the jumble of food on my cot. I thought of this woman reaching Betsie's cell, reducing it again to four walls and a prison cot. A chill wind was blowing through Scheveningen, cleaning, ordering, killing.

It was this tall, ramrod-straight woman who unlocked the door to my cell one afternoon in the second half of June and admitted Lieutenant Rahms. At the severity in his face I swallowed the greeting that had almost burst from me.

'You will come to my office,' he said briefly. 'The notary has come.'

We might as well have been total strangers. 'Notary?' I said stupidly.

'For the reading of your Father's will.' He made an impatient gesture; obviously this minor matter had interrupted a busy day. 'It's the law – family present when a will is opened.'

Already he was heading from the cell and down the corridor. I broke into a clumsy run to keep up with the strides of the silent woman beside me. The law? what law? And since when had the German occupation government concerned itself with Dutch legal procedures? Family. Family present . . . No, don't let yourself think of it!

At the door to the courtyard the matron turned, erect and impassive, back along the corridor. I followed Lieutenant Rahms into the dazzling early summer afternoon. He opened the door for me into the fourth hut. Before my eyes adjusted to the gloom I was drowning in Willem's embrace.

'Corrie! Corrie! Baby sister!' It was fifty years since he had called me that.

Now Nollie's arm was around me too, the other one still clinging to Betsie, as though by the strength of her grip she would hold us together forever. Betsie! Nollie! Willem! I did not know which name to cry first. Tine was in that little room too – and Flip! And another man; when I had time to look I recognized the Haarlem notary who had been called in on the watchshop's few legal consultations. We held each other at arm's length to look, we babbled questions all at once.

Betsie was thin and prison-pale. But it was Willem who shocked me. His face was gaunt, yellow, and pain-haunted. He had come home this way from Scheveningen, Tine told me. Two of the eight men crowded into his tiny cell had died of jaundice while he was there.

Willem! I could not bear to see him this way. I crooked my arm through his, standing close so that I did not have to look at him, loving the sound of his deep rolling voice. Willem did not seem aware of his own illness: his concern was all for Kik. This handsome blond son had been seized the month before while helping an American parachutist reach the North Sea. They believed he had been on one of the recent prison trains into Germany.

As for Father, they had learned a few more facts about his last days. He had apparently become ill in his cell and been taken by car to the municipal hospital in The Hague. There, no bed had been available. Father had died in a corridor, separated somehow from his records or any clue to his identity. Hospital authorities had buried the unknown old man in the paupers' cemetery. The family believed they had located the particular grave.

I glanced over at Lieutenant Rahms. He was standing with his back to us as we talked, staring down at the cold unlit stove. Swiftly I opened the package that Nollie had pressed into my hand with the first embrace. It was what my leaping heart had told me: a Bible, the entire Book in a compact volume, tucked inside a small pouch with a string for wearing around the neck as we had once carried our identity cards. I dropped it quickly over my head and down my back beneath my blouse. I couldn't even find words with which to thank her: the day before, in the shower line, I had given away my last remaining Gospel.

'We don't know all the details,' Willem was saying in a low voice to Betsie, 'just that after a few days the soldiers were taken off guard duty at the Beje and police stationed there instead.' The fourth night, he believed, the chief had succeeded in assigning Rolf and another of our group to the same shift. They had found all the Jews well, though cramped and hungry, and seen them to new hiding places.

'And now?' I whispered. 'They're all right now?'

Willem lowered his deep-sunk eyes to mine. He had never been good at concealing difficult truths. 'They're all right, Corrie – all except Mary.' Old Mary Itallie, he said, had been arrested one day walking down a city street. Where she had been going and why she had exposed herself this way in broad daylight, nobody knew.

'The time is up.' Lieutenant Rahms left his perusal of the stove and nodded to the notary. 'Proceed with the reading of the will.'

It was a brief, informal document: the Beje was to be home for Betsie and me as long as we wanted it; should there ever be any money realized from the sale of house or watch shop, he knew we would recall his equal love for us all; he committed us with joy to the constant care of God.

In the silence which followed, we all suddenly bowed our heads. 'Lord Jesus,' Willem said, 'we praise You for these moments together under the protection of this good man. How can we thank him? We have no power to do him any service. Lord, allow us to share this inheritance from our father with him as well. Take him too, and his family, into Your constant care.'

Outside, a guard's footsteps sounded on the crunchy gravel walk.

12

Vught

'Get your things together! Get ready to evacuate! Collect all possessions in pillowcases!' The shouts of the guards echoed up and down the long corridor.

I stood in the center of my cell in a frenzy of excitement. Evacuate! Then – then something was happening! We were leaving the prison! The counter-invasion must have begun!

I snatched the pillowcase from the little wad of straw I had stuffed into it. What riches this coarse bit of muslin had been in the two weeks since it had been provided: a shield for my head from the scratch and smell of the bedding. It almost didn't matter that the promised sheets had never arrived.

With trembling hands I dropped my few belongings into it, the blue sweater, the pajamas – covered now back and front with embroidered figures – toothbrush, comb, a few remaining crackers wrapped in toilet paper. My Bible was in its pouch on my back where it remained except when I was reading it.

I put on my coat and hat and stood at the iron door clutching the pillowcase in both hands. It was still early in the morning; the tin breakfast plate had not yet been removed from the shelf in the door. Getting ready had taken no time at all.

An hour passed. I sat on the cot. Two hours. Three. It was warm in the cell this late June day. I took off my hat and coat and folded them next to me on the cot.

More time passed. I kept my eyes on the ant hole, hoping for a last visit from my small friends, but they did not appear. Probably I had frightened them by my early dashing about.

I reached into the pillowcase, took one of the crackers and crumbled it about the little crack. No ants. They were staying safely hidden.

And suddenly I realized that this too was a message, a last wordless communication among neighbours. For I too had a hiding place when things were bad. Jesus was this place, the Rock cleft for me. I pressed a finger to the tiny crevice.

The afternoon sun appeared on the wall and moved slowly across the cell. And then all at once there was a clanging out in the corridor. Doors scraped. Bolts banged. 'Out! *Schnell*! All out! No talking!'

I snatched up my hat and coat.

My door screeched open. 'Form ranks of five — ' the guard was already at the next cell.

I stepped out into the hall. It was jammed from wall to wall: I had never dreamed so many women occupied this corridor. We exchanged looks. 'In-va-sion,' we mouthed silently, the soundless word sweeping through the massed women like an electric charge. Surely the invasion of Holland had begun! Why else would they be emptying the prison!

Where would we be taken? Where were we headed? Not into Germany! Dear Jesus, not Germany.

The command was given and we shuffled forward down the long chill halls, each carrying a pillowcase, with her belongings forming a little bulge at the bottom. At last we emerged into the wide courtyard inside the front gate of the prison and another long wait began. But this wait was pleasant with the late afternoon sun on our backs. Far to the right I could see the columns of the men's section. But crane my neck though I would, I could not see Betsie anywhere.

At last the huge gate swung in and a convoy of gray transport buses drove through. I was herded aboard the third one. The seats had been removed, the windows painted over. The bus lurched dreadfully as it started up but we were standing too close together to fall. When the bus ground to a stop we were at a freight yard somewhere on the outskirts of the city.

Again we were formed into ranks. The guards' voices were tense and shrill. We had to keep our heads facing forward, eyes front. Behind us we could hear buses arriving, then lumbering away again. It was still light, but I knew by the ache in my stomach that it was long past suppertime.

And then, ahead and to the left of me, in the newest group of arriving prisoners. I spotted a chestnut bun. Betsie! Somehow, some way, I was going to get to her! Now instead of wanting the day to end, I prayed that we stayed where we were until dark.

Slowly the long June day faded. Thunder rumbled and a few drops of rain fell. At last a long row of unlit coaches rolled slowly over the tracks in front of us. They banged to a stop, rolled forward a little farther, then stopped again. After a while they began backing. For an hour or more the train switched back and forth.

By the time the order came to board, it was pitch dark. The ranks of prisoners surged forward. Behind us the guards shouted and cursed: obviously they were nervous at transporting so many prisoners at one time. I wriggled and shoved to the left. Elbows and shoulders were in my way but I squirmed past. At the very steps of the train I reached out and seized Betsie's hand.

Together we climbed onto the train, together found seats in a crowded compartment, together wept tears of gratitude. The four months in Scheveningen had been our first separation in fifty-three years; it seemed to me that I could bear whatever happened with Betsie beside me.

More hours passed as the loaded train sat on the siding. For us they flew, there was so much to share. Betsie told me about each of her cellmates – and I told her about mine and the little hole into which they scrambled at any emergency. As always, Betsie had given to others everything she had. The Bible that Nollie had smuggled to her she had torn up and passed around, book by book.

It must have been 2:00 or 3:00 in the morning that the train at last began to move. We pressed our faces to the glass, but no lights showed and clouds covered the moon. The thought uppermost in every mind was: Is it Germany? At one point we made out a tower that Betsie was sure was the cathedral at Delft. An hour or more later the clack of the train changed pitch: we were crossing a trestle. But – a very long one! As the minutes passed and still we had not reached the other side Betsie and I exchanged looks. The Moerdijk Bridge! Then we were headed south. Not east into Germany, but south to Brabant. For the second time that night we wept tears of joy.

I leaned my head back against the wooden slats of the seat and shut my eyes, reliving another train trip to Brabant. Mama's hand had gripped Father's, then, as the train swayed. Then, too, it was June – the June of the First Sermon, of the garden back of the manse, of Karel . . .

I must have fallen asleep, back in that other June, for when I opened my eyes the train had stopped. Voices were shouting at us to move: *Schneller*! *Aber schnell*! An eerie glare lit the windows. Betsie and I stumbled after the others along the aisle and down the iron steps. We seemed to have stopped in the middle of a wood. Floodlights mounted in trees lit a broad rough-cleared path lined by soldiers with leveled guns.

Spurred by the shouts of the guards Betsie and I started up the path between the gun barrels. '*Schneller*!' Close ranks! Keep up! Five abreast!' Betsie's breath was coming short and hard and still they yelled at us to go faster. It had rained hard here, for there were deep puddles in the path. Ahead of us a white-haired woman stepped to the side to avoid one; a soldier struck her in the back with a gun butt. I took Betsie's pillowcase along with mine, hooked my other arm through hers and hauled her along beside me.

The nightmare march lasted a mile or more. At last we came to a barbed-wire fence surrounding a row of wooden barracks. There were no beds in the one we entered, only long tables with backless benches pulled up to them. Betsie and I collapsed onto one of these. Under my arm I could feel the irregular flutter of her heart. We fell into an exhausted sleep, our heads on the table.

The sun was streaming through the barracks windows when we woke up. We were thirsty and hungry: we had had nothing to eat or drink since the early meal at Scheveningen the morning before. But all that day no guard or any official person appeared inside the barracks. At last, when the sun was low in the sky, a prisoner crew arrived with a great vat of some thick steamy substance that we gobbled ravenously.

And so began our stay in this place that, we learned, was named Vught after the nearest small village. Unlike Scheveningen, which had been a regular Dutch prison, Vught had been constructed by the occupation especially as a concentration camp for political prisoners. We were not yet in the camp proper but in a kind of quarantine compound outside. Our biggest problem was idleness, wedged together as we were around the long rows of tables with nothing to do. We were guarded by the same young women who had patrolled the corridors at Scheveningen. They had been adequate enough as long as we were behind locked doors; here they seemed at a loss. Their only technique for maintaining discipline was to shriek obscenities and hand out punishments to all alike. Half rations for the entire barracks. An extra roll call at rigid attention. A ban on talking for twenty-four hours.

Only one of our overseers never threatened or raised her voice. This was the tall, silent head matron from Scheveningen. She appeared in Vught the third morning during the predawn roll call and at once something like order seized our rebellious and untidy ranks. Lines straightened, hands were clamped to sides, whispers ceased as those cold blue eyes swept across us.

Among ourselves we nicknamed her 'The General.' During one long roll call a pregnant woman at our table slumped to the floor, striking her head against the edge of the bench. The General did not so much as pause in her expressionless reading of names.

We had been in this outer camp at Vught almost two weeks when Betsie and I along with a dozen others were called out by name during morning roll call. When the rest had been dismissed The General distributed typewritten forms among us and instructed us to present them at the administration barracks at 9:00 o'clock.

A worker on the food crew – a long-term prisoner from the main camp – smiled encouragingly as he ladled out our breakfast. 'You're free!' he whispered. 'Those pink forms mean release!'

Betsie and I stared disbelievingly at the sheets of paper in our hands. Free? Free to leave – free to go home? Others crowded around, congratulating us, embracing us. The women from Betsie's cell at Scheveningen wept unabashedly. How cruel to have to leave all these behind!

'Surely the war will be over very soon,' we told them. We emptied our pillowcases, passing out our few belongings among those who had to stay.

Long before 9:00 we were standing in the big wooden anteroom of Administration. At last we were summoned to an inner office where our forms were examined, stamped, and handed over to a guard. We followed this man down a corridor into another office. For hours the process continued as we were shuttled from one room and official to another, questioned, fingerprinted, sent on to the next post. The group of prisoners grew until there were forty or fifty of us standing in line beside a high anchor-chain fence topped with barbed wire. On the other side of the fence was a white birch wood, above our heads the blue Brabant sky. We too belonged to that wide free world.

The next barracks we entered held a row of desks with women clerks seated behind them. At one of these I was handed a brown paper envelope. I emptied it into my hand and the next moment was staring in disbelief at my Alpina watch. Mama's ring. Even my paper guilders. I had not seen these things since the night we arrived at Scheveningen. Money . . . why, that belonged to the world of shops and trolley cars. We could go to a train station with this money. Two fares to Haarlem, please . . .

We marched along a path between twisted rolls of barbed wire and through a wide gate into a compound of low tin-roofed barracks. There were more lines, more waits, more shuffling from desk to desk, but already the camp and its procedures had become unreal to me.

Then we were standing before a high counter and a young male clerk was saying, 'Leave all personal effects at the window marked "C".'

'But they just gave them back to me!'

'Watches, purses, jewelry . . .'

Mechanically, like a machine with no will of its own, I handed watch, ring, and money through the small barred window. A uniformed woman swept them into a metal box. 'Move along! Next!'

Then – were we not to be released? Outside this building a florid-faced officer formed us into a double column and marched us across a broad parade ground. At one end of it a crew of men with shaved heads and striped overalls were digging a ditch. What did it mean? What did any of it mean, this whole long day of lines and waits? Betsie's face was gray with weariness and she stumbled as we marched.

Through another fence we arrived in a yard surrounded on three sides by low concrete buildings. A young woman in a military cape was waiting for us.

'Prisoners halt!' barked the red-faced officer. 'Explain to the newcomers, *Fraulein*, the function of the bunkers.'

'The bunkers,' the girl began in the bored voice of a museum guide, 'are for the accommodation of those who fail to cooperate with camp rules. The rooms are cozy, if a bit small: about the size of a gym locker. To hasten the educational process the hands are tied above the head . . .'

Even as the horrid recital continued, two guards came out of the bunker, carrying between them the form of a man. He was alive, for his legs were moving, but he seemed to have no conscious control over them. His eyes were sunken and rolled back in his head.

'Not everyone,' the girl observed in the same detached drawl, 'seems to appreciate the accommodations at the bunkers.'

I seized Betsie's arm as the command to march came again, more to steady myself than her. It was Father's traincase once again. Such cruelty was too much to grasp, too much to bear. Heavenly Father, carry it for me!

We followed the officer down a wide street lined with barracks on either side and halted at one of the gray, featureless sheds. It was the end of the long day of standing, waiting, hoping: we had simply arrived in the main camp at Vught.

The barracks appeared almost identical with the one we had left this morning, except that this one was furnished

with bunks as well as tables and benches. And still we were
not allowed to sit: there was a last wait while the matron
with maddening deliberateness checked off our documents
against a list.

'Betsie!' I wailed, 'how long will it take?'

'Perhaps a long, long time. Perhaps many years. But what
better way could there be to spend our lives?'

I turned to stare at her. 'Whatever are you talking about?'

'These young women. That girl back at the bunkers.
Corrie, if people can be taught to hate, they can be taught
to love! We must find the way, you and I, no matter how long
it takes . . .'

She went on, almost forgetting in her excitement to keep
her voice to a whisper, while I slowly took in the fact that she
was talking about our guards. I glanced at the matron seated
at the desk ahead of us. I saw a gray uniform and a visored
hat; Betsie saw a wounded human being.

And I wondered, not for the first time, what sort of a person
she was, this sister of mine . . . what kind of road she followed
while I trudged beside her on the all-too-solid earth.

A few days later Betsie and I were called up for work
assignments. One glance at Betsie's pallid face and fragile
form, and the matron waved her contemptuously back inside
the barracks where the elderly and infirm spent the day
sewing prison uniforms. The women's uniform here in Vught
was a blue overall with a red stripe down the side of the leg,
practical and comfortable, and a welcome change after our
own clothes that we had worn since the day of our arrest.

Apparently I looked strong enough for harder work; I was
told to report to the Phillips factory. This 'factory' turned out
to be no more than another large barracks inside the camp
complex. Early in the morning though it was, the tar beneath
the shingled roof was beginning to bubble in the hot July sun.
I followed my escort into the single large room where several
hundred men and women sat at long plank tables covered with
thousands of tiny radio parts. Two officers, one male, one
female, were strolling the aisles between the benches while
the prisoners bent to their tasks.

I was assigned a seat at a bench near the front and given the job of measuring small glass rods and arranging them in piles according to lengths. It was monotonous work. The heat from the roof pressed like a weight on my head. I longed to exchange at least names and home towns with my neighbors on either side, but the only sound in the room was the clink of metal parts and the squeak of the officers' boots. They reached the door across from where I sat.

'Production was up again last week,' the male officer said in German to a tall slender man with a shaved head and a striped uniform. 'You are to be commended for this increase. However we continue to receive complaints of defective wiring. Quality control must improve.'

The shaved-headed man made an apologetic gesture. 'If there were more food, *Herr Officier*,' he murmured. 'Since the cutback in rations I see a difference. They grow sleepy, they have trouble concentrating . . .' His voice reminded me a little of Willem's, deep, cultivated, the German with only a trace of Dutch accent.

'Then you must wake them up! Make them concentrate on the penalties! If soldiers on the front can fight on half-rations, then these lazy — '

At a terrible look from the woman officer, he stopped and ran his tongue over his lips. 'Ah – that is – I speak of course merely as an example. There is naturally no truth in the rumor that rations at the front are reduced. So! I – I hold you responsible!' And together they stalked from the building.

For a moment the prisoner-foreman watched them from the doorway. Slowly he raised his left hand, then dropped it with a slap to his side. The quiet room exploded. From under tables appeared writing paper, books, knitting yarn, tins of biscuits. People left their benches and joined little knots of chattering friends all over the room. Half a dozen crowded around me: Who was I? Where was I from? Did I have any news of the war?

After perhaps half an hour of visiting among the tables, the foreman reminded us that we had a day's quota to meet and people drifted back to their places. The foreman's name, I learned, was Moorman and he had been headmaster of a

Roman Catholic boys' school. He himself came over to my workbench the third day I was there; he had heard that I had followed the entire assembly line through the barracks, tracing what became of my dull little piles of rods. 'You're the first woman worker,' he said, 'who has ever shown any interest in what we are making here.'

'I am very interested,' I said. 'I'm a watchmaker.'

He stared at me with new interest. 'Then I have work you will enjoy more.' He took me to the opposite end of the huge shed where the final assembly of relay switches was done. It was intricate and exacting work, though not nearly so hard as watch repair, and Mr Moorman was right. I enjoyed it and it helped make the eleven-hour workday go faster.

Not only to me but to all the Phillips workers, Mr Moorman acted more as a kindly older brother than a crew boss. I would watch him, ceaselessly moving among his hundreds of charges, counseling, encouraging, finding a simpler job for the weary, a harder one for the restless. We had been at Vught more than a month before I learned that his twenty-year-old son had been shot here at the camp the week Betsie and I arrived.

No trace of this personal tragedy showed in his care for the rest of us. He stopped frequently at my bench, the first weeks, more to check my frame of mind than my work. But eventually his eyes would travel to the row of relay switches in front of me . . .

'Dear watch lady! Can you not remember for whom you are working? These radios are for their fighter planes!' And reaching across me he would yank a wire from its housing or twist a tiny tube from an assembly.

'Now solder them back wrong. And not so fast! You're over the day's quota and it's not yet noon.'

Lunchtime would have been the best time of day if I could have spent it with Betsie. However, Phillips workers were not allowed to leave the factory compound until the workday ended at 6:00. Prisoners on kitchen detail lugged in great buckets of gruel made of wheat and peas, tasteless but nourishing. Apparently there had been a cutback in rations recently: still the food was better and more plentiful than at Scheveningen where there had been no noonday meal at all.

After eating we were free for a blessed half hour to stroll about within the Phillips compound in the fresh air and the glorious Brabant sun. Most days I found a spot along the fence and stretched out on the warm ground to sleep (the days started with roll call at 5:00 A.M.). Sweet summer smells came in the breezes from the farms around the camp; sometimes I would dream that Karel and I were walking hand in hand along a country lane.

At 6:00 in the evening there was another roll call, then we marched back to our various sleeping barracks. Betsie always stood in the doorway of ours waiting for me; each evening it was as though a week had passed, there was so much to tell one another.

'That Belgian boy and girl at the bench next to mine? This noon they became engaged!'

'Mrs Heerma – whose granddaughter was taken to Germany – today she let me pray with her.'

One day Betsie's news touched us directly. 'A lady from Ermelo was transferred to the sewing detail today. When I introduced myself, she said, "Another one!"'

'What did she mean?'

'Corrie, do you remember, the day we were arrested, a man came to the shop? You were sick and I had to wake you up.'

I remembered very well. Remembered the strange roving eyes, the uneasiness in the pit of my stomach that was more than fever.

'Apparently everyone in Ermelo knew him. He worked with the Gestapo from the first day of occupation. He reported this woman's two brothers for Resistance work, and finally herself and her husband too.' When Ermelo had finally caught on to him he had come to Haarlem and teamed up with Willemse and Kapteyn. His name was Jan Vogel.

Flames of fire seemed to leap around that name in my heart. I thought of Father's final hours, alone and confused, in a hospital corridor. Of the underground work so abruptly halted. I thought of Mary Itallie arrested while walking down a street. And I knew that if Jan Vogel stood in front of me now I could kill him.

Betsie drew the little cloth bag from beneath her overalls and held it out to me, but I shook my head. Betsie kept the Bible during the day, since she had more chance to read and teach from it here than I did at the Phillips barracks. In the evenings we held a clandestine prayer meeting for as many as could crowd around our bunk.

'You lead the prayers tonight, Betsie. I have a headache.'

More than a headache. All of me ached with the violence of my feelings about the man who had done us so much harm. That night I did not sleep and the next day at my bench scarcely heard the conversation around me. By the end of the week I had worked myself into such a sickness of body and spirit that Mr Moorman stopped at my bench to ask if something were wrong.

'Wrong? Yes, something's wrong!' And I plunged into an account of that morning. I was only too eager to tell Mr Moorman and all Holland how Jan Vogel had betrayed his country.

What puzzled me all this time was Betsie. She had suffered everything I had and yet she seemed to carry no burden of rage. 'Betsie!' I hissed one dark night when I knew that my restless tossing must be keeping her awake. Three of us now shared this single cot as the crowded camp daily received new arrivals. 'Betsie, don't you feel anything about Jan Vogel? Doesn't it bother you?'

'Oh yes, Corrie! Terribly! I've felt for him ever since I knew – and pray for him whenever his name comes into my mind. How dreadfully he must be suffering.'

For a long time I lay silent in the huge shadowy barracks restless with the sighs, snores, and stirrings of hundreds of women. Once again I had the feeling that this sister with whom I had spent all my life belonged somehow to another order of things. Wasn't she telling me in her gentle way that I was as guilty as Jan Vogel? Didn't he and I stand together before an all-seeing God convicted of the same sin of murder? For I had murdered him with my heart and with my tongue.

'Lord Jesus,' I whispered into the lumpy ticking of the bed,

'I forgive Jan Vogel as I pray that You will forgive me. I have done him great damage. Bless him now, and his family . . .' That night for the first time since our betrayer had a name I slept deep and dreamlessly until the whistle summoned us to roll call.

The days in Vught were a baffling mixture of good and bad. Morning roll call was often cruelly long. If the smallest rule had been broken, such as a single prisoner late for evening check-in, the entire barracks would be punished by a 4:00 A.M. or even a 3:30 call and made to stand at parade attention until our backs ached and our legs cramped. But the summer air was warm and alive with birds as the day approached. Gradually, in the east, a pink-and-gold sunrise would light the immense Brabant sky as Betsie and I squeezed each other's hands in awe.

At 5:30 we had black bread and 'coffee,' bitter and hot, and then fell into marching columns for the various work details. I looked forward to this hike to the Phillips factory. Part of the way we walked beside a small woods, separated only by a roll of barbed wire from a glistening world of dew-drops. We also marched past a section of the men's camp, many of our group straining to identify a husband or a son among the ranks of shaved heads and striped overalls.

This was another of the paradoxes of Vught. I was endlessly, daily grateful to be again with people. But what I had not realized in solitary confinement was that to have companions meant to have their griefs as well. We all suffered with the women whose men were in this camp: the discipline in the male section was much harsher than in the women's; executions were frequent. Almost every day a salvo of shots would send the anguished whispers flying: How many this time? Who were they?

The woman next to me at the relay bench was an intense Communist woman named Floor. She and her husband had managed to get their two small children to friends before their arrest, but she worried aloud all day about them and about Mr Floor, who had tuberculosis. He worked on the rope-making crew in the compound next to Phillips and each noon they managed to exchange a few words through the barbed wire separating the two enclosures. Although she was expecting a third child in September she would never eat her morning allotment of bread but passed it through the fence to him. She was dangerously thin, I felt, for an expectant mother, and several times I brought her a portion of my own breakfast bread. But this too was always set aside for Mr Floor.

And yet in spite of sorrow and anxiety – and no one in that place was without both – there was laughter too in the Phillips barracks. An impersonation of the pompous, blustering second lieutenant. A game of blind-man's buff. A song passed in rounds from bench to bench until —

'Thick clouds! Thick clouds!' The signal might come from any bench which faced a window. The factory barracks was set in the center of the broad Phillips compound; there was no way a camp official could approach it without crossing this open space. In an instant every bench would be filled, the only sound the businesslike rattle of radio parts.

One morning the code words were still being relayed down the long shed when a rather hefty *Aufseherin* stepped through the door. She glanced furiously about, face flushing scarlet as she applied 'thick clouds' to her appearance. She shrieked and ranted for a quarter of an hour, then deprived us of our noontime break in the open air that day. After this we adopted the more neutral signal 'fifteen.'

'I've assembled fifteen dials!'

During the long hot afternoons pranks and talk died down as each one sat alone with his own thoughts. I scratched on the side of the table the number of days until September 1. There was nothing official about that date, just a chance remark by Mrs Floor to the effect that six months was the usual prison term for ration-card offenders. Then, if that were the charge and if they included the time served at Scheveningen, September 1 would be our release date.

'Corrie,' Betsie warned one evening when I announced triumphantly that August was half over, 'we don't know for sure.'

I had the feeling, almost, that to Betsie it didn't matter. I looked at her, sitting on our cot in the last moments before lights out, sewing up a split seam in my overalls as she'd so often sat mending under the lamplight in the dining room. Betsie by the very way she sat evoked a high-backed chair behind her and a carpet at her feet instead of this endless row of metal cots on a bare pine floor. The first week we were here she had added extra hooks to the neck of her overalls so that she could fasten the collar high around her throat and, this propriety taken care of, I had the feeling she was as content to be reading the Bible here in Vught to those who had never heard it as she'd been serving soup to hungry people in the hallway of the Beje.

As for me, I set my heart every day more firmly on September 1.

And then, all of a sudden, it looked as though we would not have to wait even this long. The Princess Irene Brigade was rumored to be in France, moving toward Belgium. The Brigade was part of the Dutch forces that had escaped to England during the Five-Day War; now it was marching to reclaim its own.

The guards were noticeably tense. Roll call was an agony. The old and the ill who were slow reaching their places were beaten mercilessly. Even the 'red light commando' came in for discipline. These young women were ordinarily a favored group of prisoners. Prostitutes, mostly from Amsterdam, they were in prison not for their profession – which was extolled as a patriotic duty – but for infecting German soldiers. Ordinarily, with the male guards anyway, they had a bold, breezy manner; now even they had to form ruler-straight lines and stand hours at frozen attention.

The sound of the firing squad was heard more and more often. One lunchtime when the bell sounded to return to work, Mrs Floor did not appear at the bench beside me. It always took a while for my eyes to readjust to the dim factory after the bright sun outside: it was only gradually that I saw the hunk of black bread still resting at her place on the bench. There had been no husband to deliver it to.

And so hanging between hope and horror we waited out the days. Rumor was all we lived on. The Brigade was across the Dutch border. The Brigade was destroyed. The Brigade had never landed. Women who had stayed away from the whispered little prayer service around our cot now crowded close, demanding signs and predictions from the Bible.

On the morning of September 1 Mrs Floor gave birth to a baby girl. The child lived four hours.

Several days later we awoke to the sound of distant explosions. Long before the roll-call whistle the entire barracks was up and milling about in the dark between the cots. Was it bombs? Artillery fire? Surely the Brigade had reached Brabant. This very day they might be in Vught!

The scowls and threats of the guards when they arrived daunted us not at all. Everyone's mind had turned homeward, everyone talked of what she would do first. 'The plants will all be dead,' said Betsie, 'but we'll get some cuttings from Nollie! We'll wash the windows so the sun can come in.'

At the Phillips factory Mr Moorman tried to calm us. 'Those aren't bombs,' he said, 'and certainly not guns. That's demolition work. Germans. They're probably blowing up bridges. It means they expect an attack but not that it's here. It might not come for weeks.'

This dampened us a bit, but as the blasts came closer and closer nothing could keep down hope. Now they were so near they hurt our ears.

'Drop your lower jaw!' Mr Moorman called down the long room. 'Keep your mouth open and it will save your eardrums.'

We had our midday meal inside with the doors and windows closed. We'd been working again for an hour – or sitting at our benches, no one could work – when the order came to return to dormitories. With sudden urgency women embraced husbands and sweethearts who worked beside them at Phillips.

Betsie was waiting for me outside our barracks. 'Corrie! Has the Brigade come? Are we free?'

'No. Not yet. I don't know. Oh, Betsie, why am I so frightened?'

The loudspeaker in the men's camp was sounding the signal for roll call. No order was given here and we drifted about aimlessly, listening we scarcely knew for what. Names were being read through the men's speaker, though it was too far away to make them out.

And suddenly an insane fear gripped the waiting women. A deathlike silence now hung over both sides of the vast camp. The loudspeaker had fallen silent. We exchanged wordless looks, we almost feared to breathe.

Then rifle fire split the air. Around us women began to weep. A second volley. A third. For two hours the executions went on. Someone counted. More than seven hundred male prisoners were killed that day.

There was little sleeping in our barracks that night and no roll call the following morning. About 6:00 A.M. we were ordered to collect our personal things. Betsie and I put our belongings into the pillowcases we had brought from Scheveningen: toothbrushes, needle and thread, a small bottle of Davitamon oil that had come in a Red Cross package, Nollie's blue sweater which was the only thing we had brought with us when we left the quarantine camp ten weeks before. I transferred the Bible in its bag from Betsie's back to my own; she was so thin it made a visible bump between her shoulders.

We were marched to a field where soldiers were passing out blankets from the backs of open trucks. As we filed past, Betsie and I drew two beautiful soft new ones; mine was white with blue stripes, Betsie's white with red stripes – obviously the property of some well-to-do family.

About noon the exodus from camp began. Through the drab streets of barracks we went, past the bunkers, through the maze of barbed-wire compounds and enclosures, and at last onto the rough dirt road through the woods down which we had stumbled that rainy night in June. Betsie hung hard to my arm; she was laboring for breath as she always did when she had to walk any distance.

'March! *Schnell!* Double-time!'

I slipped my arm beneath Betsie's shoulders and half-carried her the final quarter-mile. At last the path ended and we lined up facing the single track, over a thousand women standing toe to heel. Farther along, the men's section was also at the siding; it was impossible to identify individuals among the shaved heads glistening in the autumn sun.

At first I thought our train had not come; then I realized that these freight cars standing on the tracks were for us. Already the men were being prodded aboard, clambering up over the high sides. We could not see the engine, just this row of small, high-wheeled European boxcars stretching out of sight in both directions, machine guns mounted at intervals on the roof. Soldiers were approaching along the track, pausing at each car to haul open the heavy sliding door. In front of us a gaping black interior appeared. Women began to press forward.

Clutching our blankets and pillowcases we were swept along with the others. Betsie's chest was still heaving oddly after the rapid march. I had to boost her over the side of the train.

At first I could make out nothing in the dark car; then in a corner I saw a tall, uneven shape. It was a stack of bread, dozens of flat black loaves piled one on top of another. A long trip then . . .

The small car was getting crowded. We were shoved against the back wall. Thirty or forty people were all that could fit in. And still the soldiers drove women over the side, cursing, jabbing with their guns. Shrieks rose from the center of the car but still the press increased. It was only when eighty women were packed inside that the door thumped shut and we heard iron bolts driven into place.

Women were sobbing and many fainted, although in the tight-wedged crowd they remained upright. Just when it seemed certain that those in the middle must suffocate or be trampled to death, we worked out a kind of system where, by half-sitting, half-lying with our legs wedged around one another like members of a sledding team, we were able to get down on the floor of the car.

'Do you know what I am thankful for?' Betsie's gentle voice startled me in that squirming madhouse. 'I'm thankful that Father is in heaven today!'

Father. Yes! Oh Father, how could I have wept for you?

The warm sun beat down on the motionless train, the temperature in the packed car rose, the air grew foul. Beside me someone was tugging at a nail in the ancient wood of the wall. At last it came free; with the point she set to work gouging the hole wider. Others around the sides took up the idea and in a while blessed whiffs of outside air began to circle about us.

It was hours before the train gave a sudden lurch and began to move. Almost at once it stopped again, then again crawled forward. The rest of the day and into the night it was the same, stopping, starting, slamming, jerking. Once when it was my turn at the air-hole I saw in the moonlight trainmen carrying a length of twisted rail. Tracks ahead must be destroyed. I passed the news. Maybe they would not be able to repair them. Maybe we would still be in Holland when liberation came.

Betsie's forehead was hot to my hand. The 'red light' girl between whose legs I was wedged squeezed herself into an even tighter crouch so that Betsie could lie almost flat across my lap. I dozed too, from time to time, my head on the shoulder of the friendly girl behind us. Once I dreamed it was storming. I could hear the hailstones on Tante Jans's front windows. I opened my eyes. It really was hailing. I could hear it rattling against the side of the car.

Everyone was awake now and talking. Another storm of hail. And then we heard a burst of machine-gun fire from the roof of the train.

'It's bullets!' someone shouted. 'They're attacking the train.'

Again we heard that sound like tiny stones striking the wall, and again the machine guns answered. Had the Brigade reached us at last? The firing died away. For an hour the train sat motionless. Then slowly we crawled forward.

At dawn someone called out that we were passing through the border town of Emmerich.

We had arrived in Germany.

13

Ravensbruck

For two more incredible days and two more nights we were carried deeper and deeper into the land of our fears. Occasionally one of the loaves of bread was passed from hand to hand. But not even the most elementary provision had been made for sanitation and the air in the car was such that few could eat.

And gradually, more terrible than the crush of bodies and the filth, the single obsession was: something to drink. Two or three times when the train stopped, the door was slid open a few inches and a pail of water passed in. But we had become animals, incapable of plan or system. Those near the door got it all.

At last, the morning of the fourth day, the train stopped again and the door was opened its full width. Like infants, on hands and knees, we crawled to the opening and lowered ourselves over the side. In front of us was a smiling blue lake. On the far side, among sycamore trees, rose a white church steeple.

The stronger prisoners hauled buckets of water from the lake. We drank through cracked and swollen lips. The train was shorter; the cars carrying the men had disappeared. Only a handful of soldiers – some of them looking no older than fifteen – were there to guard a thousand women. No more were needed. We could scarcely walk, let alone resist.

After a while they got us into straggly columns and marched us off. For a mile the road followed the shore of the lake, then left it to climb a hill. I wondered if Betsie could make it to the top, but the sight of trees and sky seemed to have revived her and she supported me as much as I her. We passed a number of local people on foot and in horsedrawn wagons. The children especially seemed wonderful to me, pink-cheeked and healthy. They returned my stares with wide-eyed interest; I noticed, however, that the adults did not look at us but turned their heads away as we approached.

From the crest of the hill we saw it, like a vast scar on the green German landscape; a city of low gray barracks surrounded by concrete walls on which guard towers rose at intervals. In the very center, a square smokestack emitted a thin gray vapor into the blue sky.

'Ravensbruck!'

Like a whispered curse the word passed back through the lines. This was the notorious women's extermination camp whose name we had heard even in Haarlem. That squat concrete building, that smoke disappearing in the bright sunlight – no! I would not look at it! As Betsie and I stumbled down the hill, I felt the Bible thumping between my shoulder blades. God's good news. Was it to this world that He had spoken it?

Now we were close enough to see the skull-and-crossbones posted at intervals on the walls to warn of electrified wiring along the top. The massive iron gates swung in; we marched between them. Acres of soot-gray barracks stretched ahead of us. Just inside the wall was a row of waist-high water spigots. We charged them, thrusting hands, arms, legs, even heads, under the streams of water, washing away the stench of the boxcars. A squad of women guards in dark blue uniforms rushed at us, hauling and shouting, swinging their short, hard crops.

At last they drove us back from the faucets and herded us down an avenue between barracks. This camp appeared far grimmer than the one we had left. At least, in marches about Vught, we had caught sight of fields and woods. Here, every vista ended in the same concrete barrier; the camp was set down in a vast man-made valley rising on every side to those towering wire-topped walls.

At last we halted. In front of us a vast canvas tent-roof –

no sides – covered an acre or more of straw-strewn ground. Betsie and I found a spot on the edge of this area and sank gratefully down. Instantly we were on our feet again. Lice! The straw was literally alive with them. We stood for a while, clutching blankets and pillowcases well away from the infested ground. But at last we spread our blankets over the squirming straw and sat on them.

Some of the prisoners had brought scissors from Vught: everywhere beneath the huge tent women were cutting one another's hair. A pair was passed to us. Of course we must do the same, long hair was folly in such a place. But as I cut Betsie's chestnut waves, I cried.

Toward the evening there was a commotion at one end of the tent. A line of S. S. guards was moving across it, driving women out from under the canvas. We scrambled to our feet and snatched up our blankets as they bore down on us. Perhaps a hundred yards beyond the tent the chase stopped. We stood about, uncertain what to do. Whether a new group of prisoners had arrived or what the reason was for driving us from the tent, no one knew. Women began spreading their blankets on the hard cinder ground. Slowly it dawned on Betsie and me that we were to spend the night here where we stood. We laid my blanket on the ground, stretched out side by side and pulled hers over us.

'The night is dark and I am far from home . . .' Betsie's sweet soprano was picked up by voices all around us. 'Lead Thou me on . . .'

We were waked up some time in the middle of the night by a clap of thunder and a deluge of rain. The blankets soaked through and water gathered in puddles beneath us. In the morning the field was a vast sodden swamp: hands, clothes, and faces were black from the cinder mud.

We were still wringing water from our blankets when the command came to line up for coffee. It was not coffee but a thin liquid of approximately the same color and we were grateful to get it as we shuffled double-file past the makeshift field kitchen. There was a slice of black bread for each prisoner too, then nothing more until we were given a ladle of turnip soup and a small boiled potato late in the afternoon.

In between we were kept standing at rigid attention on the soggy parade ground where we had spent the night. We were near one edge of the huge camp here, close enough to the outer wall to see the triple row of electric wires running along the top. Two entire days we spent this way, stretching out again the second night right where we stood. It did not rain again but ground and blankets were still damp. Betsie began to cough. I took Nollie's blue sweater from my pillowcase, wrapped it around her and gave her a few drops of the vitamin oil. But by morning she had agonizing intestinal cramps. Again and again throughout that second day she had to ask the impatient woman monitor at the head of our row for permission to go to the ditch that served as sanitary facility.

It was the third night as we were getting ready to lie down again under the sky when the order came to report to the processing center for new arrivals. A ten-minute march brought us to the building. We inched along a corridor into a huge reception room. And there under the harsh ceiling lights we saw a dismal sight. As each woman reached a desk where some officers sat she had to lay her blanket, pillowcase, and whatever else she carried onto a growing pile of these things. A few desks further along she had to strip off every scrap of clothes, throw them onto a second pile, and walk naked past the scrutiny of a dozen S. S. men into the shower room. Coming out of the shower she wore only a thin prison dress and a pair of shoes. Nothing more.

But Betsie needed that sweater! She needed the vitamins! Most of all, we needed our Bible. How could we live in this place without it? But how could I ever take it past so many watchful eyes without the overalls covering it?

We were almost at the first desk. I fished desperately in my pillowcase, drew out the bottle of vitamins and closed my fist around them. Reluctantly we dropped the other things on the heap that was fast becoming a mountain. 'Dear God,' I prayed, 'You have given us this precious Book. You have kept it hidden through checkpoints and inspections. You have used it for so many — '

I felt Betsie stagger against me and looked at her in alarm. Her face was white, her lips pressed tight together. A guard was passing by; I begged him in German to show us the toilets. Without so much as a glance, he jerked his head in the direction of the shower room.

Timidly Betsie and I stepped out of line and walked to the door of the big, dank-smelling room with its row on row of overhead spigots. It was empty, waiting for the next batch of fifty naked and shivering women to be admitted.

'Please,' I said to the S. S. man guarding the door, 'where are the toilets?'

He did not look at me either. 'Use the drainholes!' he snapped, and as we stepped inside he slammed the door behind us. We stood alone in the room where a few minutes later we would return stripped even of the clothes on our backs. Here were the prison things we were to put on, piled just inside the door. From the front and back of each otherwise ordinary dress a large 'X' had been cut and replaced with cloth of another color.

And then we saw something else, stacked in the far corner, a pile of old wooden benches. They were slimy with mildew, crawling with cockroaches, but to me they seemed the furniture of heaven itself.

'The sweater! Take the sweater off!' I hissed, fumbling with the string at my neck. Betsie handed it to me and in an instant I had wrapped it around the Bible and the vitamin bottle and stuffed the precious bundle behind the benches.

And so it was that when we were herded into that room ten minutes later we were not poor, but rich. Rich in this new evidence of the care of Him who was God even of Ravensbruck.

We stood beneath the spigots as long as the flow of icy water lasted, feeling it soften our lice-eaten skin. Then we clustered dripping wet around the heap of prison dresses, holding them up, passing them about, looking for approximate fits. I found a loose long-sleeved dress for Betsie that would cover the blue sweater when she would have a chance to put it on. I squirmed into another dress for myself, then reached behind the benches and shoved the little bundle quickly inside the neck.

It made a bulge you could have seen across the Grote

Markt. I flattened it out as best I could, pushing it down, tugging the sweater around my waist, but there was no real concealing it beneath the thin cotton dress. And all the while I had the incredible feeling that it didn't matter, that this was not my business, but God's. That all I had to do was walk straight ahead.

As we trooped back out through the shower room door, the S.S. men ran their hands over every prisoner, front, back, and sides. The woman ahead of me was searched three times. Behind me, Betsie was searched. No hand touched me.

At the exit door to the building was a second ordeal, a line of women guards examining each prisoner again. I slowed down as I reached them but the *Aufseherin* in charge shoved me roughly by the shoulder. 'Move along! You're holding up the line!'

And so Betsie and I arrived at Barracks 8 in the small hours of the morning, bringing not only the Bible, but a new knowledge of the power of Him whose story it was. There were three women already asleep in the bed assigned to us. They made room for us as best they could but the mattress sloped and I kept sliding to the floor. At last all five of us lay sideways across the bed and managed to get shoulders and elbows arranged. The blanket was a poor threadbare affair compared with the ones we had given up, but at least the overcrowding produced its own warmth. Betsie had put on the blue sweater beneath her long-sleeved dress and wedged now between me and the others, her shivering gradually subsided and she was asleep. I lay awake a while longer, watching a searchlight sweep the rear wall in long regular arcs, hearing the distant calls of soldiers patrolling the walls . . .

Morning roll call at Ravensbruck came half an hour earlier than at Vught. By 4:30 A.M. we had to be standing outside in the black predawn chill, standing at parade attention in blocks of one hundred women, ten wide, ten deep. Sometimes after hours of this we would gain the shelter of the barracks only to hear the whistle.

'Everybody out! Fall in for roll call!'

Barracks 8 was in the quarantine compound. Next to us –

perhaps as a deliberate warning to newcomers – were located the punishment barracks. From there, all day long and often into the night, came the sounds of hell itself. They were not the sounds of anger, or of any human emotion, but of a cruelty altogether detached: blows landing in regular rhythm, screams keeping pace. We would stand in our ten-deep ranks with our hands trembling at our sides, longing to jam them against our ears, to make the sounds stop.

The instant of dismissal we would mob the door of Barracks 8, stepping on each others' heels in our eagerness to get inside, to shrink the world back to understandable proportions.

It grew harder and harder. Even within these four walls there was too much misery, too much seemingly pointless suffering. Every day something else failed to make sense, something else grew too heavy. 'Will You carry this too, Lord Jesus?'

But as the rest of the world grew stranger, one thing became increasingly clear. And that was the reason the two of us were here. Why others should suffer we were not shown. As for us, from morning until lights-out, whenever we were not in ranks for roll call, our Bible was the center of an ever-widening circle of help and hope. Like waifs clustered around a blazing fire, we gathered about it, holding out our hearts to its warmth and light. The blacker the night around us grew, the brighter and truer and more beautiful burned the word of God. 'Who shall separate us from the love of Christ? Shall tribulation, or distress, or persecution, or famine, or nakedness, or peril, or sword? . . . Nay, in all these things we are more than conquerors through him that loved us.'

I would look about us as Betsie read, watching the light leap from face to face. More than conquerors . . . It was not a wish. It was a fact. We knew it, we experienced it minute by minute – poor, hated, hungry. We are more than conquerors. Not 'we shall be.' We are! Life in Ravensbruck took place on two separate levels, mutually impossible. One, the observable, external life, grew every day more horrible. The other, the life we lived with God, grew daily better, truth upon truth, glory upon glory.

Sometimes I would slip the Bible from its little sack with hands that shook, so mysterious had it become to me. It was new; it had just been written. I marveled sometimes that the ink was dry. I had believed the Bible always, but reading it now had nothing to do with belief. It was simply a description of the way things were – of hell and heaven, of how men act and how God acts. I had read a thousand times the story of Jesus' arrest – how soldiers had slapped Him, laughed at Him, flogged Him. Now such happenings had faces and voices.

Fridays – the recurrent humiliation of medical inspection. The hospital corridor in which we waited was unheated, and a fall chill had settled into the walls. Still we were forbidden even to wrap ourselves in our own arms, but had to maintain our erect, hands-at-sides position as we filed slowly past a phalanx of grinning guards. How there could have been any pleasure in the sight of these stick-thin legs and hunger-bloated stomachs I could not imagine. Surely there is no more wretched sight than the human body unloved and uncared for. Nor could I see the necessity for the complete undressing: when we finally reached the examining room a doctor looked down each throat, another – a dentist presumably – at our teeth, a third in between each finger. And that was all. We trooped again down the long, cold corridor and picked up our X-marked dresses at the door.

But it was one of these mornings while we were waiting, shivering, in the corridor, that yet another page in the Bible leapt into life for me.

He hung naked on the cross.

I had not known – I had not thought . . . The paintings, the carved crucifixes showed at the least a scrap of cloth. But this, I suddenly knew, was the respect and reverence of the artist. But oh – at the time itself, on that other Friday morning – there had been no reverence. No more than I saw in the faces around us now.

I leaned toward Betsie, ahead of me in line. Her shoulder blades stood out sharp and thin beneath her blue-mottled skin.

'Betsie, they took *His* clothes too.'

Ahead of me I heard a little gasp. 'Oh, Corrie. And I never thanked Him . . .'

Every day the sun rose a little later, the bite took longer to leave the air. It will be better, everyone assured everyone else, when we move into permanent barracks. We'll have a blanket apiece. A bed of our own. Each of us painted into the picture her own greatest need.

For me it was a dispensary where Betsie could get medication for her cough. 'There'll be a nurse assigned to the barracks.' I said it so often that I convinced myself. I was doling out a drop of the Davitamon each morning on her piece of black bread, but how much longer could the small bottle last? 'Especially,' I would tell her, 'if you keep sharing it around every time someone sneezes.'

The move to permanent quarters came the second week in October. We were marched, ten abreast, along a wide cinder avenue and then into a narrower street of barracks. Several times the column halted while numbers were read out – names were never used at Ravensbruck. At last Betsie's and mine were called: 'Prisoner 66729, Prisoner 66730.' We stepped out of line with a dozen or so others and stared at the long gray front of Barracks 28. Half its windows seemed to have been broken and replaced with rags. A door in the center let us into a large room where two hundred or more women bent over knitting needles. On tables between them were piles of woolen socks in army gray.

On either side doors opened into two still larger rooms – by far the largest dormitories we had yet seen. Betsie and I followed a prisoner-guide through the door at the right. Because of the broken windows the vast room was in semi-twilight. Our noses told us, first, that the place was filthy: somewhere plumbing had packed up, the bedding was soiled and rancid. Then as our eyes adjusted to the gloom we saw that there were no individual beds at all, but great square piers stacked three high, and wedged side by side and end to end with only an occasional narrow aisle slicing through.

We followed our guide single file – the aisle was not wide enough for two – fighting back the claustrophobia of these platforms rising everywhere above us. The tremendous room was nearly empty of people; they must have been out on various work crews. At last she pointed to a second tier in the center of a large block. To reach it we had to stand on the bottom level, haul ourselves up, and then crawl across three other straw-covered platforms to reach the one that we would share with – how many? The deck above us was too close to let us sit up. We lay back, struggling against the nausea that swept over us from the reeking straw. We could hear the women who had arrived with us finding their places.

Suddenly I sat up, striking my head on the cross-slats above. Something had pinched my leg.

'Fleas!' I cried. 'Betsie, the place is swarming with them!'

We scrambled across the intervening platforms, heads low to avoid another bump, dropped down to the aisle, and edged our way to a patch of light.

'Here! And here another one!' I wailed. 'Betsie, how can we live in such a place!'

'Show us. Show us how.' It was said so matter of factly it took me a second to realize she was praying. More and more the distinction between prayer and the rest of life seemed to be vanishing for Betsie.

'Corrie!' she said excitedly. 'He's given us the answer! Before we asked, as He always does! In the Bible this morning. Where was it? Read that part again!'

I glanced down the long dim aisle to make sure no guard was in sight, then drew the Bible from its pouch. 'It was in First Thessalonians,' I said. We were on our third complete reading of the New Testament since leaving Scheveningen. In the feeble light I turned the pages. 'Here it is: "Comfort the frightened, help the weak, be patient with everyone. See that none of you repays evil for evil, but always seek to do good to one another and to all . . ."' It seemed written expressly to Ravensbruck.

'Go on,' said Betsie. 'That wasn't all.'

'Oh yes: ". . . to one another and to all. Rejoice always, pray constantly, give thanks in all circumstances; for this is the will of God in Christ Jesus — "'

'That's it, Corrie! That's His answer. "Give thanks in all circumstances!" That's what we can do. We can start right now to thank God for every single thing about this new barracks!'

I stared at her, then around me at the dark, foul-aired room.

'Such as?' I said.

'Such as being assigned here together.'

I bit my lip. 'Oh yes, Lord Jesus!'

'Such as what you're holding in your hands.'

I looked down at the Bible. 'Yes! Thank You, dear Lord, that there was no inspection when we entered here! Thank You for all the women, here in this room, who will meet You in these pages.'

'Yes,' said Betsie. 'Thank You for the very crowding here. Since we're packed so close, that many more will hear!' She looked at me expectantly. 'Corrie!' she prodded.

'Oh, all right. Thank You for the jammed, crammed, stuffed, packed, suffocating crowds.'

'Thank You,' Betsie went on serenely, 'for the fleas and for — '

The fleas! This was too much. 'Betsie, there's no way even God can make me grateful for a flea.'

'"Give thanks in *all* circumstances,"' she quoted. 'It doesn't say, "in pleasant circumstances." Fleas are part of this place where God has put us.'

And so we stood between piers of bunks and gave thanks for fleas. But this time I was sure Betsie was wrong.

They started arriving soon after 6:00 o'clock, the women of Barracks 28, tired, sweat-stained, and dirty from the long forced-labor details. The building, we learned from one of our platform mates, had been designed to hold four hundred. There were now fourteen hundred quartered here with more arriving weekly as concentration camps in Poland, France, Belgium, Austria, as well as Holland were evacuated toward the center of Germany.

There were nine of us sharing our particular square, designed for four, and some grumbling as the others discovered they would have to make room for Betsie and me. Eight acrid and overflowing toilets served the entire room; to reach them we had to crawl not only over our own bedmates but over those on the other platforms between us and the closest aisle, always at the risk of adding too much weight to the already sagging slats and crashing down on the people beneath. It happened several times, that first night. From somewhere in the room would come a splintering sound, a shriek, smothered cries.

Even when the slats held, the least movement on the upper platforms sent a shower of dust and straw over the sleepers below – followed by a volley of curses. In Barracks 8 most of us had been Dutch. Here there was not even a common language and among exhausted, ill-fed people quarrels erupted constantly.

There was one raging now as the women sleeping nearest the windows slammed them shut against the cold. At once scores of voices demanded that they be raised again. Brawls were starting all up and down that side of the room; we heard scuffling, slaps, sobs.

In the dark I felt Betsie's hands clasp mine. 'Lord Jesus,' she said aloud, 'send Your peace into this room. There has been too little praying here. The very walls know it. But where You come, Lord, the spirit of strife cannot exist . . .'

The change was gradual, but distinct. One by one the angry sounds let up.

'I'll make you a deal!' The voice spoke German with a strong Scandinavian accent. 'You can sleep in here where it's warmer and I'll take your place by the window!'

'And add your lice to my own!' But there was a chuckle in the answer. 'No thanks.'

'I'll tell you what!' The third voice had a French burr. 'We'll open them halfway. That way we'll be only half-frozen and you'll be only half-smothered.'

A ripple of laughter widened around the room at this. I lay back on the sour straw and knew there was one more circumstance for which I could give thanks. Betsie had come to Barracks 28.

Roll call came at 4:30 A.M. here as it had in quarantine. A whistle roused us at 4:00 when, without even shaking the straw from clothes and hair, the stampede began for the ration of bread and coffee in the center room. Latecomers found none.

The count was made in the *Lagerstrasse*, the wide avenue leading to the hospital. There we joined the occupants of other barracks – some 35,000 at that time – stretching out of sight in the pale glow of the street lamps, feet growing numb on the cold cinder ground.

After roll call, work crews were called out. For weeks Betsie and I were assigned to the Siemens factory. This huge complex of mills and railroad terminals was a mile and a half from the camp. The 'Siemens Brigade,' several thousand of us, marched out the iron gate beneath the charged wires into a world of trees and grass and horizons. The sun rose as we skirted the little lake; the gold of the late fall fields lifted our hearts.

The work at Siemens, however, was sheer misery. Betsie and I had to push a heavy handcart to a railroad siding where we unloaded large metal plates from a boxcar and wheeled them to a receiving gate at the factory. The grueling workday lasted eleven hours. At least, at noontime we were given a boiled potato and some thin soup; those who worked inside the camp had no midday meal.

Returning to camp we could barely lift our swollen and aching legs. The soldiers patrolling us bellowed and cursed, but we could only shuffle forward inches at a step. I noticed again how the local people turned their eyes another way.

Back at the barracks we formed yet another line – would there never be an end to columns and waits? – to receive our ladle of turnip soup in the center room. Then, as quickly as we could for the press of people, Betsie and I made our way to the rear of the dormitory room where we held our worship 'service.' Around our own platform area there was not enough light to read the Bible, but back here a small light bulb cast a wan yellow circle on the wall, and here an ever larger group of women gathered.

They were services like no others, these times in Barracks 28. A single meeting might include a recital of the Magnificat in Latin by a group of Roman Catholics, a whispered hymn by some Lutherans, and a sotto-voce chant by Eastern Orthodox women. With each moment the crowd around us would swell, packing the nearby platforms, hanging over the edges, until the high structures groaned and swayed.

At last either Betsie or I would open the Bible. Because only the Hollanders could understand the Dutch text we would translate aloud in German. And then we would hear the life-giving words passed back along the aisles in French, Polish, Russian, Czech, back into Dutch. They were little previews of heaven, these evenings beneath the light bulb. I would think of Haarlem, each substantial church set behind its wrought-iron fence and its barrier of doctrine. And I would know again that in darkness God's truth shines most clear.

At first Betsie and I called these meetings with great timidity. But as night after night went by and no guard ever came near us, we grew bolder. So many now wanted to join us that we held a second service after evening roll call. There on the *Lagerstrasse* we were under rigid surveillance, guards in their warm wool capes marching constantly up and down. In was the same in the center room of the barracks: half a dozen guards or camp police always present. Yet in the large dormitory room there was almost no supervision at all. We did not understand it.

Another strange thing was happening. The Davitamon bottle was continuing to produce drops. It scarcely seemed possible, so small a bottle, so many doses a day. Now, in addition to Betsie, a dozen others on our pier were taking it.

My instinct was always to hoard it – Betsie was growing so very weak! But others were ill as well. It was hard to say no to eyes that burned with fever, hands that shook with chill. I tried to save it for the very weakest – but even these soon numbered fifteen, twenty, twenty-five . . .

And still, every time I tilted the little bottle, a drop appeared at the tip of the glass stopper. It just couldn't be! I held it up to the light, trying to see how much was left, but the dark brown glass was too thick to see through.

'There was a woman in the Bible,' Betsie said, 'whose oil jar was never empty.' She turned to it in the Book of Kings, the story of the poor widow of Zarephath who gave Elijah a room in her home: 'The jar of meal wasted not, neither did the cruse of oil fail, according to the word of Jehovah which he spoke by Elijah.'

Well – but – wonderful things happened all through the Bible. It was one thing to believe that such things were possible thousands of years ago, another to have it happen now, to us, this very day. And yet it happened, this day, and the next, and the next, until an awed little group of spectators stood around watching the drops fall onto the daily rations of bread.

Many nights I lay awake in the shower of straw dust from the mattress above, trying to fathom the marvel of supply lavished upon us. 'Maybe,' I whispered to Betsie, 'only a molecule or two really gets through that little pinhole – and then in the air it expands!'

I heard her soft laughter in the dark. 'Don't try too hard to explain it, Corrie. Just accept it as a surprise from a Father who loves you.'

And then one day Mien pushed her way to us in the evening food line. 'Look what I've got for you!'

Mien was a pretty young Dutch woman we had met in Vught. She was assigned to the hospital and often managed to bring to Barracks 28 some stolen treasure from the staff room – a sheet of newspaper to stuff in a broken window, a slice of bread left untouched on a nurse's plate. Now we peered into the small cloth sack she carried.

'Vitamins!' I cried, and then cast an apprehensive glance at a policeman nearby. 'Yeast compound!' I whispered.

'Yes!' she hissed back. 'There were several huge jars. I emptied each just the same amount.'

We gulped the thin turnip water, marveling at our sudden riches. Back at the bunk I took the bottle from the straw. 'We'll finish the drops first,' I decided.

But that night, no matter how long I held it upside down, or how hard I shook it, not another drop appeared.

On the first of November a coat was issued to each prisoner. Betsie's and mine were both of Russian make, probably once trimmed with fur: threads showed where something had been torn from the collars and cuffs.

Call-ups for the Siemens factory had ceased and we

speculated that it had been hit in one of the bombing raids that came within earshot almost nightly now. Betsie and I were put to work leveling some rough ground just inside the camp wall. This too was back-breaking labor. Sometimes as I bent to lift a load my heart cramped strangely; at night spasms of pain gripped my legs.

But the biggest problem was Betsie's strength. One morning after a hard night's rain we arrived to find the ground sodden and heavy. Betsie had never been able to lift much; today her shovels-ful were microscopic and she stumbled frequently as she walked to the low ground where we dumped the loads.

'*Schneller!*' a guard screamed at her. 'Can't you go faster?'

Why must they scream, I wondered as I sank my shovel into the black muck. Why couldn't they speak like ordinary human beings? I straightened slowly, the sweat drying on my back. I was remembering where we had first heard this maniac sound. The Beje. In Tante Jans's rooms. A voice coming from the shell-shaped speaker, a scream lingering in the air even after Betsie had leapt to shut it off . . .

'Loafer! Lazy swine!'

The guard snatched Betsie's shovel from her hands and ran from group to group of the digging crew, exhibiting the handful of dirt that was all Betsie had been able to lift.

'Look what Madame Baroness is carrying! Surely she will over-exert herself!'

The other guards and even some of the prisoners laughed. Encouraged, the guard threw herself into a parody of Betsie's faltering walk. A male guard was with our detail today and in the presence of a man the women guards were always animated.

As the laughter grew, I felt a murderous anger rise. The guard was young and well fed – was it Betsie's fault that she was old and starving? But to my astonishment, Betsie too was laughing.

'That's me all right,' she admitted. 'But you'd better let me totter along with my little spoonful, or I'll have to stop altogether.'

The guard's plump cheeks went crimson. 'I'll decide who's

to stop!' And snatching the leather crop from her belt she slashed Betsie across the chest and neck.

Without knowing I was doing it I had seized my shovel and rushed at her.

Betsie stepped in front of me before anyone had seen. 'Corrie!' she pleaded, dragging my arm to my side. 'Corrie! keep working!' She tugged the shovel from my hand and dug it into the mud. Contemptuously the guard tossed Betsie's shovel toward us. I picked it up, still in a daze. A red stain appeared on Betsie's collar; a welt began to swell on her neck.

Betsie saw where I was looking and laid a bird-thin hand over the whip mark. 'Don't look at it, Corrie. Look at Jesus only.' She drew away her hand: it was sticky with blood.

In mid-November the rains started in earnest, chill, drenching, daylong downpours that left beads of moisture even on the inside walls. The *Lagerstrasse* was never dry now; even when the rain let up, deep puddles stood in the road. We were not allowed to step around them as the ranks were formed: often we stood in water up to our ankles, and at night the barracks reeked with rotting shoe leather.

Betsie's cough began to bring up blood. We went to sick call at the hospital, but the thermometer registered only 102°, not enough to admit her to the wards. Alas for my fantasies of a nurse and a dispensary in each barracks. This large bare room in the hospital was where all the sick in the camp had to assemble, often standing outside in the rain for hours just to get through the door.

I hated the dismal place full of sick and suffering women, but we had to go back, again and again, for Betsie's condition was growing worse. She was not repelled by the room as I was. To her it was simply a setting in which to talk about Jesus – as indeed was everyplace else. Wherever she was, at work, in the food line, in the dormitory, Betsie spoke to those around her about His nearness and His yearning to come into their lives. As her body grew weaker, her faith seemed to grow bolder. And sick call was 'such an important place, Corrie! Some of these people are at the very threshold of heaven!'

At last one night Betsie's fever registered over the required 104°. There was another long wait until a nurse appeared to lead her and half a dozen others into the hospital proper. I stayed with them as far as the door to the ward, then made my way slowly back to the barracks.

As usual, as I stood in the door of the dormitory, it reminded me most of an anthill. Some women were already asleep after the long workday, but most were stirring about, some waiting for a turn at the toilets, others picking lice off themselves and their neighbors. I twisted and squirmed through the crowded aisles to the rear where the prayer service was just ending. Nights when Betsie and I reported to sick call we left the Bible with Mrs Wielmaker, a saintly Roman Catholic woman from The Hague who could render the Dutch words in German, French, Latin, or Greek. Women crowded around me, asking after Betsie. How was she? How long would she have to stay?

Lights-out blew and the scramble into the bunks began. I hoisted myself to the middle tier and crawled across those already in place. What a difference since Betsie had come to this room! Where before this had been the moment for scuffles and cursing, tonight the huge domitory buzzed with 'Sorry!' 'Excuse me!' And 'No harm done!'

I found our section in the dark and squeezed into a spot in the middle. From the doorway a searchlight swept the room, lingering on blocks where anything stirred. Someone's elbow dug into my back, another woman's feet were two inches from my face. How was it possible, packed so close, to be so utterly and miserably alone?

The Blue Sweater

In the morning a cold wet mist hung over the *Lagerstrasse*. I was grateful that Betsie did not have to stand outside.

All day the blanketing fog hung over Ravensbruck, an eerie day when sound was muffled and the sun never rose. I was on potato detail, one of a crew hauling baskets of potatoes to long trenches to be covered with dirt against the freezing weather ahead. I was glad of the hard physical work that drove some of the damp from my bones and for the occasional bite of raw potato when guards were not watching.

Next day when the white pall still lay over the camp, my loneliness for Betsie became too much to bear. As soon as roll call was dismissed, I did a desperate thing. Mien had told me a way to get into the hospital without passing the guardpost inside the door. The latrine at the rear, she said, had a very large window too warped to close tight. Since no visiting was permitted in the hospital, relatives of patients often took this way of getting inside.

In the dense fog it was easy to get to the window unseen. I hoisted myself through it, then clapped my hand to my nose against the stinging odor. A row of lidless, doorless toilets stretched along one wall in the pool of their overflow. I dashed for the door, then stopped, my flesh crawling. Against this opposite wall a dozen naked corpses lay side by side on their backs. Some of the eyes were open and seemed to stare unblinkingly at the ceiling.

I was standing there, lead-footed with horror, when two men pushed through the door carrying a sheet-wrapped bundle between them. They did not even glance at me and I realized they took me for a patient. I ducked round them into the hall and stood a moment, stomach knotting with the sight I had seen. After a while I started aimlessly off to the left.

The hospital was a maze of halls and doors. Already I was not sure of the way back to the latrine. What if the potato crew left before I got back? And then a corridor looked familiar. I hurried, almost running from door to door. At last. The ward where I left Betsie! No hospital personnel was in sight: I walked eagerly down the aisles of cots looking from face to face.

'Corrie!'

Betsie was sitting up in a cot near the window. She looked stronger, eyes bright, a touch of color in her sunken cheeks. No nurse or doctor had seen her yet, she said, but the chance to lie still and stay indoors had already made a difference.

Three days afterward, Betsie returned to Barracks 28. She still had received no examination or medicine of any kind and her forehead felt feverish to my touch. But the joy of having her back outweighed my anxiety.

Best of all, as a result of her hospitalization, she was given a permanent assignment to the 'knitting brigade,' the women we had seen the very first day seated about the tables in the center room. This work was reserved for the weakest prisoners, and now overflowed into the dormitories as well.

Those working in the sleeping rooms received far less supervision than those at the tables, and Betsie found herself with most of the day in which to minister to those around her. She was a lightning knitter who completed her quota of socks long before noon. She kept our Bible with her and spent hours each day reading aloud from it, moving from platform to platform.

One evening I got back to the barracks late from a wood-gathering foray outside the walls. A light snow lay on the ground and it was hard to find the sticks and twigs with which a small stove was kept going in each room. Betsie was waiting for me, as always, so that we could wait through the food line together. Her eyes were twinkling.

'You're looking extraordinarily pleased with yourself,' I told her.

'You know we've never understood why we had so much freedom in the big room,' she said. 'Well – I've found out.'

That afternoon, she said, there'd been confusion in her knitting group about sock sizes and they'd asked the supervisor to come and settle it.

'But she wouldn't. She wouldn't step through the door and neither would the guards. And you know why?'

Betsie could not keep the triumph from her voice: 'Because of the fleas! That's what she said, "That place is crawling with fleas!"'

My mind rushed back to our first hour in this place. I remembered Betsie's bowed head, remembered her thanks to God for creatures I could see no use for.

Though Betsie was now spared heavy outdoor labor, she still had to stand the twice-daily roll call. As December temperatures fell, they became true endurance tests and many did not survive. One dark morning when ice was forming a halo around each street lamp, a feeble-minded girl two rows ahead of us suddenly soiled herself. A guard rushed at her, swinging her thick leather crop while the girl shrieked in pain and terror. It was always more terrible when one of these innocent ones was beaten. Still the *Aufseherin* continued to whip her. It was the guard we had nicknamed 'The Snake' because of the shiny dress she wore. I could see it now beneath her long wool cape, glittering in the light of the lamp when she raised her arm. I was grateful when the screaming girl at last lay still on the cinder street.

'Betsie,' I whispered when the The Snake was far enough away, 'what can we do for these people? Afterward I mean. Can't we make a home for them and care for them and love them?'

'Corrie, I pray every day that we will be allowed to do this! To show them that love is greater!'

And it wasn't until I was gathering twigs later in the morning that I realized that I had been thinking of the feeble-minded, and Betsie of their persecutors.

Several days later my entire work crew was ordered to the hospital for medical inspection. I dropped my dress onto the pile just inside the door and joined the file of naked women. Ahead of us, to my surprise, a doctor was using a stethoscope with all the deliberateness of a real examination.

'What is this for?' I whispered to the woman ahead of me.

'Transport inspection,' she hissed back, not moving her head. 'Munitions work.'

Transport! But they couldn't! They mustn't send me away! Dear God, don't let them take me away from Betsie!

But to my terror I passed one station after another – heart, lungs, scalp, throat – and still I was in the line. Many were pulled out along the way, but those who remained looked hardly stronger. Swollen stomachs, hollow chests, spindly legs: how desperate for manpower Germany must be!

I halted before a woman in a soiled white coat. She turned me around to face a chart on the wall, her hand cold on my bare shoulder. 'Read the lowest line you can.'

'I – I can't seem to read any of them. (Lord forgive me!) Just the top letter. That big E.' The top letter was an F.

The woman seemed to see me for the first time. 'You can see better than that! Do you want to be rejected?'

At Ravensbruck, munitions transport was considered a privilege; food and living conditions in the factories were said to be far better than here in the camp.

'Oh yes, Doctor! My sister's here at Ravensbruck! She's not well! I can't leave her!'

The doctor sat down at her table and scrawled something on a piece of paper. 'Come back tomorrow to be fitted for glasses.'

Catching up to the line, I unfolded the small blue slip of paper. Prisoner 66730 was instructed to report for an optical fitting at 6:30 the following morning. Six-thirty was the time the transport convoys were loaded.

And so as the huge vans rumbled down the *Lagerstrasse*

the next day, I was standing in a corridor of the hospital waiting my turn at the eye clinic. The young man in charge was perhaps a qualified eye doctor, but his entire equipment consisted of a box of framed glasses, from gold-rimmed bifocals to a plastic-framed child's pair. I found none that fitted and at last was ordered back to my work detail.

But, of course, I had no work assignment, having been marked down for transport. I walked back uncertainly toward Barracks 28. I stepped into the center room. The supervisor looked up over the heads of the knitting crew.

'Number?' she said.

I gave it and she wrote it in a black-covered book. 'Pick up your yarn and a pattern sheet,' she went on. 'You'll have to find a place on one of the beds, there's no room here.' And she turned back to the pile of finished socks on the table.

I stood blinking in the center of the room. Then grabbing a skein of the dark gray wool I dashed through the dormitory door. And thus began the closest, most joyous weeks of all the time in Ravensbruck. Side by side, in the sanctuary of God's fleas, Betsie and I ministered the word of God to all in the room. We sat by deathbeds that became doorways of heaven. We watched women who had lost everything grow rich in hope. The knitters of Barracks 28 became the praying heart of the vast diseased body that was Ravensbruck, interceding for all in the camp – guards, under Betsie's prodding, as well as prisoners. We prayed beyond the concrete walls for the healing of Germany, of Europe, of the world – as Mama had once done from the prison of a crippled body.

And as we prayed, God spoke to us about the world after the war. It was extraordinary; in this place where whistles and loudspeakers took the place of decisions, God asked us what we were going to do in the years ahead.

Betsie was always very clear about the answer for her and me. We were to have a house, a large one – much larger than the Beje – to which people who had been damaged by concentration-camp life would come until they felt ready to live again in the normal world.

'It's such a beautiful house, Corrie! The floors are all inlaid wood, with statues set in the walls and a broad staircase sweeping down. And gardens! Gardens all around it where they can plant flowers. It will do them such good, Corrie, to care for flowers!'

I would stare at Betsie in amazement as she talked about these things. She spoke always as though she were describing things that she saw – as if that wide, winding staircase and those bright gardens were the reality, this cramped and filthy barracks the dream.

But it wasn't a dream. It was really, achingly, endlessly true, and it was always during roll calls that the accumulated misery threatened to overwhelm me.

One morning three women from Barracks 28 lingered inside a few minutes to avoid the cold. All the following week the entire barracks was punished by an extra hour at attention. The lights on the *Lagerstrasse* were not even lit when we were driven from our bunks at 3:30 A.M.

It was during this preinspection lineup one morning that I saw what I had till then refused to believe. Headlights appeared at the far end of the long street, wavering over the snow. Trucks with open flat-beds in the rear were approaching, spattering slush as they passed. They pulled up at the front door of the hospital. The door opened and a nurse appeared, supporting an old woman whose legs buckled as she limped down the steps. The nurse lifted her gently onto the back of a truck. They were pouring out the door now, leaning on the arms of nurses and hospital helpers, the old, the ill. Last of all came orderlies with stretchers between them.

Our eyes took in every detail of the scene; our brains refused. We had known, of course, that when overcrowding reached a certain point, the sickest were taken to the brick building at the foot of the great square smokestack. But, that these women here in front of us – these very ones . . . It was not possible. Above all I could not put it together with the kindly behavior of the nurses. That one in the truck just ahead, bending solicitously, even tenderly, over her patient . . . What was passing through her mind just now?

And all the while, it grew colder. One night during evening roll call a platoon somewhere far down the *Lagerstrasse* began a rhythmic stamping. The sound grew as others picked it up. The guards did not stop us and at last the entire street was marching in place, pounding tattered shoes against the frozen ground, driving circulation back into numb feet and legs. From now on this was the sound of roll call, the stamping of thousands of feet on the long dark street.

And as the cold increased, so did the special temptation of concentration-camp life: the temptation to think only of oneself. It took a thousand cunning forms. I quickly discovered that when I maneuvered our way toward the middle of the roll-call we had a little protection from the wind.

I knew this was self-centered: when Betsie and I stood in the center, someone else had to stand on the edge. How easy it was to give it other names! I was acting only for Betsie's sake. We were in an important ministry and must keep well. It was colder in Poland than in Holland; these Polish women probably were not feeling the chill the way we were.

Selfishness had a life of its own. As I watched Mien's bag of yeast compound disappear I began taking it from beneath the straw only after lights-out when others would not see and ask for some. Wasn't Betsie's health more important? (You see, God, she can do so much *for* them! Remember that house, after the war!)

And even if it wasn't right – it wasn't so *very* wrong, was it? Not wrong like sadism and murder and the other monstrous evils we saw in Ravensbruck every day. Oh, this was the great ploy of Satan in that kingdom of his: to display such blatant evil that one could almost believe one's own secret sins didn't matter.

The cancer spread. The second week in December, every occupant of Barracks 28 was issued an extra blanket. The next day a large group of evacuées arrived from Czechoslovakia. One of them assigned to our platform had no blanket at all and Betsie insisted that we give her one of ours. So that evening I 'lent' her a blanket. But I didn't 'give' it to her. In my heart I held onto the right to that blanket.

Was it coincidence that joy and power imperceptibly drained from my ministry? My prayers took on a mechanical ring.

Even Bible reading was dull and lifeless. Betsie tried to take over for me, but her cough made reading aloud impossible.

And so I struggled on with worship and teaching that had ceased to be real. Until one drizzly raw afternoon when just enough light came through the window to read by, I came to Paul's account of his 'thorn in the flesh.' Three times, he said, he had begged God to take away his weakness, whatever it was. And each time God had said, Rely on Me. At last Paul concluded – the words seemed to leap from the page – that his very weakness was something to give thanks for. Because now Paul knew that none of the wonders and miracles which followed his ministry could be done by his own virtues. It was all Christ's strength, never Paul's.

And there it was.

The truth blazed like sunlight in the shadows of Barracks 28. The real sin I had been committing was not that of inching toward the center of a platoon because I was cold. The real sin lay in thinking that any power to help and transform came from me. Of course it was not *my* wholeness, but Christ's that made the difference.

The short winter day was fading: I could no longer separate the words on the page. And so I closed the Bible and to that group of women clustering close I told the truth about myself – my self-centeredness, my stinginess, my lack of love. That night real joy returned to my worship.

Each roll call the wind seemed sharper. Whenever she could, Mien smuggled newspapers from the staff room at the hospital, which we placed inside our clothes. Nollie's blue sweater beneath Betsie's dress was black with newsprint.

The cold seemed to be affecting Betsie's legs. Sometimes in the morning she could not move them at all and two of us would have to carry her between us. It was not hard – she weighed no more than a child. But she could no longer stamp her feet as the rest of us did to keep the blood flowing. When we returned to the dormitory I would rub her feet and hands, but my own only picked up the chill from hers.

It was the week before Christmas that Betsie woke up unable to move either legs or arms. I shoved my way through the crowded aisles to the center room. The Snake was on duty.

'Please!' I begged. 'Betsie is ill! Oh please, she's got to get to the hospital!'

'Stand at attention. State your number.'

'Prisoner 66730 reporting. Please, my sister is sick!'

'All prisoners must report for the count. If she's sick she can register at sick call.'

Maryke de Graaf, a Dutch woman on the tier above ours, helped me form a cradle with our arms and carry Betsie outside. The rhythmic stamping had already begun in the *Lagerstrasse*. We carried her to the hospital, then stopped. In the light of the street lamps, the sick-call line stretched to the edge of the building and out of sight around the corner. In the sooty snow alongside, three bodies lay where they had fallen.

Without a word Maryke and I turned and carried out load back to the *Lagerstrasse*. After roll call we got her back into bed. Her speech was slow and blurred, but she was trying to say something.

'A camp, Corrie – a concentration camp. But we're . . . in charge . . .' I had to bend very close to hear. The camp was in Germany. It was no longer a prison, but a home where people who had been warped by this philosophy of hate and force could come to learn another way. There were no walls, no barbed wire, and the barracks had windowboxes. 'It will be so good for them . . . watching things grow. People can learn to love, from flowers . . .'

I knew by now which people she meant. The German people. I thought of The Snake standing in the barracks door that morning. 'State your number. All prisoners must report for the count.'

I looked into Betsie's shrunken face. 'We are to have this camp in Germany instead, Betsie? Instead of the big house in Holland?'

'Oh no!' she seemed shocked. 'You know we have the house first! It's ready and waiting for us . . . such tall, tall windows! The sun is streaming in — '

A coughing fit seized her; when finally she lay still, a stain of blood blackened the straw. She dozed fitfully during the day and night that followed, waking several times with the excitement of some new detail about our work in Holland or Germany.

'The barracks are gray, Corrie, but we'll paint them green! Bright, light green, like springtime.'

'We'll be together, Betsie? We're doing all this together? You're sure about that?'

'Always together, Corrie! You and I . . . always together.'

When the siren blew next morning. Maryke and I again carried Betsie from the dormitory. The Snake was standing at the street door. As we started through it with our fragile burden she stepped in front of us. 'Take her back to the bunks.'

'I thought all pris — '

'Take her back!'

Wonderingly, we replaced Betsie on the bed. Sleet rattled against the windows. Was it possible that the atmosphere of Barracks 28 had affected even this cruel guard? As soon as roll call was dismissed I ran back to the dormitory. There, beside our bed, stood The Snake. Beside her two orderlies from the hospital were setting down a stretcher. The Snake straightened almost guiltily as I approached. 'Prisoner is ready for transfer,' she snapped.

I looked at the woman more closely: Had she risked fleas and lice to spare Betsie the sick-call line? She did not stop me as I started after the stretcher. Our group of knitters was just entering the big room. As we passed, a Polish friend dropped to her knees and made the sign of the Cross.

Sleet stung us as we reached the outside. I stepped close to the stretcher to form a shield for Betsie. We walked past the waiting line of sick people, through the door and into a large ward. They placed the stretcher on the floor and I leaned down to make out Betsie's words.

'. . . must tell people what we have learned here. We must tell them that there is no pit so deep that He is not deeper still. They will listen to us, Corrie, because we have been here.'

I stared at her wasted form. 'But when will all this happen, Betsie!'

'Now. Right away. Oh, very soon! By the first of the year, Corrie, we will be out of prison!'

A nurse had caught sight of me. I backed to the door of the room and watched as they placed Betsie on a narrow cot close to the window. I ran around to the outside of the building. At last Betsie caught sight of me; we exchanged smiles and soundless words until one of the camp police shouted at me to move along.

About noontime I put down my knitting and went out to the center room. 'Prisoner 66730 reporting. Request permission to visit the hospital.' I stood ramrod straight.

The Snake glanced up, then scrawled out a pass. Outside it was still sleeting. I reached the door of the ward but the horrible nurse would not let me enter, even with my pass. So I went again to the window next to Betsie's cot. I waited until the nurse left the room, then tapped gently.

Betsie's eyes opened. Slowly she turned her head.

'Are you all right?' I formed with my lips.

She nodded.

'You must get a good rest,' I went on.

She moved her lips in reply but I could not follow. She formed the words again. I bent my head to one side, level with hers. The blue lips opened again:

'. . . so much work to do . . .'

The Snake was off duty during the afternoon and evening and though I asked the other guards repeatedly, I did not again get permission to leave. The minute roll call was dismissed the following morning, I headed for the hospital, permission or no.

I reached the window and cupped my eyes to peer in. A nurse was standing directly between me and Betsie. I ducked out of sight, waited a minute, then looked again. A second nurse had joined the first, both now standing where I wanted to see. They stepped to the head and foot of the bed: I gazed curiously at what lay on it. It was a carving in old yellow ivory. There was no clothing on the figure; I could see each ivory rib, and the outline of the teeth through the parchment cheeks.

It took me a moment to realize it was Betsie.

The nurses had each seized two corners of the sheet. They

lifted it between them and carried the bundle from the room before my heart had started to beat in my chest.

Betsie! But – she had too much to do! She could not —

Where were they taking her? Where had they gone? I turned from the window and began running along the side of the building, chest hurting me as I breathed.

Then I remembered the washroom. That window at the rear – that was where . . .

My feet carried me mechanically around to the back of the building. And there, with my hand on the windowsill, I stopped. Suppose she was there? Suppose they had laid Betsie on that floor?

I started walking again. I walked for a long time, still with that pain in my chest. And each time my feet took me back to the washroom window. I would not go in. I would not look. Betsie could not be there.

I walked some more. Strangely enough, although I passed several camp police, no one stopped me.

'Corrie!'

I turned around to see Mien running after me. 'Corrie, I've looked for you everywhere! Oh, Corrie, come!'

She seized my arm and drew me toward the back of the hospital.

When I saw where she was headed I wrenched my arm free. 'I know, Mien. I know already.'

She didn't seem to hear. She seized me again, led me to the washroom window, and pushed me in ahead of her. In the reeking room stood a nurse. I drew back in alarm, but Mien was behind me.

'This is the sister,' Mien said to the nurse.

I turned my head to the side – I would not look at the bodies that lined the far wall. Mien put an arm around my shoulder and drew me across the room till we were standing above that heart-breaking row.

'Corrie! Do you see her!'

I raised my eyes to Betsie's face. Lord Jesus – what have You done! Oh Lord, what are You saying! What are You giving me!

For there lay Betsie, her eyes closed as if in sleep, her

face full and young. The care lines, the grief lines, the deep hollows of hunger and disease were simply gone. In front of me was the Betsie of Haarlem, happy and at peace. Stronger! Freer! This was the Betsie of heaven, bursting with joy and health. Even her hair was graciously in place as if an angel had ministered to her.

At last I turned wonderingly to Mien. The nurse went silently to the door and opened it for us herself. 'You can leave through the hall,' she said softly.

I looked once more at the radiant face of my sister. Then Mien and I left the room together. A pile of clothes was heaped outside in the hallway; on top lay Nollie's blue sweater.

I stooped to pick it up. The sweater was threadbare and stained with newsprint, but it was a tangible link with Betsie. Mien seized my arm. 'Don't touch those things! Black lice! They'll all be burned.'

And so I left behind the last physical tie. It was just as well. It was better. Now what tied me to Betsie was the hope of heaven.

15

The Three Visions

The beauty of Betsie's face sustained me over the next days, as I went from one to another of the women who had loved her, describing to them her peace and her joy.

Two mornings after her death the count was off at roll call. The other barracks were dismissed, 28 remained in ranks, eyes front. The loudspeaker beeped and a voice came on: a woman was missing; the entire barracks would stand on the *Lagerstrasse* until she was found. Left, right, left, right, endlessly tramping to drive the chill from weary legs. The sun came up, a wan wintry sun that did not warm. I looked down at my feet: my legs and ankles were swelling grotesquely. By noontime there was no feeling in them. Betsie, how happy you are today! No cold, no hunger, nothing between you and the face of Jesus!

The dismissal order came in the afternoon. We learned later that the missing woman had been found dead on one of the upper platforms.

It was the following morning when over the loudspeaker during roll call came the words: 'Ten Boom, Cornelia!'

For an instant I stood stupidly where I was. I had been Prisoner 66730 for so long that I almost failed to react to my name. I walked forward.

'Stand to the side!'

What was going to happen? Why had I been singled out? Had someone reported the Bible?

The roll call dragged on. From where I stood I could see almost the entire *Lagerstrasse*, tens of thousands of women stretching out of sight, their breath hanging white in the night air.

The siren blew for dismissal; the guard signaled me to follow her. I splashed through the slush, trying to keep up with the strides of her tall boots. My legs and feet were still painfully swollen from the long count the day before, my shoes were held together with bits of string.

I hobbled behind the guard into the administration barracks at the opposite end of the *Lagerstrasse* from the hospital. Several prisoners were standing in line at a large desk. An officer seated behind it stamped a paper and handed it to the woman in front of him.

'*Entlassen!*' he said.

Entlassen? Released? Was – was the woman free then? Was this – were we all —

He called a name and another prisoner stepped to the desk. A signature, a stamp:

'*Entlassen!*'

At last 'Ten Boom, Cornelia,' was called. I stepped to the desk, steadying myself against it. He wrote, brought down the stamp, and then I was holding it in my hand: a piece of paper with my name and birthdate on it, and across the top in large black letters: CERTIFICATE OF DISCHARGE.

Dazed, I followed the others through a door at our left. There at another desk I was handed a railway pass entitling me to transportation through Germany to the Dutch border. Outside this office a guard pointed me down a corridor into still another room. There the prisoners who had been ahead of me were tugging their dresses over their heads and lining up against the rear wall.

'Clothing over here!' a smiling prison trusty told me. '*Entlassen* physical,' she explained.

I drew the Bible over my head along with the dress, rolled them together and buried the bundle at the bottom of the clothing pile. I joined the others, the wooden wall rough against my bare back. Strange how the very word 'Release' had made the procedures of prison a hundred times more hateful. How often Betsie and I had stood like this. But the thought of freedom had stirred in me

and the shame of this inspection was greater than all the
others.

At last the doctor arrived, a freckle-faced boy in a military
uniform. He glanced along the lineup with undisguised contempt. One by one we had to bend, turn around, spread our
fingers. When he reached me his eyes traveled down to my
feet and his lips puckered in disgust.

'Edema,' he said. 'Hospital.'

He was gone. With one other woman who had not 'passed'
I scrambled back into my clothes and followed the trusty from
the building. Day had broken, a sullen gray sky spitting snow.
We started up the *Lagerstrasse*, past the endless streets of
barracks.

'Then – we're not – aren't we to be released?'

'I imagine you will be, as soon as the swelling in your legs
goes down,' the trusty said. 'They only release you if you're
in good condition.' I saw her look at the other prisoner: the
woman's skin and eyes were a dull dark yellow.

Sick call stretched around the side of the hospital, but
we walked straight through the door and into a ward at the
rear. The room was crammed with double-decker cots. I was
assigned a place on an upper bunk next to a woman whose
body was covered with erupting pustules. But at least it was
near a wall where I could keep my swollen legs elevated. That
was what mattered now: to get the swelling down, to pass the
inspection.

Whether that ray of freedom shed a new, relentless light on
Ravensbruck, or whether this was truly the most savage place
yet, I could not tell. The suffering was unimaginable. Around
me were survivors of a prison train which had been bombed
on its way here. The women were horribly mutilated and in
terrible pain, but at each moan two of the nurses jeered and
mimicked the sounds.

Even in the other patients I saw that stony indifference to
others that was the most fatal disease of the concentration
camp. I felt it spread to myself: how could one survive if
one kept on feeling! The paralyzed and the unconscious kept
falling out of the crowded narrow cots; that first night four

women fell from upper bunks and died on the floor. It was better to narrow the mind to one's own need, not to see, not to think.

But there was no way to shut out the sounds. All night women cried out a German word I didn't know. *'Schieber!'* Over and over from rasping throats: *'Schieber!'*

Finally I realized that they were calling for bedpans. It was out of the question for most of the women in this room to make it to that filthy latrine next door. At last, reluctant to lower my legs, I climbed down from my cot and set about the chore. The gratitude of the patients was heart-wrenching. 'Who are you. Why are you doing this?' – as though cruelty and callousness were the norm, ordinary decency the marvel.

As a wintry dawn crept through the windows, I realized it was Christmas Day.

I went each morning to the clinic at the front of the hospital where I could hear the tramping of feet on the *Lagerstrasse* outside. Each time the verdict was 'Edema of the feet and ankles.' Many of those who attended the clinic were, like myself, discharged prisoners. Some had been released months ago: their discharge papers and railway passes were ragged from opening and refolding. And – what if Betsie were still alive? Surely our prison term would have been up together. But Betsie would never, never have passed the physical. What if she were here with me? What if I were to pass the inspection and she . . .

There are no 'ifs' in God's kingdom. I could hear her soft voice saying it. His timing is perfect. His will is our hiding place. Lord Jesus, keep me in Your will! Don't let me go mad by poking about outside it.

I kept looking for someone to give the Bible to. How easy it would be, back in Holland, to get another – a hundred others. There were not many Hollanders in the ward who would be able to read the Dutch text, but at last I slipped it around the neck of a grateful young woman from Utrecht.

The sixth night I spent in the ward both bedpans were suddenly and mysteriously missing. In an upper bunk on the center aisle were two Hungarian gypsies whose muttering

was part of the babble of the room. I never walked past
their cot because one of them had a gangrenous foot which
she would thrust in the face of anyone who came near. Now
someone screamed out that the gypsies had the bedpans,
hidden under their blankets to save them the trip to the
toilets. I went to their cot and pleaded with them – though
I didn't know whether they understood German or not.

Suddenly in the dark something wet and sticky coiled round
my face. The woman had taken the bandage from her foot and
flung it at me. I ran sobbing down the corridor and washed and
washed beneath the wall spigot in the latrine. I would never
step into that aisle again! What did I care about the wretched
bedpans! I couldn't bear . . .

But of course I did go back. I had learned much, in the past
year, about what I could and could not bear. As the gypsies
saw me heading down the aisle toward them, both bedpans
clattered onto the floor.

The next morning the doctor on duty at the clinic stamped
the medical approval on my discharge form. Events that had
dragged so slow now moved with bewildering speed. In a
dressing shed near the outer gate of the camp I was outfitted
with clothes. Underthings; a woolen skirt: a truly beautiful
silk blouse; sturdy, almost-new shoes; a hat, an overcoat. I
was handed a form to sign stating that I had never been ill at
Ravensbruck, never had an accident, and that the treatment
had been good. I signed.

In another building I received a day's bread ration and food
coupons for three additional days. I was also given back my
watch, my Dutch money, and Mama's ring. And then I was
standing with a group of ten or twelve just inside the gate.

The heavy iron doors swung open; at the heels of a woman
guard we marched through. We climbed the little hill: now I
could see the lake, frozen from shore to shore. The pines and
the distant church steeple sparkled in the winter sun like an
old-fashioned Christmas card.

I could not believe it. Perhaps we were only going to the
Siemens factory; tonight we would march back to camp. But at
the top of the hill we turned left, toward the center of the small

town. I could feel my feet swelling in the tight new shoes, but I bit my lip and made myself stride along. I imagined the guard turning around, pointing a scornful finger: 'Edema! Send her back to camp!'

At the small train station the guard turned and left us without a backward glance. Apparently we were all traveling as far as Berlin, then each pursuing her separate route home. There was a long wait on cold iron benches.

The feeling of unreality persisted. Only one thing seemed familiar, the hungry hollow in my stomach. I put off getting into my bread allowance as long as I could, but at last reached into my overcoat pocket. The packet was gone. I sprang up from the bench, looking beneath it, retracing my steps through the station. Whether I had dropped it or it had been stolen, the bread was gone, and with it the ration coupons.

At last a train pulled into the station and we crowded eagerly to it but it was for military personnel only. Late in the afternoon we were allowed aboard a mail train, only to be put off two stops farther on to make room for a food shipment. The trip became a blur. We reached the huge, bomb-gutted terminal in Berlin sometime after midnight.

It was New Year's Day, 1945. Betsie had been right: she and I were out of prison . . .

Snow drifted down from a shattered skylight as I wandered, confused and frightened, through the cavernous station. I knew that I must find the train to Uelzen, but months of being told what to do had left me robbed of initiative. At last someone directed me to a distant platform. Each step now was agony in the stiff new shoes. When I reached the platform at last, the sign said not Uelzen but Olsztyn, a town in Poland in exactly the opposite direction. I had to cross those acres of concrete floors again.

Ahead of me an elderly man, pink-cheeked from working in the roofless station, was raking bomb rubble into a pile. When I asked him for directions he took me by the arm and led me himself to the proper platform. 'I was to Holland once,' he said, voice wistful with recollection. 'When the wife was alive, you know. Right on the sea we stayed.'

A train was standing on the track and I climbed aboard. It

was hours before anyone else arrived, but I did not dare get off for fear I would not find my way back again. By the time the train started up I was dizzy for lack of food. At the first stop outside Berlin I followed the other passengers into the station café. I showed the woman behind the cash-box my Dutch guilders and told her I had lost my coupons.

'That's an old story! Get out of here before I call the police!'

The trip was endless. Many miles of track could be traveled only at a crawl. Some sections were gone altogether and there were interminable, long detours and many changes of train. Often we did not stop in a station at all, for fear of air raids, but exchanged freight and passengers in the countryside.

And all the while, out my window passed once-beautiful Germany. Fire-blackened woods, the gaunt ribs of a church standing over a ruined village. Bremen especially brought tears to my eyes. In all that wasteland I saw one human being, an old woman poking at a heap of bricks.

In Uelzen there was a long wait between trains. It was late at night, the station was deserted. As I dozed in an empty coffee bar my head dropped forward until it rested on the small table in front of me. A blow on my ear sent me sprawling almost to the floor.

'This is not a bedroom!' the furious station agent shrieked. 'You can't use our tables to sleep on!'

Trains came. Trains didn't come. I climbed on and off. And then I was standing in a line at a customs shed and the sign on the little station building said *Nieuwerschans*. As I left the building a workman in a blue cap and blue overalls stepped up to me. 'Here! You won't get far on those legs! Hang onto my arm.'

He spoke Dutch.

I clung to him and hobbled across some tracks to where another train was waiting, engine already puffing smoke. I was in Holland.

We jerked forward. Flat, snow-covered fields glided past the window. Home. It was still occupied Holland, German soldiers still stood at intervals along the tracks – but it was home.

The train was going only as far as Groningen, a Dutch city not far from the border. Beyond that rails were torn up and all except government travel banned. With the last of my strength I limped to a hospital near the station.

A nurse in a sparkling white uniform invited me into a little office. When I had told my story, she left the room. In a few minutes she was back with a tray of tea and rusk. 'I left the butter off,' she said. 'You're suffering from malnutrition. You must be careful what you eat.'

Tears tumbled into the hot tea as I drank. Here was someone who felt concern for me. There were no available beds in the hospital, she said, but one of the staff was away and I was to have her room. 'Right now I have a hot tub running.'

I followed her down gleaming corridors in a kind of happy dream. In a large bathroom clouds of steam were rising from a glistening white tub. Nothing in my life ever felt as good as that bath. I lay submerged to my chin, feeling the warm water soothe my scab-crusted skin. 'Just five minutes more!' I would beg each time the nurse rapped at the door.

At last I let her hand me a nightgown and lead me to a room where a bed was turned down and waiting. Sheets. White sheets top and bottom. I could not get enough of running my hands over them. The nurse was tucking a second pillow beneath my swollen feet. I struggled to stay awake: to lie here clean and cared for was such joy I did not want to sleep through a minute of it.

I stayed in the hospital at Groningen ten days, feeling my strength return. For most meals I joined the nurses in their own dining room. The first time I saw the long table set with silverware and glasses, I drew back in alarm.

'You're having a party! Let me take a tray to my room!' I did not feel ready yet for laughter and social chatter.

The young woman beside me laughed as she pulled out a chair for me. 'It's not a party! It's just supper – and skimpy enough at that.'

I sat down blinking at knives, forks, tablecloth – had I once eaten like this, every day in the year? Like a savage watching his first civilized meal I copied the leisurely gestures of the others as they passed bread and cheese and unhurriedly stirred their coffee.

The ache in my heart was to get to Willem and Nollie – but how could it be done with the travel ban? Telephone service, too, was more limited than ever, but at last the girl at the hospital switchboard reached the telephone operator in Hilversum with the news of Betsie's death and my release.

In the middle of the second week, hospital authorities arranged a ride for me on a food truck headed south. We made the illegal trip at night and without headlights: the food had been diverted from a shipment headed for Germany. In the gray early morning the truck pulled up to Willem's big brick nursing home. A tall, broad-shouldered girl answered my knock, and then went dashing down the hallway with the news that I was here.

In a moment my arms were around Tine and two of my nieces. Willem arrived more slowly, limping down the corridor with the help of a cane. We held each other a long time while I told them the details of Betsie's illness and death.

'Almost,' said Willem slowly, 'almost I could wish to have this same news of Kik. It would be good for him to be with Betsie and Father.' They had had no word of this tall blond son since his deportation to Germany. I remembered his hand on my shoulder, guiding me on our bicycles through the blacked-out streets to Pickwick's. Remembered his patient coaching: 'You *have* no cards, Tante Corrie! There *are no Jews*.' Kik! Are the young and brave as vulnerable as the old and slow?

I spent two weeks in Hilversum, trying to adjust to what my eyes had told me that first moment. Willem was dying. Only he seemed unaware of it as he hobbled along the halls of his home bringing comfort and counsel to the sick people in his care. They had over fifty patients at the moment, but what I could not get over was the number of young women in help: nurse's aides, kitchen helpers, secretaries. It was several days before I perceived that most of these 'girls' were young men in hiding from the forced-labor conscription which had grown more ruthless than ever.

And still something in me could not rest until I got back to Haarlem. Nollie was there, of course. But it was the Beje, too, something in the house itself that called me, beckoned me, told me to come home.

The problem, again, was getting there. Willem had the use of an official car for nursing-home business, but only within a radius of Hilversum. Finally, after many relayed phone calls, he told me the trip had been arranged.

The roads were deserted as we set out; we passed only two other cars all the way to the rendezvous spot with the car from Haarlem. Ahead, pulled off onto the snow at the side of the road, we saw it, a long black limousine with official government plates and curtained rear windows. I kissed Willem goodbye and then stepped quickly, as instructed, into the rear of the limousine. Even in the curtained gloom the ungainly bulk beside me was unmistakable.

'Oom Herman!' I cried.

'My dear Cornelia.' His great hand closed around both of mine. 'God permits me to see you again.'

I had last seen Pickwick sitting between two soldiers on the prison bus in The Hague, his poor bald head bruised and bleeding. Now here he was, waving aside my sympathy as though that had been an incident too trivial to recall.

He seemed as well informed as ever about everything that went on in Haarlem, and as the uniformed driver sped us along the empty roads, he filled me in on all the details I ached to know. All of our Jews were safe except for Mary Itallie, who had been sent to Poland following her arrest in the street. Our group was still operating, although many of the young men were in hiding.

He warned me to expect changes at the Beje. After the police guard had been removed, a series of homeless families had been housed there, although at the moment he believed the living quarters above the shop were empty. Even before the house was unsealed, loyal Toos had returned from Scheveningen and reopened the watch business. Mr Beukers, the optician next door, had given her space in his shop from which she had taken orders to give to our repairmen in their homes.

As my eyes adjusted to the dim light I made out my friend's face more clearly. There was perhaps an extra knob or two on the misshapen head, teeth were missing – but to that vast, kindly ugliness the beating had made no real difference at all.

Now the limousine was threading the narrow streets of Haarlem. Over the bridge on the Spaarne. Across the Grote Markt in the shadow of St Bavo's, into the Barteljorisstraat. I was out of the car almost before it stopped, running down the alley, through the side door, and into Nollie's embrace. She and her girls had been there all morning, sweeping, washing windows, airing sheets for my homecoming. Over Nollie's shoulder I saw Toos standing in the rear door to the shop, laughing and sobbing both at once. Laughing because I was home; crying because Father and Betsie, the only two people she had ever allowed herself to love, would never be.

Together we trooped through the house and shop, looking, stroking – 'Remember how Betsie would set out these cups?' 'Remember how Meta would scold Eusie for leaving his pipe here?' I stood on the landing outside the dining room and ran my hand over the smooth wood of the Frisian clock. I could see Father stopping here, Kapteyn at his heels.

'We mustn't let the clock run down . . .'

I opened the glass face, moved the hands to agree with my wristwatch, and slowly drew up the weights. I was home. Life, like the clock, started again: mornings repairing watches in the workshop, noons most often bumping on my tireless bicycle out to Bos en Hoven Straat.

And yet . . . in a strange way, I was not home. I was still waiting, still looking for something. I spent days prowling the alleys and canal banks nearby, calling Maher Shalal Hashbaz by name. The elderly vegetable lady three stores down told me that the cat had mewed at her door the night of our arrest and she had taken him in. For months, she said, the small children of the neighborhood had banded together to bring food to 'Opa's kitty.' They had brought scraps from garbage pails and even tidbits from their own scanty plates smuggled past watchful mothers, and Mr Hashbaz had remained sleek and fat.

It was mid-December, she said, when he had not appeared one night to her call, nor had she seen him since. And so I searched, but with a sinking heart: in this winter of Holland's hunger, all my searching brought not one single cat or dog to my call.

I missed more than the cat; the Beje needed people to fill its rooms. I remembered Father's words to the Gestapo chief in The Hague: 'I will open my door to anyone in need . . .' No one in the city was in greater need than its feeble-minded. Since the start of the Nazi occupation they had been sequestered by their families in back rooms, their schools and training centers shut down, hidden from a government which had decided they were not fit to live. Soon a group of them was living at the Beje. They still could not go out on the streets, but here at least they had new surroundings and a program of sorts with the time I could take from the shop.

And still my restlessness continued. I was home, I was working and busy – or was I? Often I would come to with a start at my workbench to realize that I had sat for an hour staring into space. The repairmen Toos had found – trained under Father – were excellent. I spent less and less time in the shop; whatever or whoever I was looking for was not there.

Nor upstairs. I loved the gentle people in my care, but the house itself had ceased to be home. For Betsie's sake I bought plants for every windowsill, but I forgot to water them and they died.

Maybe I missed the challenge of the underground. When the national group approached me with a request, I agreed eagerly. They had false release papers for a prisoner in the Haarlem jail. What could be simpler than to carry this document around the corner and through those familiar wooden doors.

But as the doors closed behind me my heart began to race. What if I couldn't get out? What if I was trapped?

'Yes?' A young police lieutenant with bright orange hair stepped from behind the reception desk. 'You had an appointment?'

It was Rolf. Why was he being so stiff with me? Was I under arrest? Were they going to put me in a cell? 'Rolf!' I said. 'Don't you know me?'

He peered at me as though trying to refresh his memory. 'Of course!' he said smoothly. 'The lady at the watch shop! I heard you were closed down for a while.'

I gaped at him. Why, Rolf knew perfectly – and then I recalled where we were. In the central foyer of the police station with half a dozen German soldiers looking on. And I had greeted one of our group by name, practically admitted a special relationship between us, when the cardinal rule of the underground was . . . I ran my tongue over my lips. How could I have been so stupid?

Rolf took the forged papers from my shaking hands and glanced through them. 'These must be passed upon by the police chief and the military overcommand together,' he said. 'Can you return with them tomorrow afternoon at four? The chief will be in a meeting until — '

I heard no more. At the words 'tomorrow afternoon' I had bolted for the door. I stood thankfully on the sidewalk until my knees stopped knocking. If I had ever needed proof that I had no boldness or cleverness of my own, I had it now. Whatever bravery, or skill I had ever shown were gifts of God – sheer loans from Him of the talent needed to do a job. And it was clear, from the absence of such skills now, that this was no longer His work for me.

I crept meekly back to the Beje. And it was at that moment, as I stepped into the alley, that I knew what it was I was looking for. It was Betsie.

It was Betsie I had missed every moment of every day since I ran to the hospital window and found that she had left Ravensbruck forever. It was Betsie I had thought to find back here in Haarlem, here in the watchshop and in the home she loved.

But she was not here. And now for the first time since her death, I remembered. 'We must tell people, Corrie. We must tell them what we learned . . .'

That very week I began to speak. If this was God's new work

for me, then He would provide the courage and the words. Through the streets and suburbs of Haarlem I bumped on my bicycle rims, bringing the message that joy runs deeper than despair.

It was news that people needed to hear that cheerless spring of 1945. No Bride of Haarlem tree filled the air with fragrance; only the stump had been too big to haul off for firewood. No tulips turned fields into carpets of color: the bulbs had all been eaten. No family was without its tragedy. In churches and club rooms and private homes in those desperate days I told the truths Betsie and I had learned in Ravensbruck.

And always at these meetings, I spoke of Betsie's first vision: of a home here in Holland where those who had been hurt could learn to live again unafraid. At the close of one of these talks a slender, aristocratic lady came up to me. I knew her by sight: Mrs Bierens de Haan whose home in the suburb of Bloemendaal was said to be one of the most beautiful in Holland. I had never seen it, only the trees at the edge of the huge park in which it was set, and so I was astonished when this elegantly dressed lady asked me if I were still living in the ancient little house on the Barteljorisstraat.

'How did you – yes, I do. But — '

'My mother often told me about it. She went there frequently to see an aunt of yours who, I believe, was in charitable work?'

In a rush it all came back. Opening the side door to let in a swish of satin and rustle of feathers. A long gown and a plumed hat brushing both sides of the narrow stairs. Then Tante Jans standing in her doorway with a look that froze in the bones the thought of bouncing a ball.

'I am a widow,' Mrs Bierens de Haan was saying, 'but I have five sons in the Resistance. Four are still alive and well. The fifth we have not heard from since he was taken to Germany. As you spoke just now something in me kept saying, "Jan will come back and in gratitude you will open your home for this vision of Betsie ten Boom."'

It was two weeks later that a small boy delivered a scented

envelope to the side door; inside in slanted purple letters was a single line, 'Jan is home.'

Mrs Bierens de Haan herself met me at the entrance to her estate. Together we walked up an avenue of ancient oaks meeting above our heads. Rounding the final bend, we saw it, a fifty-six-room mansion in the center of a vast lawn. Two elderly gardeners were poking about the flowerbeds.

'We've let the gardens go,' Mrs Bierens de Haan said. 'But I thought we might put them back in shape. Don't you think released prisoners might find therapy in growing things?'

I didn't answer. I was staring up at the gabled roof and the leaded windows. Such tall, tall windows . . .

'Are there — ' my throat was dry. 'Are there inlaid wood floors inside, and a broad gallery around a central hall, and – bas-relief statues set along the walls?'

Mrs Bierens de Haan looked at me in surprise. 'You've been here then! I don't recall — '

'No,' I said. 'I heard it from — '

I stopped. How could I explain what I did not understand?

'From someone who's been here,' she finished simply, not understanding my perplexity.

'Yes,' I said. 'From someone who's been here.'

The second week in May the Allies retook Holland. The Dutch flag hung from every window and the 'Wilhelmus' was played on the liberated radio day and night. The Canadian army rushed to the cities the food they had stockpiled along the borders.

In June the first of many hundreds of people arrived at the beautiful home in Bloemendaal. Silent or endlessly relating their losses, withdrawn or fiercely aggressive, every one was a damaged human being. Not all had been in concentration camps; some had spent two, three, even four years hidden in attic rooms and back closets here in Holland.

One of the first of these was Mrs Kan, widow of the watch-shop owner up the street. Mr Kan had died at the underground address; she came to us alone, a stooped, white-haired woman who startled at every sound. Others came to Bloemendaal, scarred body and soul by bombing raids or loss of family or any of the endless dislocations of war. In 1947 we began to receive Dutch people who had been prisoners of the Japanese in Indonesia.

Though none of this was by design, it proved to be the best possible setting for those who had been imprisoned in Germany. Among themselves they tended to live and relive their special woes; in Bloemendaal they were reminded that they were not the only ones who had suffered. And for all these people alike, the key to healing turned out to be the same. Each had a hurt he had to forgive: the neighbor who had reported him, the brutal guard, the sadistic soldier.

Strangely enough, it was not the Germans or the Japanese that people had most trouble forgiving; it was their fellow Dutchmen who had sided with the enemy. I saw them frequently in the streets, NSBers with their shaved heads and furtive eyes. These former collaborators were now in pitiful condition, turned out of homes and apartments, unable to find jobs, hooted at in the streets.

At first it seemed to me that we should invite them too to Bloemendaal, to live side by side with those they had injured, to seek a new compassion on both sides. But it turned out to be too soon for people working their way back from such hurt: the two times I tried it, it ended in open fights. And so as soon as homes and schools for the feeble-minded opened again around the country I turned the Beje over to these former NSBers.

This was how it went, those years after the war, experimenting, making mistakes, learning. The doctors, psychiatrists, and nutritionists who came free of charge to any place that cared for war victims, sometimes expressed surprise at our loose-run ways. At morning and evening worship people drifted in and out, table manners were atrocious, one man took a walk into Haarlem every morning at 3:00 A.M. I could not bring myself to sound a whistle or to scold, or to consider gates or curfews.

And, sure enough, in their own time and their own way, people worked out the deep pain within them. It most often started, as Betsie had known it would, in the garden. As flowers bloomed or vegetables ripened, talk was less of the bitter past, more of tomorrow's weather. As their horizons broadened, I would tell them about the people living in the Beje, people who never had a visitor, never a piece of mail. When mention of the NSBers no longer brought on a volley of self-righteous wrath, I knew the person's healing was not far away. And the day he said, 'Those people you spoke of – I wonder if they'd care for some homegrown carrots,' then I knew the miracle had taken place.

I continued to speak, partly because the home in Bloemendaal ran on contributions, partly because the hunger for Betsie's story seemed to increase with time. I traveled all over Holland, to other parts of Europe, to the United States.

But the place where the hunger was greatest was Germany. Germany was a land in ruins, cities of ashes and rubble, but more terrifying still, minds and hearts of ashes. Just to cross the border was to feel the great weight that hung over that land.

It was at a church service in Munich that I saw him, the former S.S. man who had stood guard at the shower room door in the processing center at Ravensbruck. He was the first of our actual jailers that I had seen since that time. And suddenly it was all there – the roomful of mocking men, the heaps of clothing, Betsie's pain-blanched face.

He came up to me as the church was emptying, beaming and bowing. 'How grateful I am for your message *Fraulein*,' he said. 'To think that, as you say, He has washed my sins away!'

His hand was thrust out to shake mine. And I, who had preached so often to the people in Bloemendaal the need to forgive, kept my hand at my side.

Even as the angry, vengeful thoughts boiled through me, I saw the sin of them. Jesus Christ had died for this man; was I going to ask for more? Lord Jesus, I prayed, forgive me and help me to forgive him.

I tried to smile, I struggled to raise my hand. I could not. I felt nothing, not the slighest spark of warmth or charity. And so again I breathed a silent prayer. Jesus, I cannot forgive him. Give me Your forgiveness.

As I took his hand the most incredible thing happened. From my shoulder along my arm and through my hand a current seemed to pass from me to him, while into my heart sprang a love for this stranger that almost overwhelmed me.

And so I discovered that it is not on our forgiveness any more than on our goodness that the world's healing hinges, but on His. When He tells us to love our enemies, He gives, along with the command, the love itself.

It took a lot of love. The most pressing need in postwar Germany was homes; nine million people were said to be without them. They were living in rubble heaps, half-standing buildings, and abandoned army trucks. A church group invited me to speak to a hundred families living in an abandoned factory building. Sheets and blankets had been hung between the various living quarters to make a pretense of privacy. But there was no insulating the sounds: the wail of a baby, the din of radios, the angry words of a family quarrel. How could I speak to these people of the reality of God and go back to my quiet room in the church hostel outside the city? No, before I could bring a message to them, I would have to live among them.

And it was during the months that I spent in the factory that a director of a relief organization came to see me. They had heard of my rehabilitation work in Holland, he said, and they wondered – I was opening my mouth to say that I had no professional training in such things, when his next words silenced me.

'We've located a place for the work,' he said. 'It was a former concentration camp that's just been released by the government.'

We drove to Darmstadt to look over the camp. Rolls of rusting barbed wire still surrounded it. I walked slowly up a cinder path between drab gray barracks. I pushed open a creaking door; I stepped between rows of metal cots.

'Windowboxes,' I said. 'We'll have them at every window. The barbed wire must come down, of course, and then we'll need paint. Green paint. Bright yellow-green, the color of things coming up new in the spring . . .'

TRAMP FOR THE LORD

Tramp for the Lord

Corrie ten Boom with Jamie Buckingham

Hodder & Stoughton
LONDON SYDNEY AUCKLAND

Tramp for the Lord

Copyright © 1974 by Corrie ten Boom and Jamie Buckingham.

First published as a single volume 1974 by Hodder and Stoughton.
Second edition 1975.

The right of Corrie ten Boom and Jamie Buckingham to be
identified as the authors of this work has been asserted by them in
accordance with the Copyright, Designs and Patents Act 1988.

All rights reserved.

Unless otherwise identified, Scripture references in this book are
from the King James Version of the Bible.

Scripture references identified PHILLIPS are from The New Testament
in Modern English translated by J. B. Phlips, 1958.

Scripture references identified NEB are from *The New English Bible*.
Copyright © The Delegates of the Oxford University Press and the
Syndics of the Cambridge University Press 1961 and 1970. Reprinted by
permission.

Scripture references identified LB are from The Living Bible. Copyright
© 1971 by Tyndale House Publishers, Wheaton, Illinois 60187. All
rights reserved.

The poem 'Royal Scars' is from *Wings* by Amy Carmichael published by
SPCK, London.

Excerpts from *War on the Saints* by Jessie Penn-Lewis. The Overcomer
Literature Trust, Parkstone, Poole, and Christian Literature Crusade,
Fort Washington. Used by Permission.

Contents

Foreword

My wife Jackie and I met Tante (Aunt) Corrie and her pretty, blond secretary, Ellen de Kroon, at the airport in Melbourne, Florida. Ellen had called the night before saying they were flying in, but that Corrie had been having some severe heart pains. At eighty years of age, that's serious business.

We met the plane and whisked them to our house which is just minutes from the airport 'I'm very tired,' Tante Corrie said. 'I like to rest a while.'

Moments later she was stretched out on our daughter's lavender bedspread. I opened the window so the soft, tropical breeze could blow in from the lake behind the house. Gently closing the door, I cautioned the children to speak in whispers, and tiptoed into the kitchen to join Jackie and Ellen.

Ellen had brought us some Gouda cheese and we sliced it, reminiscing over my first meal in Corrie's house in Holland. Ellen couldn't wait to tell Jackie about the expression on my face when Corrie informed me I had a choice of two dishes for lunch: raw mullet dipped in onion, or smoked eel.

Talking softly and munching on cheese and crackers, I glanced up to see Tante Corrie coming down the hall, her eyes sparkling.

'Aren't you going to rest?' I asked.

'Oh, I have already a good sleep,' she answered in her thick, Dutch accent. 'Ten minutes is all you need when God gives the sleep.'

It is this remarkable power of recuperation which has allowed Tante Corrie, at more than eighty years of age, to tramp the world for the Lord. I saw that same power at work in her life a year later in Pittsburgh. We were both on the programme for a Bible conference at the Pittsburgh Theological Seminary. She had spoken three times that day to a congregation made up of everybody from bearded Jesus People to university professors. I was out late that night and, when I returned to the dormitory, I saw Ellen running down the hall 'Tante Corrie is having a heart attack,' she said

I raced to Corrie's room. She was stretched out on her bed, her face grey from the pain 'God has told me my time is not yet up,' she whispered. 'I have sent for a minister to pray that I may be healed.'

Moments later, as the young minister arrived and laid his hands on her, I saw her features relax and the colour return to her cheeks. 'Thank You, Lord,' she said softly, 'for taking away the pain.' Then, signifying she was ready for us to leave, she said, 'I go to sleep now.'

The next morning at eight o'clock she was behind the pulpit speaking to a thousand persons in the great auditorium – as though nothing extraordinary had happened.

I am convinced that the secret of Tante Corrie's great recuperative power, as well as the secret of her popularity as a speaker, lies in her childlikeness. As a little girl believes her Daddy can do anything, so Corrie ten Boom trusts in God – even more. She is living proof of what happens when a woman – when *any* person – is filled with the Holy Spirit.

JAMIE BUCKINGHAM

Introduction

The World Is My Classroom

The school of life offers some difficult courses, but it is in the difficult class that one learns the most – especially when your teacher is the Lord Jesus Himself.

The hardest lessons for me were in a cell with four walls. The cell in the prison at Scheveningen, Holland, was six paces in length, two paces in breadth, with a door that could be opened only from the outside. Later there were four barbed-wire fences, charged with electricity, enclosing a concentration camp in Germany. The gates were manned by guards with loaded machine guns. It was there in Ravensbruck that more than ninety-six thousand women died.

After that time in prison, the entire world became my classroom. Since World War II, I have travelled around it twice, speaking in more than sixty countries on all continents. During these three decades I have become familiar with airports, bus stations, and passport offices. Under me have been wheels of every description: wheels of automobiles, trains, jinrikishas, horse-drawn wagons, and the landing gear of airplanes. Wheels, wheels, wheels! Even the wheels of wheelchairs.

I have enjoyed hospitality in a great number of homes and have slept in many times more than a thousand beds. Sometimes I have slept in comfortable beds with foam rubber mattresses in the United States, and sometimes on straw mats on dirt floors in India. There have been clean rooms and dirty rooms.

One bathroom in Hollywood had a view of exotic plants and flowers from the sunken Roman bathtub; while a bathroom in Borneo was simply a mud hut equipped with nothing but a barrel of cold water. Once, while staying with a group of young Jewish girls in Israel, I had to climb over a mountain of building materials, and walk through a junk-filled field to make my way to a tiny outhouse which was nothing more than a hole in the ground. Such a place would have been impossible to find at night.

Always in my travels, even now that I am in my ninth decade of life, I have carried in my hand and in my heart the Bible – the very Word of Life which is almost bursting with Good News. And there has been plenty for everyone. I often feel as the disciples must have felt as they fed more than five thousand with five loaves and two fishes. The secret was that they had received it from the blessed hand of the Master. There was abundance for all and twelve basketfuls of fragments left over.

There has been plenty for the dying ones in the concentration camps – plenty for the thousands gathered in universities, in town halls, and in churches all over the world. Sometimes I have spoken to a few men in prison who stood behind bars and listened hungrily. Once to a group of six missionaries in Japan who offered me hospitality during a twenty-eight-hour rainstorm in which more than a thousand persons perished around us. Groups of hundreds and crowds of thousands have listened under pandals in India and in theatres in South America. I have spoken to tens of thousands at one time in the giant stadiums of America and retreated to the mountains of North Carolina to spend time with a small group of girls in a summer camp.

'God so loved the world . . .' (John 3:16) Jesus said. And that is why I keep going, even into my eightieth years, because we've a story to tell to the nations, a story of love and light.

God has plans – not problems – for our lives. Before she

died in the concentration camp in Ravensbruck, my sister Betsie said to me, 'Corrie, your whole life has been a training for the work you are doing here in prison – and for the work you will do afterward.'

The life of a Christian is an education for higher service. No athlete complains when the training is hard. He thinks of the game, or the race. As the Apostle Paul wrote:

In my opinion, whatever we may have to go through now is less than nothing compared with the magnificent future God has planned for us. The whole creation is on tiptoe to see the wonderful sight of the sons of God coming into their own. The world of creation cannot as yet see reality, not because it chooses to be blind, but because in God's purpose it has been so limited – yet it has been given hope. And the hope is that in the end the whole of created life will be rescued from the tyranny of change and decay and have its share in that magnificent liberty which can only belong to the children of God!

It is plain to anyone with eyes to see that at the present time all created life groans in a sort of universal travail. And it is plain, too, that we who have a foretaste of the Spirit are in a state of painful tension, while we wait for that redemption of our bodies which will mean that at last we have realized our full sonship in him.

Romans 8:18–23 PHILLIPS

Looking back across the years of my life, I can see the working of a divine pattern which is the way of God with His children. When I was in a prison camp in Holland during the war, I often prayed, 'Lord, never let the enemy put me in a German concentration camp.' God answered *no* to that prayer. Yet in the German camp, with all its horror, I found many prisoners who had never heard of Jesus Christ. If God had not used my sister Betsie and me to bring them to Him, they would never have heard of Him. Many died, or were killed, but many died with the Name of Jesus on their lips. They were well worth all our suffering. Faith is like radar which sees through the fog

– the reality of things at a distance that the human eye
cannot see.

My life is but a weaving, between my God and me,
I do not choose the colours, He worketh steadily,
Oftimes He weaveth sorrow, and I in foolish pride,
Forget He sees the upper, and I the underside.
Not till the loom is silent, and shuttles cease to fly,
Will God unroll the canvas and explain the reason why
The dark threads are as needful in the skilful Weaver's
     hand,
As the threads of gold and silver in the pattern He has
     planned.

                                        ANONYMOUS

Although the threads of my life have often seemed knotted, I
know, by faith, that on the other side of the embroidery there
is a crown. As I have walked the world – a tramp for the Lord
– I have learned a few lessons in God's great classroom. Even
as I share these things with those of you who read this book, I
pray the Holy Spirit will reveal something of the divine pattern
in God's plan for you also.

                                        CORRIE TEN BOOM
                                        Baarn, Holland

1

A Strange Place to Hope

Rank upon rank we stood that hot September morning in 1944, more than a thousand women lining the railroad siding, one unspoken thought among us: *Not Germany!*

Beside me my sister Betsie swayed. I was fifty-two, Betsie fifty-nine. These seven months in a prison and concentration camp since we had been caught concealing Jews in our home had been harder on her. But prisoners though we were, at least till now we had remained in Holland. And now when liberation must come any day, where were they taking us?

Behind us guards were shouting, prodding us with their guns. Instinctively my hand went to the string around my neck. From it, hanging down my back between my shoulder blades, was the small cloth bag that held our Bible, that forbidden Book which had not only sustained Betsie and me throughout these months, but given us strength to share with our fellow prisoners. So far we had kept it hidden. But if we should go to Germany . . . We had heard tales of the prison inspections there.

A long line of empty boxcars was rolling slowly past. Now they clanged to a halt and a gaping freight door loomed in front of us. I helped Betsie over the steep side.

The dark boxcar grew quickly crowded. We were pressed against the wall. It was a small European freight car; thirty or forty people jammed it. And still the guards drove women in, pushing, jabbing with their guns. It was only when eighty women were packed inside that the heavy door slid shut and we heard the iron bolts driven into place outside.

Women were sobbing and many fainted, although in the tightly wedged crowd they remained upright. The sun beat down on the motionless train; the temperature in the packed car rose. It was hours before the train gave a sudden lurch and began to move. Almost at once it stopped again, then again crawled forward. The rest of that day and all night long it was the same – stopping, starting, slamming, jerking. Once through a slit in the side of the car I saw trainmen carrying a length of twisted rail. Maybe the tracks ahead were destroyed. Maybe we would still be in Holland when the liberation came.

But at dawn we rolled through the Dutch border town of Emmerich. We were in Germany.

For two more incredible days and two more nights we were carried deeper and deeper into the land of our fears. Worse than the crush of bodies and the filth, was the thirst. Two or three times when the train was stopped the door was slid open a few inches and a pail of water passed in. But we had become animals, incapable of plan. Those near the door got it all.

At last, on the morning of the third day, the door was hauled open its full width. Only a handful of very young soldiers was there to order us out and march us off. No more were needed. We could scarcely walk, let alone resist. From the crest of a small hill we saw it – the end of our journey – a vast gray barracks city surrounded by double concrete walls.

'*Ravensbruck*!

Like a whispered curse, the word passed back through the line. This was the notorious women's death camp itself, the very symbol to Dutch hearts of all that was evil. As we stumbled down the hill, I felt the little Bible bumping on my back. As long as we had that, I thought, we could face even hell itself. But how could we conceal it through the inspection I knew lay ahead?

It was the middle of the night when Betsie and I reached the processing barracks. And there, under the harsh ceiling lights, we saw a dismaying sight. As each woman reached the head of the line she had to strip off ever scrap of clothes, throw them all onto a pile guarded by soldiers, and walk naked past the scrutiny of a dozen guards into the shower room. Coming out of the shower room she wore only a thin regulation prison dress and a pair of shoes.

Our Bible! How could we take it past so many watchful eyes?

'Oh, Betsie!' I began – and then stopped at the sight of her pain-whitened face. As a guard strode by, I begged him in German to show us the toilets. He jerked his head in the direction of the shower room. 'Use the drain holes!' he snapped.

Timidly Betsie and I stepped out of line and walked forward to the huge room with its row on row of overhead spigots. It was empty, waiting for the next batch of fifty naked and shivering women.

A few minutes later we would return here stripped of everything we possessed. And then we saw them, stacked in a corner, a pile of old wooden benches crawling with cock-roaches, but to us the furniture of heaven itself.

In an instant I had slipped the little bag over my head and, along with my woolen underwear, had stuffed it behind the benches.

And so it was that when we were herded into that room ten minutes later, we were not poor, but rich – rich in the care of Him who was God even of Ravensbruck.

Of course when I put on the flimsy prison dress, the Bible bulged beneath it. But that was His business, not mine. At the exit, guards were feeling every prisoner, front, back, and sides. I prayed, 'Oh, Lord, send your angels to surround us.' But then I remembered that angels are spirits and you can see through them. What I needed was an angel to shield me so the guards could not see me. 'Lord,' I prayed again, 'make your angels untransparent.' How unorthodox you can pray when you are in great need! But God did not mind. He did it.

The woman ahead of me was searched. Behind me, Betsie was searched. They did not touch or even look at me. It was as though I was blocked out of their sight.

Outside the building was a second ordeal, another line of guards examining each prisoner again. I slowed down as I reached them, but the captain shoved me roughly by the shoulder. 'Move along! You're holding up the line.'

So Betsie and I came to our barracks at Ravensbruck. Before long we were holding clandestine Bible study groups for an ever-growing group of believers, and Barracks 28 became known throughout the camp as 'the crazy place, where they hope'.

Yes, hoped, in spite of all that human madness could do. We had learned that a stronger power had the final word, even here.

(Reprinted by permission from GUIDEPOSTS MAGAZINE, Copyright 1972 by Guideposts Associates Inc., Carmel, New York 10512.)

. . . and . . . you shall be My witnesses
both in Jerusalem, and in all Judea, and
Samaria . . .
Acts 1:8 RSV

2

Witnesses Unto Me

It was a week after Betsie had died in Ravensbruck that I took
my place in the ranks of women prisoners standing together
in the icy cold of the early morning.

'66730!'

'That is my number,' I said weakly as we took our places
for roll call.

'ten Boom, Cornelia.'

'That is my name,' I thought. How strange that they
would call me by name when they always addressed us by
number!

'Come forward.'

We were falling in line for the roll call. Ten in a line, every
one hundredth woman one step forward. My friends looked
at me sadly.

'What does it mean?' I asked inwardly. 'Punishment . . .
freedom . . . the gas chamber . . . sent to another concentration camp?'

There was but one thought that comforted me. 'What a joy
that Betsie is in heaven. No matter what terrible things now
happen, she will not have to bear it.'

The guard, a young German girl, shouted at me. 'Nr.
66730!'

I stepped forward, stood at attention and repeated the

necessary words. '*Schutzhaftling ten Boom, Cornelia, meldet sich.*'

'Stand on Number 1 on the roll call.'

I went to the place to the far right, where I could overlook the entire square of the bleak camp. Standing in the crowd I could not feel the draft, but now, standing in the bitter cold, the wind whipped through my ragged prison dress. Another girl, young and frightened, was sent to stand beside me. Roll call took three hours and we were almost frozen. She saw how cold I was and rubbed my spine when the guards were not looking.

'Why must I stand here?' I asked through chattering teeth.

Her answer was barely audible as it came from her blue lips. 'Death sentence.'

I turned back to the Lord. 'Perhaps I'll see you soon face-to-face, like Betsie does now, Lord. Let it not be too cruel a killing. Not gas, Lord, nor hanging. I prefer shooting. It is so quick. You see something, you hear something, and it is finished.'

I looked back at the young girl beside me. 'Lord, this is perhaps the last chance I will have to bring someone to You before I arrive in heaven. Use me, Lord. Give me all the love and wisdom I need.'

'What is your name?' I asked her softly, glancing always to see if the guards were looking.

'Tiny.'

'I am Corrie,' I whispered. 'How long have you been here?'

'Two years.'

'Did you ever read the Bible?'

'No, I never did.'

'Do you believe God exists?'

'I do. I wish I knew more about Him. Do you know Him?'

'I do. Jesus, His Son, came to this world to carry our punishment. He died on the cross, but He rose from the dead and has promised to be with us always. My sister died here. She suffered so much. I, too, have suffered. But Jesus is always with us. He did a miracle in taking away all my hatred and bitterness for my enemies. Jesus is willing to bring into our hearts God's love through His Holy Spirit.'

Tiny listened. For almost three hours we talked while the guards completed the roll call. It was a miracle, for I had a chance to explain many things about Jesus. The prisoners behind us listened, too. I felt happy. Perhaps this was my last chance in life, but what joy!

I continued. 'Jesus wants to live in your heart. "Behold, I stand at the door and knock", He says. "If anyone opens the door, I'll come in." Will you open the door of your heart and let Him come in and change you?'

'I will,' she said.

'Then talk to Him. Tell Him whatever you think. Now you have a Friend who never leaves you alone.'

The siren sounded and the guards shouted at the prisoners. 'Get to work!'

Thousands of women prisoners were running to their places where they had to march to their work. Tiny disappeared from sight. Only I was left standing in my place where I had been ordered not to move. I still did not know what fate awaited me.

I did know, however, that the God who never slumbers nor sleeps was now with Tiny. And Tiny knew it, too. Neither of us knew at that time how important that was going to be to her in the next few days. But above the din of the concentration camp, I thought I heard the singing of the angels.

Then I heard my name called. Was it death? Oh, thank God, no. It was life. I was being released. I later learned it was through an administrative blunder, but even then I knew it was not the end of an era – it was just the beginning. Ahead of me was the world.

Then he turned my sorrow into joy! He took
away my clothes of mourning . . .
Psalms 30:11 LB

3

Release!

When you are dying – when you stand at the gate of eternity – you see things from a different perspective than when you think you may live for a long time. I had been standing at that gate for many months, living in Barracks 28 in the shadow of the crematorium. Every time I saw the smoke pouring from the hideous smokestacks I knew it was the last remains of some poor women who had been with me in Ravensbruck. Often I asked myself, 'When will it be my time to be killed or die?'

But I was not afraid. Following Betsie's death, God's Presence was even more real. Even though I was looking into the valley of the shadow of death, I was not afraid. It is here that Jesus comes the closest, taking our hand, and leading us through.

One week before the order came to kill all the women of my age, I was free. I still do not understand all the details of my release from Ravensbruck. All I know is, it was a miracle of God.

I stood in the prison yard – waiting the final order. Beyond the walls with their strands of barbed wire stood the silent trees of the German forest, looking so much like the grey-green sets on the back of one of our theatre stages in Holland.

Mimi, one of the fellow prisoners, came within whispering

distance. 'Tiny died this morning,' she said without looking at me. 'And Marie also.'

Tiny! 'Oh, Lord, thank You for letting me point her to Jesus who has now ushered her safely into Your Presence.' And Marie. I knew her well. She lived in my barracks and had attended my Bible talks. Like Tiny, Marie had also accepted Jesus as her Lord. I looked back at the long rows of barracks. 'Lord, if it was only for Tiny and Marie – that they might come to know You before they died – then it was all worthwhile.'

A guard spoke harshly, telling Mimi to leave the yard. Then he said to me, 'Face the gate. Do not turn around.'

The gate swung open and I glimpsed the lake in front of the camp. I could smell freedom.

'Follow me,' a young girl in an officer's uniform said to me.

I walked slowly through the gate, never looking back. Behind me I heard the hinges squeak as the gate swung shut. I was free, and flooding through my mind were the words of Jesus to the church at Philadelphia:

> Behold, I have set before thee an open door, and no man can shut it . . .
>
> Revelation 3:8

First that door directed me back to Holland. The train ride took three days. Another prisoner, Claire Prins, had been released with me. Her leg was alarmingly swollen and of course both of us were mere skin and bones. But we were *free*!

Arriving in Groningen, we made our way to a Christian hospital called the Deaconess House, where I asked to speak to the superintendent. Perhaps they would help us until I could return to Haarlem, I thought.

'Sister Tavenier cannot come at the moment,' the attendant said. 'She is helping conduct a Christian service in one of the wards. I'm afraid you will have to wait.'

'Would you mind,' I said, looking at the attendant, 'if I attended the service also?'

She looked at me tenderly, sensing, perhaps, some of my

suffering. 'Why, of course. You may rest in the waiting room
until it starts. I'll come after you.'

'Nurse . . .,' I hesitated to ask, 'have you anything for me
to drink?'

Again the look of compassion crossed her face. 'I'll bring
you some tea,' she said gently.

A few minutes later she placed it before me, saying, 'I have
not put butter on the toast for I see you are sick. The dry
toast and tea will be good for you.'

I was deeply touched by this tiny show of consideration.
A moment later I was lying in a comfortable chair with my
legs outstretched on a bench. A wonderful feeling of rest
descended on me. I was in the Netherlands, among good
people. My suffering was over.

A nurse came for me, to take me to the ward where
the service was to be held. Chairs had been arranged in
a semicircle between the beds, facing a table. An elderly
minister walked in and a hymnal was handed me. I could
see the nurses and patients glancing stealthily at me. My
clothes were ragged and filthy, hanging from my gaunt body
like rags on a scarecrow. Yet I was so thankful to be free I
cared not.

The minister spoke in a well-modulated voice. Then we
joined in singing. I could not help but make comparisons: the
dirty prison dormitory, infection-ridden and filthy, the beds
full of lice, and now this. Clean sheets and pillow cases and
a spotless floor. The hoarse voices of the slave drivers and
the mature, melodious voice of the minister. Only the singing
was the same, for we had sung at Ravensbruck. Singing was
one of the ways we kept up our courage.

Following the service the nurse took me to the superintendent's office. 'Miss Prins has been taken care of,' she
said, 'and is already in a fresh bed. You both must have
had a horrible experience. But now, what must be done
with you?'

I sat in a chair across from her desk. For more than
a year I had not been allowed to make a decision. All
I could do was follow orders. It was difficult even to
think. 'I don't know, Sister,' I said. It was enough just

to be surrounded by people who were not angry with me.

'I know what,' she said, as she touched a bell. 'First we'll give you a warm dinner.'

A young nurse appeared and took my arm, guiding me down a hall towards the dining room. 'I understand you have just been released from Ravensbruck,' she said. 'Where are you going? Where is your home?'

'I am going to Haarlem,' I replied.

'Oh, Haarlem,' she said with excitement. 'Do you know Corrie ten Boom who lives there?'

I looked at her. She was one of the YWCA leaders I had worked with before the war. 'Truus Benes!' I exclaimed in delight.

'Why, yes, that is my name,' she said, bewildered. 'But I don't believe I know you.'

'I am Corrie ten Boom.'

The nurse stopped abruptly in the hall, staring at me. 'Oh, no, that is impossible. I know Corrie ten Boom very well. I have been in girls' camps with her several times. She is much younger than you.'

'But, really, I am Corrie ten Boom,' I argued. Then I thought of how I must have looked. My face was thin and pale, my mouth wide, like skin stretched across a skull. My hair fell queerly about my face. My eyes were hollow. My coat was dirty, for I had at times slept on the floor of the train as we travelled out of Germany. The belt of my dress sagged, for I had not had the energy to fasten it.

The nurse reached out tenderly and touched my chapped hand. 'Yes . . . yes . . . it is you. It *is*!' And then we both broke into laughter.

In the dining room we sat opposite each other at a small table and I asked about our mutual acquaintances. Was Mary Barger still living? Jeanne Blooker and . . .? It was ridiculous to ask such questions, but I wanted to know everything. The world, for me, had stopped while I had been in the concentration camp. Now it was beginning to turn again and I had so much catching up to do.

Then I was eating. Potatoes, brussels sprouts, meat and

gravy, and for dessert, pudding with currant juice and an apple!

'I have never seen anyone eat so intensely,' one of the nurses from a nearby table commented. I cared not. With every mouthful of food I could feel new life streaming into my body. I had once said to Betsie in camp, 'When we get home we shall have to eat carefully, taking only small amounts at a time until our stomachs are ready.'

'No,' Betsie had said, 'God will see to it that we shall be able to retain all sorts of food right from the start.'

She was right. How wonderfully good that food did taste. I shall remember that meal as long as I live.

Then came a warm bath. They could hardly get me out of it. My poor sick skin, damaged by lice, seemed to grow softer the moment I slipped into that warm tub.

Afterwards they dressed me. Several of the ex-leaders of the Netherlands Girls' Clubs were among the nurses – girls that I had known before the war. They dressed me up as if I were a doll. One of them had lingerie, another shoes, another a dress and pins for my hair. I felt so happy that I laughed for sheer joy. How sweet they were to me.

These young women had been trained in kindness. How opposite from the concentration camp where men had been trained in cruelty.

I was then taken to a cozy bedroom so I could rest. How lovely was the combination of colours. I was starved for colour. In the concentration camp everything was grey. But here in Holland the colours were vivid again. My eyes could not seem to get enough to satisfy them.

And the bed! Delightfully soft and clean with thick woollen blankets. One of the little nurses brought an extra pillow and tucked it under my swollen feet. I wanted to laugh and cry at the same time.

On a shelf was a row of books. Outside I heard the whistle of a boat on a canal and the merry sound of little children calling to one another as they skipped down the street. Far in the distance I heard the sound of a choir singing and then, oh, joy, the chimes of a carillon. I closed my eyes and tears wet my pillow. Only to those who have been in prison does freedom have such great meaning.

Later that afternoon one of the nurses took me up to her room where for the first time in many months I heard the sound of a radio. Gunther Ramin was playing a Bach trio. The organ tones flowed about and enveloped me. I sat on the floor beside a chair and sobbed, unashamedly. It was too much joy. I had rarely cried during all those months of suffering. Now I could not control myself. My life had been given back as a gift. Harmony, beauty, colours, and music. Only those who have suffered as I, and have returned, can fully understand what I mean. I knew my life had been given back for a purpose. I was no longer my own. This time I had been ransomed and released. I knew that God would soon be sending me out as a tramp for the Lord. But right now, He was letting me enjoy the luxury of thanksgiving. I was drinking from a fountain I knew would never run dry – the fountain of praise.

One of the first places I visited, after my release from the concentration camp, was the *Grote Kerk* in Haarlem. Since it was so close to where I had grown up in the Beje, I counted it as much of an old friend as I did the watch-maker's shop.

'May I show you through?' the old usher said as he met me at the door.

'If it is all right,' I said, 'I would like to be alone.'

He nodded, understandingly, and disappeared into the shadows of the sanctuary. I walked over the gravestones that formed the floor of the ancient building. My shoes made a strange, scraping sound that gave forth a hollow echo in the empty cathedral. I remembered the many times I had played here as a child.

My cousin Dot was my closest friend. She was the youngest daughter of my Uncle Arnold who was the previous usher – the caretaker – of the *Grote Kerk*.

Dot and I did everything together, but our favourite pastime was to play hide-and-seek in the big church. There were many wonderful places to hide: pews, old doors giving entrance to spiral staircases, and many closets. There was a world-famous pipe organ in the cathedral and sometimes when there was a concert, Uncle Arnold would allow members of his family to come into the church, sit on a wooden bench without a back and lean against the cold, moist stone wall to hear the magnificent music.

The cathedral was a symphony in grey tones during the day, both inside and outside. In the evening, when the gas lamps were lit in the side transepts, we could see the pillars and ceilings pointing upwards, as the shadows danced about in a mysterious glow.

Only one place was absolutely 'off limits' as we played hide-and-seek. That was the old pulpit. We never went there, but for the rest – what a playground that old church was! When we shouted, the echo would ring from transept to transept and our laughter never, never seemed to be sacrilegious. Unlike some of the stern adults who sometimes frowned on our frolics, I had always thought that the laughter of the little children in an empty cathedral was the most beautiful of all hymns of praise. And so we grew up, knowing only a God who enjoyed our presence as we skipped, ran, and played through this building which was built for His glory.

One afternoon we played very late and before we knew it, the darkness of the cathedral swallowed us up. I looked around. Through the beautiful stained-glass windows I saw a little light coming in from the streets around. Only the silhouettes of the Gothic pillars stood out in the darkness as they reached upward and upward.

'Let's go home,' whispered Dot. 'I'm scared.'

I was not. Slowly I went to the usher's door that opened out to where Uncle Arnold lived. There was a Presence that comforted me, a deep peace in my heart. Even in the darkness, smelling the dust and dampness of the church building, I knew that the 'Light of the World' was present. Was the Lord preparing me for some time in the future when I would need to know that His light is victorious over all darkness?

It was forty-five years later. Betsie and I walked to the square where roll call was being held in the concentration camp. It was still early, before dawn. The head of our barracks was so cruel that she had sent us out into the very cold outdoors a full hour too early.

Betsie's hand was in mine. We went to the square by a different way from the rest of our barracks-mates. We were three as we walked with the Lord and talked with Him. Betsie spoke. Then I talked. Then the Lord spoke. How? I do not know. But both of us understood. It was the same Presence I had felt years before in the old cathedral in Haarlem.

The brilliant early morning stars were our only light. The cold winter air was so clear. We could faintly see the outlines of the barracks, the crematorium, the gas chamber, and the towers where the guards were standing with loaded machine guns.

'Isn't this a bit of heaven!' Betsie had said. 'And, Lord, this is a small foretaste. One day we will see You face-to-face, but thank You that even now You are giving us the joy of walking and talking with You.'

Heaven in the midst of hell. Light in the midst of darkness. What a security!

4

A Song in the Night

The war was over. Even before I left the concentration
camp, I knew I would be busy helping those who had lost
their way. Now I found myself starting just such a work in
Bloemendaal. It was more than a home for the homeless; it
was a refuge for those who had lost their way spiritually as
well as physically.

Yet, because I had lived so close to death, looking it in the
face day after day, I often felt like a stranger among my own
people – many of whom looked upon money, honour of men,
and success as the important issues of life. Standing in front
of a crematorium, knowing that any day could be your day,
gives one a different perspective on life. The words of an old
German motto kept flashing in my mind:

What I spent, I had; what I saved, I lost; what I gave, I
have.

How well I understood the feeling of the artist who painted
the picture of the corpse of a once wealthy man and entitled
it, *Sic transit gloria mundi* – So passes the glory of this world.
The material things of this world no longer excited me – nor
would they ever again.

It was during this time that I visited Haarlem, the town

where I had spent more than fifty years of my life. It was late in the evening as I walked through the streets. Waiting before a traffic light, I had a strange feeling that the people should fall in line five by five, as in the concentration camp. Instead, they chatted about insignificant things and when the light changed, they moved on without anyone shouting at them.

Walking the streets that night, however, I felt growing in me a tremendous desire to tell all men, especially those in bondage to material things, of the One who can set us free from all prisons: Jesus.

It was after midnight when I finally made my way to the Barteljorisstraat. There were few streetlights but the moon and many stars were visible above the ancient rooftops of the familiar houses on the short street. I paused in front of the Beje on the corner of the small alley that came out in the midst of the street. I let my fingertips run across the door of the watchmaker's shop. Even though the Beje was no longer my home, it was still part of my heart. Little did I dream that one day it would be set aside as a museum to commemorate my family and the hiding place of those precious Jews who had been saved from certain death at the hands of the Nazis.

I stood alone in the darkness, allowing myself the sweet luxury of remembering. How often had I put the shutters before the show window. Through this door I had walked on my first day of school, almost fifty years ago. Oh, what an unwilling pupil I had been, crying in fear of leaving the dear old house whose warmth in winter had protected me, whose windows had kept out the rain and mist, whose cheery fire had welcomed me and others in the family each night after the dinner dishes had been put away. Yet my father, knowing my fear, took me by the hand and led me through this door and out into the world of learning, into an unknown world of teachers and classrooms.

Now Father was dead. Only My Heavenly Father remained. I ran my hand over the door, letting my fingers explore the cracks. It was no longer my hiding place. Others lived here now, and the world was my classroom, and my only security

came in knowing that underneath were the Everlasting Arms.
How thankful I was for my Heavenly Father's strong hand
around mine.

I looked into the small alley. It was almost pitch dark. I
strained my ears, and in the far off recesses of my heart,
could imagine the voices of Father, Betsie, and the others.
Had it been only a year ago? It seemed like centuries. 'What
an honour,' Father had said, 'to give my life for God's chosen
people, the Jews.'

I felt the wall with my hands, then gently pressed my face
against the cold stones. No, I was not dreaming. It was
reality. The old Beje, the old hiding place, was no longer
mine. Ravensbruck had taught me much I needed to learn.
My hiding place was now in Jesus alone. Even though I was
wandering the streets at midnight in a town that used to be
my home, but was now only a town, I knew the Presence of
the Heavenly Father.

Suddenly the cathedral started to play its nostalgic chimes.
Day and night through my lifetime I had heard the beautiful
music from the *Grote Kerk*. It was not a dream, as I
had often experienced in the concentration camp. It was
real. I walked out of the shadows of the alley and made
my way down the Barteljorisstraat to the *Grote Markt*.
I paused to look at the cathedral which was silhouetted
against the dark sky, framed into place by a million twinkling stars.

'Thank You, Jesus, that I am alive,' I said.

In my heart I heard Him reply, 'Lo, I am with you always,
even unto the end of the world' (Matthew 28:20).

I stayed there for long minutes as the hands on the face
of the great clock moved towards the hour. Then the
chimes in the cathedral tower pealed forth once again, this
time with the sounds of Luther's famous hymn 'A Mighty
Fortress Is Our God'. I listened and heard myself singing
the hymn, not in Dutch, but in German: *'Ein' feste Burg ist
unser Gott.'*

'How like You, Lord,' I half-chuckled, 'that You would
remind me of Your grace by letting me hear a German
hymn.'

A policeman passed, looked at me, and spoke a friendly word.

I said, 'Good-night, Policeman. A mighty fortress is our God.'

I was free.

*By faith Abraham, when he was called to
go out into a place which he should after
receive for an inheritance, obeyed; and he
went out, not knowing whither he went.*
Hebrews 11:8

5

A Great Discovery

When my parents were married, many years ago, they
claimed Psalm 32:8 as their 'life verse', the promise which
they felt was God's assurance for them.

I will instruct thee and teach thee in the way which thou
shalt go: I will guide thee with mine eye.

Now that Father and Mother were gone, this promise
became the special directive for my life as well – God's
pledge to guide me in all my journeys. It was especially
needed as I set out for my first trip to America.

The war had only been over a short time, and many
Europeans wanted to go to America. However, few, if any,
wanted to go for the same reason I did – to carry the Gospel
as a missionary to the Americans. For all of us, however, it
was the same story when we applied for passage to America:
'It is impossible to obtain papers.'

I prayed, 'Lord, if it is Your will that I go to America, then
You must provide the necessary papers.'

I soon discovered that man's importunity is God's opportunity. He uses our problems as building materials for His
miracles. I began to understand that this was my first lesson

in learning to trust Him completely, my first steps on the path to complete dependence on, and obedience to, His guidance. How much I had to learn!

At last all my papers were approved, except the final one – the most important one. I sat alone on a hard wooden bench in the hall of the Immigration Office in The Hague. Everyone coming out of the office warned those of us waiting in the hall, 'That fellow in there is as hard as flint. He passes no one.'

'Lord,' I prayed silently, 'I am willing to go or stay. It is up to You.'

'Hello, there! Don't we know each other?' It was the voice of a middle-aged woman standing in front of me. I looked up into her face, trying vainly to recognize her.

'You're Corrie ten Boom,' she laughed. 'I'm one of your cousins and this is Jan, my husband. I haven't seen you for years, and of course, Jan has never seen you since we were married only six years ago.'

'Are you trying to go to America, also?' I asked.

'Oh no,' she laughed. 'I'm visiting Jan. He has his office in this building.'

'Then perhaps you can help me,' I said, shaking his hand. I told him my story.

He was polite but said, 'I'm sorry. I would like to be of service to my brand-new cousin, but that's not my department. However, if you have trouble, ring me up.' He gave me his telephone number and we shook hands again as he left.

I continued to wait. The 'man of flint' left the office for coffee and a young clerk took his place. Then it was my turn.

'You had better wait until my boss returns,' the clerk said when I told him where I wanted to go and why.

My shoulders sagged. 'I cannot wait any longer. Won't you please call this number?' I handed him the card that Jan had handed me earlier.

I prayed while he placed the call. Moments later he hung up. 'All is arranged. I am approving your passport. You may make your trip to America.'

From there I travelled to Amsterdam to try to arrange passage on a ship of the Holland–America Line. However, another mountain loomed before me. The agent told me they would only put my name on the waiting list. 'We will notify you in about a year,' he said.

'A year! But I must go now.' The agent just shrugged his shoulders and returned to his work.

Disappointed, I returned to the square in the centre of the city. God had told me to go America – of that I was certain. All my papers were in order. God had seen to that also. Now was up to Him to move this mountain. Glancing across the street I noticed a sign: AMERICAN EXPRESS COMPANY. Stepping into the office I enquired, 'Have you passenger accommodations on any of your freighters to America?'

The old clerk looked over his glasses and said, 'You may sail tomorrow, Madam, if your papers are in order.'

'Oh, tomorrow is too sudden,' I said, hardly believing what I heard. 'What about next week?'

'That, too, can be arranged,' he said. 'We don't have very many women your age who ship out on freighters. But if you are willing, so are we.'

Several weeks before I had met an American businessman who was visiting relatives in Holland. When I told him of my plans to visit American he tried to discourage me. 'It's not easy to make one's way in America,' he said.

'I believe you,' I told him. 'But God has directed me and I must obey.'

He then gave me two cheques, one small and one larger. 'If you need it, use it,' he said. 'You can repay me later.' I tucked them away for safekeeping.

So I arrived in New York as a missionary to America. I was only allowed to bring in fifty dollars, and of course, I knew no one. However, I found my way to the YWCA where I found a room and a place to leave my bags.

I had the address of a group of Hebrew–Christian immigrants who were meeting in New York. I made a phone call and they invited me to come and speak. Since they were German, I could not use the English lectures I had prepared on board the ship, but had to speak to them in their native language. It was better perhaps, for my English was rather hard to understand.

At the end of the week after wandering around the city in a rather helpless daze, I went downstairs in the YWCA to pay my bill. The clerk looked at me sympathetically. 'I am sorry, but our accommodations are so restricted that we cannot allow you to stay here any longer. One week is our limit. Do you have a forwarding address?'

'Yes. I just don't know what it is, yet.'

'I don't understand,' she said, perplexed.

'God has another room for me,' I explained. 'He just hasn't told me what the address is. But I am not worried. He led me through Ravensbruck. He will surely see me through America as well.'

Suddenly the clerk remembered. 'By the way, a letter came for you.'

Strange, I thought, as she handed me the envelope. *How could I receive a letter? No one knows where I am staying.* But there it was. I read it hurriedly and then turned to the clerk. 'My forwarding address will be this house on 190th Street.'

'But why didn't you tell me that before?' she asked.

'I didn't know. It was in this letter. A woman that I do not know writes, "I heard you speak to the Jewish congregation. I am aware that it is almost impossible to get a room in New York City. My son happens to be in Europe, so you are welcome to use his room as long as you are in New York."'

The lady at the desk was more amazed than I. However, I reasoned, perhaps she had not experienced miracles before.

I rode the subway to 190th Street. The house at the address was a large, multistoried building occupied by many families. I found the correct apartment at the end of a hall, but no one was home. Certainly my hostess did not expect her invitation to be an eleventh-hour answer to my problem. I arranged myself among my suitcases on the floor, and leaning against the wall, soon began to drift off to sleep.

In those last moments before sleep took over, my mind drifted back to Ravensbruck. I could feel Betsie's bony hand touching my face. It was pitch black in Barracks 28 where seven hundred other prisoners were asleep. Each day hundreds of women died and their bodies were fed to the ovens. Betsie had grown so weak, and we both knew that death was always moments away.

'Are you awake, Corrie?' Her weak voice sounded so far away.

'Yes, you wakened me.'

'I had to. I need to tell you what God has said to me.'

'Shhh. We hinder the sleep of the girls around us. Let us lie with our faces toward each other.'

The cot was so small. We could only lie like spoons in a box, our knees bumping against the knees of the other. We used our two coats as covers along with the thin black blanket provided by the Nazis.

I pulled the coat over our heads so we could whisper and not be heard 'God showed me,' Betsie said, 'that after the war we must give to the Germans that which they now try to take away from us: our love for Jesus.'

Betsie's breath was coming in short gasps. She was so weak, her body wasted away until there was nothing but her thin skin stretched over brittle bones. 'Oh, Betsie,' I exclaimed, 'you mean if we live we will have to return to Germany?'

Betsie patted my hand under the blanket. 'Corrie, there is so much bitterness. We must tell them that the Holy Spirit will fill their hearts with God's love.'

I remembered Romans 5:5. Only that morning some of the women in the barracks had huddled with us in the corner while I read from our precious Bible. But I shuddered. Germany. If I were ever released from this horrible place could I ever return to Germany?

Betsie's weak voice whispered on. 'This concentration camp here at Ravensbruck has been used to destroy many, many lives. There are many other such camps throughout Germany. After the war they will not have use for them anymore. I have prayed that the Lord will give us one in Germany. We will use it to build up lives.'

No, I thought. *I will return to my simple job as a watchmaker in Holland and never again set my boot across the border.*

Betsie's voice was quivering so I could barely understand her. 'The Germans are the most wounded of all the people in the world. Think of that young girl guard who swore in such filthy language yesterday. She was only seventeen or eighteen years old, but did you see how she was beating that poor old woman with a whip? What a job there is to do after the war.'

I found a place where I could put my hand. It was such a stupid problem, I thought, yet it was a small cot and it was difficult to position my hands and arms. My hand rested on Betsie's left side, just on her heart. I felt her ribs – only skin and bones. How long would she be able to live? Her heart was fluttering inside the rib cage like a dying bird, as though it would stop any moment.

I rested and thought. How close to God's heart was Betsie. Only God could see in such circumstances the possibility for ministry in the future – ministry to those who even now were preparing to kill us. Most of all, to see in such a place as Ravensbruck an opportunity to bless and build up the lives of our enemies. Yes, only the Lord Jesus could have given Betsie such a vision.

'Must we live with them in Germany?' I whispered.

'For a while,' Betsie answered. 'Then we will travel the whole world bringing the Gospel to all – our friends as well as our enemies.'

'To *all* the world? But that will take much money.'

'Yes, but God will provide,' Betsie said. 'We must do nothing else but bring the Gospel and He will take care of us. After all, He owns the cattle on a thousand hills. If we need money we will just ask the Father to sell a few cows.'

I was beginning to catch the vision. 'What a privilege,' I said softly, 'to travel the world and be used by the Lord Jesus.'

But Betsie did not answer. She had fallen asleep. Three days later she was dead.

Going to bed the night after Betsie died was one of the most difficult tasks of my life. The one electric light bulb was screwed into the ceiling toward the front of the room. Only a feeble ray reached my narrow cot. I lay in the semi-darkness – thinking – remembering – trying to recon-struct Betsie's vision.

There was a shuffle of feet near my bed and I looked up. A
Russian woman, thin and gaunt, was shuffling down the aisle
between the beds looking for a place to sleep. The Russians
were not received kindly and everyone turned away. As she
neared me I saw the hunted look in her eyes. How awful to
be in prison and not have even a place to sleep!

Betsie's place beside me was vacant. I motioned to the
woman and threw back the blanket for her. She crept in,
gratefully, and stetched out beside me. We were sharing the
same pillow and with our faces so close I wanted to speak.
But I did not know her language.

'*Jesoes Christoes?*' I asked softly.

'Oh!' she exclaimed. Quickly making the sign of the cross,
she threw her arms about me and kissed me.

She who had been my sister for fifty-two years, with whom
I had shared so much of weal and woe, had left me. A Russian
woman now claimed my love. And there would be others, too,
who would be my sisters and brothers in Christ all across
the world.

I was awakened by a gentle hand shaking my shoulder. It was
after midnight and I realized I had fallen asleep in the midst of
my suitcases, sitting on the floor, and leaning against the wall
of the hallway.

'Come,' my new friend said softly as she opened the door,
'the floor is no place for a child of the King.' I rose from my
cramped, huddled position and entered her apartment. I was
her guest for the next five weeks.

As the weeks passed, however, I realized I was running out of money. Jan ten Have (the publisher of my
little book in Holland) was visiting New York. He helped
me as much as he could, and I spent most of my time
looking up addresses given me in Holland. The Americans
were polite and some of them were interested, but none
wanted me to come to speak. They were all busy with
their own things. Some even said I should have stayed in
Holland.

As the weeks slipped by, I found more and more resistance
to my ministry. No one was interested in a middle-aged

spinster woman from Holland who wanted to preach. 'Why did you come to America?' people began to ask.

'God directed me. All I could do was obey.'

'That's nonsense,' they answered. 'There is no such thing as direct guidance from God. Experience proves we must use our common sense. If you are here and out of money, then it is your fault, not God's.'

I tried to argue back in God's defence. 'But God's guidance is even more important than common sense. I am certain He told me to bring His message to America. I can declare that the deepest darkness is outshone by the light of Jesus.'

'We have ministers to tell us such things,' was the reply.

'Certainly, but I can tell from my experience in a concentration camp that what such ministers say is true.'

'It would have been better for you to have remained in Holland. We don't need any more preachers. Too many Europeans come to America. They should be stopped.'

I was growing discouraged. Perhaps the Americans were right. Perhaps I should return to Holland and go back to my job as a watchmaker. My money was gone, and all that remained was the second cheque given me by the American businessman. Yet I was hesitant to cash it without his approval. I found his address and arrived in an imposing business office in Manhattan. Only this time his face was not as friendly as it had been in Holland.

'Do you mind if I cash your second cheque?' I asked.

'How do I know if you can return the money?' he asked. 'You've been in America five weeks and have found there is no work. I think it would be better if you simply returned the cheque.'

Mustering all my courage I said, 'I am sure God has work for me here. I am in His will, and will somehow return all your money.'

He snorted, tore up the cheque and then wrote out another – for a much smaller amount.

I was embarrassed and humbled. I had money in Holland – a balance left from my first book and a small income from the business I had sold. But these funds could not be brought to America. I returned to my room and closed the door. It was time for a long consultation with my Heavenly Father.

Kneeling beside the bed I prayed, 'Father, You must help me out. If I must borrow money to return to Holland people will say, "There, you see, the promises of the Bible are not real. Direct guidance does not exist." Father, for Your honour's sake. You must help me out.'

I fell weeping across the bed. Then, slowly, like a deep realization that dawns in a person's heart, the answer came: 'Do not worry about My honour. I will take care of that. In days to come you will give thanks for these days in New York.'

A great ocean separated me from my homeland. I had no money. Nobody wanted to hear my lectures. All I had was an inner word from God that He was guiding me. Was it enough? All I could do was press on – and on – and on – for His Name's sake.

Before going to sleep I opened my Bible, my constant companion. My eyes fell on a verse from the Psalms, 'The Lord taketh pleasure . . . in those that hope in His mercy' (147:11). It was a thin web – a tiny filament – stretching from heaven to my little room on 190th Street in New York. I fell asleep holding on to it with all my strength.

The next day I attended a Dutch service in a New York church. Dr Barkay Wolf was the speaker and many Hollanders were present, meeting afterward for coffee in the vestry. The Reverend Burggraaff, who had baptized our Canadian-born princess, was presented to me.

'ten Boom,' he mused when he heard my name. 'I often tell the story of a nurse by that name. She experienced a miracle in a concentration camp with a bottle of vitamins that never ran out. I tell it to prove that God still performs miracles today, as in Bible times. Do you happen to know that nurse? Is she related to you?'

I felt joy springing in my heart. 'She is not a nurse,' I replied. 'She is a watchmaker. And you are looking at her. It was I who had that experience in 1944.'

'Then you must come with me to Staten Island and tell your story to my congregation,' he exclaimed.

I spent the next five days in this pleasant parsonage with Rev and Mrs Burggraaff. What a joy to eat good Dutch food again. I had been trying to find out how long one could exist on Nedick's ten-cent breakfast which consisted of a cup of coffee, a doughnut, and a small glass of orange juice, eaten while standing at a counter. Now God was re-supplying me, not only with food, but with new hope. I could see that the Lord does take pleasure in those that hope in His mercy!

A week later I returned to Manhattan. Walking down the street I saw a church with a notice on the door. Drawing closer I saw it was an invitation to attend the Lord's Supper next Sunday morning, Easter.

Following the service, the minister gave me the address of Irving Harris, the editor of a Christian magazine called *The Evangel*. He encouraged me to go by and see him.

I did. In fact, the very next morning I went up to his office and talked to him. 'I know I am walking in the way God has led me,' I told him, 'but so many declare there is no such thing as direct guidance.'

'Pay no attention to them,' Mr Harris advised. 'The Bible contains many promises that God will lead those who obey Him. Have you ever heard of a good shepherd who does not lead his sheep?'

Mr Harris asked if I had any material which he might use in his magazine. I gave him a copy of one of my lectures and told him to use as much as he could.

'There is one drawback,' he explained. 'We cannot pay. This paper exists only to spread the Gospel, not for financial profit.'

'Wonderful!' I exclaimed. 'I am in the presence of an American who sees money in its proper perspective.'

Mr Harris gave me a name and address in Washington, DC. He strongly urged me to make an appointment and go down to see Mr Abraham Vereide. I knew nothing of Mr Vereide at the time, although I have since discovered he was one of the great Christian leaders of America. I was suspicious, afraid I was being shrugged off again. But I felt I could trust Mr Harris and followed through, taking a chance and making a phone call to Washington.

Mr Vereide received me graciously, inviting me to Washington as his guest. At dinner three other guests were present, all professors who plied me with questions throughout the evening. I felt like a schoolgirl who had been invited out by her headmistress. My English was crude and my mistakes seemed more glaring than ever before. How could I compete with such learned men?

The next afternoon, however, I was asked to address a group of women. They asked specifically that I share my prison experiences with them. This time I felt at home. Certainly I could tell them what the Lord had done in my life.

They received me warmly – enthusiastically in fact. 'Corrie,' one of the ladies said afterwards, 'this is your message. Share it wherever you go.' She then handed me a cheque that enabled me to return all the money I had borrowed in New York.

Suddenly the tables were turned. Instead of no work, I had to guard against overwork. Abraham Vereide's recommendation brought in calls from everyplace, asking me to come and share my testimony. The calls came from villages and towns, as well as from the big cities. I spoke in churches, universities, schools, and clubs. For almost ten months I travelled America, everywhere telling the story that Jesus Christ is reality, even in darkest days. I told them that He is the answer to all the problems in the hearts of men and nations. I knew it was so, because of what He had done for me.

As the year drew to a close I began to sense God wanted me to return to Europe. I was homesick for Holland, but this time I felt Him leading me in another direction – Germany. The one land I dreaded.

When I left the German concentration camp I said, 'I'll go anywhere God sends me, but I hope never to Germany.' Now I understand that was a statement of disobedience. F. B. Meyer said, 'God does not fill with His Holy Spirit those who believe in the fullness of the Spirit, or those who desire Him, but those who obey Him.' More than anything I desired to be filled with God's Spirit. I knew I had no choice but to go to Germany.

> *I will sing of the mercies of the Lord for ever: with my mouth will I make known thy faithfulness to all generations.*
> Psalms 89:1

6

Music From Broken Chords

The Germans had lost face in defeat. Their homes had been destroyed and when they heard the enormity of Hitler's crimes (which many Germans knew nothing about) they were filled with despair. As they returned to their Fatherland they felt they had nothing to live for.

Friends in Darmstadt helped me rent a former concentration camp to use as a home for displaced persons. It was not big, but there was room for about one hundred and sixty refugees and soon it was full with a long waiting list. I worked closely with the refugees programme of the Lutheran Church ('*das Evangelische Hilfswerk*') in the Darmstadt camp. Barbed wire disappeared. Flowers, light-coloured paint and God's love in the hearts of the people changed a cruel camp into a refuge where people would find the way back to life again.

Marienschwestern, the Lutheran Sisterhood of Mary, whose members had dedicated their lives to serving the Lord and spiritually hungry people, assisted with the children's and women's work. Pastors and members of different churches helped by building homes. I was travelling and helping raise money for the work.

The camp was crowded. Some rooms were jammed with several families. Noise and bedlam were everywhere as families, many without men because they had been killed in the war, tried to carry on the most basic forms of living. Often I would walk through the camp talking with the lonely, defeated people and trying to bring them hope and cheer.

One afternoon I spotted an elderly woman huddled in the corner of a big room. She was obviously new to the camp. She had been put in the big room along with three other families and told she could set up housekeeping in the corner. There she crouched, like a whipped child, her faded, worn dress pulled tightly around her frail, wasted body. I could sense she was distressed by the bedlam of all the crying children, but most of all defeated by life itself.

I went to her, sat beside her on the floor, and asked who she was. I learned she had been a professor of music at the Dresden Conservatory before the war. Now she had nothing.

I asked her to tell me about her life, knowing that sometimes it helps just to have someone willing to listen. She told me that a minister in a nearby town had given her permission to play his piano. She had also learned of several farmers' children nearby who wanted to receive music lessons. But the minister's home was miles away and the only way to get there was on foot. It all seemed so hopeless.

'You were a professor of piano?' I asked excitedly. 'I am a great lover of Germany's master musician, Johann Sebastian Bach.'

For an instant her eyes lighted up. 'Would you care to accompany me to the minister's home?' she asked with great dignity. 'I would be most happy to play for you.'

It was a great privilege, and even though we had to walk many miles, I sensed God was doing something special.

She seated herself at the battered piano. I looked at the instrument. Even though it had been saved from the bombing it had not been protected from the rain. The strings were exposed through the warped frame and I could see they were rusted. Some were broken and curled around the others. The pedals had long been broken off and the keyboard was almost entirely without ivory. If any of the notes played it would be a miracle.

Looking up the old woman said, 'What would you like me to play?'

Silently I prayed, knowing that failure at this moment could crush her forever. Then, to my own amazement, I heard myself saying, 'Would you please play the "Chromatic Phantasy" of Bach?'

I was aghast. Why had I picked one of the most difficult of all piano pieces for this old woman to play on such a ruined instrument? Yet the moment I said it, I saw a light flicker behind her eyes and a slight, knowing smile played across her tired face. She nodded, and with great finesse, put her fingers on the broken keyboard.

I could hardly believe my ears. From that damp, battered old piano flowed the beautiful music of Bach as her skilled fingers raced up and down the broken, chipped keys. Tears came to my eyes and ran down my cheeks as I thought of wounded Germany, left with only the remnants of the past, still able to play beautiful music. Such a nation will survive to create again, I thought.

As the notes of Bach faded from the air the words of an old Gospel song, written by the blind composer Fanny J. Crosby, came to mind:

> Down in the human heart, crush'd by the tempter,
> Feelings lie buried that grace can restore;
> Touched by a loving heart, wakened by kindness
> Chords that were broken will vibrate once more.

As we walked back to the former concentration camp my companion had a new spring in her step. 'It has been many years since I played the "Chromatic Phantasy",' she said. 'Once I was a concert pianist and many of my pupils are now outstanding musicians. I had a beautiful home in Dresden that was destroyed by the bombs. I had to flee and was not able to take one thing with me.'

'Oh, no, you are wrong,' I said. 'You took with you your most prized possession.'

'And what is that?' she asked, shocked.

'Your music. For that which is in your heart can never be taken from you.'

Then I told her of what I had learned in Ravensbruck, of Betsie's vision, and that God's love still stands when all else has fallen. 'In the concentration camp they took all we had, even made us stand naked for hours at a time without rest, but they could not take Jesus from my heart. Ask Jesus to come into your life. He will give you riches no man can take away from you.'

We returned to the camp in silence, but I knew the Holy Spirit was pricking her heart, reminding her of the things that man cannot snatch from us. Soon it was time for me to leave the camp and move on to other fields. The day I left she was sitting in that same corner of the room. A boy was playing his mouth organ, a baby was crying, there were the sounds of shouts and the pounding of a hammer against a wooden crate. The room was full of discord and disharmonic noises, but her eyes were closed and there was a faint smile on her face. I knew God had given her something that no one could ever take from her – ever again.

After the war, Germany was filled with wounds and scars – not all of them on the surface. In one tiny cubicle in the camp at Darmstadt, I found a German lawyer. He was sitting miserably in a wheelchair, the stumps of his legs poking out from under a lap blanket. He was filled with bitterness, hatred, and self-pity. He told me he had once been an active member of his Lutheran church and as a boy had rung the church bell in the village where he lived. Now the horrible injustice of war had taken his legs, and he was bitter against God and man.

I felt attracted to him since some of his experiences were similar to mine. One morning I made a special trip to his room to tell him something of my life.

I found him sitting in his wheelchair, staring at a blank wall. His face was grey, his eyes lifeless. I never was one for introductions so I got right to the point of my visit.

'The only way to get rid of bitterness is to surrender it,' I said.

He turned slowly and looked at me. 'What do you know about bitterness?' he asked. 'You still have your legs.'

'Let me tell you a story,' I said. 'In Holland, during the war, a man came to me begging me to help him liberate his wife. I felt compassion for him and gave him all my money. I also convinced my friends to do the same. But the man was a quisling, a traitor. The only reason he came to me was to trap me so he could have me arrested. Not only did he betray me, but he betrayed my entire family and friends. We were all sent to prison where three members of my family died. You ask me about bitterness and hatred. You only hate circumstances, but I hated a man. Sitting in the prison in my homeland, waiting to be transferred to a concentration camp in Germany, hatred and bitterness filled my heart. I wanted that man to die. I know what it is like to hate. That is why I can understand you.'

The lawyer turned his chair to face me. He was listening. 'So you have hated also. What do you suggest I do about my hate?'

'What I have to say is of no importance. Let me tell you what the Son of God had to say. 'For if ye forgive men their trespasses, your Heavenly Father will also forgive you. But if ye forgive not men their trespasses, neither will your Father forgive your trespasses.' (*See* Matthew 6:14, 15.) If we forgive other people, our hearts are made fit to receive forgiveness.'

The lawyer shifted uneasily in his wheelchair. I could see the muscles in his neck stand out as he pushed with his hands to change position. 'When we repent,' I continued, 'God forgives us and cleanses us. That is what I did, believing that if I confessed my sin God would be faithful and just to cleanse my sin and forgive me from all unrighteousness.'

The lawyer looked at me and shook his head. 'That is easy to say, but my hatred is too deep to have it washed away.'

'No deeper than mine,' I said. 'Yet when I confessed it, not only did Jesus take it away, He filled me with love – even the ability to love my enemy.'

'You mean you actually loved the man who betrayed you and who was responsible for the death of your family?'

I nodded. 'After the war, when that man was sentenced to death, I corresponded with him and God used me to show him the way of salvation before he was executed.'

The lawyer shook his head. 'What a miracle! What a miracle! You mean Jesus can do that to a person? I shall have to give this much thought.'

Since I have learned not to push a person beyond where God has left him, I bade my friend good-bye and returned to my room.

A year later I was in Darmstadt again. My friends had given this man a car with special fixtures so he could drive without legs. He met me at the train station to bring me to the camp. As I got in the car, he laughed at my startled look.

'You taught me that Jesus is victor,' he said. 'Now surely you are not afraid to drive with a man who has no legs.'

'You are right,' I answered. 'I shall not be afraid. I am so glad to see you again. How are you?'

'Fine. I must tell you at the very beginning that I have surrendered my bitterness to God. I repented and the Lord did just as you said. He forgave me and filled my heart with His love. Now I am working in the refugee camp and am praising God that He can use even a legless man if he is surrendered.'

He paused, and then continued. 'But there is something I must know. After you forgave your enemies, was it settled once and for all?'

'Oh no,' I answered. 'Just this month I had a sad experience with friends who behaved like enemies. They promised something but did not keep their promise. In fact, they took great advantage of me. However, I surrendered my bitterness to the Lord, asked forgiveness and He took it away.'

We were bouncing over a bumpy road but the lawyer was more intent on me than his driving. 'Was the bitterness gone for good, then?'

'No, just the next night, at four o'clock, I awoke and my heart was filled with bitterness again. I thought, *How could my dear friend behave as she did?* Again I brought it to the Lord. He filled my heart with His love. But the next night it came back again. I was so discouraged. God had used me often to help people to love their enemies, and I could always give my testimony about what He had done in my life; but now I felt defeated.

'Then I remembered Ephesians 6:10–20 where Paul describes the "armour of God". He said that even after you have come to a standstill, still stand your ground. I was at a standstill, so I decided to stand my ground and the bitterness and resentment fell away before me.

'Corrie ten Boom without the Lord Jesus cannot be victorious. I need the Lord every moment. And I have learned that I am absolutely dependent on Him. Because of this He has made me rich.'

We were just arriving at the refugee camp and my lawyer friend parked before the building, turned off the motor, and looked at me with a grin. 'I am glad to hear that,' he said. 'For sometimes my old bitterness returns. Now I shall just stand my ground, claim the victory of Jesus over fear and resentment, and love even when I don't want to.'

My friend had learned well the secret of victory. It comes through obedience.

7

Love Your Enemy

It was in a church in Munich that I saw him – a balding, heavy-set man in a grey overcoat, a brown felt hat clutched between his hands. People were filing out of the basement room where I had just spoken, moving along the rows of wooden chairs to the door at the rear. It was 1947 and I had come from Holland to defeated Germany with the message that God forgives.

It was the truth they needed most to hear in that bitter, bombed-out land, and I gave them my favourite mental picture. Maybe because the sea is never far from a Hollander's mind, I liked to think that that's where forgiven sins were thrown. 'When we confess our sins,' I said, 'God casts them into the deepest ocean, gone forever. And even though I cannot find a Scripture for it, I believe God then places a sign out there that says, NO FISHING ALLOWED.'

The solemn faces stared back at me, not quite daring to believe. There were never questions after a talk in Germany in 1947. People stood up in silence, in silence collected their wraps, in silence left the room.

And that's when I saw him, working his way forward against the others. One moment I saw the overcoat and the brown hat; the next, a blue uniform and a visored cap with its skull and crossbones. It came back with a rush: the huge room with its harsh overhead lights; the pathetic pile of dresses and shoes in the centre of the floor; the shame of walking naked past this man. I could see my sister's frail form ahead of me, ribs sharp beneath the parchment skin. *Betsie, how thin you were!*

The place was Ravensbruck and the man who was making his way forward had been a guard – one of the most cruel guards.

Now he was in front of me, hand thrust out: 'A fine message, Fraulein! How good it is to know that, as you say, all our sins are at the bottom of the sea!'

And I, who had spoken so glibly of forgiveness, fumbled in my pocketbook rather than take that hand. He would not remember me, of course – how could he remember one prisoner among those thousands of women?

But I remembered him and the leather crop swinging from his belt. I was face-to-face with one of my captors and my blood seemed to freeze.

'You mentioned Ravensbruck in your talk,' he was saying. 'I was a guard there.' No, he did not remember me.

'But since that time,' he went on, 'I have become a Christian. I know that God has forgiven me for the cruel things I did there, but I would like to hear it from your lips as well. Fraulein,' – again the hand came out – 'will you forgive me?'

And I stood there – I whose sins had again and again to be forgiven – and could not forgive. Betsie had died in that place – could he erase her slow terrible death simply for the asking?

It could not have been many seconds that he stood there – hand held out – but to me it seemed hours as I wrestled with the most difficult thing I had ever had to do.

For I had to do it – I knew that. The message that God forgives has a prior condition: that we forgive those who have injured us. 'If you do not forgive men their trespasses,' Jesus says, 'neither will your Father in heaven forgive your trespasses.'

I knew it not only as a commandment of God, but as a daily experience. Since the end of the war I had had a home in

Holland for victims of Nazi brutality. Those who were able to forgive their former enemies were able also to return to the outside world and rebuild their lives, no matter what the physical scars. Those who nursed their bitterness remained invalids. It was as simple and as horrible as that.

And still I stood there with the coldness clutching my heart. But forgiveness is not an emotion – I knew that too. Forgiveness is an act of the will, and the will can function regardless of the temperature of the heart. 'Jesus, help me!' I prayed silently. 'I can lift my hand. I can do that much. You supply the feeling.'

And so woodenly, mechanically, I thrust my hand into the one stretched out to me. And as I did, an incredible thing took place. The current started in my shoulder, raced down my arm, sprang into our joined hands. And then this healing warmth seemed to flood my whole being, bringing tears to my eyes.

'I forgive you, brother!' I cried. 'With all my heart.'

For a long moment we grasped each other's hands, the former guard and the former prisoner. I had never known God's love so intensely as I did then. But even so, I realized it was not my love. I had tried, and did not have the power. It was the power of the Holy Spirit as recorded in Romans 5:5, '. . . because the love of God is shed abroad in our hearts by the Holy Ghost which is given unto us.'

*And Jesus being full of the Holy Ghost
returned from Jordan, and was led by the
Spirit into the wilderness . . . And Jesus
returned in the power of the Spirit into
Galilee: and there went out a fame of him
through all the region round about.*
Luke 4:1; 14

8

In the Power of the Spirit

As I stood in the railroad station in Basel, Switzerland, waiting
for my luggage, I suddenly realized that I did not know where
I was supposed to go. For ten years, after my release from
prison, I had been travelling all over the world at the direction
of God. Many times I did not know why I was to go to a certain
place until I arrived. It had become almost second nature not
to make my plans and then ask for God's signature. Rather,
I had learned to wait for God's plan and then write my name
on the schedule.

But this time was different. Suddenly I was in Basel and
had no idea why, or whom I was to contact. Besides, I was
tired. Sleeping each night in a different bed and always living
out of a suitcase had worn me down. I felt a sensation of panic
in my heart and sat down, trying to remember to whom I was
going. At sixty-three years of age could it be that I was so
overworked that I was losing my memory? Or even worse,
had God withdrawn His conscious Presence from me and was
letting me walk alone for a season?

Inside my suitcase I found an address. It had no meaning
to me but it was all I had to go on. I took a taxi to the place

but the people at that address were complete strangers and had never heard of me. By now I was desperate – and a little bit frightened.

The people told me of another man I might contact. Perhaps he would know who I was and why I had come to Basel. I took another taxi but this gentleman, too, was unfamiliar with my work.

For ten years the Lord had guided me step-by-step. At no time had I been confused or afraid. Now I was both – unable to recognize the Presence of God. Surely He was still guiding me, but like the pilot who flies into the clouds, I was now having to rely on instruments rather than sight. I decided to turn around and go back home to Holland, there to await further orders.

Because of a severe storm the planes were not flying. I had to travel by train. Arriving at Haarlem, I started towards the phone near the station to call Zonneduin, the house where I was to stay in the outskirts of the city in Bloemendaal.

But on the way to the phone booth I slipped on the wet pavement and before I knew it I was sprawled in the street. A sharp pain shot through my hip and I was unable to stand.

'Oh, Lord,' I prayed, 'lay Your hand on my hip and take away this horrible pain.'

Instantly the pain disappeared, but I was still unable to get up. Kind people assisted me to a taxi where a policeman asked if he could help.

'What is your name?' he asked.

'Corrie ten Boom.'

He looked surprised and questioned me further. 'Are you a member of the family of that name whom we arrested about ten years ago?'

'That is right.'

During the war many of the good Dutch policemen had been in the service of the Gestapo, remaining there for the express purpose of helping political prisoners. This man had been on duty that day my family was arrested.

'I am so sorry about your accident,' he said sympathetically, 'but I am glad to see you again. I will never forget that night in the police station. You were all sitting or lying on the floor of the station. Your old father was there with all his children and many of your friends. I have often told my colleagues that there was an atmosphere of peace and joy in our station that night, as if you were going to a feast instead of prison and death.'

He paused and looked at me kindly as if trying to remember my face. 'Your father said before he tried to sleep, "Let us pray together." And then he read Psalm 91.'

'You remember!' I exclaimed. After ten years that policeman had remembered which psalm my father had read.

For a fleeting moment, sitting in that old taxi on a Haarlem street while the rain pelted the roof, I allowed myself that pain of looking backwards. It was in this same city that we had been arrested. In fact, the prison was only a short distance from where I was now sitting. That was the last time our family had been together. Within ten days Father was dead. Then later Betsie. All gone. Now, ten years later this policeman still remembered.

He that dwelleth in the secret place of the most High shall abide under the shadow of the Almighty.

verse 1

Now the message was clear. Although there was no light to guide me, I was still in God's will. Actually, when one is abiding under the shadow of the Almighty there will be no light, but that is only because God's Presence is so near.

I leaned back in the seat. 'Dear God, when this shadow came over me I thought You had departed. Now I understand it was because You were drawing closer. I eagerly await whatever You have planned for me.'

Eager I was, but not so patient. An X-ray showed my hip was not broken, only badly bruised. The doctor said I would have to remain in bed for several weeks for it to heal. I was taken from the clinic to Zonneduin where I was put to bed, unable to move or turn over without the help of a nurse.

I was a very impatient patient. I had only five days to get to a student conference in Germany and as the days slipped by and I realized my hip was not healing fast enough to make the conference, I grew irritable.

'Is there not a Christian in all Haarlem who can pray for me to be healed?' I asked.

My friends sent for a particular minister in the city who was known to have laid hands on the sick for healing. That same afternoon he came to my room.

Standing beside my bed he said, 'Is there any unconfessed sin in your life?'

What an odd question, I thought. I understood he had agreed to come and pray for my healing, but was it his job to get so personal about my sins and attitudes? However, I did not have far to look. My impatience and demanding attitude which I had displayed towards my nurse had been wrong – very wrong. I asked her to come to the room and I repented of my sin, asking both her and God to forgive me.

Satisfied, this gentle man then reached over and laid his hands on my head. Only the year before my sister Nollie had died. Ever since my heart had been broken with mourning. I had the feeling of being left all alone and knew that the insecurity which I had experienced had contributed to my being here in this bed, rather than in Germany with the students. Yet as this tall, handsome man laid his hands on me and prayed, I felt a great stream of power flowing through me. Such great joy. The mourning left and I wanted to sing with David:

> Thou hast turned for me my mourning into dancing: thou has put off my sackcloth, and girded me with gladness.
>
> Psalms 30:11

I felt the Presence of the Lord Jesus all around me and felt His love flowing through me and over me as if I were being immersed in an ocean of grace. My joy became so intense that I finally prayed, 'No more, Lord, no more.' My heart felt it was about to burst, so great was the joy. I knew it was that wonderful experience promised by Jesus – the Baptism in the Holy Spirit.

I looked at the man who had prayed for me. 'Can I walk now?' I asked.

He smiled. 'I do not know. All I know is you asked for a cupful and God gave you an ocean.'

Ten days later I was on my way to Germany, late, but still filled with joy overflowing. Only after I arrived did I realize why God chose this particular time to fill me with His Holy Spirit. For in Germany, for the first time, I came face-to-face with many people who were demonized. Had I gone in my own power I would have been consumed. Now, going in the power of the Holy Spirit, God was able to work much deliverance through me as we commanded demons to be cast out in the Name of the Lord Jesus Christ.

Jesus specifically warned His followers not to try to minister in His Name without His power. As I found out from my experience in Basel, trying to do the Lord's work in your own strength is the most confusing, exhausting, and tedious of all work. But when you are filled with the Holy Spirit, then the ministry of Jesus just flows out of you.

It was the beginning of a new spiritual blessing that each day brings me into a closer walk with the Lord Jesus. Now, whether I am walking in the bright light of His Presence, or abiding under the *shadow* of the Almighty, I know that He is not only with me, He is in me.

. . . greater is he that is in you, than he that is in the world.

1 John 4:4

9

Conny

After twelve years of travelling alone, someone joined me
in my worldwide travels. The Lord saw and supplied my
need in the person of Conny van Hoogstraten, a beautiful,
young, Dutch woman who became my first constant travelling
companion. I met her on one of my visits to England. We
worked well as a team (not to say we did not have difficulties
– as always happens when people work so close together).
However, those hard moments were used to bring us closer
to Jesus as we learned to walk in the light with each other.
Yes, 1 John 1:7–9 became a reality, and the Lord used Conny
in the lives of countless people all over the world to show and
teach them the joy of walking in the light.

We laughed much together for the Lord had given Conny
an infectious sense of humour and a happy laughter. One of
Conny's special gifts was the ability to change a house into a
home. People always found an open door and quickly became
friends. We were both so different but the Lord moulded
us into a team fit to do His work. I will never forget the
day, now almost eight years ago, that Conny told me of the
someone else who had come into her life and that we would
have to pray for a new partner. That was one of those very
difficult days and the best thing I could do was to go for a
long walk. I experienced more than ever before that I was
so dependent upon Conny and that I loved her like a sister.
I could not understand the Lord's purpose, but during that

walk I surrendered Conny to the Lord, and I also surrendered myself in a new way and entrusted my whole being to Him who knew best. Conny was in good hands so why not trust Him for the future? Those last years together were so different from all other years.

In that final year together, the Lord made it clear to me to go to Viet Nam. Conny and I talked it over and Conny shared with me that her fiancé was not in favour of her going there so we had to look around for someone else. It was early spring and I happened to meet a good brother in the Lord who shared that he had been called to go to Viet Nam also. I rejoiced and thanked the Lord as we made plans to go together. The young man was Brother Andrew and he proved to be a very good travelling companion. In Viet Nam, the Lord gave me a very nice nurse who worked with the W.E.C. and she took care of me when I travelled while Brother Andrew was away on other trips to very dangerous places.

I will never forget the tremendous needs I saw in the hospitals and other places I visited, but instead of taking all those needs to Jesus, I kept them in my heavy and overburdened heart. How silly I could be! With that heavy heart and aching body I had to go on to Indonesia. Oh, the Lord worked in spite of me, and the people were very kind to me and helped me in many ways, but the happiest moment came when we landed in Amsterdam. We quickly drove to Soestdijk where a very dear friend, Elisabeth van Heemstra (who was working in Jerusalem at that time) had made her apartment available to me. That was a great gift from the Lord! I had no place I could really call home but now I had one – and what a haven it was! Beautiful surroundings in a quiet section of town. There Conny and I spent our last months together and it was a precious time. Conny was busy with marriage preparations and the new house she and her husband would move into. Many old-time friends came by to say hello. We talked and prayed much and we trusted that the Lord would supply a new partner before Conny's marriage.

How marvellous are His ways! The Lord answered our prayers and gave me another Dutch companion. Her name is Ellen de Kroon, a registered nurse, who loves the Lord very much. I will never forget the first time Ellen visited me. Conny and her fiancé were there also. It was a nice day in June and we decided to sit outside on the balcony. After talking for some time, Ellen noticed that I was getting cold, so she got up, asked me where she could find a shawl and put it around my shoulders. I noticed Conny's face, just beaming, with eyes that seemed to say, 'See! You prayed for that "someone" who would take care of you and love you and here she is.' It was a testimony for Conny as well, knowing that Ellen would take her place.

On Conny's wedding day, September 1, 1967, the Lord filled the empty place left behind by Conny with Ellen, the tall, fair-haired nurse. Conny and her husband lived not far from us and she took much time to help Ellen with the work. Almost a year after Conny was married, her husband had to go to India for several weeks. During that time, Conny accompanied me to the United States to start the work on the book *The Hiding Place* while Ellen took care of the work in Holland. Yes, it was Conny who started to type that book which has already blessed so many lives all over the world. I knew that she loved the work we were doing but she also missed her husband. It was so good to bring him daily before the Lord. Our prayers were answered and Conny's husband returned safely to Holland while I continued my travels with my new companion, Ellen.

Two years had passed when we learned that Conny had been taken ill. We returned to Holland and were on our way to visit Conny in the hospital. I knew that she was very ill, because she had received treatment that would indicate terminal illness unless the Lord would perform a miracle. When we entered Conny's room, it was like stepping into a flower garden and in the midst of it was Conny, almost asleep. Her husband was sitting beside her. That day, her specialist had informed her of her illness and that there was no hope. Conny was prepared to go and be with her Lord and Saviour but to take that trip all by herself was so difficult for her. Would Jesus ask that of her?

Slowly she said, 'I have taken many trips in my lifetime but there was always someone with me. Mother was there when

I was small, Corrie was with me during many of them, and now my husband is with me. But on this trip, who is going to go with me?'

Her husband gently took her hand and said, 'Conny, here is my hand and as soon as Jesus comes for you, I will surrender your hand to Him!'

Conny did not answer but her face looked content. Suddenly she turned to us and asked us to sing Psalm Twenty-Three for her. I swallowed the lump in my throat and asked the Lord to help me in joining the others in the singing, but the phrase we left out was, 'though I walk through the valley of the shadow of death . . .'

When we finished Conny said, 'You forgot one phrase – please sing it!'

So we sang, 'though I walk through the valley of the shadow of death' while the tears rolled down our cheeks. Then Conny thought of all the friends all over the world whom we had come to know and love, and she asked me to greet them. We began to pray and Conny laid her hands on Ellen's head and said, 'Be . . . faithful unto death and I will give thee a crown of life' (Revelation 2:10).

Conny died a victorious death. Her life bore much fruit, and she prepared many people to meet the Master, our Lord Jesus Christ, who came to call her home to be with Him forever.

*And these signs shall follow them
that believe;
In my name shall they cast out
devils . . .*
Mark 16:17

10

Authority Over Demons

For weeks I had been travelling through Eastern Europe: Russia, Poland, Czechoslovakia – speaking in many home groups and even, on occasion, in a church. Many churches were still open in Eastern Europe, although the Communists were very strict about who could speak – and what they said. However, as a harmless old Dutch woman I was allowed to sometimes speak in one of the churches.

As if by a miracle, I was invited to speak in a series of meetings in a great cathedral in a large Communist city. I found that the pastors loved the Lord and had a heavy burden for lost souls.

The first several nights I spoke about the abundant life in Jesus Christ – the joy, the unspeakable love, and the peace that passes all understanding. It was as though I was carried by the Holy Spirit through the joyful storehouse of abundance that we possess when we know Jesus. I described in great detail the precious promises made available to us in Christ.

But something was wrong. Although some of the people rejoiced, most of them simply sat rooted to their benches. They were like chained animals, dying of hunger but unable to reach the food. And the more I tried to give them the more

I was aware their hearts were shackled so they could not taste the food I was offering them.

Each night I would return to my room with a heavy heart for I knew that although these dear people wanted to receive what I was giving them, they could not. 'It is as if the devil keeps a fence around these people that you cannot reach them,' my travelling companion said.

'Could it be that demons keep them in bondage?' I wondered.

I opened my Bible and read, 'In my name shall they cast out devils.'

'Lord, what must I do?' I cried out.

'Obey Me!' came the answer.

'But how, Lord? There are so many who are bound by demon powers and I cannot meet with each of them individually.'

'Where did I say that you can deal only with individuals?' He asked.

I was confused and returned to His Word. It became apparent that the Lord wanted me to send all the evil spirits away in His Name. Yet I knew this type of ministry was forbidden in Communist lands.

That night was the final night of the meetings. The great cathedral was crowded with people, but it was the same as on all the other nights. They were not able to receive what I was giving them. I spoke again on Jesus the Victor. 'In the world you will have tribulation, but be of good courage, I have overcome the world.' (*See* John 16:33.) They sat like stone images, unable to grasp the joy of the Lord.

I knew God was calling on me to act. I trembled, but I had no choice. 'I must interrupt my message for a moment, friends,' I said. 'Many of you cannot grasp the richness the Lord offers us this evening. The servants of Satan are keeping you in bondage.'

Then I obeyed. Taking a deep breath and offering one last quick prayer I said in a loud voice, 'In the Name of Jesus I command all dark powers keeping people from the blessings of God to disappear. Go away! Get out of the hearts of these people. Get out of this church. Go to the place where God sends you.'

Then, closing my eyes I raised my hands upward and prayed, 'Lord, will You now protect us with Your precious blood. *Amen.*'

I was afraid but I felt secure. I knew God had told me to do it. Then, as I opened my eyes and looked out over the huge congregation, I saw a miracle happen. The people who had been in bondage came alive. They began to rejoice and as I continued my message I could sense their eager hearts drinking in the living water as I poured it out before them.

After the service I was scheduled to meet with a large group of local pastors who had attended the meeting. By the time I was able to break away from the crowd of people who came forward to speak to me, and get to the back room, the pastors were already meeting. Their conversation was very serious.

'How could you do that?' one pastor asked as soon as I entered the room. 'Communists do not allow people to speak about demons!'

'I had to obey God,' was my only answer.

The pastors resumed their discussion about the meeting. They, too, had seen the bondage. They had also sensed the release when the demons were cast out. But there were some who had studied psychology and others who had studied demonology. They entered into a heated argument about the subject. I had studied none of these. All I knew was God had told me to use my authority in the Name of Jesus. So I sat back while the argument swirled around me.

At last one of the pastors said, 'We know God's promises and God's command, but who among us has ever been willing to obey Mark 16:17: "And these signs shall follow them that believe; In my name shall they cast out devils . . ."'

There was a long, uncomfortable silence. When the Bible interferes with man's theology, it always causes a strain. The pastor then continued, 'God has this evening given Corrie the grace to take the authority of Jesus and in His Name cast out devils. We should be thankful instead of all this arguing.'

That was the end of the pastors' meeting, but, oh, what a

lesson I learned that night. It is tragic to be around people, especially men of God, who do not recognize the fact that we are surrounded, not only by angels, but also by the powers of darkness.

Someone once asked my opinion of the missionaries in a certain country. My answer was, 'They have given all, but they have not taken all. They have given homeland, time, money, luxury, and more; but they have not taken all of the boundless resources of God's promises. Many do not know about two precious weapons: the power of the blood of Jesus – and every Christian's legal right to use the wonderful Name of Jesus to cast out demons.'

In *War on the Saints*, Mrs Jessie Penn-Lewis wrote, '. . . when the existence of evil spirits is recognized by the heathen, it is generally looked upon by the missionary as "superstition" and ignorance; whereas the ignorance is often on the part of the missionary, who is blinded by the prince of the power of the air to the revelation given in the Scriptures, concerning the satanic powers.'

We need to recognize the enemy in order to overcome him. But let us beware of the mistakes that C. S. Lewis described in *Screwtape Letters*. He says, 'There are two equal and opposite errors into which our race can fall about the devils. One is to disbelieve in their existence, the other is to believe and to feel an unhealthy interest in them! They themselves are equally pleased by both errors, and they hail a materialist or a magician with the same delight.'

We have a good safeguard and guide – the Bible – God's Word. Here we find not only the necessary information about Satan and demons, but also the weapons and the armour that we need for this battle.

God wants and expects us to be conquerors over the powers of darkness – not only for the sake of personal victory and the liberation of other souls – but for His glory, so that His triumph and victory over His enemies may be demonstrated!

First, then, let us see what the Bible says about the powers of darkness. The devil (or Satan) is introduced to us as a person who opposes God and His work. He is the 'god of this world' who blinds the minds of the people to the truths of God's Word. Having rebelled against God, he was cast out of heaven; then, he caused man's fall in paradise. Jesus calls him 'the father of lies, a liar, a murderer.' (*See* John 8:44.) He works often as an 'angel of light', seeking the ruin of the elect. But he was cursed of God. Jesus triumphed over him at the Cross of Calvary and in His Resurrection. He has been condemned and will finally be destroyed.

There are many kinds of demons, and they afflict people in various ways. They also bring false doctrine, trying to seduce the elect by oppressing, obsessing, and possessing. They know Jesus, recognize His power, and tremble before Him. For them, hell is the final destination, as it is for Satan.

Second, the Bible gives us direction concerning the stand we have to take against these powers. It is most important to realize that ours is the position *in Christ*. We are called to resist the devil in the 'whole armour of God', by virtue of the blood of Jesus, by faith, prayer, and fasting.

I remember in Ravensbruck, for instance, when we had very little to eat, my sister Betsie said, 'Let us dedicate this involuntary fast to the Lord that it may become a blessing.' Almost immediately we found we had power over the demons that were tormenting us and were able to exercise that power to cast them out of our barracks.

Let us remember that God's Word stands forever, and that His commandments mean for us today exactly the same as for His disciples twenty centuries ago. Those who act on them, in obedience, will in the same way prove God's almighty power. Yes, Jesus said, 'In my name shall they cast out devils.' And that means us today.

Our fight is not against a physical army, a political party, an atheistic organization – or anything like that. Our fight is against organizations and powers that are spiritual. Demons may come in as a result of occult sin, even from years back. This includes contact with hypnotism, astrology charts, fortune-telling, Ouija boards and other forms of occultism, sometimes entered into 'just for fun'. These demons will remain until they are cast out in Jesus' Name.

We are up against the unseen power that controls this dark

world and the spiritual agents are from the very headquarters of evil. Therefore, we must wear the 'whole armour of God', that we may be able to resist evil in its day of power, and that even when we have fought to a standstill, we may still stand our ground.

Conny and I had travelled throughout Poland. Conny was then my constant companion, and we met many wonderful Christians in that Iron Curtain country. It encouraged us to know that God was using us to bring comfort and strength to the men and women of God. However, the longer we stayed in Poland, the more exhausted we became.

'I do not understand it,' Conny said one morning as we were getting up. 'I have just wakened from a full night's sleep but already I am weak and tired.'

I, too, felt the same way. We thought perhaps it was some kind of sickness we had picked up; yet neither of us seemed to be really sick.

Then in Warsaw one day we happened to meet an old friend from Holland. Kees was in Poland with his wife, travelling with his camping trailer.

'What a joy to meet you,' he said. 'How are things going?'

I looked at Conny and she looked at me. 'You know, Kees, we both feel so tired. It is as if our legs are heavy, like when you have the flu. Yet we are not ill, just tired.'

Kees looked at us intently. 'Is this your first time to work in Poland?'

'Yes,' I answered. 'But what does that have to do with it?'

'Let me explain,' Kees said. 'Your tiredness is nothing less than an attack of the devil. He does not like your work in Poland, for the antichrist is busy here, arranging his army.'

Reaching out, he put his hand on my arm. 'Corrie and Conny, you must remember you have the protection of the blood of Jesus. Whenever you experience these attacks from the dark powers, you must rebuke them in the Name of Jesus.'

I knew what Kees was saying was right. We sat in his car while he read from the Bible. 'They overcame him by the blood of the lamb, and by the word of their testimony, and they loved not their lives unto the death' (Revelation 12:11).

Then Kees prayed with us, laying his hands on us in the Name of Jesus and rebuking the dark powers that would attack us. Even as he was praying I felt the darkness leave. By the time the prayer was over, we both felt covered by the blood of the Lamb and all our tiredness had disappeared.

God had taught us a valuable lesson that we would remember in many other areas of the world. We learned that in a country where a godless philosophy reigns, that only by claiming the blood of Jesus can you stand and not fall. The same is true in a city, or school, or even a church building. If Jesus Christ is not recognized as Supreme, then darkness rules.

Since then we have travelled in many countries and felt this same tiredness coming over us. Often I have felt it in American cities. Now I know it simply means that I am in a place where Satan rules. But praise the Lord! I can be an overcomer when I stand in the power of the blood of the Lamb.

*But I say unto you, Love your enemies,
bless them that curse you, do good to them
that hate you, and pray for them which
despitefully use you, and persecute you.*
Matthew 5:44

11

Lights From Darkest Africa

Thomas was a tall black man who lived in a round hut together
with his big family in the middle of Africa. He loved the Lord
and loved people – an unbeatable combination.

Thomas's neighbour, who lived across the dirt street, hated
God – and hated men like Thomas who loved God. The hatred
grew stronger and stronger until the man began sneaking over
at night and setting fire to the straw roof on Thomas's hut,
endangering his small children. Three nights in a row this
happened and each time Thomas was able to rush out of his
hut and put out the flames before they destroyed the roof
and the walls. The fact that he never said an unkind word to
his neighbour, only showing him love and forgiveness, made
his neighbour hate him even more.

One night the neighbour sneaked across the street and
set fire to Thomas's roof. This night, however, a strong
wind came up and as Thomas rushed to beat out the fire,
the sparks blew across the street and set the neighbour's
house on fire. Thomas finished putting out the fire on his
roof and then rushed across the street to put out the fire on
his neighbour's roof. He was able to extinguish the flames,
but in the process he badly burned his hands and arms.

Other neighbours told the chief of the tribe what had

happened. The chief was so furious that he sent his police to arrest the neighbour and throw him into prison.

That night Thomas came to the meeting where I was speaking (as he had done each night). I noticed his badly burned hands and asked him what had happened. Reluctantly he told me the story.

'It is good that this man is now in prison,' I said. 'Now your children are no longer in danger and he cannot try again to put your house in flames.'

'That is true,' he said. 'But I am so sorry for that man. He is an unusually gifted man and now he must live together with all those criminals in a horrible prison.'

'Then let us pray for him,' I said.

Thomas dropped to his knees and holding up his burned and bandaged hands, he began to pray. 'Lord, I claim this neighbour of mine for You. Lord, give him his freedom and do the miracle that in the future he and I will become a team to bring the Gospel in our tribe. *Amen.*'

Never had I heard such a prayer.

Two days later I was able to go to the prison. I spoke to the prisoners about God's joy and God's love. Among the group who listened intently was Thomas's neighbour. When I asked who would receive Jesus in his heart, that man was the first one to raise his hand.

After the meeting I told him how Thomas loved him, how he had burned his hands trying to put out the fire to save his house, and how he had prayed that they might become a team to spread the Gospel. The man wept big tears and nodded his head saying, 'Yes, yes, that is how it shall be.'

The next day I told Thomas. He praised God and said, 'You see, God has worked a miracle. We never can expect too much from Him.' He left, running off down the path, his face beaming with joy.

I had been in Africa for three weeks when I finally got to visit the prison on the outside of the city. I inquired to the warden if I could talk to the prisoners.

'Impossible,' he said, 'the prison is on restriction for an entire month due to an uprising that has broken out among the prisoners. Nobody is allowed in to see the men, much less give a sermon.'

I felt discouraged but knew that God had brought me to that place for some reason. So, I just stood – looking at the warden.

He grew very uncomfortable (having me stand and look at him). At last he said, 'There are some political prisoners who have been sentenced to death. Would you like to speak to them?'

'Certainly,' I said.

The warden called three heavily armed soldiers who escorted me down a long hall past many barred doors and into a cell where one man was sitting on a low bench which was also his bed. There was absolutely nothing else in the cell. The only light came from a small window high above the floor that let just a little spot of sunlight fall on the hardpacked dirt floor in that dreary place.

I leaned against the wall. He was a young man with black skin and very white teeth. He looked up, his eyes filled with sadness. What could I say? 'Lord, give me some light to pass on to this man who sits in such darkness.'

Finally I asked him a question. 'Do you know about Jesus?'

'Yes,' he said slowly, 'I have a Bible at home. I know that Jesus died on a cross for the sins of the world. Many years ago I accepted Him as my Saviour and followed Him for some time until political affairs absorbed all my time. Now I wish I could start again and live a surrendered life, but it is too late. This week I die.'

'It is not too late, my friend,' I said. 'Do you know the ones responsible for your death sentence?'

'I could give you the entire list of those who have put me here,' he answered, gritting his teeth. 'I know all their names and hate them.'

I opened my Bible and read, 'But if you do not forgive men their trespasses, neither will your Father forgive your trespasses.' Then I closed the Bible and looked at him. 'Do you want your Father to forgive you before you die?'

'Of course I want that,' he said. 'More than anything else

in the world. But I cannot meet the conditions. I am not able
to forgive. I am young, strong, and healthy. I have a wife and
children. These men have wronged me and now this very
week they will take away my life. How do I forgive that?'

The man looked at me with eyes full of despair and
hopelessness. I felt such a great compassion in my heart,
yet I knew I must be stern for much depended on it.

'Let me tell you a story,' I said. And then I told him of my
experience in the church in Berlin when my former guard
from the concentration camp asked me to forgive him.

'That moment I felt a great bitterness swelling in my heart,'
I said. 'I remembered the sufferings of my dying sister. But
I knew that unforgiveness would do more harm to me than
the guard's whip. So I cried out to the Lord, "Lord, thank
You for Romans 5:5:

> The love of God is shed abroad in our hearts by the Holy
> Ghost which is given unto us.

Thank You, Lord, that Your Love in me can do that which I
cannot do."

'At that moment a great stream of love poured through me
and I said, "Brother, give me your hand. I forgive all."'

I looked down at the African man sitting on the bench. 'I
could not do it. I was not able. Jesus in me was able to do it.
You see, you never touch so much the ocean of God's love
as when you love your enemies.'

The man listened as I told him more of Jesus. Then
promising to meet him on the other shore, I prayed with
him and left.

The next day a missionary friend came by the place where
I was staying. He told me that as soon as I left the prison
the prisoner had sent a message to his wife saying, 'Don't
hate the people who brought me here and who will cause my
death. Love them. Forgive them. I cannot, and neither can
you, but Jesus in us can do it.'

I slept well that night, knowing why God had brought me
to Africa.

*　　*　　*

I had spoken in many prisons in my travels across the world, but the prison in Ruanda, Africa, was the dreariest, darkest prison I had ever seen. The men were all black, their uniforms were black and they were sitting in the mud on the ground.

I had just entered the prison gate with my interpreter, a missionary lady. Steam (the aftermath of a hard tropical rain) was rising from the mud. The men were sitting on pieces of paper, branches, banana leaves, their legs caked with mud up to their knees.

'Why don't we go into the building' I asked my interpreter.

'Impossible,' she whispered, obviously afraid of the men. 'There are so many prisoners that even during the night only half of them can go inside.'

I looked at their faces. Like their skin, their eyes were dark. It was the look I had seen so many times in Ravensbruck – the look of those whose hope had died. Unhappiness. Despair. Hopelessness. Anger. How could I speak to them? What could I, an old Dutch woman, say to these miserable men that would help their lives?

'Lord,' I prayed, 'I am not able to overcome this darkness.'

'Take My promise of Galatians 5:22,' I heard an inner voice say.

Quickly I took my Bible and opened it to that passage. 'But the fruit of the Spirit is love . . .'

'Thank You, Lord,' I whispered. 'But I have a great love for these men already or I would not be here.'

I read on. 'But the fruit of the Spirit is love, joy . . .'

'Joy?' I asked. 'In these surroundings?' Then I remembered what Nehemiah said, 'The joy of the Lord is my strength.'

'Yes, Lord,' I cried out. 'That is what I need. That is what I claim. I claim the promise of joy.'

Even as I spoke the words I felt a wonderful, lifting sensation in my heart. It was joy – more joy than I had ever felt. It poured like a river out of my inner being; like the rising tide it covered the salt flats of my depression and turned the ugly mud of despair into a shimmering lagoon of blessedness. Moments later I was introduced to the prisoners who all sat, staring at me in hatred. The steam rose around them and the stinging insects swarmed their mud-coated ankles and legs.

I began to talk of the joy that is ours when we know Jesus. What a Friend we have in Him. He is always with us. When we are depressed, He gives us joy. When we do wrong. He gives us the strength to be good. When we hate, He fills us with His forgiveness. When we are afraid, He causes us to love.

Several faces changed and I saw that some of my joy was spilling over on them. But I knew what the rest were thinking. *After your talk you can go home, away from this muddy, stinking prison. It is easy to talk about joy when you are free. But we must stay here.*

Then I told them a story.

'Morning roll call at Ravensbruck was often the hardest time of the day. By 4:30 A.M. we had to be standing outside our barracks in the black pre-dawn chill, in blocks of one hundred women, ten wide, ten deep.

'Names were never used in the concentration camp. It was part of the plan to dehumanize the prisoners – to take away their dignity of life – their worth before God and man. I was known simply as Prisoner 66730.

'Roll call sometimes lasted three hours and every day the sun rose a little later and the icy-cold wind blew a little stronger. Standing in the grey of the dawn I would try to repeat, through shivering lips, that verse of Scripture which had come to mean so much to me: 'Who shall separate us from the love of Christ? Shall tribulation, or distress, or persecution, or famine, or nakedness, or peril, or sword? As it is written, for thy sake we are killed all the day long; we are accounted as sheep for the slaughter" (Romans 8:35, 36). In all this there was an overwhelming victory through Jesus who had proved His love for me by dying on the cross.

'But there came a time when repeating the words did not help. I needed more. "Oh God," I prayed, "reveal Yourself somehow."

'Then one morning the woman directly in front of me sank to the ground. In a moment a young woman guard was standing over her, a whip in her hand.

'"Get up," she screamed in a rage. "How dare you think you can lie down when everyone else is standing!"

'I could hardly bear to see what was happening in front of me. *Surely this is the end of us all,* I thought. Then suddenly a skylark started to sing high in the sky. The sweet, pure notes of the bird rose on the still cold air. Every head turned upward, away from the carnage before us, listening to the song of the skylark soaring over the crematorium. The words of the psalmist ran through my mind: "For as the heaven is high above the earth, so great is [God's] mercy towards them that fear Him (Psalms 103:11).'"

I looked out at the men who were sitting in front of me. No longer were their faces filled with darkness and anger. They were listening – intently – for they were hearing from someone who had walked where they were now walking. I continued.

'There in that prison I saw things from God's point of view. The reality of God's love was just as sure as the cruelty of men.

> O love of God, how deep and great,
> Far deeper than man's deepest hate.

'Every morning for the next three weeks, just at the time of roll call, the skylark appeared. In his sweet song I heard the call of God to turn my eyes away from the cruelty of men to the ocean of God's love.

'A Jewish doctor, Viktor Frankl, who went through far more suffering in the concentration camps than I, wrote a book. He ends the book with these words: ". . . we have come to know man is that being who has invented the gas chambers of Auschwitz; however, he is also that being who has entered those gas chambers upright with the Lord's Prayer or the *Shema Yisroel* on his lips."'

Although I was speaking through an interpreter, God's Spirit was working through both of us. I saw joy appearing on the faces of nearly all the men sitting before me.

'Say, men,' I said, 'do you know Jesus is willing to live in your hearts? He says, "I stand at the door of your heart and knock. If anyone hears my voice and opens the door, I come in." Just think: that same Jesus loves you and will live in your heart and give you joy in the midst of all this mud. He who is willing, raise his hand.'

I looked around. All the men, including the guards, had raised their hands. It was unbelievable, but their faces showed a joy that only the Holy Spirit could produce. As I left the prison and returned to the car, all the men accompanied me. The guards did not seem worried or anxious that they swarmed around me. In fact, they did not even prevent them from going out the gate to stand around my car. As I opened the door and got in, the men began to shout and chant something, repeating the same words over and over.

'What do they shout?' I asked my interpreter. She smiled and said, 'They shout, "Old woman, come back. Old woman, come back and tell us more of Jesus."'

The missionary turned to me as we drove off. 'I must confess to you that I thought this place was too dark for the light of the Gospel. I had been here once before and was so frightened I said I would never come back. Now, because I had to come to interpret for you, I have seen what the Holy Spirit can do. The joy of the Lord is available, even for such a place as this. From now on I shall return every week to tell them about Jesus.'

Months later I received a letter from her in which she said, 'The fear is gone. The joy remains.'

Carry neither purse, nor scrip, nor shoes:
and salute no man by the way . . . And
in the same house remain, eating and
drinking such things as they give: for the
labourer is worthy of his hire . . .
Luke 10:4, 7

12

God Will Provide

The people in America seem to feel I should not hesitate to ask
for money for my ministry, which supports other ministries
such as Bible and book translations in many parts of the
world. However, from the very beginning of my ministry
I have felt it was wrong to ask for money – even to ask
for travel expenses. I did not want to be paid for 'services
rendered'. I simply wanted to preach the Gospel and let the
Lord provide for me.

I learned this lesson very early in my travelling ministry. I
was in New England and spoke, among other things, about
the former concentration camp where I helped refugees in
Germany. My hosts had asked me to do this, saying they
knew the American people would like to help support it.
After the meeting a dignified, well-dressed lady came up and
handed me a cheque for a rather large sum of money. It was
designated to my work in Europe.

'It was so very interesting to hear about your work,'
she said.

'What did you think about the other things I said?' I asked.
'Did you find them important also?'

She gave me a quizzical look. I continued. 'Of course it is

a very good thing to give money for evangelistic work, but today I also spoke about conversion. God does not want a little bit of your money. He wants all of your heart. He wants to possess you completely. God will not let me take your cheque.' I handed it back to her.

As I was speaking I noticed a haughty, proud look come into her eyes. Very deliberately she pulled her fur cape around her neck. Then, without answering at all, she arrogantly walked away.

When I got back to my room I looked sadly at the other cheques which had been given me. Was God speaking to me? Was it wrong to speak of my own work while at the same time I urged people to be converted or to forgive their enemies? Was it wrong to listen to these Americans who were urging me to receive collections for my ministry? I dropped to my knees in prayer. God knew my needs.

The answer was very clear from the Lord. 'From now on you must never again ask for money.'

Great joy entered my heart and I prayed, 'Heavenly Father, You know that I need more money than ever before. But from this day on I shall never ask for a penny. No guarantees before I come to speak. No travel expenses. Not even a place to stay. I will trust in You believing that You will never forsake me.'

That very day I received two letters. One was from a woman in Switzerland. 'Corrie, God told me that from now on you must never again ask for money.'

The other letter was from my sister in Holland. She wrote, 'When I prayed for your work this morning God made it clear to me that you should not ask anybody for financial support. He will provide everything.'

I thought of the night in the concentration camp when my sister Betsie had talked with me about our plans for the future. 'Corrie, we should never worry about money,' she said. 'God is willing to supply our every need.'

Many years later, when I faced a severe hardship, I was forced to remember this principle. I felt I had received a direct command from the Lord to go to Russia. The price of our tickets and expenses would be five thousand guilders.

However, when I looked at my cheque book I found we had only three thousand guilders in the bank.

'Lord,' I prayed, 'what must I do? You have commanded me to go to Russia but I need two thousand more guilders.'

I thought that this time God would let me write a few wealthy friends, telling them of my need, and asking them to send the money for the plane ticket. Instead I heard a very clear directive from God: 'Give away two thousand guilders.'

'Oh, no, Lord,' I said, as I sat at the table in my apartment in Baarn, Holland. 'You did not understand. I did not say I wanted to *give* away two thousand guilders. I said I needed someone to give me that amount so I could go to Russia.'

However, God seldom listens to my arguments. He waited for me to get through with my objections, and then repeated His original command. This time, though, it was even more specific. I was to give two thousand guilders to a certain mission group that had an immediate need.

I could not understand how anyone's need could be more immediate than my own, but foregoing the 'wisdom of the wise', I sat down and wrote a cheque to this mission group, depleting my bank account down to one thousand guilders.

Later that day I went back down to see if I had received any mail. Among the letters was one from the American publishing company that was to publish *The Hiding Place*. For some months I had been writing back and forth and only two weeks before I had finally signed the contract. I brought the letter back upstairs and opened it. As I pulled it out, a cheque fluttered to the floor. It was an advance from the publisher, money which I did not think I was going to get until the manuscript was completed. I looked at the figure. It amounted to more than I needed!

God takes His prohibition of asking for money very seriously, just as He means it seriously when He says He will care for and protect us. However, if we seek to raise our own money then God will let us do it – by ourselves. Many times we will be able to raise great amounts of money by human persuasion or downright perseverance in asking. But we will miss the far greater blessing of letting Him supply all our needs according to His own riches. And, as I found out in the case of the guilders needed for the trip to Russia, God always has more for us than we would think of asking.

I would much rather be the trusting child of a rich Father, than a beggar at the door of worldly men.

Yes, the Lord is not only my shepherd; He is my treasurer. He is very wealthy. Sometimes He tries my faith, but when I am obedient then the money always comes in just in time.

My last stop on my first trip to the Orient was Formosa. It was time for me to move on so I went to the travel agency in Taipei and gave the girl a list of all the places I needed to go on the next leg of my journey. Hong Kong, Sydney, Auckland, then back to Sydney, on to Cape Town, Tel Aviv and finally to Amsterdam.

The travel agent wrote it all down and then asked, 'What is your final destination?'

'Heaven,' I answered simply.

She gave me a puzzled look. 'How do you spell that?

'H-E-A-V-E-N,' I spelled out slowly.

After she had written it down she sat looking at the paper. At last she looked up. 'Oh, now I understand,' she said with a smile. 'But I did not mean that.'

'But I meant it,' I said. 'And you do not need to write it down because I already have my ticket.'

'You have a ticket to *heaven*?' she asked, astonished. 'How did you receive it?'

'About two thousand years ago,' I said, noting her genuine interest, 'there was One who bought my ticket for me. I only had to accept it from Him. His name is Jesus and He paid my fare when He died on the cross for my sins.'

A Chinese clerk, working at the next desk, overheard our conversation and joined in. 'What the old woman says is true,' he told his companion.

I turned and looked at the Chinese man. 'Have you a reservation for heaven?' I asked him.

His face lit up in a smile. 'Yes, I have,' he said, nodding enthusiastically: 'Many years ago, as a child on the mainland, I received Jesus as my Saviour. That makes me a child of God with a place reserved in the house of the Father.'

'Then you are also my brother,' I said, shaking his hand. Turning back to the other clerk I said, 'When you do not have a reservation for a seat on the plane, and try to get aboard, you face difficulty. But when you do not have a place reserved for you in heaven, and the time comes for you to go, you end up in far greater difficulty. I hope my young brother here will not rest until you have made your reservation in heaven.'

The Chinese clerk smiled broadly, and nodded. I felt confident he would continue to witness to his fellow worker now that I had opened the door.

I left the travel agency with a good feeling in my heart. Surely God was going to bless this trip since I was already off to such a good start. However, when I arrived in my room and checked my ticket, I found the girl had made a mistake in the route. Instead of sending me from Sydney to Cape Town to Tel Aviv, as I had requested, she had routed me from Sydney to Tel Aviv and then to Cape Town. I went immediately to the phone and called her.

'Why have you changed my schedule?' I asked. 'My Chief has told me I must go first to Cape Town and after that to Tel Aviv. However, you have changed the sequence. God is my Master and I must obey Him.'

'Then God has made a mistake,' she said, half-seriously. 'There is no direct flight from Australia to Africa since there is no island in the Indian Ocean for the plane to land and refuel. That is why you must first go overland to Tel Aviv and then down to Cape Town.'

'No,' I argued. 'I cannot follow that route. I must do what my Chief has told me. I'll just have to pray for an island in the Indian Ocean.'

We both laughed and hung up. 'Lord,' I prayed, 'if I have made a mistake in hearing Your direction, please show me. But if I heard correctly, then open the way.'

An hour later the girl called back. 'Did you really pray for an island in the Indian Ocean?' she asked, incredulous. Before I could answer she continued, 'I just received a telegram from Qantas, the Australian airline. They have just begun to use the

Cocos Islands for a refueling station and beginning tomorrow will have a direct flight from Sydney to Cape Town.'

I thanked her and hung up. It was good to know that God does not make a mistake in His plans.

However, I am stubborn and never seem to learn my lessons well. Just a few days later, after I got to Sydney and was to make a short trip to Auckland, New Zealand, and back, I ran into another situation which would have been much easier on me had I remembered the lesson I should have learned back in Formosa.

Since I was only going to be in Auckland for four days before returning to Sydney and then on to Cape Town, I packed all my essential items into one suitcase which I would carry with me. I left the other suitcases with my friends in Sydney, planning to pick them up when I came back through on my way to Africa. Besides my essential clothing, I also took with me my notebooks, Bibles, literature, and coloured slides. My slides, taken in many lands, and the manuscripts of my sermons are all very valuable to me. Although I seldom read from my notes when I speak, I feel more comfortable when I have them before me. I have been accused by my friends of ascending the platform with three Bibles and five notebooks. I think it is hardly that bad, but I have met so many people and jotted down so many ideas that I cannot remember them all. So I try to carry all my notes with me.

As I started to leave the Sydney airport for the plane, one of the pilots spotted me struggling along with my heavy suitcase. He volunteered to help me. 'I have to stop by the radio room first,' he said, 'but then I shall bring your bag directly to your seat.'

I hesitated to turn loose my bag, however, since it was filled with everything I needed for the rest of my journey, not to mention a lifetime of treasures.

'You can trust me,' he insisted. 'I will arrive at the plane before you and shall leave your bag on your seat.'

Reluctantly I parted from my suitcase and watched the pilot as he walked out of the door. Several minutes later we boarded the plane and I rushed to my seat. The bag was not there. Alarmed, I called the stewardess. She assured me that the bag had been stowed with the rest of the luggage and was perfectly safe. I tried to settle back in my seat as we took off, yet I had an uncomfortable feeling inside.

The plane made a stop in Melbourne before heading out over the Tasman Sea for New Zealand. However, when we landed in Melbourne there was a radio message waiting for me. Like Job, the thing which I greatly feared had come upon me. The message was from Sydney. A bag, belonging to Corrie ten Boom, had been left in the radio room.

I was frustrated – and angry. 'Can they send it to me?' I asked the ticket agent.

'I'm sorry,' he said, shaking his head. 'The only way we can get it to you is to send it on our next plane to London. From there it will go to Rome, then Tel Aviv, and then . . .'

'Oohhh,' I groaned, waving him quiet. 'It will never make it. It contains all my earthly treasures and it is not even locked. Tell them just to hold it for me in Sydney. I shall pick it up when I return in four days. In the meantime, I have nothing, not even a toothbrush.'

I reboarded the plane and slumped in my seat, dejected, angry, and full of resentment. On the flight from Sydney to Melbourne I had witnessed to the stewardess about my faith in Jesus Christ. I had told her that Jesus was victor in every situation and that He gave us the power to praise Him in all situations. Now, however, I did not feel very much like praising Him at all.

I looked up and the stewardess was bending over me. 'How wonderful it must be to be a Christian at a time like this,' she said. 'Most people would be full of anger and resentment.'

I forced a smile and said, 'Well, it must be for some reason; nothing happens by chance to a child of God.'

Even though I was speaking the truth, I was not walking in the victory. Victory would mean that I had no resentment at all, and at that moment I was overflowing with it.

It was late evening as the plane took off from Melbourne. It would be a night flight to Auckland and I tried to make myself comfortable. Below us was the sea with only the engines of the plane to hold us in the sky. I dozed, fitfully, and then woke to the smell of smoke in the cabin. The other passengers were awake also, and some of them were up in the aisle, expressing alarm. Moments later the stewardess was at my seat.

'I have good news for you,' she said softly. 'We are returning to Sydney to pick up your bag.'

'Yes, indeed, good news for me,' I said. 'But tell me, are we not in great danger?'

'No,' she said, smiling sweetly and patting my pillow, 'we are just having some hydraulic difficulties. There is no danger.'

I followed her with my eyes as she went from seat to seat, assuring all the passengers that there was no danger. I leaned across the aisle and asked the man in the next seat what was meant by hydraulic difficulties.

'It is bad news,' he said. 'All the mechanism on the plane depends on the hydraulic system. The wing flaps, the steering mechanism, even the landing gear is controlled by the hydraulic system. Since the fire is in that system it means the pilot could lose control of the plane at any moment.'

I sat back in my seat and tried to look out the window. Below was the blackness of the Tasman Sea. The smell of smoke was still very strong in the cabin. I was not afraid of death. Often, as a prisoner I had faced it. I remembered the words of Dwight Moody, 'The valley of the shadow of death holds no darkness for the child of God. There must be light, else there could be no shadow. Jesus is the Light. He has overcome death.'

Yet I knew I was not right with God because I was not right with man. I still held resentment in my heart and knew it had to be removed before I could even pray. I leaned back in my seat and opened my heart to God, confessing my resentment over my suitcase (which was worthless to me now that we might crash into the sea) and asking Him to forgive me. Then I prayed, 'Lord, perhaps I shall see You very soon. I thank You that all my sins have been cleansed by the blood of the Lamb.'

I opened my eyes and looked around me. 'What of the others?' I wondered. 'Are they prepared to die?' No one was sleeping. All were sitting, alert in their seats. I noticed a woman busy applying lipstick and shook my head. How silly to feel you have to enter eternity with painted lips! I had the strongest urge to stand up and say to the people around me, 'Friends, perhaps in a few minutes we shall all enter eternity. Do you know where you are going? Are you prepared to appear before God? There is still time to accept the Lord Jesus . . .'

But I could say nothing. I wanted to stand and urge them to come to Jesus, but I could not. I was ashamed of the Gospel of our Lord Jesus Christ. And not only that, but there was fear in my heart.

We finally made a landing – safe landing – in Sydney. My bag was returned to me, but there was no joy in my heart. Even though I had been forgiven of my resentment, I had been ashamed of the Lord Jesus. I found a seat in the lounge and sat with my head bowed, my eyes closed.

'Dear Lord, I am not fit to be a missionary. I stood before the very portals of eternity and warned no one.'

I opened one of my notebooks and read on the margin of a page a note I had made many years before. 'To travel through the desert with others, to suffer thirst, to find a spring, to drink of it, and not tell the others that they may be spared is exactly the same as enjoying Christ and not telling others about Him.'

'Oh, Lord,' I moaned. 'Send me back home. Let me repair watches. I am not worthy to be Your evangelist.'

As I sat there, like Jeremiah, trying to resign my commission, I saw a man coming towards me. He introduced himself as a Jewish doctor who had been aboard my flight. 'I watched you all through those hours on the plane when our lives were in great danger,' he said. 'You were neither afraid nor anxious. What is your secret?'

A ray of light. Perhaps God was giving me another chance. 'I am a Christian,' I said joyfully. 'I know the Messiah, Jesus, the Son of God. He died on the cross for my sins, and yours also. If our burning plane had fallen into the sea I had the assurance of going to Heaven.'

We sat and talked for a long time before he excused himself. But a few minutes later he was back again. 'I must hear more about this Jesus who gives you such peace,' he said.

Four times he got up and left, and yet he kept coming back. Each time his request was the same. 'Tell me more about Jesus.'

I told him how Jesus gives us authority over Satan. How Jesus has promised us mansions in heaven. How He gives to all who believe the power to become the sons of God.

The Jewish doctor drank it all in and finally left saying I had given him much to think about. I sat back in my chair. The Lord, my treasurer, had given me just enough of His wealth that I might share it with one of His hungry children. I had been found worthy to evangelize after all. And in the process I had learned another valuable lesson in the school of life. When I am weak, then am I strong (2 Corinthians 12:10).

13

A Place to Be

Everyone needs a place to be. One of the great joys of heaven is that it is a place, a prepared place. I am thankful that there I will have a special house that is reserved just for me.

When I was born, Father and Mother were living on the Korte Prinsegracht, a typical Amsterdam canal. I was born prematurely and my skin was blue. Uncle Hendrik, Tante Jans's husband, looked at me and exclaimed, 'I hope the Lord will quickly take this poor little creature to His home in heaven.'

But my parents and Tante Anna did not agree with him. They surrounded me with love and care. However, since there were no incubators in those early days, I cried much from the cold. Tante Anna, knowing I missed the warmth of the special place under my mother's heart from which I had come, rolled me in her apron and tied me against her stomach. There I was warm and quiet.

Many years later I was in a primitive house in Africa. The bathtub was made from an old oil drum that had been sawed in half. Missionaries lived there and they invited me in to eat with them. Walking into the kitchen, I saw an African woman with the white missionary child strapped tightly to her back.

'Hey, how nice she has your baby on her back,' I said to the missionary mother.

The white mother smiled and said, 'The baby was so fearful this morning. All she would do was cry. When the African cook came to the house she took one look at the baby and said, "Ah, Missee, give me the baby. I will keep her quiet." So she strapped her on her back and the baby has slept all morning while the cook has been busy around the kitchen.'

I could understand that feeling of having a place – of belonging. I was often afraid as a small child. Sleeping beside my sister, Nollie, who was a year and a half older than me, I begged to be able to hold her hand at night. She refused, and instead gave me the hem of her nightgown. By and by she did not even like me holding on to that, but told me to hold on to the hem of my doll's nightgown.

Then, when I was five years old, the Lord Jesus became a great reality to me. My mother told me how He loved little children and was even willing to live in my heart if I asked Him in. I did, and a feeling of peace and security took the place of the fear I had so often felt. From then on I could go to sleep at night and not be afraid.

As a child I prayed a nursery rhyme:

> Ik ga slapen, ik ben moe;
> 'k Sluit mijn oogjes beiden toe.
> Heere, houd ook deze nacht
> Weder over mij de wacht.
>
> (I'm going to sleep, I am tired;
> I close both my little eyes.
> Lord, watch over me again
> The whole night long.)

In all these years that I have been a 'tramp for the Lord', I have often been afraid. But in those moments I have always reached up and touched the hem of Jesus' garment. He has never failed to wrap me close to Him. Yet, I still long for that time when I shall have a mansion in heaven.

Here on earth, at the age of seventy-seven, for the first time I found a place of my own – a beautiful apartment in Baarn, Holland. Even though I am seldom there (for I intend to keep on travelling until I die in harness), it is still a place to hang up my pictures on the walls and put the few sticks of furniture that I have saved from my days in the Beje. Yet, even with this 'home' here on earth, I still long most of all for my heavenly mansion.

When I was a child, Tante Jans composed a children's song. I remember two lines:

> 'k zou zoo graag eens komen, Heiland,
> In dat heerlijk Vaderhuis.
>
> (I should just like to come, Saviour,
> In that beautiful Father-house.)

As a child, however, I always got the words mixed up when I sang the song. Instead of singing, 'to come', I would sing 'to peek'. The older people laughed at my mistake but I thought they were very stupid. With all my heart I meant what I was singing. As a little child I did not want to go to heaven, I just wanted to peek for a moment. Now, though, that my days have grown long, I no longer sing as I did as a child. Now my greatest desire is to come for all eternity into the beautiful Father-house.

14

Obedience

Obedience is easy when you know you are being guided by a God who never makes mistakes.

Conny and I were in Africa and one day during my Quiet Time I began to feel that God was telling me it was time to leave Africa.

'Lord, where do You want us to go?' I asked.

'Argentina,' came the answer deep in my heart.

Argentina? I had never been to Argentina. I could not speak a word of Spanish. In those days air travel was sometimes poor in Africa and to fly across the Atlantic Ocean to Buenos Aires would be a trying ordeal. Yet as I sat before the Lord the word *Argentina* became even stronger.

'Yes, but . . .,' I started to answer Him. Then I remembered that obedience never says, 'Yes, but . . .' Rather it always says, 'Yes, Lord!' Some months before a missionary by the name of Breson had written me, asking if I would be willing to speak in his church if I ever came to Argentina. I did not know Breson very well, so I had not thought much about the invitation. Now, however, with God speaking to me so strongly, I sat down and wrote Mr Breson a letter, asking if he could meet us in Buenos Aires and arrange some meetings for me.

We waited almost a month, but there was no answer. 'Are you sure it is the Lord's guidance for us to go to Argentina?' Conny asked. 'Perhaps this man Breson no longer lives in

Buenos Aires. What if we go and there is no one to meet us? Then what will we do?'

I reached out and touched Conny's hand. 'Yes, I know it is God's will for us to go to Argentina. Some years ago God spoke to me and told me to go to Japan. I had no money. I knew no one in Japan. I could not speak the language. Yet I knew God had led me. I finally saved up enough money to fly to Tokyo and stepped off the plane on a dark, rainy night in that strange land and said, "Lord, here I am. Now what?" I remembered that David Morken was there with Youth for Christ. He found me a room and because of my obedience God opened many doors of ministry. I was alone on that trip, but this time I have you. No, I know we should go to Argentina.'

The plane flight was much longer than we expected. Connections were very bad and we had to spend one whole day in a hot, dirty African airport awaiting a connecting flight that would take us on to West Africa for our flight across the ocean. It was almost midnight when we caught our last plane and I could sense Conny's anxiety. However, I was sure of God's guidance.

We finally arrived in the busy Buenos Aires airport. I looked out across the hundreds of hurrying people, hoping I might see Mr Breson's face. There was no one.

Conny and I struggled with our luggage and at the ticket desk a man asked us, in broken English, if he could send our bags to our address.

'I do not yet know my address,' I said. Conny looked worried. I knew her thoughts. *Do you know for sure it is Argentina where God would have you work?* We were both exhausted from all-night plane rides which had been added to the ordeal of waiting in all those African airports. We carried our suitcases to the kerb and I sat down. 'See if you can find a taxi,' I said to Conny. 'Perhaps there is a YWCA hotel nearby.'

But there were no taxis. The air was heavy and hot. I finally asked a man, 'Do you know where there is a YWCA hotel?'

The man gave me a blank stare and moved on. I could speak Dutch, German, and English, but none of those languages helped me here. We sat on our suitcases looking at the streams of traffic passing down the street.

'Aunty, Tante Corrie, are you sure that God's guidance brought us to Argentina?'

I looked at Conny. Her face was dirty and creased with lines of exhaustion. I, too, was hot and tired and unhappy. But I was also sure of God's leadership. 'Yes,' I said wearily. 'I am sure.'

'I don't like Argentine mosquitos,' Conny said, slapping her arm. 'They are just as cruel as African mosquitos.'

We looked at each other and laughed. Here we were in a strange country with a strange language. Holland was far, far away, yet we were laughing.

Then I heard a man's voice from the other side of the street shouting, *'Bent u Corrie ten Boom?'* ('Are you Corrie ten Boom?')

My name. My language. What joy! I could barely see the man on the far side of the streaming traffic, but he was waving his arms as he shouted.

'Ja, dat ben ik,' I shouted back.

The man had to wait for the traffic to thin before he could run across the street. Finally, after dodging cars, he stepped on to the kerb. 'I am Reverend Mees,' he said, extending his hand. 'I did not think you would be here but felt I should come and check just the same.'

'Do you know Mr Breson?' I asked. 'I had hoped he would meet us.'

'Did you not receive Breson's letter?' Reverend Mees asked. There was a look of alarm on his face.

'No, we heard nothing from him.'

Reverend Mees put his hand on his forehead and looked towards the sky. 'Oh, this is too bad. He wrote you a letter telling you not to come. He could not arrange any meetings and is now on a mission tour in the jungle. He will not be back for two months.'

I sat back down on my suitcases, feeling even more tired than before.

'Do you know if there is a YWCA hotel in the city?' I asked, as if this would solve all our problems.

Reverend Mees smiled, 'No, I do not know of a YWCA hotel, but a dear friend of mine, a woman doctor, knew about the possibility of your coming. She asked me to bring you to her hospital and from there she will take you to her home. She has a spare bedroom and a little apartment where you can be very comfortable.'

Dr Gwen Shepherd received us graciously at the hospital. I knew at once that she was one of God's precious children and therefore my sister also. She took us to her car and for the first time I experienced what traffic in Buenos Aires is like. Travelling in the jungles of Africa was nothing to the streets of Buenos Aires. There were no traffic lights. At every intersection the cars came racing together, four abreast. Those who arrived first were the first ones through. I never saw an accident (but perhaps that was because I kept my eyes closed most of the time!). However, after bouncing and speeding down the streets, we finally reached her home where she provided wonderful hospitality. That night she invited a number of youth group leaders to her home and I had an opportunity to share with them. The next day another invitation came for me to speak and before long I was even busier than I had been in any other place on the earth. Dr Shepherd had a wonderful gift of administration and arranged much ministry for me. It was indeed God's guidance for me to come to Argentina. What a joy I would have missed had I disobeyed.

Perhaps the greatest joy of the entire trip, however, happened one afternoon in Dr Shepherd's hospital. I was allowed into a ward where polio patients were being treated. One room was filled with people in iron lungs. I had never seen the wheezing, gasping iron lungs before and they scared me.

'Do you wish to talk to some of the patients?' a kind nurse asked me.

I looked around and said, 'No, I think I am unable to talk. I just want to go off somewhere and cry.'

Always when I say that I am not able, I get the same answer from the Lord. He says, 'I know you can't. I have known it already a long time. I am glad now you know it for yourself for now you can let Me do it.'

'All right, Lord, You do it,' I said. And surely the Lord did. I went from one iron lung to another telling the men and women about the Lord Jesus Christ who breathes into each one of us His Holy Spirit.

Then I came to a man on a rocking bed. He had a different kind of polio and instead of being in a lung he was on a bed that rocked up and down. When his head was up he could breathe in. When his head went down he breathed out. The nurse told me he was Jewish.

'Ah,' I said, 'I am happy to meet one of God's chosen people. My old father, my dear sister, and some others in my family died in concentration camps because we loved the Jews. I, too, was in prison for helping Jews. But tell me, do you know the Jew, Jesus, as your personal Messiah?'

The bed rocked up and down and he shook his head for he could not speak. He had a long tube in his nose and could only move one hand slightly to write tiny notes.

'Then is it all right if I tell you about him?' I asked.

He picked up his stubby pencil and scribbled on a small note-book on the side of his moving bed, 'I am ready to listen.'

I stayed beside that rocking bed and told my Jewish friend about the great Messiah, the one whom the prophet called, 'Wonderful, Counsellor, The mighty God, The everlasting Father, The Prince of Peace' (Isaiah 9:6).

I finished speaking and from my bag took a small embroidery. On one side was stitched a beautiful crown. The other side was quite mixed up. 'When I see you on this bed,' I said, 'not speaking, not moving, I think of this embroidery.' I held up the back side of the embroidery. 'Your life is like this. See how dark it is. See how the threads are knotted and tangled, mixed up. But when you turn it around then you can see that God is actually weaving a crown for your life. God has a plan for your life and He is working it out in beauty.'

He picked up his pencil and wrote again:

thanks God
I am already
seeing the
beautiful side

Thanks God I am already seeing the beautiful side.

What a miracle. He understood God did not want him to become a Gentile. Rather he would become a completed Jew. I prayed and thanked the Lord with him. Then it was time to go and Dr Shepherd once again took me to her beautiful home.

The next day I returned to the polio ward and asked the nurse if I could speak with my Jewish friend.

'I am sorry,' she said, 'but your Jewish friend on the rocking bed is no longer with us. Just five minutes after you left he beckoned me to come to his side. There was a wonderful light shining in his eyes and he wrote on a little paper, "For the first time I prayed in Jesus' name." Then he closed his eyes and died.'

'Then I am not sorry,' I answered. 'I am glad. I know he has his own crown of life. Praise God.'

God has a divine pattern for each of His children. Although the threads may seem knotted – as they did when we were sitting outside the airport in Buenos Aires – on the other side is a crown.

*For my thoughts are not your thoughts,
neither are your ways my ways, saith
the Lord.*
Isaiah 55:8

15

The Real Corrie ten Boom

While in Havana, Cuba, I was asked to speak at a youth
rally in the Salvation Army hall. Of course this was before
the Communist take-over so there was still freedom to talk
openly about the Lord Jesus Christ.

It was a hot June night and the hall was small and stifling.
The meeting was scheduled to begin at seven o'clock, but
more and more groups continued to arrive from other parts
of the city, so no one seemed to be in a hurry to start. As
in most Latin American countries everything was, '*Mañana,
mañana*', even the church services.

Finally, I was seated on the platform between two men
with huge drums. One of them, an old Negro with white hair,
tried to show his love for the Lord by vigorously beating one
of the drums. The sound was almost unbearable. The captain
had a very sharp voice and led the singing by shouting, waving
his hands, and pounding on the top of the pulpit. The young
Cubans sang loudly with much clapping of hands and stomping
of feet. By nine o'clock I was already worn out, and all I had
done was sit and listen. There was a terrific ringing in my
ears and my head was splitting with a headache from the
crashing sounds of the drums. Finally, though, I was called
on to speak and the hall grew silent. I was grateful for the
few moments of peace.

After I spoke the captain introduced a missionary who had brought his slides. The lights were turned out and we all sat in the miserable heat while the missionary began his long slide presentation. Like many missionaries, he had been called upon to do some medical work in the field, so many of his slides dealt with that. He had photograph after photograph of drugs and medicines which had been given him by various doctors. 'This particular bottle of pills was given me by Dr Smith,' he droned on. Then flipping to his next slide he said, 'And this box of medicines was sent me by Dr Jones.'

The young people in the hall were not the least bit interested in seeing these boxes, bottles, and jars. The noise grew louder and louder and finally reached such volume that the missionary had to shout to make himself heard. It was ten-thirty when he finally finished his presentation and the lights came back on.

Now the room was filled with flying bugs, moths, insects, and some kind of huge flying beetle which buzzed around the exposed light bulbs and then dropped to the floor or in people's laps. The young people were climbing over the backs of the benches, babies were asleep on the floor, and everybody was sweating profusely. I did not think I could stand much more.

Then the captain came to the front again and began to preach. A flying insect went in my ear and another was caught in my hair. I looked for some way to escape, but I was boxed in by the huge drums on either side. Finally the captain gave an invitation for people to come forward and be saved.

'Surely no one is in a mood to do anything but go home,' I said to myself. Then I thought, *I hope nobody comes to the front, I long to get out of here and go to bed.*

Yet, to my great surprise, people began getting up from their seats and coming to the front. They were kneeling around the altar rail. Twenty of them. I saw tears in the eyes of some of the young Cubans and listened as the captain spoke with great persuasion, his voice full of love.

A startling realization swept over me. I was selfish. I had hoped nobody would be saved because of my own weariness. My sleep was more important than the salvation of sinners.

Oh, what a terrible egotist I was. Suddenly my bed was no longer important. I was willing to stay up all night if God was working. But what could I do with my guilty feeling for having been so selfish?

Then I began to praise God, for I had learned what to do with my sin. I confessed it to the Heavenly Father in Jesus' Name and I claimed His forgiveness. With joy I was able to get up and pray with the twenty young people who had made the important decision to commit their lives to Jesus Christ. It was eleven-thirty when the meeting finally came to a close.

The next morning, Sunday, I spoke in a beautiful church which was filled with the most prominent people in Havana. As I entered the imposing building I was given a copy of the parish magazine which had been handed to all the other people. In it I read an introductory article about my ministry. It said, 'Corrie ten Boom is a most popular world evangelist . . . She is tireless and completely selfless in her absolute dedication to the cause of the Gospel . . .'

Oh, Lord, I thought, *if only these people knew who the real Corrie ten Boom is, they would not have come out this morning to hear me.*

'Tell them,' the Lord answered immediately.

By that time I was seated on the platform looking out over the sea of faces before me. 'But Lord, if I tell them, they will reject me.'

'Can I bless a lie?' the Lord asked me in my heart. 'I can only bless the truth. You do want My blessing, don't you?'

Then it was time for me to speak. The gracious minister gave a flowery introduction and asked me to come to the pulpit. Before I could give my message, however, I knew what I had to do.

Reading first from the parish paper I then said, 'Sometimes I get a headache from the heat of the halo that people put around my head. Would you like to know what Corrie ten Boom is really like?' Then I told them what happened the evening before – how my own sleep had been more important in my eyes than the salvation of young people. 'That,' I said, 'was Corrie ten Boom. What egotism! What selfishness! But the joy is that Corrie ten Boom knew what to do with her sins.

When I confessed them to the Father, Jesus Christ washed them in His blood. They are now cast into the deepest sea and a sign is put up that says, NO FISHING ALLOWED. Corrie ten Boom is lazy, selfish, and filled with ego. But Jesus in Corrie ten Boom is just the opposite of all these things.'

Then I waited. Surely now that the congregation knew what kind of person I was, they would no longer want to hear me. Instead I sensed them all leaning forward, eager to hear what I might say. Instead of rejecting me, they accepted me. Instead of a beautiful church with prominent members and a popular world evangelist, we were all sinners who knew that Jesus died to lift us out of the vicious circle of ego into the light of His love.

God had blessed the truth!

*For the Son of man is come to seek and to
save that which was lost.*
Luke 19:10

16

Checkpoint Charlie

Conny and I stood in line, along with other people, outside
Checkpoint Charlie, the gate for foreigners into East Berlin.
Many of those in line were Dutch and I saw they were being
passed without difficulty. Everything seemed routine: Hand
your passport to a guard, walk down the line, and receive
your passport back with a stamp that allowed you to spend
the one day in East Berlin. I hoped it would be as easy for
us when it was our turn to be checked.

Finally we were in front of the window. The guard looked
at our passports, looked in a book, and then turned and said
something to another man behind him.

'Is there a problem?' I asked the man.

He turned and gave me a stern look. 'Come with me,' he
said, motioning for Conny and me to follow him into a small
room to one side. We were questioned and then they opened
my handbag. There they found two books. One of them was
one of my books which had been published in East Germany.
The other was a copy of Billy Graham's *Peace With God* which
had also been translated into German.

The officer picked up Billy Graham's book and shouted,
'What? A book by that machine gun of God!'

I laughed. 'I like the name you give to Billy Graham. I will
tell him what you called him the next time I see him – God's
Machine Gun. However, if I am not allowed to take the books

with me into East Berlin, I will just give them to you and you can let us go on.'

'Oh, no,' he said sternly, 'it is not that easy. First we have to write up your deposition.'

He searched me to see if I had hidden more books before he began his inquisition. I did not like his rough, crude manner and told him so.

'I really feel as if I am in the hands of the Gestapo again,' I said.

'No,' he said, abashed, 'I am no Gestapo.'

'You surely have the same manners,' I said bluntly.

He softened his approach but still kept us in the inquisition room for more than three hours. A woman typist copied everything I said and wrote it into a 'protocol'. I learned that my name was on the blacklist for East Germany, which was the reason I was being so thoroughly questioned. However, I was primarily upset because we had only a few hours to visit the Christians in East Berlin and our time was being wasted here in the guard station.

'Lord,' I complained silently, 'why are You keeping us here when we need to be about Your business in East Berlin?'

Then slowly it came through my stubborn Dutch mind that God had us in the guard office for a purpose. He not only loved the Christians in East Berlin but He loved these Communist guards also – the officer and the uniformed typist. What a sad mistake we sometimes make when we think that God only cares about Christians. Although God desires that all people become Christians, He does not love one group more than another. In fact, it was for the world that God gave His only begotten Son, and Jesus Himself said He had not come to call the righteous but sinners to repentance (*See* Matthew 9:13). I remembered the words of Jesus when He said, 'You will be led before kings and governors for My name's sake. This will be a time, an opportunity, for you to bear testimony. Resolve and settle it in your minds, not to meditate and prepare beforehand how you are to answer.' (*See* Matthew 10:18,19.)

Suddenly my attitude towards the officer changed. Instead of an enemy, I saw him as one of those for whom Christ died.

Now I answered every question testifying of my faith in Jesus. It became almost a kind of game.

I asked the officer, 'Did you ever read the Bible?'

'No, I am a Marxist,' he said stubbornly.

'The Bible was written especially for Marxists,' I said. 'It says that God so greatly loved the Marxists that He gave His only begotten Son so that any Marxist who believes in Him shall not perish, but have eternal life.'

Both the officer and the woman typist were listening with serious faces. I went ahead to talk about the two problems of the human race – sin and death – and stated that the Bible gives us the answer to these problems by telling us about Jesus.

'Why don't you keep my books and read them?' I said. 'I will be glad to autograph my book for you and the book by Billy Graham will answer many of your questions.'

'Must I read it?' the officer said.

'It will not do you any harm,' I laughed.

The officer laughed too, but then, catching himself, became very serious and businesslike again.

'I see, Fraulein, that you are carrying chocolate with you? What is your reason?'

'I am taking it for the minister's children in East Berlin. Don't you bring chocolate with you when you visit a family with children?'

'No, I take flowers with me,' he said seriously.

'Flowers are nice for parents, but children prefer chocolate. Besides, I often preach about chocolate.'

'What crazy people we have here today,' the officer said. 'You carry books by a man who talks like a machine gun and then tell me you preach about chocolate. Tell me, what kind of sermon do you get from a chocolate bar, old woman?'

'Several years ago,' I answered, 'I spoke to a group of Germans who prided themselves as intellectuals. They would not receive me because they felt that they were more profound in their theology than I. So, my last time with them I brought them all some Dutch chocolates. Since chocolate was very rare after the war, they eagerly accepted my gift. Later, when I stood to speak to them, I told them, "No one has said anything to me about the chocolate."

'They disagreed, saying that they had all thanked me for it.

'"I did not mean that," I said. "I mean no one questioned me about it. No one asked whether it had been manufactured in Holland or Germany, what quantities it contained of cocoa, sugar, milk, or vitamins. Instead of analysing it, you just ate it."

'Then I picked up my Bible and said, "It is the same with this Book. If you try to analyse it as a book of science or even a book of theology, you cannot be nourished by it. Like chocolate, it is to be eaten and enjoyed, not picked apart bit by bit."'

I stopped talking and noticed, once again, that the officer and the typist were deeply interested in what I was saying. Then the officer straightened up, cleared his throat, and said to the typist, 'Please type Fraulein ten Boom's protocol and we will let her pass.' With that he stood and left the room, never looking back.

I sat quietly while the typist finished typing her report. Moments later the officer was back. He pulled the paper from the typewriter and read aloud. 'When in prison Corrie ten Boom received from God the commission to bring the Gospel of Jesus Christ over the whole world. Her church has taught her to bring chocolate when she visits families with children.'

The officer nodded and excused himself, saying he had to read it to his superior officer before I could be approved for entrance into East Berlin. While he was gone I talked with the typist, urging her to accept Jesus as her Lord. She listened intently, reading through some of the pages in my book. However, when the officer returned she straightened up and returned to her typewriter.

I handed Billy Graham's book to the officer. 'Sir, be sure and take this book by God's Machine Gun home with you. It will change your life.'

He tried to look severe, but behind his eyes I could sense both hunger and thirst. Without saying a word he took the book and slipped it into his briefcase. He handed my book to the typist and motioned her to put it in her purse. Then he opened the door and pointed in the direction of East Berlin. 'I am sorry to have detained you so long, Fraulein,' he said. 'But what we have been doing here is even more important than your visit to your friends.'

I shook his hand and Conny and I entered the Communist city, wondering if the officer actually realized the truth of his last statement. What we had to do in East Berlin was important, but even more important was bringing the Good News of Jesus to those who walk in darkness.

17

Facing Death

Watchman Nee once said, 'When my feet were whipped my
hands suffered pain.'

Christians all over the world are bound together as the body
of Christ. Many Americans, in particular, do not realize it, but
a part of that body is suffering the most terrible persecution
and tribulation in the history of mankind. If we are members
of that same body – and we are – then we must suffer with
them, pray for them, and where it is possible, help them.

I remember hearing of a missionary – a single woman – who
turned her back on all her possessions at home and went to
China. 'Are you not afraid?' a friend asked as she prepared
to board the ship. 'I am afraid of only one thing,' she said,
'that I should become a grain of wheat not willing to die.'

How much more like Christ that is than the churches who
gather at Thanksgiving to sing:

Let thy congregation escape tribulation!

Several years ago I was in Africa in a little country where
an enemy had taken over the government. There was great
oppression against the Christians by the new government.
The first night I was there some of the native Christians were

commanded to come to the police station to be registered. When they arrived they were arrested and during the night they were secretly executed. The next day the same thing happened with other Christians. The third day it was the same. By that time the entire district realized that the Christians were being systematically murdered. It was the intent of the new government to eradicate them all – men, women, and children – much as Hitler tried to eradicate all the Jews.

I was to speak in a little church on Sunday morning. The people came, but I could see fear and tension written on every face. All during the service they looked at each other, their eyes asking the same questions: 'Will this one I am sitting beside be the next one to be killed? Will I be the next one?'

I looked out on that congregation of black and white faces. The room was hot and stuffy. Moths and other insects came through the screenless windows and swirled around the naked light bulbs hanging over the bare, wooden benches upon which the natives sat. They were all looking at me, expecting, hoping, that I could bring them a word from God for this tragic hour.

I opened my Bible and read 1 Peter 4:12–14 (PHILLIPS).

And now, dear friends of mine, I beg you not to be unduly alarmed at the fiery ordeals which come to test your faith, as though this were some abnormal experience. You should be glad, because it means you are called to share Christ's sufferings. One day, when he shows himself in full splendour to men, you will be filled with the most tremendous joy. If you are reproached for being Christ's followers, that is a great privilege, for you can be sure that God's Spirit of glory is resting upon you.

I closed the Book and began to talk, simply, as an aunt would talk to her nieces and nephews. 'When I was a little girl,' I said, 'I went to my father and said, "Daddy, I am afraid that I will never be strong enough to be a martyr for Jesus Christ."

'"Tell me," Father said, "when you take a train trip from

Haarlem to Amsterdam, when do I give you the money for the ticket? Three weeks before?"

"'No, Daddy, you give me the money for the ticket just before we get on the train.'

"'That is right,' my father said, 'and so it is with God's strength. Our wise Father in heaven knows when you are going to need things too. Today you do not need the strength to be a martyr; but as soon as you are called upon for the honour of facing death for Jesus, He will supply the strength you need – just in time.'"

I looked out at my African friends. Many of them had already lost loved ones to the firing squad or the headman's axe. I knew that others would surely die that week. They were listening intently.

'I took great comfort in my father's advice,' I said. 'Later I had to suffer for Jesus in a concentration camp. He indeed gave me all the courage and power I needed.'

My African friends were nodding seriously. They, too, believed God would supply all their needs, even the power to face death bravely.

'Tell us more, Tante Corrie,' one grizzled old black man said. It was as though they were storing up all the truth they could so they could draw on it in the day of trial.

I told them of an incident that had taken place in the concentration camp at Ravensbruck. 'A group of my fellow prisoners had approached me, asking me to tell them some Bible stories. In the concentration camp the guards called the Bible *das Lügenbuch* – the book of lies. Cruel death punishment had been promised for any prisoner who was found possessing a Bible or talking about the Lord. However, I went to my little cot, found my Bible, and returned to the group of prisoners.

'Suddenly I was aware of a figure behind me. One of the prisoners formed the words with her lips, "Hide your Bible. It's Lony." I knew Lony well. She was one of the most cruel of all the *aufseherinen* – the women guards. However, I knew that I had to obey God who had guided me so clearly to bring a Bible message to the prisoners that morning. Lony remained motionless behind me while I finished my teaching and then I said, "Let's now sing a hymn of praise."

'I could see the worried, anxious looks on the faces of the prisoners. Before it had been only me speaking. Now they, too, were going to have to use their mouths to sing. But I felt God wanted us to be bold, even in the face of the enemy. So – we sang.

'When the hymn was finished I heard a voice behind me. "Another song like that one," she said. It was Lony. She had enjoyed the singing and wanted to hear more. The prisoners took heart and we sang again – and again. Afterwards I went to her and spoke to her about the Lord Jesus Christ. Strangely, her behaviour began to change until, in a crude sort of way, she became a friend.'

I finished my story and stood silently while the words took their effect on my African friends. 'Let me tell you what I learned from that experience,' I told them. 'I knew that every word I said could mean death. Yet never before had I felt such peace and joy in my heart as while I was giving the Bible message in the presence of mine enemy. God gave me the grace and power I needed – the money for the train ticket arrived just the moment I was to step on the train.'

The faces before me broke into broad grins. Gone were the wrinkles of fear and anxiety. Once again their eyes were flashing with joy and their hearts were filled with peace. I closed the service by reading a poem by Amy Carmichael.

> We follow a scarred Captain,
> Should we not have scars?
> Under His faultless orders
> We follow to the wars.
> Lest we forget, Lord, when we meet,
> Show us Thy hands and feet.

The meeting was over and the Africans stood to leave. Then softly, in the back of the room, someone began singing an old gospel song.

There's a land that is fairer than day.
And by faith we can see it afar.
For the Father waits over the way,
To prepare us a dwelling place there.
In the sweet by and by, we shall meet on that
   beautiful shore.
In the sweet by and by, we shall meet on that
   beautiful shore.

I don't know how many were killed that week, but someone told me that more than half those who had attended that service met a martyr's death – and thus received a martyr's crown. But I know that God's Spirit of glory had been resting upon them. (*See* 1 Peter 4:14.)

. . . and a little child shall lead them.
Isaiah 11:6

18

Saved by a Newborn Infant

One of my greatest privileges is visiting with missionaries all over the world. Those of us who live in the comfort and security of our homes cannot begin to imagine what the life of a missionary is like. Many of them have no fresh water and only simple food. They constantly face the threat of sickness and infection. Some live in primitive places where their very lives are in danger. Much to my sadness, yet to the glory of God, the list is growing longer each day of men and women who are literally laying down their lives for Jesus' sake on the mission field. These men and women stand on the front lines, often in lonesome places, but knowing that their Master who has placed them there will also stand with them.

Once in a primitive spot in Africa I visited a missionary couple. Their small home was located in a delightful spot that gave a beautiful view of lakes and mountains. They had very little of this world's goods, but were rich in God's grace and had been given a homesite that many wealthy people would pay thousands of dollars to have as their own. Crowded into this tiny shack were six children, the youngest just a few months old. 'Come with me,' the missionary wife said as she picked up the baby and walked outside. 'I want to tell you a story.'

We sat on a bench overlooking an awesome scene of grandeur. Spreading before us was a mighty view of the mountains, covered with deep jungle and spotted with lakes and waterfalls.

'To have many little children can be a burden for a missionary,' she said. 'There comes a time when you have to send them to the homeland because there are no good schools here. But while they are small you try to enjoy them.'

She paused and looked down at the sweet baby asleep in her arms. Her voice was tense with emotion as she continued. 'But when I learned I was going to have another baby, I rebelled against God. We already had five small children and it did not seem fair that we should have to bear another. My health was not good and I looked upon having another child with great sorrow and unhappiness.'

Tears were streaming down her face as she talked. 'Was it not enough to have five children? Oh, how my heart cried out at God and there were times when I wished He would take the baby from me.

'The time for the birth was here. I was very weak and there were no doctors nearby. We had no one to leave the other children with, so my husband put us all in the car and drove us into a town where there was a good mission hospital. There we stayed until the baby was born.'

The tiny child stirred in her arms, stretched her little arms and yawned. How precious she looked! The mother's voice grew soft. 'When we returned to our house with the new baby we learned that in the short days we had been gone the dreaded Mau Mau had come. They had murdered every white person in the entire area. Had we been home we would have all been killed.'

She hugged the little baby to her breast, tears flowing down her face. 'This little darling was sent by God to save all our lives. Never again shall I rebel against His ways for our lives.'

19

Miracles Every Day

It was my first time in India and I was to speak at a conference of missionaries in Vellore. However, when my plane arrived in Bangkok I was told the next plane to Vellore did not leave for three days.

'But this means I will have to miss the first three days of the conference,' I said.

'We are sorry, but there is no way,' the man at the ticket counter told me. However, the airlines did make arrangements for me to stay at a hotel until the next plane left.

Arriving at the hotel I asked the kindly Indian man who was in charge of my arrangements, 'Is there no possibility that I can catch another plane to Vellore?'

'The airlines are making every effort,' he assured me.

'Then we must pray that God will help them,' I said.

'Do you *profess* to be a Christian?' he asked with a startled look on his face.

'Yes, I do,' I answered. 'I am a *professor* of Jesus Christ. And what about you?'

He hung his head. 'I have been, but I am what you call a lost sheep.'

'Hallelujah!' I said. 'Then you are just the one sheep for whom the Shepherd left the ninety-nine to find.'

We talked a long time in the lobby of the hotel. Finally I asked the man if he would be willing to come back to Jesus.

'Oh, yes,' he said. 'For I believe God kept you here just for this reason.'

We prayed together in the hotel and then I said to him, 'Now that God has used me for this miracle will you pray with me for another miracle – that I might arrive in Vellore in time for the conference?'

The man leaped to his feet. 'While you pray I must run an errand. I'll be back shortly.' With that he was out of the door, leaving me sitting among my suitcases.

Half-an-hour later he was back. 'Make quickly ready for the plane,' he said. 'I think God has performed your miracle. We have discovered another plane going by a different route to Vellore.'

'Did you arrange that?' I asked.

'I did,' he smiled as he hoisted my bags to his back. 'But don't thank me. I must thank you for bringing me back to the Shepherd.'

We rushed madly to the airport and I found the plane was supposed to have left long before. However, they were holding it just for me. Panting, I climbed the steps to the plane.

'Ah, Professor,' the stewardess said as she closed the door behind me, 'we were afraid we would have to leave you.'

'Professor?' I asked. 'What's this?'

'Oh,' she smiled sweetly. 'We know all about you. Our hotel agent told us that you are an important *professor* from Holland who has to give significant speeches in Vellore. That is why we have held the plane on the ground until you arrived.'

I took my seat near a window. Outside the once-lost sheep was grinning and waving. I waved back. *Surely*, I thought, *God not only had a special reason for keeping me in Bangkok, but He must have an equally important reason for wanting me in Vellore*.

I was right. My first talk to the missionary conference in Vellore was the next morning. I spoke on the reality of God's promises in the Bible. After the service I slipped away from the crowd and strolled in a beautiful garden near the conference centre. It was alive with colour: green and red crotons mixed their rich colours with the dark orange of the copper plants and the rainbow hues of the flowering shrubs. *How wonderful*, I thought, *to be in the centre of God's will*.

'Excuse me,' a shy voice said from behind.

I turned and recognized one of the English missionary ladies. Her body seemed weak. She hesitated to speak but at last said, 'Do you really believe in God's promises?'

'Yes, I do,' I said.

'Do you believe the Lord still heals the sick?'

'Of course,' I answered. I motioned for her to sit with me on a stone bench near a flowering hibiscus. First I read to her from the Bible where Jesus said we would lay hands on the sick and they would be healed (*See* Mark 16:18–20). Then I told her of a recent experience in Indonesia.

'I was staying in the house of a dear Chinese pastor and his wife,' I said. 'Since we were so busy the wife had no time to cook, so a member of their church, another Chinese lady, came every day in a rickshaw to fix me a good Chinese meal.

'One morning I was sitting in the house and looked out of the window. I saw this dear woman stumbling up the pathway. Her head was bleeding and her dress badly torn. I rushed out to meet her and helped her into the house. Her rickshaw had collided with another rickshaw and she had been badly injured, hitting her head against a metal part of the primitive vehicle. Since Chinese people were not popular in Indonesia at that time, no doctor would come to see her. Instead they just brought her to the house and let her out.

'I knew her condition was serious and also knew that the doctor would not come to the Chinese pastor's house either. Therefore, I just laid my hands on her and prayed in Jesus' Name that she be healed. She was restored instantly.'

The missionary lady was listening intently. 'Must you know a person's type of sickness before you pray for them?' she asked.

'No, I'm not a doctor. I do not heal. It is the Lord who heals.'

'I am very ill,' she said quietly. 'Will you lay hands on me and pray?'

'I will,' I said. She slipped off the bench and knelt in that beautiful garden while I put my hands on her head and prayed for her to be healed in the Name of Jesus Christ.

She rose slowly to her feet. 'Now I will tell you my sickness,' she said. 'I have leprosy.'

I had been in leper colonies and suddenly I was filled with great fear. *Oh*, I thought, *this is far too difficult for the Lord. I wish now she had told me ahead of time so I would have known not to pray for her*.

Then I felt ashamed and asked forgiveness for my small faith and unbelief. After all, it was not I who said He would heal the sick – but He who had said it.

Some years passed and I lost the name and address of the lady missionary, although many times I remembered that time in the garden and continued to pray for her. Five years later I was back in India, staying with friends of the Pocket Testament League. One afternoon there was a knock at my hotel door. 'Do you remember me?' a beautiful lady asked.

I looked at her and said, 'I have seen you before but I do not remember who you are.'

'Do you remember a time in Vellore when you laid hands on a leper patient and prayed in Jesus' Name that she be healed?'

'Oh, yes,' I exclaimed. 'I surely remember you. But you are a different person.'

She smiled. 'The Lord wonderfully healed me. The doctors say I am absolutely healed from leprosy.'

'Thank You, Lord,' I said aloud. 'Your Name be glorified! You are always ready to meet our needs, even when our faith is small.'

*The grass withereth, the flower fadeth: but
the word of our God shall stand for ever.*
Isaiah 40:8

20

God's Word, the Sword – God's
Perfect Weapon

It had been a hectic half year. I had flown from New Zealand
to Korea where I had spoken in more than two hundred and
fifty meetings in a three-month period. I then returned to
Hamilton, New Zealand, for a brief visit before continuing
to India.

In New Zealand I had stayed with a family who were
memorizing verses of Scripture, using the Navigators' system. I was thrilled to find so many of the new converts
in New Zealand studying this course. Since I knew less
Scripture in English than I did in Dutch, I, too, determined
to start memorizing Scripture. I knew that once the Word of
God was hidden in my heart it would be with me always.

Leaving New Zealand full of new zeal, I arrived in the state
of Kerala, India, where I was to speak in a series of small
conferences far back in the jungle. My Indian companion met
me at the airport and took me to a small place on the river
where a canoe was waiting. We climbed in and started our
slow trip down the peaceful river. Slowly our little craft glided
over the shallow waters. Except for the rhythmic sound of the
paddle and the occasional murmur of the soft wind in the trees
there was nothing to be heard.

My Indian companion was the leader of a home group.
Twice a year the home groups in the area come together

in a conference to study the Bible, pray, and plead for revival. I was to speak three times a day in several such conferences which would be held in a *pandal* – a wide roof protecting the congregation from the hot sun. There are no walls so the breeze may pass through and the people sit on the grassy floor.

As the coolie paddled our canoe down the river, my Indian companion told me of the great longing in his heart to win souls for Jesus Christ.

'Yet I am not successful,' he said. 'I always give my testimony, but I am not able to persuade people to make a decision.'

'Do you use the Sword of the Spirit, the Word of God?' I asked him.

'I fear I am not very adept at handling that Sword,' he admitted. 'Just at the critical moment I am never able to find a text that fits the situation.'

'Yes, I can understand that,' I confessed. 'I sometimes have the same problem. However, I am now memorizing certain verses of Scriptures which I call my First Aid Course. These are emergency Scriptures which I apply to the wound until I can look up the rest of the Scriptures which will bring further healing.'

My Indian companion brightened and then I told him of a recent experience in Canada where I had learned that it was not me, but the Word of God coming through me, that won people to Christ anyway.

'I had just finished speaking to a class of university students,' I told him as the canoe glided down the quiet river. 'I was relaxing on the veranda of one of the dormitories when a very educated woman, who had attended my lectures, sat down with me.

'"What you just told the students was very interesting," she said. "But you are too narrow. I am an expert on world religions. I have travelled to many countries and have had long discussions with the leaders of many religious groups. I have discussed the road of life through time and eternity with Muslims, Brahmins, Shintoists, and many others. All of them know God, even though they do not believe in Jesus Christ.

I am sorry to have to disagree with your talk this afternoon, but you put too much emphasis on Jesus Christ and do not allow that other religions are just as good as Christianity."

'I was embarrassed,' I told my Indian companion. Then I remembered something a friend had once told me. "You are not called to convince anyone," he had said. "You are simply called to be an open channel for the Spirit of God to flow through. You can never be anything else, even though you may think so at times. Follow the pathway of obedience, let the Word of God do its own work, and you will be used by God far beyond your own powers."

'Therefore, I said to the woman, "Your argument is not with me, but with the Bible. It is not I who say these things, it is the Word of God. Jesus said that no man can come to the Father but by him. (*See* John 14:6.) If you wish to dispute someone, dispute Him."'

I looked at my Indian friend. His eyes were fixed on my face as he drank in what I was saying. I continued with the story. 'Some time later a reception was held in Ottawa, Canada, for all who wished to meet Prince Bernhard of the Netherlands. It was a pleasure to see so many Hollanders together. The prince looked tired, but he was cheerful and kind to us all. I met many old acquaintances and then, suddenly, I was face-to-face with this same lady who had so adamantly disputed with me some time before.

'"I am glad to see you," she said genuinely. "I have never been able to forget what you said when you spoke at our university when you quoted Jesus, 'No man cometh unto the Father but by me.' I have tried to argue with that from every angle, but am unable to get away from the fact that Jesus said it. I can argue with you, but I am having a difficult time arguing with Him."

'"How wonderful," I told her. "Now you are listening to the voice of God. Keep listening. He has much more to say to you."

'"Yes," she said. "I believe He does."

'We parted and I have not seen her since, but I know the Sword of the Spirit is still doing its work in her life.'

I turned and looked at my Indian friend. He was nodding

his head in understanding. 'If we diligently read the Bible, the Holy Spirit will give us the right words and Scripture references.' I said. 'If we depend on Him, we are like the branches of these vines along the river which bear fruit. However, if the branches are broken off, then no fruit will appear.'

By this time the forest had thinned out on either side of the river. We could see narrow paths which permitted the people to tread single file through the trees. It was almost dark and I saw, coming down the paths, files of Indian people carrying torches of lighted palm leaves in their hands. The white clothes they wore gave the scene a strange, ethereal appearance as though they were pilgrims walking to heaven. Many had gathered already in the *pandal* away in the distance and were singing a gospel song in a monotone, chanting it over and over as the white-robed pilgrims made their way to the meeting place.

After the meeting that night I lay in my little thatched hut, praising God for the power of the Word of God which had not only drawn these people together, but which had won them to the Lord Jesus Christ. In my mind I listed five reasons why I believe the Bible is inspired:

(1) It says so. '. . . holy men of God spake as they were moved by the Holy Ghost' (2 Peter 1:21).
(2) The effect it has upon all who believe and follow it.
(3) Though some of it was written more than two thousand years before Jesus arrived on earth, yet all the writers agree.
(4) The authors do not offer any excuses for their own faults or sins.
(5) The writers record some of the most harrowing scenes which affected them greatly, yet they never express one word of emotion. The Holy Spirit wanted the facts recorded, and not their feelings about the facts.

Many persons make the mistake of thinking they can measure the certainty of their salvation by their feelings. It is the Word of God that is their foundation and therefore it is essential for the new convert in Christ to have a practical knowledge of the Bible. More than anyone else it is the new convert who will come under the fire of the enemy. He needs the knowledge of the Sword of the Spirit. As the Lord Jesus used this Sword to overcome the evil one in His temptation experiences, so we must learn to defend ourselves against every sort of attack.

But lay up for yourselves treasures in heaven . . . For where your treasure is, there will your heart be also.
Matthew 6:20, 21

21

Where Is Heaven?

Happiness is not dependent on happenings, but on relationships in the happenings.

My father taught me this when I was just a child. He often told me of the early days of his marriage. He had opened a small jewellery store in a narrow house in the heart of the Jewish section of Amsterdam. Poor Mother! She had dreamed of a home with a little garden. She loved beautiful things and spacious views. 'I love to see the sky,' she often said. Instead, she found herself on a narrow street, in an old house – the kind with only a single room on each story – with worn-out furniture which they had inherited from Grandmother. Yet they were both happy, not because of the circumstances but because of the relationships in the circumstances.

There, in Amsterdam in that narrow street in the ghetto, they met many wonderful Jewish people. They were allowed to participate in their sabbaths and in their feasts. They studied the Old Testament together and, on occasion, even the New Testament.

I have remembered, many times, the lessons I learned from my father about happiness and happenings. But never was it so clear as when I was in Korea many, many years later.

I had been in the Orient for three months, spending much of the time in Korea. While there I spoke in many meetings in schools, orphanages, children's homes, and churches. One day, after I had spoken in a university, a theological student came to me. I had never seen such gloom on the face of a man who said he wanted to be a minister of the risen Christ.

'Why is it that you are so full of unhappiness?' I asked.

'I have lost my way,' he said sadly. 'When I first became a Christian my pastor taught me the Bible is true. In those days I had great happiness. But now I am studying the famous scholar, Rudolph Bultmann, who says our Bible is full of myths and fables. I have lost my way and no longer know where heaven is.'

I was angry. It did not seem right that the simple boys of Korea had to struggle through this horrible theology. They studied many hours at the universities, going to school twice as long as students in America, yet because of what they studied they often lost their faith. I answered his question about heaven by telling him what I had just seen and heard the day before while driving through the countryside.

There I saw the poorest shack I had ever seen. It was a tiny lean-to, made from materials collected from the garbage heap – pieces of cardboard, tin cans which had been smashed flat, old boards . . . As we drove past, though, I heard the beautiful voice of a woman singing. Seldom, even in the concert halls of Europe had I heard such a sweet voice. We stopped the car and listened, for it was like the song of a skylark.

I said to the missionary who was travelling with me, 'Do you know that song?'

'Yes,' she said, 'it says, *Where Jesus is, 'tis heaven there.*'

Oh, how my heart leaped for joy as I heard this beautiful song coming from such a poor place. It is one thing to hear such a song in a dignified church, or pouring through the speakers of an expensive stereo set. But when one hears it coming from the poorest shack in the midst of such poverty, then it means something else.

I looked at the young theological student before me. 'Jesus said, 'The Kingdom of heaven is within you' (Luke 17:21). Bultmann is wrong and Jesus is right. Heaven is not a myth or fairy story: heaven is a prepared place for prepared people. Theology in the hands of the Holy Spirit is a beautiful science.

But in the hands of unbelievers it is death. If you want to find where heaven is, get out of your stuffy classroom and go back out into the countryside. Listen to the simple faith of those who read only the Bible and trust only in God, not in material things. What do they care if some theologian says that heaven is a fable. They have found Jesus, and where Jesus is, 'tis heaven there.'

22

When You Are Tempted to Quit

The enemy tries to make everything work out for the worst.
Usually it is not the big problems which depress me, but the
multitude of inconveniences which stack up like small rocks
to form an immovable mountain. Recently a series of such
small incidents almost caused me to resign my commission
from the Lord.

In my journeyings I often have to cross borders between
countries. Knowing that smuggling is sin, I do not do
it. My first irritation came through an encounter with a
customs official.

'Do you have anything to declare?' he asked rudely.

'Yes,' I replied. 'Nylon stockings.'

I had put them on top of my luggage to show him, for
I knew that at that time it was necessary to pay duty on
such items.

'There are four pair here,' he said. 'You told me one
pair.'

'No, I did not!' I answered.

But he did not believe me. For the next hour he searched
my baggage. He tried all the little boxes to see if they had
false bottoms. He squeezed my tooth-paste tube to see if it
contained diamonds. He checked my shoes for false heels
which might contain drugs. He felt the hem of my dresses
to see if I had sewn pearls into them. He almost pulled the

lining out of my suitcases. Of course he found nothing at all and finally allowed me to pass – after paying the duty on the four pair of stockings. I was both offended and unhappy.

Later I understood why this incident had made me so upset. I had not surrendered my self-righteousness. I was so sure of my own honesty that I suffered from the consequence of wounded pride. It is easier to surrender one's sins than one's virtue!

Unaware of the reason for my depression, I then discovered that I had missed my plane connections due to the delay in the customs office. I was forced to sleep on a couch in the ladies' room at the airport. However, I am a good sleeper and enjoyed a sound slumber. When I awoke, the amazed cleaning woman (who was sweeping the floor around my couch) said with admiration, 'How wonderful to be able to sleep so soundly with so much noise going on around you.'

Eventually the plane on which I was travelling flew into a storm making me feel airsick. Then the night following my arrival there was an earthquake. I hate earthquakes for they remind me of the bombs that fell during the war.

Then the kind people who should have arranged my meetings greeted my arrival with, 'We thought you needed a holiday and rest so we have not organized anything.' Sometimes this is God's plan, but more often is it just a sign of people's laziness to make preparation. So I did not appreciate the fact they had not arranged any meetings for me.

The final inconvenience – one which caused me almost to give up completely – had to do with my room. My hosts put me in a small room that had no writing table. Ordinarily this would not have disturbed me for I am used to writing on my knee, but on top of everything else that had happened, I crumpled like the camel loaded with straw. I blew up.

The reason was not hard to find. Self-pity had come into my heart. Self-pity is a nasty sin and the devil uses it and always starts his talks with 'Poor Corrie.'

This time he began by saying, 'Why must you always live out of your suitcases? Stay at home and then you won't have trouble with customs officials, passports, luggage,

plane connections, and other things. Every night you will
be able to sleep in the same comfortable bed; and there
are no earthquakes in Holland. After all, you are no longer
young. You've lived like a tramp for many, many years. It
is time to hang up your harness and retire into a nice green
pasture. Let someone else do the work. You've earned your
reward.'

By this time I was nodding. 'Yes, yes, Satan, you are
right.' So, having listened to his advice I wrote a friend in
Holland who managed an international guest house where at
the time I had a room kept for me with my own few pieces
of furniture.

'I believe the time has now come for me to work in Holland,'
I wrote. 'I am tired of all this travelling and I cannot stand
having wheels beneath me any longer. Will you arrange to
have a desk – a big one – put in front of the window in my
room; and an easy chair – a very easy one – on the right . . .'
In my fantasy I had worked out a lovely dream of heaven here
on earth, and me in the middle of it!

That afternoon I posted the letter and then came back to
my room to look over my calendar. I jotted down all the names
of people I would have to write, cancelling my appointments.
Everyone would understand. Had not many said, 'My, you
must be tired at your age!'?

Everything would have gone all right (or perhaps I should
be truthful and say 'all wrong') had I not picked up my Bible.
This old, black Bible has been my guidebook in times of light
and in times of darkness. I began to read, asking, 'Lord, what
would You have me do?'

I opened to the Book of Romans, chapter 10. 'How shall
they call on Him in whom they have not believed? And how
shall they believe in Him of whom they have not heard? And
how shall they hear without a preacher? . . . As it is written,
how beautiful are the feet of them that preach the Gospel
of peace, and bring glad tidings of good things.' (*See* verses
14, 15.)

I remembered the words of a paratrooper instructor. He
said that when he had his men in the plane and they were
over the battlefield he gave four commands.

FIRST Attention! *Lift up your eyes* (John 4:35).

SECOND Stand in the door! *Look upon the fields, for they are white already to harvest* (John 4:35).

THIRD Hook up! *Be ye filled with the Holy Spirit* (See John 20:22).

FOURTH Follow me! *I will make you fishers of men* (Mark 1:17).

I sat for a long time – thinking. It is not our task to give God instructions. We are to simply report for duty.

I laid my Bible on the bed and picked up pen and paper. Balancing the pad clumsily on my knee I wrote my friend in Holland.

Forget about that last letter I wrote. I am not coming home to Holland. I refuse to spend the rest of my life in a pasture when there are so many fields to harvest. I hope to die in harness.

*And so, dear brothers, I plead with you
to give your bodies to God. Let them be a
living sacrifice . . .*
Romans 12:1 LB

23

I'll Go Where You Want Me to Go, Dear Lord . . . but Not Up Ten Flights of Stairs

I had spoken that Sunday morning in a church in Copenhagen, Denmark, urging the people to present their bodies as living sacrifices to the Lord. I had said even though I was an old woman that I wanted to give myself completely to Jesus and do whatever He wanted me to do, go wherever He wanted me to go – even if it meant dying.

After the church time, two young nurses approached me. They invited me up to their apartment to have a cup of coffee. I was very tired. At almost eighty years of age I found that standing on my feet for long periods of time was beginning to be exhausting. The cup of coffee sounded good so I accepted their invitation.

But I was not prepared for the walk up to their apartment. Many of the houses in Copenhagen are old, high houses with no elevators. The nurses lived on the tenth floor of such a house and we had to walk up the steps.

'O Lord,' I complained as I looked up at the high building, 'I do not think I can make it.' But the nurses wanted me to come up so badly that I consented to try.

By the time we reached the fifth floor my heart was pounding wildly and my legs were so tired I thought they could not take another step. In the corridor of the fifth floor

I saw a chair and pleaded with the Lord, 'Lord, let me stay here a time while the nurses go on up the stairs. My heart is so unhappy.

The nurses waited patiently as I collapsed into the chair, resting. 'Why, O Lord, must I have this stair climbing after this busy day of speaking?'

Then I heard God's voice, even louder than my pounding heart. 'Because a great blessing is waiting you, a work which will give joy to the angels.'

I looked up at the steps, towering above me and almost disappearing into the clouds. Perhaps I am leaving this earth to go to heaven, I thought. Surely that will give joy to the angels. I tried to count the steps. It seemed there were at least one hundred more to climb. However, if God said that the work would give joy to the angels, then I had to go. I rose from my chair and once again started trudging up the long flights of stairs, one nurse in front of me, the other behind me.

We finally reached the apartment on the tenth floor and on entering I found a room with a simple lunch already prepared on the table. Serving the lunch were the mother and father of one of the girls.

I knew there was only a short time and also knew that a blessing of some kind was waiting us. So, without many introductions, I started asking immediate questions.

'Tell me,' I asked the nurse's mother, 'is it long ago that you found Jesus as your Saviour?'

'I have never met Him,' she said, surprised at my question.

'Are you willing to come to Him? He loves you. I have travelled in more than sixty countries and have never found anyone who said they were sorry they had given their hearts to Jesus. You will not be sorry either.'

Then I opened my Bible and pointed out the verses about salvation. She listened intently. Then I asked them, 'Shall we now talk with the Lord?'

I prayed, then the two nurses prayed and finally the mother folded her hands and said, 'Lord Jesus, I know already much about You. I have read much in the Bible, but now I pray You to come into my heart. I need cleansing and salvation. I know that You died at the cross for the sins of the whole world and also for my sins. Please, Lord, come into my heart and make me a child of God. *Amen.*'

I looked up and saw tears of joy on the face of the young nurse. She and her friend had prayed so much for her parents and now the answer was given. I turned and looked at the father, who had sat quietly through all this.

'What about you?' I asked him.

'I have never made such a decision for Jesus Christ either,' he said seriously. 'But I have listened to all you have told my wife and now I know the way. I, too, would like to pray that Jesus will save me.'

He bowed his head and from his lips poured a joyful but very sincere prayer as he gave his life to Jesus Christ. Suddenly the room was filled with great rejoicing and I realized the angels had come down and were standing around, singing praises unto God.

'Thank You, Lord,' I prayed as I walked back down the long steps, 'for making me walk up all these steps. And next time, Lord, help Corrie ten Boom listen to her own sermon about being willing to go anywhere You tell me to go – even up ten flights of stairs.'

*For the earth shall be filled with the
knowledge of the glory of the Lord, as the
waters cover the sea.*
Habakkuk 2:14

24

To All the World – Beginning With One

To give a tract to someone in Russia is always a risk. If
the person you are talking to is alone, then there is a little
more freedom. However, if a third person is present both are
always uneasy – each afraid the other might turn him over to
the secret police.

Conny and I had been in a Leningrad hotel for about a week
when one morning, on our way down to breakfast, I handed
the cleaning woman a tract. It was a simple tract, written in
Russian, called 'The Way of Salvation'. It used only Scripture
verses with no commentary.

She glanced at it and then glanced at the other woman
cleaning the hall. She pushed the tract back to me, motioning
with her hand as if to say, 'That is nothing for me.'

I felt sorry for her. The answer *no* hurts when you want
to help someone. Conny and I continued on down the hall to
the elevator, heading to the dining room for breakfast. We
were the only ones on the elevator and on the way down I
cast this latest burden on the Lord. 'Father, I can't reach this
woman. Do bring her in contact with someone who can tell
her the Gospel in her own language. Lord, I claim her soul
for eternity.'

I was shocked by the boldness of my prayer. Never in all
my life had I prayed that way. Was it proper? Could I actually

claim the soul of someone else? In a kind of postscript I asked, 'Lord, was this wrong or right? May I say such a prayer?'

Then, even before I could receive His answer, I heard myself praying a prayer that frightened me even more. 'Lord Jesus, I claim all of Russia for You.'

The elevator stopped and Conny and I walked through the huge corridor to the dining room. I was bewildered. My cheeks were red and hot. 'Lord, was this right? Was this too much? But no, Lord, Your Word says, "The earth is the Lord's . . . the world and they that dwell therein" (Psalms 24:1). Surely that means Russia, too.'

Still confused, we entered the dining room. It was crowded and the waiter came up and said, 'There are only two of you. You cannot eat breakfast here since all the tables are reserved for big groups.'

We looked around. A Japanese man had heard the waiter and motioned for us to come to his table where there were two empty places. 'Just come,' he said. 'We will act as if you belong to our group.'

But the waiter saw what had happened and refused to wait on us. I felt unhappy and unwelcome. Turning to Conny I said, 'At dinner yesterday I took some white buns up to my room in my purse. They are still there and we have some Nescafé. Why should we sit here and wait? Let us go to our room.'

It was quiet and peaceful upstairs. Our breakfast tasted good although it was only dry buns and Nescafé without any cream.

Suddenly there was a knock at the door. Conny opened it and there stood the cleaning woman, the one who had refused the tract. Her hair was pulled back in a tight bun and I noticed her heavy leather shoes squeaked when she walked. She closed the door behind herself. From her lips poured a stream of Russian words, not a single one of which we could understand. Then she pointed a finger at my brown bag.

'Conny, she wants to have a tract,' I almost shouted.

Conny gave her one but it was not the same one as we had given her the first time. She looked at it, shook her head, and pointed again at the bag.

'Conny, she wants to have "The Way of Salvation".'

I got up, rummaged through my bag, and found the original tract. I smiled and handed it to her. She looked at it and her face burst into a great light of joy. Smiling and nodding in appreciation, she backed out of the room.

I was beaming with joy too, for God had answered my prayer. I had not claimed too much after all. The first prayer had already been answered and now I was sure that the second prayer, the one the Holy Spirit had prayed through me without my first thinking up the words, was going to be given a *yes* answer, too.

Conny, who was as excited as I, took her Bible and read 'For the earth shall be filled with the knowledge of the glory of the Lord, as the waters cover the sea' (Habakkuk 2:14). What a promise – the whole of Russia under the waters of God's glory!

There was another knock at the door. There stood our cleaning woman again. She entered and put a long loaf of fresh white bread on the table. Her face was still wreathed in smiles as she refused payment for it. It was her thank offering to God.

I had never had such a good breakfast in all my life.

But I hold this against you, that you have
left your first love.
See Revelation 2:4

25

Leaving My First Love

After twenty years of wandering the world as a tramp for
the Lord I was ill. At seventy-three years of age my body
had grown tired. A doctor examined me and said, 'Miss ten
Boom, if you continue at the same pace you cannot possibly
work much longer. However, if you will take a furlough for a
year then perhaps you can work for another few years.'

I consulted my Lord. He said very clearly that this advice
of the doctor was in His plan. It came to mind that I could
live during that 'Sabbath Year' in Lweza, a beautiful house in
Uganda, East Africa. Several years before I had contributed to
this place so it could be used as a house of rest for missionaries
and other workers in God's Kingdom. Now the bread I had
cast upon the waters was coming back to me. I made my plans
and soon Conny and I were safely ensconced in Africa.

Lweza was a paradise. Built on a hill in the midst of a garden
that must surely resemble Eden, it looked southward out over
Lake Victoria. The climate was ideal. Since there were many
universities, churches, prisons, and groups in Kampala, the
nearby town, I was able to speak in two or three meetings a
week. So, while my body rested, my spirit remained active.

The greatest pleasure was to sleep every night in the same
bed. During the last twenty years I had slept in more than
a thousand different beds, always living out of my suitcases.
This year I rested. I put my clothes in a drawer, hung my

dresses in a closet, and best of all, each night I laid my head on the same pillow.

In November the Sabbath Year had gone by. Conny and I took a map of the world and stretched it out across my bed, following our usual method of making plans for the next year – the same method I had used for the last twenty years. First we listened to God's plan, then we signed it. This was unlike the method I once used when I made my own plans and then asked God to sign them. Our desire was to be 'planned' by the Holy Spirit.

God's plan looked very good to Conny. There would be three months in different countries in Africa, two months in America, and then three months in Eastern Europe behind the Iron Curtain. 'Thank You, Jesus,' Conny said. But inside I was not so thankful. Conny was young, much younger than I. She loved to travel but I was getting old and was still rather tired.

After Conny left I turned to the Lord. 'I prefer to stay here,' I said stubbornly. 'There is so much to do in Kampala and Entebbe, the two nearest cities. I will work for You. I am willing to have meetings every day, counselling, writing books; but please, let me sleep every night in the same bed. Everyone can understand that at my age I should take it a bit easier.'

I got up rejoicing. This new plan of mine made me really happy.

Then Conny called. An African minister from far away Ruanda had come to visit. He started immediately to welcome me: 'We are so glad that you are willing to come to Ruanda again. Five years ago you helped us so marvellously when you told what the Lord had been to you in your great need. You said that it was not your faith that helped you through three prisons, for your faith was weak and often wavering. You said it was the Lord Himself who carried you through and that you knew from experience that Jesus' light is stronger than the deepest darkness.'

The African brother continued, 'Five years ago, however, that was just theory to us. None of us had ever been prisoners. Now there has been a civil war in our country.

Many of us have been in prison, I, myself, was in prison for two years. It was then that I remembered everything you had said. I did not have the faith of Corrie ten Boom, I did not even have faith for myself, but I knew to look to the same Jesus who gave you faith. He has also given it to me and that is why we are so happy that you are now coming again to Ruanda.'

But I was not happy at all. His words were different from what I wanted to hear. I knew that in such situations I could change the subject by asking a question. Perhaps this would make God stop reminding me of His plans and leave me alone so I could follow mine.

'How is the church in Ruanda?' I asked. 'What kind of message do they need now?'

Without hesitating one moment the brother opened his Bible and began to read:

Write this to the angel of the Church in Ephesus: These words are spoken by the one who holds the seven stars safe in his right hand, and who walks among the seven golden lampstands. I know what you have done; I know how hard you have worked and what you have endured . . . I know your powers of endurance – how you have suffered for the sake of my name and have not grown weary. But I hold this against you, that you [have lost your first love]. Remember then how far you have fallen . . .'

Revelation 2:1–5 PHILLIPS

This arrow penetrated my heart. Not only Ruanda needed that message, but also Corrie ten Boom. I had lost my first love. Twenty years before I had come out of a concentration camp – starved, weak – but in my heart there was a burning love: a love for the Lord who had carried me through so faithfully – a love for the people around me – a burning desire to tell them that Jesus is a reality, that He lives, that He is victor. I knew it from experience. For this reason I went to Germany and lived in the midst of the ruins. For this reason I had tramped the world for twenty years. I wanted everyone to know that no matter how deep we fall, the Everlasting Arms are always under us to carry us out.

And now? Now I was interested in my bed. I had lost my first love. I asked my African brother to continue to read.

> Repent and live as you lived at first. Otherwise, if your heart remains unchanged, I shall come to you and remove your lampstand from its place.

Suddenly joy came in my heart. I could bring my sin, my cold heart, my weary body to Him who is faithful and just. I did it. I confessed my sins and asked for forgiveness. And the same thing happened that always happens when I bring my sin to God in the Name of Jesus: He forgave me. Jesus cleansed my heart with His blood and refilled me with the Holy Spirit.

As God's love – the fruit of the Holy Spirit – was poured out into my heart, I set out again on my journeys – a tramp for the Lord.

What a great joy it was to experience the love of God, who gave me rivers of living water for the thirsty world of Africa, America, and Eastern Europe. Of course, it might be the will of God that some old people retire from their work. In great thankfulness to the Lord they can then enjoy their pensions. But for me, the way of obedience was to travel on, even more so than ever before.

Jesus warned us in Matthew 24:12 that the love of most men waxes cold because iniquity abounds. It is very easy to belong to the 'most men'. But the gate of repentance is always wide open. *Hallelujah*!

But if we walk in the light, as he is in the
light, we have fellowship one with another,
and the blood of Jesus Christ his Son
cleanseth us from all sin.
1 John 1:7

26

Walking in the Light

Our last few weeks in Lweza proved to be the most fruitful
of our entire time spent there, for it was in these weeks that
I learned another valuable lesson – the lesson of walking in
the light.

One afternoon Conny and I were sitting in the garden
looking at the monkeys jumping from one tree to another.
The trees and shrubs were a mass of colour and sound,
causing my heart to be filled with the glory of God's grace.

Yet Conny was discouraged. She had started a girl's club
in the YWCA in Kampala and had spent many hours work with
it. However, the girls were not interested. I was concerned
about her discouragement, feeling it went far deeper than the
problems she was having with her class.

I started to ask her about it when we were interrupted by
a man walking towards our hill. Conny squinted her eyes into
the sun and then shouted, 'It is William Nagenda!'

What a joy it was to meet that dear African saint again. I
never met an African with whom I could laugh so much and
yet learn so much at the same time.

After we exchanged greetings William said, 'When I saw
you sitting here together a question came to my mind, "Do
they walk in the light together?"'

We answered almost simultaneously. 'Oh yes, we do walk in the light together. We are a team.'

Just at that moment a boy from the house called that there was a telephone message for me. I excused myself while Conny and William remained behind to talk.

Conny was sitting in a cane and wicker chair while William squatted on his haunches beside the path, his brown knees poking up beside his face.

'I have something to confess to you,' Conny said to William.

'And what is that?' he answered gently.

'Your question gripped my heart. I must tell you that I do not really walk in the light with Tante Corrie.'

William's face broke into a wide grin and his eyes began to sparkle. 'So, that is why God had me ask that strange question.'

Conny was serious. 'Tante Corrie is so much more mature than I,' she continued. 'She has walked with Jesus for so many years. She has suffered much for Him in many ways. Thus when I see things in her life that are not right, I hesitate to speak them out to her.'

'Oh,' William said, startled. 'That is not right. The Lord wants you to be very honest with Tante Corrie. That is one reason He has put you with her. Since she is walking in the light then when you also walk in the light, you will help shed light for her path as well as yours.'

That night, after we had gone to our room together, Conny sat on the side of the bed and said, 'Tante Corrie, this is very difficult for me to say, but I now realize I must walk in the light.'

I turned and looked at her. Her face was drawn and solemn. One by one she began listing the things in my life which bothered her – the things I did which she did not believe glorified God. It was not easy for me to hear the things which I had done wrong – things which had caused a shadow to come in Conny's heart. But how wonderful it was that Conny was being completely honest with me. I apologized for the things she had listed and then thanked her for bringing them into the light. 'Let us always walk in the light together,' I said seriously.

But it was still hard for Conny. She was much younger than I and felt she was still learning. Even though I wanted her to continue to correct me, she found it very difficult. The final breakthrough came after we left Africa and flew to Brazil.

We had been in Rio de Janeiro, one of the most beautiful cities of the world, for a few weeks. As we prepared to leave – to fly south to Buenos Aires – we discovered our suitcases were overweight. The kind people in Rio had given us so many presents we were more than twenty kilograms overweight. It was going to cost us a great deal of extra money to go on to Argentina.

I unpacked my luggage and made three piles: one to send to Holland by sea, one to give away to the poor in Rio, and the smallest one to go back in my suitcase to carry on to our next destination. Finishing my repacking I hurried next door into Conny's room and unpacked her suitcase also. I went through the same procedure, sorting her belongings into three heaps and then repacking only her necessary items. I was in too much of a hurry to notice that Conny said nothing.

A week later, after a beautiful time in Buenos Aires, we were walking along a lonely stretch of beach near our cabin. I was enjoying the beautiful view over a quiet bay when Conny began to talk. Her voice was strained. 'I promised God I would walk in the light,' she said, 'and that means that I must get something settled with you. When you repacked my suitcase and decided what things to send to Holland and what to leave with me, I was not happy about it.'

How stupid and tactless I had been to rush in and interfere with Conny's life! I reached out and took her hand. 'How thoughtless I have been,' I said. 'Forgive me for not leaving it up to you.'

'I do forgive you,' Conny said. Like myself, she had learned not to play lightly with sin, but to hear another's apology and then, instead of passing it off, to forgive it. We walked on for a long time in silence and then Conny spoke again.

'Are you unhappy, Tante Corrie? You are so quiet.'

Now it was my time to walk in the light. 'There is something hindering me,' I said, 'Why did you not tell me immediately that you were disturbed? That way it could have been settled on the spot and you would not have had to carry this darkness for all these days. From now on let us both "speak the truth in love" and never let the sun go down on our misunderstandings.'

It was a good lesson. From then until Conny married in 1967 and went to live with her husband, we walked all over the world – always trying to walk in the light.

*I say therefore to the unmarried and
widows,
It is good for them if they abide even as I.*
1 Corinthians 7:8

27

Secure in Jesus

It is Satan who tries, in every way, to spoil the peace and
joy that God's servants have in their work.

Ellen, my new travelling companion, had gone with me to
a lonely mission field in Mexico. Our hostess was a lady
missionary, unmarried, in her forties. One evening while we
were alone in her little adobe, she confessed her bitterness
and resentment over being unmarried.

'Why have I been denied the love of a husband, children,
and a home? Why is it that the only men who ever paid any
attention to me were married to someone else?' Long into the
night she poured out the poison of her frustration. At last she
asked me, 'Why did you never marry?'

'Because,' I said, 'the Lord had other plans for me than
married life.'

'Did you ever fall in love and lose someone, as I have?' she
asked bitterly.

'Yes,' I said sadly. 'I know the pain of a broken heart.'

'But you were strong, weren't you,' she said in biting tones.
'You were willing to let God have His way in your life?'

'Oh, no, not at first,' I said. 'I had to fight a battle over it.
I was twenty-three. I loved a boy and believed he loved me.
But I had no money and he married a rich girl. After they were
married he brought her to me and putting her hand in mine

said, 'I hope you two will be friends.' I wanted to scream. She looked so sweet, so secure and content in his love.

'But I did have Jesus, and eventually I went to him and prayed, "Lord Jesus, You know that I belong to you one hundred per cent. My sex life is yours also. I don't know what plans You have for my life, but Lord, whatever it may be, use me to realize Your victory in every detail. I believe You can take away all my frustrations and feelings of unhappiness. I surrender anew my whole life to You."'

I looked across the little table at the bitter woman in front of me. Her face was furrowed, her eyes hard with resentment. I sensed she had been trying to run away from her frustrations. Perhaps that was even the reason she was on the mission field. Sadly, there are some of God's children who go to the mission field to escape the pain of not having a husband. I know others, back home, who spend every evening away from their families, attending Christian meetings, because they are unhappy and frustrated in their marriages. Work – even mission work – can become a wrong hiding place.

'Those called by God to live single lives are always happy in that state,' I said. 'This happiness, this contentment, is the evidence of God's plan.'

'But you loved and lost,' she exclaimed. 'Do you believe that God took away your lover to make you follow Him?'

'Oh, no,' I smiled. 'God does not take away from us. He might ask us to turn our backs on something, or someone, we should not have. God never takes away, however; God gives. If I reach out and take someone for myself and the Lord steps in between, that does not mean God takes. Rather it means He is protecting us from someone we should not have because He has a far greater purpose for our lives.'

We sat for long minutes in the semi-dark room. Only a small kerosene lamp gave its flickering light, casting faint shadows on the walls and across our faces. I thought back – remembering. I had always been content in the Lord. Back when I was in my thirties God gave me children – the children of missionaries – whom I raised. Betsie, my sister, fed and clothed them while I was responsible for their sports and music. We kept them in our home in Holland, and I found deep satisfaction in seeing them grow to maturity. I also spent a great deal of time speaking and sharing in various clubs for girls. But it was not the work that brought balance to my life, for work cannot balance our feelings. It was because my life was centred in the Lord Jesus that I had balance. Many people try to lose their feelings in work, or sports, or music, or the arts. But the feelings are always there and will eventually, as they had done tonight in this missionary, come boiling to the surface and express their resentment and discontent.

I turned to Ellen, my companion. Ellen is a tall, blond, beautiful Dutch girl then in her early thirties. She is single, yet she has learned the secret of living a balanced life. While I believe God set me apart before I was born to live a single life, Ellen was different. She did not feel that God had called her to a single life; rather she felt that one day, in God's time, she would marry. However, until that time arrived – one year or thirty years from then – I knew she was secure in Jesus and was not looking to a husband or children for her security.

I spoke to the missionary. 'There are some like me, who are called to live a single life,' I said softly. 'For them it is always easy for they are, by their nature, contented. Others, like Ellen, are called to prepare for marriage which may come later in life. They, too, are blessed, for God is using the in-between years to teach them that marriage is not the answer to unhappiness. Happiness is found only in a balanced relationship with the Lord Jesus.'

'But it is so hard,' she said, tears welling up in her eyes.

'That is so,' I said. 'The cross is always difficult. "But you are dead, and your life is hid with Christ in God" (Colossians 3:3). Dear girl, it cannot be safer. That part of you which would cling to a husband is dead. Now you can move into a life where you can be happy with or without a husband – secure in Jesus alone.'

I do not know if she really understood me, for often we set our minds on some one thing we think will make us happy – a husband, children, a particular job, or even a 'Ministry' – and refuse to open our eyes to God's better way. In fact, some believe so strongly that only this thing can bring happiness, that they reject the Lord Jesus Himself. Happiness is not found in marriage; or work; or ministry; or children. Happiness is found by being secure in Jesus.

After these things the Lord appointed other
seventy also, and sent them two and two
before his face into every city and place . . .
Luke 10:1

28

I Have Much People in This City

My second trip to Cuba was much different from the earlier
one because this time Cuba was in the hands of Communists.
Ellen was with me and we had come from Mexico with
our bags loaded with books. Friends had told us that the
Communists in Cuba were burning Bibles and confiscating
Christian literature, so I was not at all sure if we could be
allowed to bring all these books in with us. We had also
heard that most of the churches were closed and many of
the Christians were in prison – some of them for passing out
literature. Thus we were very cautious.

At the customs, in Havana, the officer pointed to my
suitcases. 'What are these books?' he asked.

'They are written by me,' I said. 'I am going to give them
to my friends.'

I saw him scowl as he picked one of them up. My heart
began to beat rapidly. 'Oh, Lord,' I prayed inwardly, 'what
must I do?'

Then I heard myself saying brashly, 'Would you like to
have one of my books? Here, I will autograph it especially
for you.'

The customs officer looked up. I took the book from his
hand and wrote my name in the front and then handed it
back. He grinned broadly and thanked me. Then, glancing

once more at my suitcase filled with books, he nodded and motioned us through the line. I closed the suitcase and stepped out on the streets. Hallelujah! The miracle had happened.

But why were we here? What kind of plans did the Lord have for us on this island? Had all our former friends been put in prison? Were any of the churches still open? These and many other questions pounded at my mind as we turned our faces towards the city.

An Intourist limousine brought us into the heart of Havana where we found a hotel room. After washing up we went out on to the streets, hoping to find some Christians. But how do you find Christians in a strange city when you cannot even speak their language? We walked up and down the sidewalks, hoping God would show us someone to speak to, but we received no guidance whatsoever.

I finally approached an old man who was leaning against the side of the building. He had a kindly face, I thought. I asked if he knew where there was a church.

He shrugged his shoulders but then, motioning us to wait, went to one of the free telephones along the street. Ellen and I stood praying. Was he going to call the police? Had we broken a law and would we be put in jail? Then we realized he was calling some of his friends, asking if they knew the whereabouts of a church. No one knew anything and he returned, saying he could be of no help.

We were discouraged and to make matters worse, it started to rain. Neither Ellen nor I had a raincoat and soon we were soaked to the skin. We had been walking for hours and I was exhausted.

'Ellen, can we try to get a taxi?' I asked.

'Well, Tante Corrie, we will need a miracle. However, we know that all things are possible with God.'

I found a little stool and sat down while Ellen walked on down the street, hoping to find a taxi. I looked out over the sea and felt as if I had just waded out of the surf, so wet was I. I thought of the words of the driver of the Intourist limousine as he had brought us from the airport. 'This is the hospital,' he had said as we drove by. 'Everyone who is ill can go there and it does not cost a penny. Here is a cemetery. When you die, we bury you and even that does not cost your relatives anything.'

I had been in many countries, but this was the first place they had offered to bury me!

We knew that the Lord had sent us to Cuba, but we had no idea of our mission. Where were the churches? We had seen some, but they were closed. Some even had trees growing in front of the doors. We had tried to call some Christians, but the ones we knew were no longer living in the area. I sat, waiting, while the water poured down my face. Then I heard a car stopping in front of me. Looking up, I saw Ellen's face in the rear window of the ancient, rusted vehicle.

'Tante Corrie,' she called above the sound of the rain, 'here I am again.' I hobbled to the taxi and got in the back door. 'Be careful where you put your feet,' Ellen laughed, 'or you will touch the street.'

The taxi took us to our hotel and soon we were in dry clothes, our wet garments hung across the fixtures in the bathroom where the steady drip, drip of water reminded us of our failure out on the street. I love to walk with Jesus, but after eight decades I realized I was not as young as I used to be. It was in such moments that I started to feel old.

Ellen could not sleep that night. We were supposed to stay in Cuba for two weeks, but if we could not find any Christians then what would we do? She arose in the middle of the night and prayed, 'Lord, give me a word so I may know we aren't in this country in vain.'

Sitting on the side of her bed, she reached for her Bible which was on the small table. She began to read where she had stopped the night before. She had learned that God does not want His children to be fearful, and the best way to overcome fear is through the Word of God.

She read Acts 18:9, 10.

Then spake the Lord to Paul . . . Be not afraid, but speak, and hold not thy peace. For I am with thee, and no man shall set on thee to hurt thee: for I have much people in this city.

What an answer!

The next morning Ellen could not wait to find all those people, and neither could I. She had one address which we had not contacted. It was the address of a small house on a side street where some Christians we had once known used to live. Walking from the hotel, she finally found the street and made her way to a dingy door, weatherbeaten and cracked. She knocked boldly.

A small man, deeply tanned and with wrinkles around his eyes, cautiously opened the door. Ellen could speak no Spanish, but she held up her Bible, and one of my books (*Amazing Love*) which had been translated into Spanish.

The man glanced at the books and then back to Ellen. Ellen smiled and pointed to my name on the book, then pointed back towards the city. Suddenly his whole face came alive. He threw open the door and shouted, 'Corrie! Corrie ten Boom *està aquì. Ella està en Havana*!'

Ellen walked in and found the room was filled with men, all kneeling on the floor. They were pastors who met each week to pray for God's help and guidance in their difficult ministry. Ellen hurried back to the hotel and soon I was meeting with these wonderful men of God. We distributed all our books and made many new friends among God's people. Indeed, God did have 'much people' in that city.

Cast thy bread upon the waters: for thou
shalt find it after many days.
Ecclesiastes 11:1

29

The Blessing Box

Many times, on my trips around the world, I am dependent
on the hospitality of Christians. From the time of my first trip
to America when I was befriended by God's people in New
York, and later by Abraham Vereide in Washington, D. C.,
I have known the love and generosity of others in the Body
of Christ.

It was on one of those continual trips, when my only home
was my suitcase (that big red one), that I was invited to stay
with friends in Colorado. I didn't feel well and needed rest.
My hostess escorted me to her lovely house with tall white
columns. Taking me up the carpeted stairs she showed me
to a beautiful room. From the windows I could see the clear,
blue sky which framed the snow-capped Rocky Mountains.
She then put her arms around me and said, 'Corrie, this is
your room. It will always be here for you.'

'This room! For me?' I could hardly believe it was true. A
place for me to unpack my suitcase! To hang up my clothes!
To spread out my writing papers and put my Bible on a desk!
Since that grey time in the concentration camp I had longed for
bright colours, as a thirsty man yearns for water. This room,
and the scenery outside, was filled with colour. I wanted to
cry, as a child cries when she is happy. But I have learned to
control my tears (most of the time, anyway) and was content
just to tell the Lord of my deep thankfulness. The Lord is so

good for He has given me so many friends, just like this, all over the world.

It was during one of my visits in this Colorado home that I received an early morning telephone call. I was already awake since we intended to leave that afternoon to fly to Washington to speak in a series of meetings arranged by Mr Vereide.

The phone call was from Alicia Davison, Mr Vereide's daughter. 'Oh, Alicia, I cannot wait to see you today. I am looking forward to it and the meetings in your fellowship house.'

There was a pause, then Alicia said, 'Tante Corrie, Dad is with the Lord.'

'Oh, Alicia . . .' I tried to speak, but nothing else would come out.

'It is all right, Tante Corrie,' she said calmly. 'I am calling to ask you to please come on to be with all of us. We will not have the meetings, but so many people are coming and we want you to be with us.'

'I shall be there this afternoon,' I said. After a brief prayer over the phone, I hung up.

I hurried to finish my packing, remembering all the kindnesses that had been poured on me by this wonderful family and their many friends. I have faced death many times, but there is always an empty place in my heart when someone I know and love leaves to be with the Lord. Nor did it ever occur to me that almost two years later I would once again fly to Washington to sit in that same Presbyterian Church not to attend a memorial for Abraham Vereide but to attend the meeting in honour of Alicia, who, although still young and beautiful, would die in Hong Kong while making a mission tour with her husband, Howard Davison.

I was warmly received by my friends in Washington. Although sad, they were rejoicing in the Lord. That night after I had gone to my room, I prayed. 'Lord,' I asked, 'Why are people so kind to me? I am just a simple old Dutch woman. Why am I treated so graciously and shown so much hospitality?'

Then the Lord reminded me of my mother's blessing box.

Our house in Haarlem was not really big but it had wide open doors.

I do not suppose that the many guests who were always coming to the Beje ever realized what a struggle it was to make both ends meet. Yet many lonesome people found a place with us and joined in our music, humour, and interesting conversation. There was always a place at the oval dinner table, although perhaps the soup was a bit watery when too many unexpected guests showed up. Our entire home was centred in the ministry of the Gospel. All people who came to us were either workers in the Kingdom of God or people who needed help.

Mother loved all her guests. She often showed her love by dropping a penny in the 'blessing box' when they arrived.

The blessing box was a small metal box that sat on the sideboard near the oval dinner table. Here money was collected for the mission that was so close to our hearts. Every time our family was blessed in a particular way, Mother would drop money in the blessing box as a thank offering to God. This was especially true if Father sold an expensive watch or received extra money for repairing an antique clock.

Whenever visitors came Mother would spread her arms wide and welcome them and then to show how she really appreciated their presence would say, 'A penny in the blessing box for your coming.' If it were a special visitor she might even put in a dime.

Then, at the dinner table, Father would always bless our visitors, thanking God that our house was privileged by their presence. It was always a special occasion for us all.

I well remember the sister-in-law of a minister who spent the night with us. The next morning Tante Anna went to her room and found her sheet twisted into a rope and lying across the bed.

'What is this?' Tante Anna asked.

The woman broke down in tears. 'I must confess. Last night I wanted to commit suicide. I made my sheet into a rope and tied it around my neck to jump from the window. But I could not forget the prayer at the dinner table, as Mr ten Boom thanked God that I could come and share in this hospitality. God spared my life through that prayer.'

After a few days in Washington I continued my travelling as a tramp for the Lord. However, fresh on my mind was the hospitality of my dear friends. And I remembered Mother's blessing box, and Father's prayers. Often I am dependent on the hospitality of Christians. God's people have been so generous to open their homes to me and many times when I lay my head on a strange pillow, which has been blessed by the love of my friends, I realize that I am enjoying the reward for the open doors and open hearts of the Beje.

Heaven will be blessed, but here on earth I already am enjoying a 'house with many mansions'.

> *If we confess our sins, he is faithful and
> just to forgive us our sins, and to cleanse
> us from all unrighteousness.*
> 1 John 1:9

30

Closing the Circle

It would seem, after having been a Christian for almost
eighty years, that I would no longer do ugly things that
need forgiving. Yet I am constantly doing things to others
that cause me to have to go back and ask their forgiveness.
Sometimes these are things I actually do – other times they
are simply attitudes I let creep in which break the circle of
God's perfect love.

I first learned the secret of closing the circle from my
nephew, Peter van Woerden, who was spending the weekend
with me in our little apartment in Baarn, Holland.

'Do you remember that boy, Jan, that we prayed for?'
Peter asked.

I well remember Jan. We had prayed for him many times.
He had a horrible demon of darkness in his life and although
we had fasted and prayed and cast out the demon in the name
of the Lord Jesus Christ, the darkness always returned.

Peter continued, 'I knew God had brought this boy to me
not only so he could be delivered, but to teach me some
lessons too.'

I looked at Peter. 'What could that boy, Jan, so filled with
darkness, teach you?'

'I did not learn the lesson from Jan,' Peter smiled. 'But from
God. Once in my intercession time for Jan the Lord told me

to open my Bible at 1 John 1:7-9. I read that passage about confessing our sin and asked the Lord what that had to do with the darkness in Jan's life.'

Peter got up and walked across the room, holding his open Bible in his hand. 'God taught me that if a Christian walks in the light then the blood of Jesus Christ cleanses him from all sin, making his life a closed circle and protecting him from all outside dark powers. But –' he turned and emphatically jabbed his finger into the pages of the Bible – 'if there is unconfessed sin in that life, the circle has an opening in it – a gap – and this allows the dark powers to come back in.'

Ah, I thought, *Peter has really learned a truth from the Lord.*

'Tante Corrie,' Peter continued, 'even though I was able to cast out the demon in Jan's life, it always crept back in through the opening in the circle – the opening of Jan's unconfessed sin. But when I led Jan to confess this sin, then the circle was closed and the dark powers could no longer return.'

That same week the wife of a good friend came to me for counselling. After I had fixed her a cup of tea she began to tell me about all the people who had prayed for her, yet she was still experiencing horrible dreams at night.

I interrupted her conversation and drew a circle on a piece of paper. 'Mary,' I said, 'do you have unconfessed sin in your life? Is this the reason the circle is still open?'

Mary said nothing, sitting with her head down, her hands tightly clasped in her lap, her feet together. I could see there was a strong battle going on in her life – a battle between spiritual forces.

'Do you really want to be free?' I urged.

'Oh, yes,' she said.

Suddenly she began telling me about a strong hatred she had for her mother. Everyone thought she loved her mother, but inside there were things that caused her actually to want to kill her. Yet, even as she spoke, I saw freedom coming into her eyes.

She finished her confession and then quickly asked Jesus to forgive her and cleanse her with His blood. I looked into her eyes and commanded the demon of hatred to leave in the name of Jesus.

What joy! What freedom!

Mary raised her hands in victory and began to praise the Lord, thanking Him for the liberation and forgiveness He had given her. Then she reached over and embraced me in a hug so tight I thought she would crack my ribs.

'Dear Lord,' she prayed, 'I thank You for closing the circle with Your blood.'

Having thus learned to close the circle by confessing my sins, I wish I could say that ever since then the circle has remained closed in my life. It is not so. For since Satan comes against us so often, then it is necessary to confess often, also. Regardless of how old a person may be, or how long he has ministered in the Name of Jesus Christ, that man still needs to confess his sins again and again – and ask forgiveness.

This truth became painfully clear to me recently when I was invited to Washington, D.C., to speak to a luncheon of businessmen and women. I love to talk to businessmen and was very excited about the meeting. When I arrived, however, I found only women present. This upset me for I felt that men needed to hear the message of forgiveness also.

After the meeting a fine-looking lady came up to me. 'I am in charge of arranging the programme for the world convention of our ladies' group,' she said. 'Some of the most influential women in the world will be present. Would you come to speak to us in San Francisco?'

I was still miffed that no men had been present for the luncheon. It's not that I disapprove of women's meetings. But I am concerned when men leave the spiritual activity to the women. God is calling *men*. Thus, I gave her a short, discourteous answer. 'No, I will not. I must speak to men also. I don't like this business of all women.'

She was very gracious. 'Don't you feel that you are the right person?' she asked.

'No,' I said, 'I am not the right person. I do not like this American system where men go about their business leaving the women to act like Christians. I will not come.' I turned and walked away.

Later that afternoon I was in my room, packing to catch the plane. The Lord began dealing with me. 'You were very rude to that woman,' He told me.

I argued with the Lord. 'But Lord, I feel that Your message is for all people, not just the women.'

'You were very rude to that woman,' He said again, gently.

He was right, of course. He always is. I had been speaking on forgiveness, but was unwilling to ask forgiveness for myself. I knew I was going to have to go to that gracious woman and apologize – confess my sin. Until I did, the circle would be open in my life and Satan would be pouring in many other dark thoughts as well.

I looked at my watch and saw I had only enough time to finish my packing and get to the airport. It made no difference. If I left Washington without closing the circle, I would be no good anywhere else. I would just have to miss my plane.

I called the front desk and found which room the woman was in. Then I went to her room. 'I must ask your forgiveness,' I said as she opened the door. 'I spoke to you rudely.'

She was embarrassed and tried to pass it off. 'Oh, no,' she said, 'you were not unkind. I understand perfectly. I, too, feel that men should be the spiritual leaders, not women.'

She was returning my unkindness with kindness, but that was not what I needed. I needed for her to admit that I was wrong about not speaking to women, and forgive me. I know it is often more difficult to forgive than to ask forgiveness, but it is equally important. To withhold forgiveness often leaves another person in bondage, unable to close the circle, and thus open to further attacks from Satan. It is as important to forgive as it is to ask forgiveness.

This sensitive woman understood. Reaching out and tenderly touching my hand, she said, 'I understand, Tante Corrie. I forgive you for your remarks about women's groups and I forgive you for being unkind to me.'

That was what I needed to hear. In the future I would indeed speak to women's groups. I would also keep a watch on my lips when tempted to speak unkindly. I missed my plane, but the circle was closed.

31

One Finger for His Glory

We arrived at her apartment by night in order to escape
detection. We were in Russia (in the region of Lithuania,
on the Baltic Sea). Ellen and I had climbed the steep
stairs, coming through a small back door into the one-room
apartment. It was jammed with furniture, evidence that
the old couple had once lived in a much larger and much
finer house.

The old woman was lying on a small sofa, propped up
by pillows. Her body was bent and twisted almost beyond
recognition by the dread disease of multiple sclerosis. Her
aged husband spent all his time caring for her since she was
unable to move off the sofa.

I walked across the room and kissed her wrinkled cheek.
She tried to look up but the muscles in her neck were
atrophied so she could only roll her eyes upward and smile.
She raised her right hand, slowly, in jerks. It was the only
part of her body she could control and with her gnarled and
deformed knuckles she caressed my face. I reached over and

kissed the index finger of that hand, for it was with this one finger that she had so long glorified God.

Beside her couch was a vintage typewriter. Each morning her faithful husband would rise, praising the Lord. After caring for his wife's needs and feeding her a simple breakfast, he would prop her into a sitting position on the couch, placing pillows all around her so she wouldn't topple over. Then he would move that ancient black typewriter in front of her on a small table. From an old cupboard he would remove a stack of cheap yellow paper. Then, with that blessed one finger, she would begin to type.

All day and far into the night she would type. She translated Christian books into Russian, Latvian, and the language of her people. Always using just that one finger – peck . . . peck . . . peck – she typed out the pages. Portions of the Bible, the books of Billy Graham, Watchman Nee and Corrie ten Boom – all came from her typewriter. That was why I was there – to thank her.

She was hungry to hear news about these men of God she had never met, yet whose books she had so faithfully translated. We talked about Watchman Nee, who was then in a prison in China, and I told her all I knew of his life and ministry. I also told her of the wonderful ministry of Billy Graham and of the many people who were giving their lives to the Lord.

'Not only does she translate their books,' her husband said as he hovered close by during our conversation, 'but she prays for these men every day while she types. Sometimes it takes a long time for her finger to hit the key, or for her to get the paper in the machine, but all the time she is praying for those whose books she is working on.'

I looked at her wasted form on the sofa, her head pulled down and her feet curled back under her body. 'Oh, Lord, why don't You heal her?' I cried inwardly.

Her husband, sensing my anguish of soul, gave the answer. 'God has a purpose in her sickness. Every other Christian in the city is watched by the secret police. But because she has been sick so long, no one ever looks in on her. They leave us alone and she is the only person in all the city who can type quietly, undetected by the police.'

I looked around at the tiny room, so jammed full of furniture from better days. In one corner was the kitchen. Beside the cupboard was her husband's 'office', a battered desk where he sorted the pages that came from her typewriter to pass them on to the Christians. I thought of Jesus sitting over against the treasury, and my heart leaped for joy as I heard Jesus bless this sick old woman who, like the widow, had given all she had.

What a warrior!

> When she enters the beautiful city
> And the saved all around her appear,
> Many people around will tell her:
> It was you that invited me here.
>
> AUTHOR UNKNOWN

Ellen and I returned to Holland where we were able to obtain a new typewriter and have it shipped to her. Now she could make carbon copies of her translations.

Today we got a letter from her husband. In the early morning hours last week she left to be with the Lord. But, he said, she had worked up until midnight that same night, typing with that one finger to the glory of God.

> *Haven't you yet learned that your body
> is the home of the Holy Spirit God
> gave you, and that he lives within you?
> Your own body does not belong to you.
> For God has bought you with a great
> price. So use every part of your body
> to give glory back to God, because he
> owns it.*
>
> 1 Corinthians 6:19, 20 LB

32

The Ding-Dong Principle

In Holland we have many churches with belfries. The bells
in the steeples are rung by hand, with a rope that is pulled
from the vestibule of the church.

One day a young Flemish girl, who had repented and
received deliverance from lust and impurity, came to me
while I was speaking in one of these churches.

'Even though I have been delivered,' she said, 'at night I
still keep dreaming of my old way of life. I am afraid I will slip
back into Satan's grasp.'

'Up in that church tower,' I said, nodding towards the
belfry, 'is a bell which is rung by pulling on a rope. But
you know what? After the sexton lets go of the rope, the
bell keeps on swinging. First *ding*, then *dong*. Slower and
slower until there's a final *dong* and it stops.

'I believe the same thing is true of deliverance. When the
demons are cast out in the name of the Lord Jesus Christ,
or when sin is confessed and renounced, then Satan's hand
is removed from the rope. But if we worry about our past

bondage, Satan will use this opportunity to keep the echoes ringing in our minds.'

A sweet light spread across the girl's face. 'You mean even though I sometimes have temptations, that I am still free, that Satan is no longer pulling the rope which controls my life?'

'The purity of your life is evidence of your deliverance,' I said. 'You should not worry about the *dings* and the *dongs*, they are nothing but echoes.'

Demons seldom leave without leaving behind their vibrations – *dings* and *dongs*. It is as though they give the clapper one big swing on the way out, scaring us into thinking they are still there. They know that, even though they have to flee at the Name of Jesus, if we grow fearful over the remaining echoes, other demons can come in and take their place.

The same is true of forgiveness. When we forgive someone, we take our hand off the rope. But if we've been tugging at our grievances for a long time, we mustn't be surprised when the old angry thoughts keep coming up for a while. They're just the *ding-dongs* of the old bell slowing down.

The Bible promises that after we confess and denounce our sins, God cleanses us from them by the blood of Jesus. Indeed, He says, 'Your sins and iniquities will I remember no more' (*See* Hebrews 8:12). However, we can do something God cannot do. We can remember our old sins. These are the *dings* and the *dongs* of our past life. When we hear them we need to remember that through Jesus' sacrifice on Calvary, Satan can no longer pull the rope in our life. We may be tempted. We may even fall back occasionally. But we have been delivered from the bondage of sin, and even though the vibrations may still sound in our lives, they will grow less and less and eventually stop completely.

Once Satan has been cast out of the house of your life, he cannot return as long as you walk in obedience. Your body is the temple of the Holy Spirit. However, that does not prevent him (or his demons) from standing outside the house and shouting through the windows, saying, 'We're still here!'

But, hallelujah, we know Satan for who he is – the prince of liars. He is *not* still here – he has been cast out. So whenever you hear one of those old echoes in your life – one of the *dings* or *dongs* – you need to stop right then and say, 'Thank You, Jesus. You have bought me with Your blood and sin has no right to sound off in my life.'

And when you stand praying, if you have a
grievance against anyone, forgive him, so
that your Father in heaven may forgive you
the wrongs you have done.
Mark 11:25 NEB

33

The Blacks and Whites of Forgiveness

I wish I could say that after a long and fruitful life, travelling
the world, I had learned to forgive all my enemies. I wish I
could say that merciful and charitable thoughts just naturally
flowed from me and on to others. But they don't. If there is
one thing I've learned since I've passed my eightieth birthday,
it's that I can't store up good feelings and behaviour – but only
draw them fresh from God each day.

Maybe I'm glad it's that way, for every time I go to Him,
He teaches me something else. I recall the time – and I
was almost seventy – when some Christian friends whom I
loved and trusted did something which hurt me. You would
have thought that, having been able to forgive the guards in
Ravensbruck, forgiving Christian friends would be child's play.
It wasn't. For weeks I seethed inside. But at last I asked God
again to work His miracle in me. And again it happened: first
the cold-blooded decision, then the flood of joy and peace. I
had forgiven my friends; I was restored to my Father.

Then, why was I suddenly awake in the middle of the night,
rehashing the whole affair again? *My friends!* I thought. *People
I loved.* If it had been strangers. I wouldn't have minded so.

I sat up and switched on the light. 'Father, I thought it was
all forgiven. Please help me do it.'

But the next night I woke up again. They'd talked so sweetly too! Never a hint of what they were planning. 'Father!' I cried in alarm. 'Help me!'

Then it was that another secret of forgiveness became evident. It is not enough to simply say, 'I forgive you.' I must also begin to live it out. And in my case, that meant acting as though their sins, like mine, were buried in the depths of the deepest sea. If God could remember them no more – and He had said, '[Your] sins and iniquities will I remember no more' (Hebrews 10:17) – then neither should I. And the reason the thoughts kept coming back to me was that I kept turning their sin over in my mind.

And so I discovered another of God's principles: We can trust God not only for our emotions but also for our thoughts. As I asked Him to renew my mind, He also took away my thoughts. He still had more to teach me, however, even from this single episode. Many years later, after I had passed my eightieth birthday, an American friend came to visit me in Holland. As we sat in my little apartment in Baarn he asked me about those people from long ago who had taken advantage of me.

'It is nothing,' I said a little smugly. 'It is all forgiven.'

'By you, yes,' he said. 'But what about them? Have they accepted your forgiveness?'

'They say there is nothing to forgive! They deny it ever happened. No matter what they say, though, I can prove they were wrong.' I went eagerly to my desk. 'See, I have it in black and white! I saved all their letters and I can show you where . . .'

'Corrie!' My friend slipped his arm through mine and gently closed the drawer. 'Aren't you the one whose sins are at the bottom of the sea? Yet are the sins of your friends etched in black and white?'

For an astonishing moment I could not find my voice. 'Lord Jesus,' I whispered at last, 'who takes all my sins away, forgive me for preserving all these years the evidence against others! Give me grace to burn all the blacks and whites as a sweet-smelling sacrifice to Your glory.'

I did not go to sleep that night until I had gone through

my desk and pulled out those letters – curling now with
age – and fed them all into my little coal-burning grate. As
the flames leaped and glowed, so did my heart. 'Forgive us
our trespasses,' Jesus taught us to pray, 'as we forgive those
who trespass against us.' In the ashes of those letters I was
seeing yet another facet of His mercy. What more He would
teach me about forgiveness in the days ahead I didn't know,
but tonight's was good news enough.

Forgiveness is the key which unlocks the door of resentment and the handcuffs of hatred. It breaks the chains of
bitterness and the shackles of selfishness. The forgiveness
of Jesus not only takes away our sins, it makes them as if
they had never been.

34

Getting Ready for the End

Some time ago, I was with a group of students in the mid-west. Some of them were new Christians, but most of them did not know the Lord. They were interested in all kinds of other things, and a Christian professor had organized weekly meetings to answer their questions. So it was that at the last evening meeting of that semester the professor said, 'Now you can hear something about Christianity in practice.'

First I spoke to those who were Christians. 'How long have you known Jesus?' I asked.

One said, 'Two weeks.' Another said, 'Three years.' And still another answered and said, 'I met Him only yesterday.'

Then I said to them, 'Well, I have good news. I have known Him seventy-five years, and I can tell you something, men. He will never let you down.'

Next I told the other students about Jesus Christ, and what He had done for me, and the great miracles also. When He tells you to love your enemies, He gives you the love that He demands from you. They were listening intently, and I was led by the Holy Spirit not to go into any doctrines or teachings other than the reality of Jesus Christ. I told them of the joy of having Jesus with me, whatever happened, and how I knew from experience that the light of Jesus is stronger than the greatest darkness. I told them of the darkness of my prison experiences, realizing that only those people who were in a German concentration camp could ever fully understand.

However, I wanted these students to know that, even though I was there where every day six hundred people either died or were killed, when Jesus is with you the worst can happen and the best remains.

Afterwards the students came up and we had coffee. One said to me, 'I would love to ask Jesus to come into my heart, but I cannot. I am a Jew.'

I said, 'You cannot ask Jesus into your heart because you are a Jew? Then you do not understand that with the Jew (Jesus) in your heart – you are a double Jew.'

He said, 'Oh, then it is possible?'

'On the divine side He was God's Son. On the human side He was a Jew. When you accept Him you do not become a Gentile. You become even more Jewish than before. You will be a completed Jew.'

With great joy the boy received the Lord Jesus as his Saviour.

There is a great new surge of interest in spiritual things. Many are interested in Jesus Christ who have never shown any interest before. Churches – which have been dead and cold like mausoleums – are coming to life. All across the world many are being saved and being filled with the Holy Spirit.

At the same time, however, many others are turning away from God. They are openly worshiping Satan. Many others are calling themselves Christians, but are involved in the occult, fortune telling, astrology, mind science, and other things of Satan.

I see over the whole world that there are two huge armies marching – the army of the Antichrist and the army of Jesus Christ. We know from the Bible that Jesus Christ will have the victory, but now the Antichrist is preparing for the time that will come before Jesus returns. The Bible says there will be a time of tribulation, and the Antichrist will take over the whole world. He will be a very 'good, religious' man, and he will make one religion for the whole world. After it has been arranged, he will proclaim himself as its god. The Bible prophesies that the time will come when we cannot buy or sell, unless we bear the sign of the Antichrist; that means that world money is coming, and people know this today. If I did not believe in the Bible before, I should believe in it now. Because what was foretold in the Bible you can now read in the newspapers.

At a student meeting in California a theological student approached me saying, 'What's all this talk about Jesus' coming again? Don't you know that men have been prophesying for years that He would come, and He never has. Even the early church could not live their religion because they were too busy looking for Christ to return. He is not coming back. It is all foolishness.'

I looked at the young man. He was so smug, so full of scoffing, and I felt sorry for him.

'Indeed, Jesus is coming again, and soon,' I said. 'And you have just proved it to me.'

He blinked his eyes. 'How did I prove it to you?'

'Because the Bible talks about it in 2 Peter 3:3, that in the last days there shall come scoffers walking after their own lusts and they will say, "Where is the promise of His Coming? Ever since the early church men have been looking for Him and He has not come." So you see, my young friend, you are one of the signs of His Coming.'

I am not afraid when I think about the Coming of the Lord Jesus. Instead I welcome it. I do not know whether it would be better for me to die and be among that great host of saints who will return with Him, or whether it would be better to remain here and listen for the sound of the trumpet. Either way I like the words of the song that says:

> God is working His purpose out,
> As year succeeds to year:
> God is working His purpose out
> And the time is drawing near –
> Nearer and nearer draws the time
> The time that shall surely be,
> When the earth shall be filled with
>   the glory of God
> As the waters cover the sea.

A. C. AINGER

I find that when Communists speak of the future of the world, they show a pattern for peace through communism. But when I ask them, 'What about when you die?' they say, 'Then everything is ended. There is no life after this life.' The Bible tells us that the Antichrist can imitate much, even the gifts of the Spirit. But there is one thing he cannot imitate, and that is the peace of God which passes all understanding.

But there are *good* things to tell about the future of the world. For instance, the Bible says the Tree of Life will be used for the healing of the nations. This means that there will be *nations* to heal, and there will be *healing*. I am so thankful that we have the Bible and can know the future of God's plan.

As the end times draw closer and closer, so does the power of God grow greater and greater. One day, on a trip to Russia, I approached the customs officer with a suitcase full of Russian Bibles. I stood in the line and saw how carefully the customs officers checked every suitcase. Suddenly a great fear swept over me. 'What will he do when he finds my Bibles? Send me back to Holland? Put me in prison?'

I closed my eyes to shut out the scene around me and said, 'Lord, in Jeremiah 1, it is written that "God watches over his word to perform it" (*See* v. 12). Lord, the Bibles in my suitcase are Your Word. Now, God, please watch over Your Word – my Bibles – so I may take them to Your people in Russia.'

Now I know that is not what Jeremiah meant, but I have found that if I pray with my hand on the promises of the open Bible that I do not have to wait until my position is doctrinally sound. God sees my heart.

The moment I prayed I opened my eyes and saw around my suitcase light beings. They were angels. It was the first and only time in my life that I had ever seen them, although I had known many, many times they were present. But this time I saw them, only for a moment, and then they were gone. But so was my fear.

I moved on through the customs line, sliding my suitcase along the stainless steel table toward the officer who was doing such a thorough inspection. At last I was before him.

'Is this your suitcase?' he asked.

'Yes, sir,' I answered politely.

'It seems very heavy,' he said, grasping it by the handle and picking it up.

'It is very heavy,' I said.

He smiled. 'Since you are the last one to come through the line I now have time to help you. If you will follow me I shall carry it for you out to your taxi.'

My heart almost overflowed with hallelujahs as I followed him through the customs gate and right out to the street where he helped me get a taxi to the hotel.

So, even though we are rapidly approaching the time when the Antichrist will try to take over the world, I am not afraid. For I have an even greater promise of the constant Presence of Jesus who is greater than anything Satan can throw against me.

The Apostle Peter said, 'Because, my dear friends, you have a hope like this before you, I urge you to make certain that such a day will find you at peace with God and man, clean and blameless in his sight' (2 Peter 3:14 PHILLIPS).

Surrender to the Lord Jesus Christ must not be partial – but total. Only when we repent and turn away from our sins (using His power, of course) does He fill us with His Holy Spirit. The fruit of the Holy Spirit makes us right with God and God's love in us makes us right with men. Through that we can forgive – even love – our enemies.

Jesus Himself makes us ready for His Coming.

(Adapted from Agape Power # 2, Copyright 1972. Logos Journal, 185 North Avenue, Plainfield, N.J. 07060. Reprinted with permission.)

. . . Suffer little children, and forbid
them not,
to come unto me: for of such is the kingdom
of heaven.
Matthew 19:14

35

Little Witness for Christ

Tante Jans lost her husband before she was forty years old.
He had been a well-known minister in Rotterdam and she
had worked faithfully beside him in the church. They had no
children and after he died it was clear that her place was to
be in our house in Haarlem. She was a poet, author, and
organizer – especially was she an organizer! Soon after she
moved into the Beje she started a club for girls where she
led the meetings and began publishing a small monthly paper
for them.

It was long before World War I started, but a detachment
of Dutch soldiers was stationed in Haarlem. Seeing many
soldiers in the streets, Tante Jans decided to open a club for
them too. She approached some wealthy people and within a
short time had enough money to build a military home. Twice a
week Tante Jans went to the house to lead in a Bible study.

Tante Jans also invited the soldiers to come to our house.
Since they were lonely and did not like the street life, many
of them accepted. Almost every evening we had soldiers in
our home.

One sergeant was a great musician and Tante Jans asked
him to teach me and my sister Nollie to play the harmonium – an old pump organ. It wasn't long before I was

joining Tante Jans at the military home to accompany the singing.

One night, in my eleventh year, a large group of soldiers had gathered for the Bible study. Before I played, Tante Jans made me sing. The song I sang was about the lost sheep which was found by the shepherd. I sang it slowly and dramatically, climaxing it with the last line:

> And the sheep that went astray was me.

As I finished singing a big blond Dutch officer reached out and pulled me to him. Picking me up and sitting me on his knee, he laughed and said, 'Tell me, young lady, how did you go astray?'

All the other soldiers laughed, and I was red with embarrassment. It did seem odd that such a little girl would describe herself as a lost sheep.

I had to confess that the line just belonged to the song and that I had never, never been a lost sheep. Then I told him that as a little girl, just five years of age, I had given my heart to Jesus Christ and could never remember not having belonged to Him.

The officer grew very serious and his eyes filled with tears. 'Ah, that is the way it should be, little Sweet-Face,' he said solemnly. 'How much better to come to Jesus as a little child, than to have to stumble, as I have, always seeking the shepherd.'

Then he closed his eyes and said softly, 'But tonight I think I shall stop seeking, and let Him find me instead.'

That night there was deep joy in the Bible meeting. The Lord had used me to lead a man to Christ. It was the first time in my life, and it had taken place not because of what I said, but because of the Holy Spirit who was in me. It was a secret I have remembered all the years of my life as I have travelled the world – a tramp for the Lord.